D1524453

In the intellectual change that took place in the seventeenth century, the role of Samuel Hartlib was of immense significance. As John Milton put it, he was sent 'hither by some good providence from a farre country to be the occasion and the incitement of great good to this Iland'.

Hartlib (originally from Elbing) settled in England in the late 1620s and lived there until his death in 1662. His aspirations formed a distinctive and influential strand in English intellectual life during those revolutionary decades. This volume reflects the variety of the theoretical and practical interests of Hartlib's circle and presents them in their continental context. The editors of the volume are all attached to the Hartlib Papers Project at the University of Sheffield, a major collaborative research effort to exploit the (largely untapped) resources of the surviving Hartlib manuscripts. In an introduction to the volume they explore the background to the Hartlib circle and provide the context in which the essays should be read.

SAMUEL HARTLIB AND UNIVERSAL REFORMATION

SAMUEL HARTLIB AND UNIVERSAL REFORMATION

Studies in intellectual communication

EDITED BY

MARK GREENGRASS, UNIVERSITY OF SHEFFIELD

MICHAEL LESLIE, RHODES COLLEGE, TENNESSEE

AND TIMOTHY RAYLOR, CARLETON COLLEGE, MINNESOTA

CAMBRIDGE
UNIVERSITY PRESS

Published by the Press Syndicate of the University of Cambridge
The Pitt Building, Trumpington Street, Cambridge CB2 1RP
40 West 20th Street, New York, NY 10011–4211, USA
10 Stamford Road, Oakleigh, Melbourne 3166, Australia

First published 1994

Printed in Great Britain at the University Press, Cambridge

A catalogue record for this book is available from the British Library

Library of Congress cataloguing in publication data

Samuel Hartlib and universal reformation: studies in intellectual communication /
edited by Mark Greengrass, Michael Leslie, and Timothy Raylor.
p.   cm.
"Published under the auspices of the Hartlib Papers Project of the University of Sheffield" –
Acknowledgements.
Includes bibliographical references and index.
ISBN 0 521 45252 x (hc)
1. Hartlib, Samuel, d. 1662.
2. England – Intellectual life – 17th century.
3. Pamphleteers – Great Britain – Biography.
4. Reformers – Great Britain – Biography.
5. Scholars – Great Britain – Biography.
I. Greengrass, Mark, 1949– .
II. Leslie, Michael.
III. Raylor, Timothy.
IV. University of Sheffield. Hartlib Papers Project.
DA378.H3S25 1994
941.06'092–dc20   94–5844   CIP

ISBN 0 521 45252 x hardback

CE

339691

Contents

Illustrations

The contributors

T. C. BARNARD has published *Cromwellian Ireland: English government and reform in Ireland, 1649–1660* (Oxford, 1975) and *The English Republic, 1649–1660* (London, 1982). He has also edited (with Jane Clark) *Lord Burlington: architecture, art and life* (London, 1994), and is currently editing a collection of essays on scholars, learning and its transmission in medieval and early modern Ireland. He is the author of numerous articles on Irish and Anglo-Irish topics and is engaged on a study of the origins, ideologies and characteristics of Irish protestant society between 1641 and 1760. Since 1976 he has been fellow and tutor of Hertford College, Oxford.

DAGMAR ČAPKOVÁ taught at the Comenius Institute of Education in the Czechoslovak Academy of Sciences in Prague before becoming a leading figure in its department for the history of education and chairing its Comenius research group. She has been awarded several prizes by the Academy of Sciences for her published work on Comenius and was awarded her DrSc by the Academy in 1991. Among her thirteen books and over two hundred articles, mostly on Comenius and the history of education, the best known are those (in Czech) on *Pre-School education in Comenius' works: his predecessors and his followers* (Prague, 1968), *The unknown diary of Comenius* (Uherský Brod, 1974) and *The philosophical and educational heritage of J. A. Comenius* (Prague, 1987).

ANTONIO CLERICUZIO graduated from the Università di Roma ('La Sapienza'), where he presented a thesis on Robert Boyle and seventeenth-century corpuscular philosophy. He has been F. A. Yates Fellow at the Warburg Institute, University of London, and honorary research fellow of the department of history and philosophy of science, University College, London. He is currently

Ricercatore in the department of philology and history of the Università di Cassino, Italy. He is the author of various articles on seventeenth-century iatrochemistry and on Robert Boyle. He is co-editor of *Alchemy and chemistry in the sixteenth and seventeenth centuries* (Hingham, MA, 1994). He is also a co-editor of the forthcoming edition of the correspondence of Robert Boyle.

STEPHEN CLUCAS, previously British Academy Postdoctoral Fellow in English at the University of Sheffield and research associate of the Hartlib Papers Project, is currently lecturer in English and humanities at Birkbeck College, University of London. He is working at present on a study of Henry Percy, ninth earl of Northumberland, and his intellectual circle.

PATRICIA COUGHLAN lectures in the English department at University College, Cork. She has written several essays and articles on seventeenth-century English writings about Ireland, and also on Anglo-Irish literature in later periods, particularly on gender. She has edited a collection of essays on *Spenser and Ireland* (Cork, 1989) and is working on a book on English colonial discourse about Ireland between 1630 and 1690.

KEVIN DUNN is associate professor of English at Yale University. He is the author of *Pretexts of authority: the rhetoric of authorship in the Renaissance preface*, forthcoming from Stanford University Press, and is presently working on a study of the rhetoric of incorporation in seventeenth-century literature.

MARK GREENGRASS is senior lecturer in modern history at the University of Sheffield and a director of the Hartlib Papers Project. He has researched and written extensively on sixteenth-century French history and is currently preparing Hartlib's diary, the *Ephemerides*, for publication.

HOWARD HOTSON, at the time of preparing his contribution to this volume, held a postdoctoral fellowship at the *Institut für Europäische Geschichte* in Mainz. He is now a junior research fellow at Brasenose College, Oxford, where he is completing two parallel studies of Johann Heinrich Alsted and the Reformed philosophical tradition; the first is a monograph, to be published by Oxford University Press and the second is a bibliographical and prosopographical study of Alsted and his sources which will be published by the Herzog August Bibliothek, Wolfenbüttel.

JOHN DIXON HUNT is currently academic adviser to the Oak Spring Garden Library, Upperville, Virginia, where he has been preparing the two-volume catalogue of the library's collections of garden design materials. He is editor of the *Journal of Garden History*, and author of various books and articles on garden history and theory: most recently, he has edited the *Oxford book of garden verse* (1993).

MARK JENNER is a lecturer and Wellcome research award-holder at the University of York. An article on John Evelyn's *Fumifugium* is forthcoming in the *Historical Journal*. He is currently revising his Oxford D.Phil. thesis, 'Early modern English conceptions of "cleanliness" and "dirt" as reflected in the environmental regulation of London, c.1530–c.1700' for publication. He is continuing his research into the history of early modern hygiene and is working on the social and medical history of London water between 1500 and 1800.

INGE KEIL studied mathematics in Munich from 1949 to 1953. She has worked since 1980 on the history of astronomy in Augsburg and on the city's scientific instrument makers. Her research on 'Johann Wiesel Augustanus Opticus' is a project of the *Institut für Europäische Kulturgeschichte* in Augsburg.

MICHAEL LESLIE was a director of the Hartlib Papers Project until taking up his present post of professor of English at Rhodes College, Memphis, Tennessee. He has published on English Renaissance literature, visual arts, and gardens, and on the applications of information technology in the humanities. He is an editor of the *Journal of Garden History* and *Word & Image*, and co-edited *Culture and cultivation in early modern England: writing and the land* (Leicester, 1992).

ANTHONY MILTON is lecturer in history at the University of Sheffield. He was educated at Clare College, Cambridge and was a research fellow at Clare Hall, Cambridge. His book, *Catholic and Reformed: the Roman and Protestant churches in English Protestant thought, 1600–1640* is forthcoming from Cambridge University Press and he is currently editing a collection of documents relating to the Synod of Dort for the Church of England Record Society.

WILLIAM R. NEWMAN is associate professor of the history of science at Harvard University. His interests include the history of alchemy and eighteenth-century chemistry, medieval and early modern science, the history of the occult sciences, early technology, and the transmission of science between different cultures. His work includes *The Summa perfectionis of pseudo-Geber* (Leiden, 1991), and *Gehennical fire: the lives of George Starkey, an American alchemist in the scientific revolution* which is due to appear from Harvard University Press in the autumn of 1994.

MALCOLM OSTER is part-time tutor in history and the history of science at the University of Oxford, where he received his D.Phil. in 1990. He has published several articles on Robert Boyle and is currently preparing a book on Boyle's life and thought, titled *Robert Boyle. Gentleman naturalist.*

RICHARD H. POPKIN's distinguished career as a historian of early modern philosophy and ideas has taken him to chairs in several North American universities before his recent retirement from Washington University, St Louis. He is presently adjunct professor at the department of history in the University of California, Los Angeles. From his earlier interests in the history of modern scepticism, his best-known published work is the *History of scepticism from Erasmus to Descartes* (London, 1964 and subsequent revised editions) and *The high road to Pyrrhonism* (San Diego, 1980). His extensive studies in the history of early modern Jewish and Christian intellectual contacts culminated in *Isaac La Peyrère: his life, work and influence* (Leiden, 1987) and *The third force in seventeenth-century thought* (Leiden, 1993).

JANA PŘÍVRATSKÁ teaches Latin and medical terminology at the Institute of Foreign Languages of the Third Medical Faculty at the Charles University in Prague. Her doctoral thesis explored Comenius' concept of language. Her interests include the historiography of linguistics, seventeenth-century language theory, universal language schemes and the philosophy of language. She has translated numerous works of Comenius into Czech and was awarded a research prize by the Czechoslovak Academy of Sciences in 1991.

VLADIMÍR PŘÍVRATSKÝ teaches in the department of biology at the Pedagogical Faculty of the Charles University in Prague. His special interests include the history and methodology of science and the philosophy of science. He has co-authored several translations of Comenius into Czech.

STEPHEN PUMFREY is lecturer in the history of science at the University of Lancaster. He co-edited and contributed to *Science, culture and popular belief in Renaissance Europe* (Manchester, 1991).

TIMOTHY RAYLOR is assistant professor of English at Carleton College, Northfield, Minnesota. From 1988 until 1992 he was British Academy/Leverhulme Trust Research Associate on the Hartlib Papers Project. He co-edited and contributed to *Culture and cultivation in early modern England: writing and the land* (Leicester, 1992), and has published articles on seventeenth-century literature and history in *English Literary Renaissance*, *Milton Quarterly*, *Renaissance Studies* and *The Seventeeenth Century*. His book *Cavaliers, clubs, and literary culture: Sir John Mennes, James Smith, and the order of the fancy* is published by the University of Delaware Press.

GERHARD F. STRASSER is an associate professor of German and comparative literature at the Pennsylvania State University. Apart from articles in teaching methodology, he has published extensively in the fields of emblematics, cryptology, universal languages and the history of science. He is the author of *Lingua universalis: Kryptologie und Theorie der Universalsprachen im 16. und 17. Jahrhundert* (Wiesbaden, 1988), and the co-editor of *Johann Joachim Becher (1635–1682)* (Wiesbaden, 1993), which both deal with aspects of closed and open languages at the time of Samuel Hartlib.

CHARLES WEBSTER is a senior research fellow at All Souls College, Oxford. He has published, among numerous studies located in the period covered by this volume, *The great instauration* (London, 1975) and *From Paracelsus to Newton* (Cambridge, 1982). More recently, he has turned his attention to the history of the British National Health Service, publishing (among other studies) the first volume of its history in *Problems of health care: the British National Health Service before 1957* (London, 1988).

Acknowledgements

This volume has been published under the auspices of the Hartlib Papers Project of the University of Sheffield. The Project was funded by the British Academy and the Leverhulme Trust. The directors of the Project acknowledge the generous support it has received from the British Academy, the Leverhulme Trust and the University of Sheffield. The success of the conference on which this work is based owed a great deal to the efforts of the research associates and assistants attached to the Project: Dr Judith Crawford, Mr W. J. Hitchens, Patricia Barry, Margaret Chambers, Gwen Smithson, Sue Wallace and John Young. Neither the Project nor this volume would have been possible without the co-operation and assistance of one of the Project Directors, Michael Hannon, the university librarian. Fig. 7.1 is reproduced with the permission and co-operation of the Herzog–August Bibliothek, Wolfenbüttel. Figs. 17.6 and 17.7 are reproduced with the permission and co-operation of the Oak Spring Garden Library, Upperville, Virginia. Fig. 17.5 is reproduced with the permission of Dumbarton Oaks, Trustees for Harvard University Garden Library. The editors are also grateful to Andrea Bevan for her assistance in preparing the text for publication.

Textual note and note on dates

In quotations, editorial intrusions have been placed in italics within square brackets. In quotations from manuscripts conventional abbreviations and contractions are silently expanded (except for those such as '&', which are still current). Other expansions are placed within square brackets. Revisions and deletions are not generally indicated. Interlineated material is placed within pointed brackets.

In 1582, Pope Gregory XIII introduced a new calendar, the Gregorian calendar or New Style, in place of the existing Julian calendar or Old Style. From 15 October 1582 the Gregorian calendar was ten days in advance of the Julian. By the time of Samuel Hartlib, the new calendar was in force throughout most of continental Europe but it did not come into use in England until 1752. In this book, therefore, events and letters in England are dated in accordance with the Old Style and events and correspondence in Europe in the New Style. Both dates are generally given for correspondence between Europe and England in accordance with contemporary seventeenth-century practice. All years are treated as beginning on 1 January.

Abbreviations

BL   The British Library

Bacon, *Works*   The Works of Francis Bacon, ed. J. Spedding, R. L. Ellis *et al.*, 14 vols. (London, 1857–74)

Boyle, *Works*   *The works of the Honourable Robert Boyle*, ed. T. Birch, 6 vols. (London, 1772)

Comenius   *Johannis Amos Comenii opera omnia* (*Diló Jana Amose Komenského*), 18 vols. in prog. (Prague, 1969–)

CSPD   *Calendar of state papers domestic*

CPW   *Complete prose works of John Milton*, ed. Don M. Wolfe *et al.*, 8 vols. (New Haven, 1953–86)

DNB   *Dictionary of national biography*

DSB   *Dictionary of scientific biography*, ed. C. C. Gillespie, 16 vols. (New York, 1970–80)

Firth & Rait   C. H. Firth and R. S. Rait, *Acts and ordinances of the Interregnum*, 3 vols. (London, 1911)

Harleian Misc.   *A copious and exact catalogue of pamphlets in the Harleian Library*, ed. W. Oldys, 10 vols. (London, 1808–12)

HDC   G. H. Turnbull, *Hartlib, Dury and Comenius: gleanings from Hartlib's papers* (London, 1947)

HP   Hartlib Papers, Sheffield University Library

Notes & records   *Notes and records of the Royal Society of London*

ODO   J. A. Comenius, *Opera didactica omnia*, 3 vols. (Amsterdam, 1657; repr. Prague, 1957)

Oldenburg   *The correspondence of Henry Oldenburg*, ed. A. R. Hall and M. B. Hall, 13 vols. (Madison, Milwaukee, London, and Philadelphia, 1965–86)

PRO	Public Records Office
Webster	Charles Webster, *The great instauration: science, medicine and reform, 1626–1660* (London, 1975)
Worthington	John Worthington, *Diary and correspondence*, ed. J. Crossley, 3 vols., Chetham Society (Manchester, 1847–86)

Introduction

Mark Greengrass, Michael Leslie and Timothy Raylor

> It is easier to find a labyrinth, then a guiding path; and truth is
> ready to glide away, while the eyes are bewitched.[1]

On 6 July 1992 over a hundred and twenty individuals from fourteen countries made their way to Sheffield to attend a conference
entitled 'Peace, Unification, and Prosperity: the Advancement of
Learning in the Seventeenth Century'. Historians of science and
medicine, specialists in the history of education and in English
literature, experts in ecclesiastical history, the history of language
and many other disciplines met and sampled some of the seventy-
two papers presented in the course of the conference. Together they
visited new worlds, entered new intellectual domains and discovered
new *epocha*. There were challenging communications on natural
history, the history of nature, order, disorder and the First Chaos,
and much more besides. John Milton, Robert Boyle, Comenius and
other well-known figures appeared in a different light. The less
familiar, such as Benjamin Worsley, became more significant. The
atmosphere was one of rich interdisciplinarity, a sense of discovery
and the advancement of learning. It would have warmed the heart
of the person who had been (albeit at a distance of 300 years)
responsible for its happening and who was, as it were, the honoured
guest at the conference table: Samuel Hartlib.

Samuel Hartlib (*c.*1600–1662) is a figure who was more or less
forgotten within a generation of his death. And yet in his own time
he was famous across Europe and well known in the emerging
colonies of North America. His energetic interventions lent him
influence in a wide variety of areas – from national and international politics, through the reform of disciplines as disparate as

---

[1] Comenius, *A reformation of schooles, designed in two excellent treatises* (1642; repr. Menston,
1969), 18.

I

education, chemistry and horticulture, through the promotion of technological development in, for instance, optics and military engineering, to public health and plantation policy. He was also valued by his contemporaries as a source of inspiration and information on matters such as medicine and the immortality of the soul.

As Kevin Dunn points out in his chapter in this volume, Hartlib neatly fits the modern critical notion of an 'author-function' in that, despite the fact that his name appears on the title pages of books and pamphlets, he was not himself the author of any significant published work.[2] Neither can he be associated with any of the great intellectual discoveries of the seventeenth century which gave impetus to the development of modern science. In the terms conventionally used to determine significance, then, and in the period of Milton, Boyle, Descartes and Comenius, Hartlib has been easy to overlook. But if we emancipate ourselves from the restrictions of our own structures – structures that derive in no small measure from the creation of canons of significant texts and authors in the fifty years following Hartlib's death – it becomes obvious why he was accorded such high status by his contemporaries.

The document epitomizing those things that render Hartlib significant is his *Ephemerides* (much cited in the following chapters), his diary of information received during his most active years as one of the key intellectual brokers of seventeenth-century Europe. To read the *Ephemerides* is to become part of the world of Hartlib, his contacts, concerns, his eclecticism. The phrase 'the Hartlib circle' is sometimes used in this volume not for reasons of intellectual laziness but precisely because that is demonstrably what there was, and the *Ephemerides* constitutes part of the proof. There was, that is to say, a range of individuals for whom Hartlib formed an important point of intersection. As well as affording a unity to a disparate group of scholars, projectors, politicians, educators and scientists, his activities offered unity to their disparate concerns: intellectual, social and technological. What makes the discussions within the Hartlib circle so important, therefore, is the commonality of their concerns, the sureness of their identification of the issues needing to be addressed, and the tenacity with which they were able to concentrate on them.

It is worth emphasizing that the overarching concern with unity – *pansophia*, the unification of the Protestant churches, the intercon-

[2] See below, chap. 9.

nection of the physical sciences, and the interpenetration of the material and spiritual worlds – stands in remarkable contrast to the intellectual and practical experience of Hartlib and his collaborators. The increasing fragmentation of intellectual disciplines was accompanied by a more marked scientific and technical specialization. In addition, by 1650, many sections of European society had lived through violent change. Hartlib and Comenius were among many who had been displaced by the Thirty Years War. As with the construction of a version of the Renaissance by those fleeing from Nazi persecution in this century, a version characterized by the idealist philosophy of Neoplatonism and the supra-national community of humanist scholars, the fierce adherence of Comenius, Hartlib and others of their acquaintance to an idealistic, unified and international vision of knowledge was surely a response to the intense pressures they were under, both political and psychological. The significance of Hartlib and his circle lies as much in the ideological implications of their motives and strategies arising from this background as it does in any of the specific projects they undertook.

With the changed environment of the Restoration and a more stable political climate in Europe after 1660, these ideological concerns faded or were transformed and Hartlib's significance became less apparent. His rediscovery is thus largely a twentieth-century phenomenon. In many respects his re-emergence is, as this volume seeks to demonstrate, still under way. This work brings together a small selection of revised papers given at the conference in 1992 in order to illustrate the main lines of that rediscovery. In an ideal world, perhaps, its proceedings would have been published in their entirety. But such unmanageable volumes fail to capture the exhilaration of the conference moment. Moreover they lack a sense of direction and coherence – more 'a labyrinth than a guiding path'. Instead, therefore, we have chosen to present a series of case-studies, each exemplifying work in progress in and around the world of Samuel Hartlib. It is these studies that are gradually reshaping our understanding of the intellectual landscape of the mid-seventeenth century. Although far from the pansophy of Hartlib's and Comenius' aspirations, being neither inclusive nor comprehensive, the volume is at least based on a perception of the organic advancement of learning of which they would have approved. It moves outwards from logic and right method to the three Books of 'the revealed Word', 'Man' and 'Nature'. To pursue Comenius' extraordinary metaphors, the volume is intended to be more like a 'perpetuall mover' or a 'living tree, with living roots, and living fruits of all the Arts, and Sciences' rather than 'a pile of wood, very neatly laid in order, with great care and diligence'.[3] The editors are acutely aware that the choices which have been made in selecting these eighteen papers from the original conference presentations imply arbitrary exclusion, and truth can glide away when trying to understand an eclectic figure such as Samuel Hartlib in a deliberately foreshortened perspective. With the various perspectives of the papers presented in this volume in mind, therefore, this introduction surveys the main contours of this emerging landscape.

The rediscovery of Samuel Hartlib in this century began with the publication in 1920 of a pamphlet by a young lecturer in education at the University of Liverpool, George Turnbull.[4] Turnbull was a classicist by training, a philosopher by inclination, and an able linguist. He had been lucky to survive the trenches around St Julien in 1917, where he was very seriously wounded. His interest in the history of German education in the seventeenth century took him to the published volumes of the *Monumenta Germaniae pedagogica*, generally ignored in England at the time; it was here, in the Comenian volumes published by Kvačala, that he first discovered Hartlib.[5] His pamphlet was a thorough biographical account, based mainly on printed sources, which rectified many errors in the *DNB* entry on Hartlib.

There matters might have rested had he not been alerted to the existence of a trunk full of manuscript papers in a solicitor's office in London in 1933. Arranged, so he recalled later, in sixty-eight tied-up bundles in a wooden chest, of indeterminate origins, these were evidently the surviving papers of Samuel Hartlib which, as Turnbull's pamphlet had indicated, had last been heard of in early 1667.[6] After Hartlib's death in penury in March 1662 they had been purchased by William, Viscount Brereton and transported to his country seat in Cheshire. It was there that Dr John Worthington

---

[3] Comenius, *A reformation of schooles*, 24.
[4] G. H. Turnbull, *Samuel Hartlib. A sketch of his life and his relations to J. A. Comenius* (Oxford, 1920).
[5] J. Kvačala, *Die pädagogische Reform des Comenius in Deutschland bis zum Ausgange des 17 Jahrhunderts*, 2 vols. (Berlin, 1903–4).
[6] *Sheffield University Gazette*, 1947.

had providentially come upon them and put them in some semblance of order:

And though my latter years have had something of the pilgrim state, yet I have had cause to acknowledge some merciful designs of providence therein. At my late being in Cheshire I met with two trunks full of Mr. Hartlib's papers, which my Lord Brereton purchased. I thought they had been put in order, but finding it otherwise, I took them out, bestrewed a great chamber with them, [*and*] put them into order in several bundles . . .[7]

It was most, though apparently not all, of these bundles that Turnbull found in 1933.

Of Brereton's involvement with Hartlib and his associates, more might be written. The Breretons of Brereton were one of a clutch of twenty-five or so major land-owning gentry families of Cheshire which constituted the cheese and salt baronetage of the Vale Royal.[8] The baronetcy was a speculative Jacobean Irish creation and the family remained inactively royalist through the Civil War.[9] William Brereton, the family heir, was tutored (thanks to the material assistance of an indulgent maternal grandfather, Sir George Goring, earl of Norwich) by John Pell, then mathematics professor to the prince of Orange at Breda.[10] Back in London in 1653, Brereton's name appears often in Hartlib's *Ephemerides*. Becoming a virtuoso was as good a way as any for a royalist to keep out of trouble, and Brereton's scientific interests rapidly became kaleidoscopic in Hartlib's varied cultural environment. Through Pell's tuition he already had a reputation as an able algebraist and mathematician. He also became a skilled musician and composer, developed a more than passing interest in the representation of language, dabbled with chemistry and became intoxicated by the possibilities of cider.[11]

---

[7] Worthington, II, 230.
[8] G. P. Higgins, 'Landownership, political authority and social status in Shropshire and Cheshire, 1500–1700', *Journal of West Midlands Studies*, 2 (1978), 444; M. D. G. Wanklyn, 'County government and society in Cheshire, 1590–1640' (MA thesis, University of Liverpool, 1973).
[9] His grandfather, Sir William Brereton, was created Baron Brereton of Leighlin, County Carlow on 11 May 1624. The parliamentary cause in Cheshire was led by Brereton's very distant kinsman, Sir William Brereton of Handforth, a military commander who proved able to muster and deploy his resources far more effectively than Sir Thomas Aston, his royalist counterpart. By the middle of 1644, only Chester remained under royalist control in the county and the Breretons of Brereton lay low throughout.
[10] Worthington, I, 212; BL Add MS 4278, fol. 104v (5/15 March 1651) records his being in the company of Sir Charles Cavendish and Hobbes.
[11] His musical abilities were noted by John Aubrey. He was directed by Mr ('Captain') Cooke, who had been in the service of the bishop of Lincoln and taught 'after the Italian

Overall he was an enthusiast for acquiring interesting bits of information and pursuing the experimental method.[12] He corresponded with, among others, Nicolaus Mercator, John Winthrop junior and John Beale.[13] In the pages of Sprat's *History of the Royal Society* he is prominently presented as one of its apolitical but pro-royalist progenitors, conveniently congruent to the author's picture of its origins.[14] Of Brereton's interest in the new experimental method, however, there is no doubt; he was a frequent attender at its meetings and a member of both the Georgical and Mechanical Committees until his retirement to Cheshire in 1669.[15] His purchase of Hartlib's papers confirms his reputation as not merely 'a lover of philosophy, but rather ... the lover of philosophers'.[16]

After his father's death in 1664, Brereton inherited both the family title and its debts. The latter were not inconsiderable. In March 1661, his father had petitioned the Crown to grant him the rent of the customs of North Wales and Chester, claiming that his faithful services to the royalist cause had so ruined his estates that 'without your Majesty's present assistance he and his numerous

mode' (HP 28/2/55A; 29/5/2A). Cooke's interests in experimental apiculture were duly fed through to Hartlib by Brereton (29/54/21A). His language interests are revealed in letters from Beale to Hartlib: 51/15A–16B (Beale to Hartlib, 10 September 1658); 67/22 (Beale to Hartlib, 2 December 1661). For his chemistry, see 16/11/41A (Friedrich Kretschmar to Hartlib, 16/26 April 1660). For his interests in cider and ale experimentation, see HP 52/137A; 64/13A; 29/4/28A.

[12] It was Brereton who told Hartlib about an indelible ink-block from the Indies (HP 29/5/7A), that Hobbes was writing a treatise on necessity and free will in 1655 (29/5/5B), and about the new French musical instrument, the *angélique* (29/5/7B). He experimented with ways to make colours fast (29/5/11B) and with coffee ('A cuphye-house or a Turkish – as it were – Ale-house is erected neere the Old Exchange. It is a Turkish-kind of drink made of water and some berry or Turkish-beane. The keeper of that shop or sellar of that drink gets 30. or 40. shill[ing]s a day. It is somewhat hot and vnpleasant but a good after relish and caused some breaking of wind in abundance' – 29/4/29B). Later, on the death of his father in 1664, he conducted a scientific investigation of the family myth that, on the death of a Brereton, débris rose to the surface of a local pond, and found it to be groundless.

[13] E.g. HP 51/97 (Beale to Brereton, 18 March 1659); 7/7/1A (Hartlib to Winthrop, 16 March 1660) and 32/1/7B (Winthrop to Hartlib); 56/1/31 (Nicolaus Mercator to Hartlib, 10 November 1655), 56/1/65 and 56/1/101 etc. Brereton would later nominate Winthrop to his fellowship of the Royal Society.

[14] Thomas Sprat, *History of the Royal Society* (London, 1667), 57 etc.

[15] Michael Hunter, *The Royal Society and its fellows 1660–1700. The morphology of an early scientific institution* (London, 1982), 36; Michael Hunter, *Establishing the new science* (Woodbridge, 1989) 98, 100, 106.

[16] The epistle dedicatory to Viscount Brereton of *Bentivoglio and Urania*, a romance by Dr Nathaniel Ingelo, cited in Worthington, I, 213.

family cannot possibly subsist'.[17] The fact was, however, that Brereton had done little to assist his present Majesty when it had counted.[18] In the 1659 royalist rising in Cheshire, he had been absent while other Cheshire families, such as the Booths of Dunham Massey and the Cholmondeleys of Vale Royal, had risked their necks. Their fortunes prospered in the 1660s while those of the Breretons languished.[19] Worthington, who had been enticed to Cheshire in 1666 by the prospects of being a household chaplain to Brereton with occasional preaching duties at Holmes Chapel (Chapel Hulme), soon realized that Brereton's financial embarrassment meant that he could not deliver what he had promised.[20] Brereton sold what ecclesiastical advowsons he had and, in 1668, parted with the jewel in the crown, his three-quarter share of the barony of Malpas.[21] It is highly likely, therefore, that, quite soon after Worthington had put the papers in order, Brereton sold them on again. From their surviving condition, however, it is clear that little or nothing was done with or to them in the intervening centuries and that they have been little disturbed.

What Turnbull found in 1933, however, was far from the totality of Hartlib's papers. Much had doubtless already disappeared in a fire which engulfed his study before his death in 1662.[22] Others were almost certainly abstracted by Worthington during his visit in 1667. The letters between Worthington and Hartlib were inevitably removed (to be copied later as part of Worthington's own manu-

---

[17] Bodleian Library, Clarendon State Papers, vol. 74, fol. 265. His request was turned down but he was granted £500 by the Council of State the following May (Cheshire Record Office, DCH/C/787).

[18] As Anthony Wood remarked, when Viscount Brereton's brother George was preferred in Oxford, the family had 'never suffered anything for the king's cause' (*The life and times of Anthony Wood*, ed. Andrew Clark, 5 vols. (Oxford, 1891–1900), I, 348).

[19] P. J. Challinor, 'The structure of politics in Cheshire, 1660–1715' (Ph.D. thesis, the Polytechnic, Wolverhampton, 1978), chap. 1.

[20] Worthington, II, 228 (Worthington to Mrs Foxcroft, 1670–1: 'I found he had not got through those difficulties he was encumbered with, nor was like to do it so soon as he promised himself. And so I saw that there was estate little enough for his necessary occasions and his family').

[21] *Notitia cestriensis, or historical notices of the diocese of Chester*, ed. F. R. Raines, Chetham Society (Manchester, 1845), VIII 248; he retained only the advowson to Brereton itself. Malpas was sold to Sir William Drake of Shardeloes, Devon for £9,493. The other quarter share was owned by the Cholmondeley family. In 1673, his contribution to the militia was reduced from 'the finding of three horses, men and arms' to 'one horse with man and arms' because of his indigence – BL Add MS 36,922, fol. 35.

[22] Turnbull, *Samuel Hartlib*, 72.

script collection); those between Seth Ward and Hartlib probably disappeared at the same time.[23] Of the items specifically mentioned by Worthington, at least one is no longer intact in the collection.[24] Other items appear to have come through the hands of Hans Sloane into the British Library. One whole bundle from the papers was dispersed from the collection and purchased for the Osborn Collection of the Beinecke Library at Yale University in 1957.[25] This left a collection of about 5,000 items, or over 20,000 folios.

No doubt some of the dispersals were innocent, but others were probably designed to manipulate the historical record. As Michael Hunter reminded the conference (with reference to the tamperings of the Boyle papers, especially by the scholar and dissenting minister, Henry Miles, in the eighteenth century), historians of ideas are more vulnerable than they often realize to the bias that may be imposed on their interpretation by such activities.[26]

What happened after this discovery in 1933 is common knowledge and quickly told. Turnbull brought the collection to Sheffield where he had been professor of education since 1922. Almost single-handedly, and despite substantial responsibilities as a senior professor in a provincial university, he began to inventory it and to transcribe some of the most significant documents it contained, including Hartlib's still unpublished diary, the *Ephemerides*. *Hartlib, Dury and Comenius*, published in 1947, was (as its sub-title suggested) merely the first fruits of this effort, the 'gleanings', a book whose subject matter endlessly overspills its biographical framework.

A larger perspective was needed, and one was offered in a lumine-

---

[23] Worthington offered to remove them on his behalf; Seth Ward replied that 'they were carelessly and perfunctorily written ..., so that it will be to my advantage to suppress them. However, sir, I leave them wholly to your disposal, either to bring them to me, when I may have the happiness to see you, or to burn them, or leave them among the rest' (Worthington, II, 226).

[24] In a letter to Dr Evans of 25 February 1666/7, Worthington commented: 'I have here met (among Mr. Hartlib's papers, in my Lord Brereton's study) with two epistles of Grotius to Crellius.' Only a fragment of the second Grotius epistle now survives in the collection (HP 11/4/1–4).

[25] Information kindly supplied by Nicholas Muellner, assistant curator of the Osborn Collection. There is no doubt that these came originally from the Hartlib collection. They consist mainly of holograph letters from Petty to Hartlib, none of which exists among the papers in Sheffield. One of the Petty letters in the Yale bundle is endorsed in the same hand that endorses other bundles in the Sheffield Hartlib Papers: 'Petty Mixt Letters & Papers of no great value [th]at I know of.'

[26] Michael Hunter, '"Not suited to the genius of the present age": historical interpretation and the problems of archival transmission'.

scent essay by H. R. Trevor-Roper (Lord Dacre), originally published in 1960.[27] Hartlib, Dury and Comenius, he argued, had to be understood within a broader intellectual tradition, and in the context of the maelstrom of Europe in the 1620s, experiencing the full fracturing force of the Reformation. It was in this light that their utopian dreams, visions of social transformation and millenarian fulfilment could be properly understood and their particular contribution to the 'English Revolution' justly appreciated. By the time Lord Dacre was preparing his article, though, Turnbull had retired from his chair at Sheffield to Prestatyn, taking Hartlib's papers with him. He died in 1961 and some say that his widow had thought of putting Hartlib's papers on the bonfire afterwards. At all events they were returned to Sheffield University in the boot of the librarian's car in May 1963, and they have remained in the University's library ever since.

The most sustained and substantial investigation and interpretation of Hartlib's papers before 1987 was, however, undertaken by Charles Webster, who began his research with Turnbull's successor as professor of education in Sheffield, W. H. G. Armytage. Charles Webster's *The great instauration* (1975) is an astonishing achievement, and the bedrock on which all subsequent studies of the world of Samuel Hartlib must build. His background and perspective was that of a historian of science reacting against the then rather dominant teleology of what constituted 'modern science'. This tended to see its origins in the Royal Society, the Restoration and the tradition of continental science established by 'highly able, professionally skilled and tough-minded men like Galileo, Kepler and Descartes'.[28] By contrast, Webster used the richness of Hartlib's papers to confirm many of the (then) much debated suppositions of the sociologist Robert Merton and, to some degree, those of the historian Christopher Hill.[29] English science 'benefited from the catalytic influence of the revolutionary intellectual and political situation' of the English Revolution.[30] This was demonstrated by the 'spectacu-

[27] H. R. Trevor-Roper, 'Three foreigners and the philosophy of the English Revolution', *Encounter*, 14 (Feb. 1960), 3–20; substantially expanded and revised in *Religion, the Reformation and social change* (London, 1967), chap. 5.
[28] A. R. Hall, 'Science, technology and Utopia in the seventeenth century', in *Science and society 1600–1900*, ed. P. Mathias (Cambridge, 1972), 44–5, cited Webster, 493.
[29] R. K. Merton, *Science, technology and society in seventeenth-century England* (New York, 1970); C. Hill, *Intellectual origins of the English Revolution* (Oxford, 1965).
[30] Webster, 487.

lar increase in scientific book production' during the 'Puritan Revolution'. The 'image of the dramatic success of the Royal Society' which was fostered by Sprat, Evelyn, Glanvill, Cowley and others unjustly minimized the Society's links with the preceding period of political upheaval. The roots of Restoration science could not be disentangled from the preceding 'Puritan' intellectual traditions. Seventeenth-century natural philosophy could not readily be divorced from either its theological roots or from its potentially utilitarian benefits. The terms 'scientist', 'technician' and 'utilitarian' were bound to be arbitrary and anachronistic if used as exclusive labels to describe individuals in the seventeenth century. Hartlib and his associates were not 'soft-headed, amateurish or incompetent' utilitarians and there was no universally applicable dividing line of conviction, status, background or interest to apply to individuals such as Wilkins, Boyle, Petty, Oldenburg, Beale or Culpeper, whose involvement with Hartlib had provided, at a critical point in their lives, an evident unity of interest and purpose.

What, then, was the significance of England's 'Puritan' intellectual traditions? Webster's central proposition was twofold. They had provided, firstly, a distinctively different approach to natural philosophy and, secondly, an alternative pattern for the organization of intellectual activity. A different attitude to natural philosophy was not merely the result of a general Calvinist asceticism. This was what Merton, following the general propositions of Troeltsch and Weber, had sought to demonstrate. There was also the impact of the particular 'eschatalogical perspective of the Puritans' which was 'significantly different from that of many other protestant groups'.[31] 'The Puritans genuinely thought that each step in the conquest of nature represented a move towards the millennial condition, and that each extension of the power of parliament reflected the special providential status of their nation.' Their 'ambitious aims and unflagging zeal ... to exploit the natural environment for the health and wealth of mankind, were sustained by an enduring expectation of intellectual and social progress. This idea of progress was religious in motivation, but it had the capacity to develop a largely secular expression.'[32]

The 'Puritan initiative for the organization of intellectual activity' was 'of the utmost importance for the growth of the English

[31] *Ibid.*, 506.   [32] *Ibid.*, 506–7.

scientific movement'. It was based on a 'Puritan' ideal of the effective deployment of vocational talent and the conviction that individual reward should be accompanied by the communication of knowledge to others. Hence 'Hartlib's tremendous network of communication became the main component in the mechanism for the exchange of information among Puritan investigators of technical and scientific problems'. Although Hartlib's schemes for an Office of Address never had any formal or official basis, it nevertheless became recognized as the nerve centre for scientific correspondency and communication in Commonwealth England.[33] 'Puritans' such as Culpeper, Beale, Worsley and Hartlib himself willingly sacrificed their proprietorial rights to their scientific knowledge, whereas 'a non-Puritan such as Evelyn, or an ambitious entrepreneur like Petty, found it extremely difficult to accept this obligation to undertake the completely uninhibited release of his scientific secrets'.[34] So although the English Revolution as a political and ecclesiastical manifestation collapsed completely in 1660 the 'Puritan Great Instauration' had an enduring effect, even if it did not live up to the great expectations that many had entertained of it.

At the time of its publication, *The great instauration* was warmly received. It was five years before a significant, if rather negative, critique of its views emerged.[35] This recognized that Webster had identified 'one strain of thought relevant to scientific endeavor in the mid-seventeenth century as utilitarian, pansophic, and inspired by providentialism and millenarianism'. It accepted that this fed into a particular brand of activity which focused on utilitarian reform endeavours, particularly of an educational disposition. But labelling this as 'Puritan' was neither illuminating nor explanatory. 'For this congeries of attitudes was shared by a wide range of English Protestants, to many of whom Webster could apply the term Puritan only at the expense of his thesis.'[36] The intellectual traditions that Webster isolated as peculiarly influencing puritan scientists – millenarianism, providentialism, utilitarianism, rational empiricism – were the common property of Protestants of all persuasions.[37] The

[33] *Ibid.*, 511. [34] *Ibid.*

[35] Lotte Mulligan, 'Puritans and English science: a critique of Webster', *Isis*, 71 (1980), 456–69.

[36] *Ibid.*, 457.

[37] It is, however, as misleading to classify modern historians of science as rigidly committed to a prescriptive pattern for the past as it is to categorize in a rigid fashion seventeenth-century intellectual patterns of thought. Webster himself has argued for the complexity of

desire to stress the continuities before and after the Restoration, to
show how the puritan traditions played an important role in shaping
and institutionalizing the English scientific community, was itself a
problematic teleology. Oster's detailed study of Boyle's millenarianism in this volume neatly exemplifies the problem.[38] Boyle's
eschatological musings were common currency among Protestants of
all persuasions. He was very sceptical of accepting more precise
millennial speculations at their face value, aware of their damaging
effects 'upon less tutored minds'; even if, in the confines of his study,
he may have allowed his mind to wander towards such matters, this
did not sustain his natural philosophy or commitment to the
advancement of learning.

Increasingly, too, the emphasis of scholarly investigation amongst
historians of science has been towards establishing the particular
baroque distinctiveness of Restoration science, its institutional
fabric and assemblage of intellectual assumptions.[39] By means of a
detailed prosopographical study of the early fellows of the Royal
Society and linked studies of the Society's early activities in relation
to a wider world of virtuoso interest, Michael Hunter has recovered
that environment and placed it in its particular context. Individuals
such as Brereton could both be captivated by the aspirations and
excitement of the world of Samuel Hartlib in the 1650s and then
have a fragmentary and discontinuous relationship with it thereafter. The inevitably selective nature of the human memory enabled
individuals to screen out what had seemed important at the time of
the Commonwealth to the advancement of learning and to remember only what they chose to remember. 'Master of Innumerable
Curiosities' is how John Evelyn recalled Samuel Hartlib, writing up
his diary in the 1680s and reliving their encounter in early
December 1655.[40] According to Hartlib's contemporaneous
account, however, Evelyn had been keen to see his revolutionary
bee-hive, designs of which had been illustrated in Hartlib's most

events in the mid-seventeenth century, 'pleading for nuance rather than rigid categoriza-
tion of groups' – see Harold J. Cook, 'Charles Webster on Puritanism and science', in
Puritanism and the rise of modern science, ed. I. Bernard Cohen (New Brunswick and London,
1990), 265–300, esp. 267ff.
[38] See below, chap. 6.
[39] This is evident from the excellent review essays of recent published work in Michael
Hunter, *Science and society in Restoration England* (Cambridge, 1981), 198–219 and *Establishing
the new science, the experience of the early Royal Society* (Woodbridge, 1989), 356–68.
[40] *The diary of John Evelyn*, ed. E. S. de Beer (London, 1959), 364. Samuel Hartlib's *Ephemerides* provides the precise date of 1 December (HP 29/5/54A).

recent publication.[41] Together they had discussed the possibilities for a 'Vniversal Mechanical Work' to which Evelyn would contribute 'all his Collections'. Between them, they planned a 'History of all Mechanical Arts'.[42] Evelyn remembered the meeting, though, only for the ingenuities which Hartlib had shown him: the '*Castles* which they set for ornament on their stoves in *Germanie* . . . which are furnished with small ordinance of silver on the battlements, out of which they discharge excellent Perfumes about the roomes' as well as 'an Inke that would give a dozen Copies, moist Sheetes of Paper being presed on it'. Hartlib remembered a co-operative pansophic enterprise of utilitarian benefit, Evelyn an afternoon's distraction with smoky stoves. The error of parallax between the two accounts is perfectly understandable and as much the result of the very different prevailing climates of opinion as of the contrasting personalities involved.

So this volume of essays does not try to look at Samuel Hartlib's world in terms of its longer-term significance to Restoration science but in itself and for its own sake. It stresses its particularity in two fundamental respects: the commitment to universal reform and the importance of 'correspondency' or human communication. In tandem, these two features made the world of Samuel Hartlib unusually distinctive. Universal reformation lay at the heart of Comenius' ideals which drew, as Professor Čapková explains, both on his intellectual upbringing and his personal suffering during the Thirty Years War.[43] 'Panorthosia' (as Comenius would term it) was a realizable goal:

I say that the task must be tackled *seriously* so that this Universal Reform (the last before its end) is not a mere shadow, but a reality whereby we may truly escape from Babylon, and truly release ourselves from the labyrinths, and be truly restored to God and attached to freedom, and truly achieve the supreme end of life, which is peace of mind.[44]

Just such a serious personal commitment was entered into by Hartlib, Dury and Comenius in their famous fraternal covenant on

[41] Timothy Raylor, 'Samuel Hartlib and the commonwealth of bees' in *Culture and cultivation in early modern England*, ed. Michael Leslie and Timothy Raylor (Leicester, 1992), chap. 5.
[42] 'Hee professed for a Vniversal Mechanical Work and that he would contribute all his Collections to one that would write the History of all Mechanical Arts' (HP 29/5/54A).
[43] See below, chap. 3.
[44] Jan Amos Comenius, *Panorthosia or universal reform*, trans. A. M. O. Dobbie (Sheffield, 1993), 14.

the eve of the English Civil War in March 1642, or the later pact between Dury, Hartlib and Clodius in August 1652.[45] The effects of universal reformation showed through, however, in many different, unlikely or even implausible ways, from the millenarian-inspired philosemitism revealed by Richard Popkin to the social and economic engineering of Benjamin Worsley analysed by Charles Webster.[46] It could camouflage the colonizing aspirations of the English in Ireland, give purpose and direction to the writing of universalist natural histories and shape the thoughts of horticultural colonizers as well.[47] Universal reformation was like the alkahest, an all-purpose solvent to be applied 'by all people, in all its aspects, and in every way', the familiar Comenian 'omnes, omnia, omnino'.[48]

The gates to universal reformation would, however, be different to different people. The Comenian strategy was majestically methodical:

Then if the reform of human states is to become possible, we must reform the individuals who comprise them. In the case of men, we should begin by reforming schools which are the factories of men; in the case of schools, we should reform books, as being the appropriate instruments for the formal education of men; in the case of books, we should reform the method of writing and producing them; and finally to enable us to reform the method fully, we must attend to the order of the material world itself, which cannot be moved since it has been framed by the skill of God and has unchangeable laws to prescribe for human understanding.[49]

For other individuals in Hartlib's circle, there were other gates to universal reformation – utilitarian and practical, mathematical and theoretical, millenarian and apocalyptical, and often uneasy combinations of several. Benjamin Worsley was both capable of seeing the path to universal reformation around the committee tables of the Rump Parliament and in the arcana of astrologically determined physical forces.[50] The most vulgar Baconians in one context turn out to be the most committed hermeticists in the next.

But within these differences there was a common emphasis upon the importance of *method*, of a 'right logick'. Stephen Clucas stresses how what Lord Dacre had dismissed as 'antiquated metaphysics' was of central importance in the Hartlib circle. Logic had kept Beale

---

[45] *HDC*, 458–60; 121–3.   [46] See below, chaps. 5 and 11.
[47] See below, chaps. 15 and 16.
[48] Comenius, *Panorthosia*, 13 and see also below, chap. 3.   [49] Comenius, *Panorthosia*, 15.
[50] See below, chaps. 11 and 12.

at his books as a student just as the possibilities of Harrison's index, mentioned by Clucas, would keep Sir Cheney Culpeper awake at night. The search for a powerful logic, a universal organizing principle to the world and to our understanding of it, seemed to be a necessary common sense, a natural extension of the way in which our minds and memories worked. John Beale recommended Viscount Brereton and Caleb Morley to recollect 'in times & leysure, in your beds and in retirem[en]ts' what had constituted 'the first impressions of your youngest yeares in your Child-hoode, & particularly such thinges, as seemed leading heades, & conduct-pipes to the sources of knowledge.' These, he suggested,

beeing found within you, & as it were by long time naturally engraffed in you, & especially if you can easily (by a fore acquired Methode) string them in order, will bee the best & truest Topiques for your future inprovem[en]t of Memorey during life. What could a Grocer, Mercer, Salter or Apothecary doe, if (when the faire is at hand) his ware were all in a heape? And if a house were overfurnished, yet the furniture soe disordered, that there could bee noe rule by which one might guess where to find bedding, linnen, bellowes, snuffers &c, in this plenty there would bee a want of all things, till reduced to fit & convenient place.[51]

The search was inevitably eclectic. But it drew at least as much upon continental logicians as upon the works of Bacon. It is difficult to escape the conclusion that what has often loosely been described as 'Baconian' in the Hartlib circle was, in reality, a tradition which came to the Hartlib circle often from intellectual sources distinct from Bacon himself. As Howard Hotson demonstrates, Hartlib, Comenius and Dury were all strongly influenced by the reformed pedagogy of Calvinist Germany. We are now much better informed about the Calvinist 'Second Reformation' there than when Trevor-Roper first published his essay and the contrasts between the experience of reformation in the Calvinist Wetterau counties or the Rhine Palatine and England are much clearer. Because of the territorial fragmentation of the German Reich, the Calvinist reformation had, in the years before the Thirty Years War, proceeded on a localized basis and been driven forward by its governing élites. Thorough Calvinist reformation had its attractions to princes anxious to enhance their authority and forge their small territories into efficiently managed units. In England, by contrast, religious and poli-

---

[51] HP 67/22/13A–14B, 13Bff (Beale to Hartlib, 2 December 1661).

tical divisions had paralysed any such developments. When the possibilities for change finally came in 1642, however, one may doubt whether the state-building aspirations of the Calvinist 'Second Reformation' principalities and the Calvinist-trained technicians who attempted to transform them were really what the parliamentarians of the Long Parliament, even the supposedly more 'apolitical' of the country gentry supporters such as Sir Cheney Culpeper, really wanted by way of reformation.

The complementary distinctiveness of the world of Samuel Hartlib – its stress upon 'communication' – was more readily acknowledged by contemporaries. Was he not the 'great Intelligencer of Europe', the 'hub of the axletree of knowledge', the 'conduit-pipe' of all learned correspondency? Within the context of universal reformation, however, the impact of intellectual communication should not be underestimated. Boundaries of language, territory, discipline, class and dogma could be, if not dissolved, at least (in the right climate) cut down in size. Jana Přívratská shows how Comenius' attempt to create a truly open, dogmatically neutral means of written communication in a universal language should be viewed within the overall patterns of universal reformation, not as a 'vast mosaic, or a summary of partial conclusions' but integrated into his methodological and philosophical system.[52] Working from a superficially denotative view of language, Comenius developed a conception of language as an essential instrument by which our ideas about the real world are taken to pieces, reassembled and compared with other ideas. In this way it became part of the relation of human phenomenon to reality and a fundamental instrument of universal reformation. Gerhard Strasser shows how cryptology, initially a means for hiding secret or arcane information, could also become a vehicle for universal, and thus far from hidden, communication.[53] The interest in language and human communication around the Hartlib circle was never a matter of purely abstract curiosity. It was fundamental to their ideals, demonstrative of their aspirations.

For the importance of 'the liberty of publique communication of the best things, which in the kingdome of God must alwaies bee inviolably observed' was central to the achievement of universal reformation. 'That every man may have liberty to make experiment

---

[52] See below, chap. 8.   [53] See below, chap. 7.

of himself of their truth', 'that every one may have liberty to use his own judgement' were the refrains of Comenius' *Reformation of schooles*.[54] An eclectic '*Libera philosophia*' lay at the heart of Hartlib's petition for the reform of the statutes of the University of Oxford in 1649.[55] It inspired Beale's suggestions for the statutes of the Dublin College, where students should be

> allowed freedome to engage in the way of Aristotle, or of the Academics or Sceptiques, as far as to notion of Ultimityes & Principles or elements or in the way of Democritus & any moderne proposalls of Ld Bacon, Gassendus, Synertus &c. And descending to the practice of Physique, whether Methodists, or Secretaryes of Chymistry & Herbarists &c. some with encouragements in Anatomy & Elements of Chirurgery. Some to bee Mathematicians To give Accompt of Ancient & Moderne Astronomy: of the ancient & Moderne Geography & Topography, of Optiques; Engines & the greate effects of the ancient Mechaniques.[56]

Although such extravagant eclecticism would eventually find more echoes in the rhetorical prefaces of scientific works of the period than in the corridors of Academe, there is no doubt that the conviction that lay behind it had unpredictable and interesting effects in corroding the ancient boundaries of established disciplines and fracturing older divisions of learning. So, for example, although Hartlib's reactions to magnetic philosophy may appear, as Stephen Pumfrey suggests, superficially naive, Hartlib nevertheless glimpsed in Gellibrand's work a window into a world of wisdom which had not been seen by the ancients.[57] Equally surprising and equally unpredictable were Hartlib's support and stimulation for John Beale's extravagant explorations of the aesthetics of the English garden, with all that they suggested of larger questions concerning wider relationships between man and the natural world. John Dixon Hunt strikingly demonstrates that the more specific concerns of Hartlib and his circle led frequently to topics as large and powerful as they are unexpected to more limited historians of science; and that debates within the circle can be seen as contributing to developments as seemingly disconnected as the history of designed landscapes.[58]

It was precisely Hartlib's eclecticism that made him the conduit-pipe for the reception of new logical methods, as Clucas demon-

---

[54] Comenius, *Reformation of schooles*, 28 and 33.   [55] Edited in Webster, 523–4.
[56] HP 31/1/77–80B, 78Aff.
[57] See below, chap. 13.   [58] See below, chap. 17.

strates.[59] In due course it would also serve as a gateway for Helmontian chemistry into England and the route by which Cartesian metaphysics and Jungian botanical taxonomy reached the Cambridge of the young Isaac Newton.[60] One of the reasons for the increasing significance of Samuel Hartlib is precisely that the more we investigate it the more often we find that his role in the transposition of intellectual ideas to the England of the mid-seventeenth century was of fundamental importance.

Behind such eclecticism lay the belief that all human knowledge was a public endowment from God to be used in the service of all humankind. As Hartlib said: 'It is nothing but the narrownes of our Spirits that makes us miserable; for if our hearts were enlarged beyond our selves, and opened to lay hold of the Advantages which God doth offer, whereby we may become joyntly serviceable unto one another in Publicke Concernments; we could not be without Lucriferous Employments for our selves; nor Unfruitful to our neighbours.'[61] Information was a commodity in which there should be, if not a free trade (military secrets and *raisons d'état* were always readily admitted as exceptions), at least a relatively uncensored flow to the greater common good. As Dunn points out, however, such notions had been percolating in England in various forms for at least a century before Samuel Hartlib.[62] Yet it was around Hartlib that the perception of knowledge as a public commodity became of central concern for the first time. As Dunn explains, this is an important context in which works as widely known as Milton's treatise *Areopagitica* should be read. As well as being a tract against censorship it is a critique of the form that censorship takes. It draws upon the Hartlibian idioms of the 'lucriferous' (Milton would prefer 'salubrious') effects of the free circulation of 'our richest Marchandize, Truth' while remaining distrustful of any suggestion that

[59] See below, chap. 2.
[60] Alan Gabbey, 'Philosophia cartesiana triumphata: Henry More (1646–1671)', in *Problems of cartesianism*, ed. Thomas M. Lennon and John W. Davis (Kingston, Ontario, 1982), 246–8 and John Gascoigne, 'A reappraisal of the role of the universities in the Scientific Revolution' in *Reappraisals of the Scientific Revolution*, ed. David C. Lindberg and Robert S. Westman (Cambridge, 1990), 217–18. For Jungian taxonomy, see the forthcoming paper by Stephen Clucas, 'Samuel Hartlib and the Hamburg scientific community, 1631–1666: a study in intellectual communications'.
[61] Hartlib's introduction to Cressy Dymock, *An essay for advancement of husbandry-learning: or the propositions for the errecting of a colledge of husbandry* (London, 1651).
[62] See below, chap. 9.

knowledge was a 'commodity' which might become subject to any publicly enforced monopoly, whether by a king or by a parliament.

For Hartlib, any patent of an invention or innovation was an open door to a monopoly unless it had a fully public framework of reference. In practice, this meant that new inventions should be publicly and demonstrably seen to work, that information regarding new devices or innovations should be publicly registered with a summary of their efficacy, and that patents themselves should be debated and agreed in the public corporations of the state. Did this not imply, Mark Jenner suggests, that Hartlib's circle came at times uncomfortably close to an environment of enterprisers whose proclaimed motives of advancement of the general good were but a thin disguise for private profit?[63] If Milton was among the monopolists, Hartlib was amidst the projectors. The fructiferous conduit-pipe of Hartlibian correspondency becomes transformed into the plausible schemes of John Lanyon for real conduit-pipes of genuine salubrity to London's citizens. Hartlib saw in Lanyon's proposals, as Mark Jenner shrewdly points out, a singularly 'convincing example to invoke when seeking to win over sceptical patrons and investors'. The results, however, belied the rhetoric. Lanyon's enterprise 'never came up to scratch and occasioned repeated complaints'. The result was one more occasion where 'it is difficult to distinguish between the schemes that Hartlib followed so avidly and parodies of projection'.

In this, Hartlib and his circle were little different from enthusiasts and inventors in all periods: the history of technological advance is strewn with examples of occasions on which the boundaries of the fantastic were difficult to draw at the time. The more serious issues, as Jenner reveals, were ideological. Hartlib and his associates were, of course, aware that the line between the 'lucriferous' imparting of knowledge to the common good and the 'luciferous' exploitation of knowledge for personal gain was a fine one, to be drawn within the consciences and attitudes of each individual. They were made aware of it, not least by the very debate about scientific method and the advancement of learning which they, and some of their more extravagant claims for its beneficial consequences, had done so much to stimulate. In a letter to Hartlib in 1649, Henry More commented critically on William Petty's recently published *Advice ... to Mr.*

[63] See below, chap. 18.

Samuel Hartlib in which lucriferous knowledge by means of the experimental method had been plainly expounded:

Though I be fully enough persuaded, that Experiments may make much for the emprovement of Physick, Cookery and wealth, yett I confesse, that the finding out the Philosophers stone (which I suppose the Hercules pillars of all Experiencers, they hope not to travayle farther if they aspire so far) if men were not unsatiably covetous, or prodigiously and mysteriously wicked and debauched, there is so many wholsome provisions already found out by the industry and art of our Ancestors, besides what Natures full breastes unforcedly spurt upon us without any squeezing or streining, that, could either the Hevenly Powers force us or our selves persuade our selves to become temperate, just, loving, and modest, innocent mankinde in these Ages of the world, need not value three straws, that so highly valued and eagerly pursude invention. Half the exploites that have been already discovered in behalf of distempered man, would make us unexpressibly happy, were they seconded but with sincereity, and unteinted morality.[64]

Until such a reformation of mankind had taken place, Henry More continued,

[*these*] great projectes seem to me, like the building of Babell against a second expected deluge, and the highest heapes of Luciferous experiments as he calles them, but the ground work of Luciferan knowledge, which the divine Light in just indignation may well thunderstrike and confound.

Similar points were made, as William Newman points out, by George Starkey, the American alchemist and virtuoso.[65] Knowledge, basely acquired, would itself be mean and base. The most refined and exquisite arcana should perhaps not be readily communicated to all and sundry lest they lose their rare efficacy in vulgar hands. So Hartlib needed to be assured of the credentials of those with whom he was dealing. To take an example, when the Protestant merchant Peter le Pruvost presented his proposal for overseas colonization by means of improved techniques of husbandry and fishing, Hartlib asked Dury to satisfy himself as to Pruvost's good intentions before pressing for the examination of the scheme by the English Parliament.[66] In due course, Dury assured him that le Pruvost was

a man free from partialitie: & Cautiously warie and prudent in his owne affaires, quiet & free from the vanitie of appearing ... & so fare as I can judge of a truly Public spirit, zealous for the Protestant cause ... And

[64] HP 18/1/2A–3B (Henry More to Hartlib, 12 March 1648/9).   [65] See below, chap. 10.
[66] HP 12/87–88B (Mr Pruvost's offer).

although the waye which he followeth doth tend to profit, yet I find him no wayes Covetously inclined or a lover of money; but contrariwise he doth discourse of the covetous practises of merchants and other men very understandingly.[67]

Dury went on to explain that there were, of course, circumstances where it was impolite to enquire too closely into another man's affairs. Universal reformation did not require those who were not 'of a communicative disposition' to be constrained against their wishes to reveal their secrets: 'I have not beene curious to know particulars of him not so much because I see him reserved, or because I would not give him cause to thinke that I desire to pry into his secretts; but merely because I am satisfied first in the mans behaviour towards me and in all wayes which I finde discreet, reall, and rationall.' It was virtues such as these that would advance universal reformation. There are many respects in which the Hartlib circle contributed unconsciously to the cultivation of the 'virtuoso'.

To lay overmuch stress on the fact that Hartlib was involved, from time to time, in what may seem to us to be technically unsound, fatally flawed technological innovation is another way of failing to look at the world of Samuel Hartlib in its own context. Among the 'sea of ingenuities' there were bound to be many 'well-principled indeavors' that would turn out to be impractical. It is easy to dismiss, for example, William Petty's engine for double writing as a fanciful or ingenious toy and thus to forget the high cost of employing London scriveners, the inevitable increase in duplicate paperwork that an advanced civil society entailed and the possible cost-benefits that the relatively inexpensive innovation of a properly designed pantograph might bring with it. That such an innovation should have apparently failed because of the difficulty in securing a reliable ink supply and well-engineered linkages in the device strengthens one's perceptions of the considerable technical difficulties of innovation in this period rather than the case for Hartlibian naivety.

The easily paraded failures have to be balanced by the (sometimes unforeseen or unlikely) successes. As Charles Webster's study of Petty's rival, Benjamin Worsley, points out, the well-advertised collapse of the saltpetre project and the inadequacies (as it turned out) of his role in the Irish Down survey have to be set against the

---

67 HP 12/66–68B (Dury to Hartlib, 30 November 1645).

practical consequences of his beliefs in the potential for universal reformation. These beliefs inspired others around him such as Robert Boyle. 'More than any other personal influence,' says Webster, 'Benjamin Worsley was responsible for establishing the deep spiritual motivation and broad horizons of Boyle's scientific activities.' They inspired Worsley to visit the Dutch Republic in 1647, fostering many of Hartlib's contacts there and sending back valuable information on a variety of subjects. They enabled him to play a far from negligible role, as secretary of the council or commission for advancing trade, in framing the 1650 Act for prohibiting trade with Virginia, the forerunner to the Navigation Act of 1651. The productive energies generated in Worsley by the interplay between beliefs and utilitarian endeavours are typical of many among Hartlib's acquaintances. It is precisely this interplay that is of critical importance to the understanding of the significance of the world of Samuel Hartlib.

The role of the Hartlib circle as a medium for technology transfer, especially from the advanced civil societies of the continental corridor running from northern Italy down the Rhine to the Netherlands, has yet to be properly investigated. In matters such as agriculture, horticulture, distillation, mining, mills, drainage, chemistry and metal-working there is still much to be learnt from the Hartlib Papers about the detailed significance of such contacts. Inge Keil has carefully documented the particular example of optical instrumentation.[68] She shows how Hartlib was particularly impressed by the potential utilitarian benefits for mankind in telescopy and microscopy. It is perhaps hardly surprising that it was while staying in Hartlib's household in London in 1641–2 that Comenius should have accorded such singular significance to optical advancement as an epitome of universal reformation in his *Via lucis*. She documents how, through his continental contacts, and particularly those in the Dutch Republic, Hartlib obtained details of the instruments manufactured by Johann Wiesel of Augsburg. In due course, Hartlib became an agent with whom orders were placed for the purchase and transport of Wiesel's telescopes and microscopes with fundamental consequences for the subsequent design features of later English-manufactured optical instruments.

No justification is needed for the existence of two essays on Ireland

[68] See below, chap. 14.

and the Hartlib circle in this volume.[69] The clustering of Anglo-Irish intellectuals at the London home of Katherine, Lady Ranelagh in the mid-1640s had given the Invisible College a pronounced Hibernian dimension. Hartlib and his friends were unlikely to overlook the opportunities Cromwellian Ireland afforded them to advance universal reformation and provide them with places of employment. The problem was that Ireland, far from offering a Hibernian 'New Atlantis', proved to be an old Atlantis full of ancient enmities and unresolved dilemmas which the Cromwellian conquest had done nothing to abate. Yet, as T. C. Barnard says, these 'untidy realities' of seventeenth-century Ireland were considerably ignored in *Irelands naturall history*, the earliest and arguably most intriguing of the Baconian-inspired topographical natural histories. A collaborative enterprise in the best Hartlibian tradition, it was also typically incomplete, patchy and badly collated. As T. C. Barnard points out, it has been more often recognized for its value as a detailed prospectus for would-be planters and investors rather than its underlying didactic purposes. Dury's preface to the work is particularly significant in this respect, affording a vision of Ireland's spiritual, moral and physical redemption to its new rulers. But when it came to the detail, its compilers saw what they chose to see and closed at least one eye to the rest. And, as Patricia Coughlan demonstrates, the degrees of prejudice and greed varied among its participants in direct proportion to the levels of intolerance or incomprehension of the uncomfortable Irish reality. So, at its most uncomprehending, *Irelands naturall history* declared that the English had always been the 'introducers of all good things into Ireland' and in various subtle and not-so-subtle ways sought to suggest that the native Irish were deficient in skills and industry. It is difficult to deny that the normally corrosive effects of the Hartlib circle's ideas and energies upon existing divisions, in the Irish context did little more than disguise many of the pre-existent boundaries and historic divisions of ethnicity, religion and enmity while in certain cases giving new grounds to reinforce the prejudices and greed that would sustain them in the future.

The absence of dogma in the Hartlib circle enabled it to foster the singular philosemitism analysed by Richard Popkin.[70] As he shows, it is a further example of the communicative energies of the Hartlib

[69] See below, chaps. 15 and 16.   [70] See below, chap. 5.

circle, especially with the Dutch Republic. These energies drew upon the common stock of millenarian, educational and scientific concerns amid the Hartlib circle and focused them on particular concrete and apparently realizable projects. John Dury's irenicism drew on similar energies and resulted in similarly specific projects for the reconciliation of confessional differences. Yet, as Anthony Milton suggests, the arguments for irenicism were well known and rehearsed in all the major confessions after the Reformation, but not always innocently advanced or accepted at face value by Dury himself or by the theologians and church leaders with whom he was negotiating.[71] The 'unchanged peace-maker', like the 'great Intelligencer of Europe', found himself eclipsed at the Restoration, forced into exile to contemplate the possibilities for inner and spiritual renewal, a personal millennium. Like Comenius, he found the escape from the *Labyrinth of the world* to lie in the 'summer house' or, as Comenius entitled the second part in the second edition of 1663, the *Paradise of the heart*.

So, like the rich fossil deposits left behind in cretaceous rocks as evidence of a distant evolution, Hartlib's papers enable us to reconstruct and, in the process, to rewrite part of the intellectual history of the seventeenth century. That process is still under way and it will shortly receive a further impetus from the publication of the electronic edition of the surviving papers in Sheffield. This edition was made possible by a substantial and exceptional grant through the auspices of the British Academy by the Leverhulme Trust to set up the Hartlib Papers Project. It was the Project that organized and sponsored the 1992 conference which in turn has resulted in this volume. Established in the spring of 1988, the first phase of the Project included the transcription of the entirety of the Hartlib Papers in the Sheffield collection and the creation of an electronic text database. This huge task has now been completed. The result is probably the largest integral text-based historical database yet constructed. The process of verifying the transcriptions is, at the time of going to press (March 1994), almost complete and the process of creating electronic images of the original documents is well in hand. In due course, these will be linked to the transcriptions, and the entire archive published on CD-ROM, with the hope and intention

[71] See below, chap. 4.

that a new and exhilarating phase of research can begin on the basis of an exciting and wholly new form of electronic edition.

This edition will not be imprisoned by the debates and questions that currently preoccupy us. Instead, thanks to the sophisticated software which has been chosen to harness it, it will encourage us to ask entirely new questions. Within the context of late twentieth-century scientific communication, we shall be replicating something of that 'living tree, with living roots, and living fruits of all the Arts, and Sciences' which had so inspired the world of Samuel Hartlib.

PART I

The cultivation of mind and soul
The search for method

Philosophical pedagogy in reformed central Europe between Ramus and Comenius: a survey of the continental background of the 'Three Foreigners'

Howard Hotson

For several centuries after his death, the world of Samuel Hartlib was a lost continent, locked away in an ancient chest full of forgotten papers and pamphlets. In the decades following the unexpected rediscovery of that chest, visitors to the strange new world it contained were few. The first to survey its uncharted terrain returned to publish a diffuse collection of random citings, principally of this new-found region's three chief inhabitants: Hartlib, Dury and Comenius. A second, drawing upon his predecessor, sketched the general intellectual landscape inhabited by these three foreigners in such vivid colours that others were persuaded to visit their world as well. Finally, a third mapped out in masterful detail the topography of a strikingly populous commonwealth of ideas: a world of unimagined breadth and diversity, extending from Bensalem to Macaria, from mining to metaphysics, from the Golden Age to the Great Instauration.[1] In the years that have followed his work, the exploration and exploitation of the seemingly inexhaustible intellectual resources of this previously unknown territory have employed whole colonies of younger scholars; and the imminent arrival of an age of unimaginably swift and easy communication throughout this entire realm will ensure that their work will continue at a still greater rate during the next generation.

Throughout this half-century of exploration, colonization and development, however, one province of Hartlib's world has

---

This chapter summarizes one of the main lines of argument of the author's D.Phil. thesis, 'Johann Heinrich Alsted: encyclopaedism, millenarianism, and the second reformation in Germany' (Oxford, 1991), a revised version of which is to be published by Oxford University Press. No attempt will be made here to give more than the most basic documentation, which the reader will soon be able to supplement with the full text.

[1] *HDC*; H. R. Trevor-Roper, 'Three foreigners: the philosophers of the puritan revolution', in *Religion, the Reformation and social change* (London, 1967; 3rd edn, London, 1984), 237–93; Webster.

remained virtual *terra incognita*. The great advancement of our
knowledge of the world which these three foreigners helped to create
in England has not been matched by any comparable enhancement
of our understanding of the world from which they came. As other
sections of G. H. Turnbull's pioneering work have gradually settled
into the revered obscurity reserved for major works of scholarship
subsequently superseded, his information on Hartlib and Dury's
early years has remained embarrassingly up to date.

The problem is not merely that we have learned so little about
Hartlib and Dury's continental origins in the past fifty years: we
now know far more about Comenius' early wanderings,[2] but we are
singularly ill prepared to make use of the knowledge we have.
Without some familiarity with the world through which they are
moving, these three figures merely cast a few wandering points of
light on an institutional and intellectual landscape that remains for
us very largely shrouded in darkness. The men who taught them –
Lauban, Mylius, Alsted – are little more than names to us. The
places where they studied – Elbing, Brieg, Herborn – are towns
which few of us could even locate unassisted on the map of central
Europe. As for the greater centres that crowned their world of
learning – Breslau, Marburg, Heidelberg – no one is yet able to
establish more than their most general intellectual and confessional
co-ordinates, somewhere in the vast cultural expanse between
Rudolph II's Prague and Theodore Beza's Geneva. Still less do we
possess any general knowledge of the pedagogical, philosophical or
theological traditions that might have prepared these three foreigners to play such central roles in the English scene. Comenius, Dury
and, above all, Hartlib step from the central European Reformed
world into the pages of English intellectual history as if from a void.

Given the traditional view of Protestant intellectual life in late
sixteenth- and early seventeenth-century Germany, this neglect is
perhaps not surprising. Its theology has always been judged, by the
standards of the previous period, as a degeneration into a second
scholasticism. Its philosophy has generally been characterized, by
the criteria of the following era, as the last gasp of a moribund
Aristotelianism. Its politics, both ecclesiastical and secular, are
inevitably interpreted in terms of the disastrous war in which they

---

[2] Most notably as surveyed in Milada Blekasted, *Comenius. Versuch eines Umrisses von Leben,
Werk und Schicksal des Jan Amos Komenský* (Oslo and Prague, 1969).

ultimately resulted. Its scientific, artistic and even literary accomplishments have never been fully integrated into a general account of the period. Indeed, many of the central features of its intellectual life fit so uneasily into the normal categories of modern academic inquiry that they have scarcely been considered worthy of historical investigation at all.

The social, political and ecclesiastical history of Reformed central Europe has, however, begun to receive more sympathetic attention in recent years and, against the backdrop of this new work, we can begin to delineate some of the main lines of intellectual development within this community.[3] Once we have left behind the narrowly construed histories of theology, metaphysics and occultism which have previously been virtually our only guides to this intellectual world, a culture begins to emerge of such variety and complexity that we can hardly speak with confidence of *the* continental background of the 'Three Foreigners' at all. Yet from a still-tangled skein of competing and often contradictory issues and influences, one tradition emerges with a sufficiently clear course of development and a sufficiently direct relevance to the topic at hand to merit summary here. We find it in one of the most unlikely places to look for intellectual innovation in the seventeenth century: the universities.

Even the most superficial comparison of German universities with their English counterparts in this period reveals something of their vitality. In place of England's two ancient universities, the empire boasted fourteen in 1500; and by 1650 another twenty foundations had been added to this total. Obviously such institutions must have been very different from their more familiar English counterparts. While Oxford remained bound to its increasingly outdated statutes and curriculum by the legacy of its fourteenth-century glory and shielded from princely interference by its ancient and unwieldy corporate structure, a sixteenth-century German university was typically a far younger, smaller and more up-to-date institution. In origin, it was generally a recent creation, founded by the local

[3] The chief synopses to date are *Die reformierte Konfessionalisierung in Deutschland – Das Problem der 'Zweiten Reformation'*, ed. Heinz Schilling (Gütersloh, 1986) and, at a still more general level, Heinrich Richard Schmidt, *Konfessionalisierung im 16. Jahrhundert*, Enzyklopädie Deutscher Geschichte, Band XII (Munich, 1992). For overviews at both levels in English, see Heinz Schilling, *Religion, political culture and the emergence of early modern Europe* (Leiden, New York and Cologne, 1992), chaps. 5–6, and R. Po-Chia Hsia, *Social discipline in the Reformation: central Europe, 1550–1750* (London and New York, 1989).

territorial prince, his father or grandfather. In scale, it was roughly
the size of an Oxbridge college, staffed by ten or twelve appointees
whose loyalties, both social and professional, were tied to the local
court. In such circumstances, the prince possessed considerable
power to reform these institutions at will; nor did he lack incentives
to stimulate such reform, or models on which to shape it anew.
Pressure to adopt the latest pedagogical innovations was generated
by sharp competition for students with an ever-increasing number
of nearby universities and by the still deadlier rivalry with confessio-
nally antagonistic neighbouring states. Exposure to educational
experiments taking place across Europe was afforded by Jesuit
pedagogues trained abroad, Reformed refugees reaching Protestant
cities from every direction, and students returning from medical and
legal studies in northern Italy, France and the Low Countries. In
response to all these incentives and opportunities, the scholastic
features of the typical German university curriculum were over-
hauled and replaced by key elements of the humanist education
programme at least once in the course of the sixteenth century.
Many universities, in fact, were reformed afresh at the accession of
each new prince.[4]

If such a picture applies to German universities in the first half of
the sixteenth century, it is still more representative of the characteristic educational institutions of the ensuing confessional age:
the academies. These new foundations, devoted as they were to
providing the pre-university level of education neglected in the
medieval period and promoted by the humanists, were innovative
by their very nature. Each of the three main confessions was quick to
adopt these institutions to its own purposes, and each enjoyed
considerable success in doing so. The Lutheran academies, typified
by Johannes Sturm's famous foundation in Strasbourg, were the
oldest; the Jesuit academies the most numerous; but there is reason
to believe that it was the younger, less fully confessionalized and
more internationally orientated Calvinist academies of Germany
that most fully embodied the reforming qualities just outlined. Such
at any rate is the impression given by the particular tradition to be

[4] Good introductions to this topic are provided by Anton Schindling, 'Schulen und Universi-
täten im 16. und 17. Jahrhundert. Bildungsexpansion und Laienbildung im Dienste der
Konfessionen', in *Wissensorganisierende und wissensvermittelnde Literatur im Mittelalter*, ed. N. R.
Wolf (Wiesbaden, 1987), 278–88; and John M. Fletcher, 'Change and resistance to change:
a consideration of the development of English and German universities during the sixteenth
century', *History of Universities*, 1 (1981), 1–36.

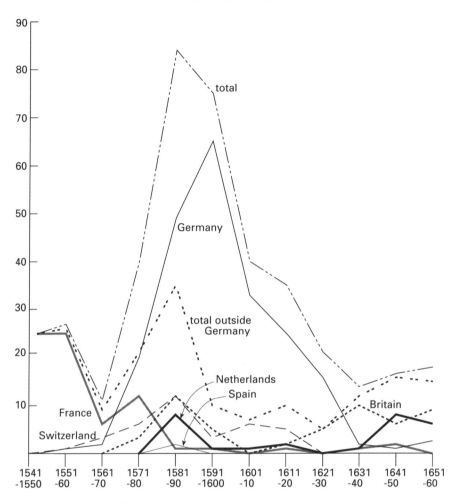

Figure 1.1 Editions of Ramus' dialectic and Talon's rhetoric before 1660
This graph is derived from the table in Walter Ong's *Ramus, method and the decay of dialogue* (296), modified where necessary by reference to his *Ramus and Talon inventory*. As the author himself is aware, the *Inventory* is imperfect, including a large number of ghosts and missing 100 or more extant editions. Given the disruption of the German library system and the exclusion of western scholars from east-central Europe during the years in which this list was compiled (see *Inventory*, 15–16), however, the proportion of German editions unrecorded here is probably higher than that for other areas.

outlined here: the tradition of philosophical pedagogy that developed within the Reformed academies between Ramus' visit to the Rhineland in 1569–70 and the first decade of the Thirty Years War.

That Petrus Ramus enjoyed his greatest measure of posthumous popularity, not in England, Scotland, France or the Netherlands, but in Reformed central Europe is a fact virtually unmentioned in the large, polyglot literature on his teaching and influence. Ramism was rediscovered by modern intellectual historians at Harvard, where it had enjoyed its longest and perhaps most unadulterated influence. After tracing its transmission back through William Ames to Cambridge puritanism, it has seemed natural to assume that Ramist influence was most strongly felt within the English-speaking world. The evidence collected in Walter Ong's *Ramus and Talon inventory*, however, suggests otherwise. Between 1570 and 1630, twenty-seven editions of Ramus' *Dialectica* and Talon's *Rhetorica* were published in English-speaking countries; presses in German-speaking countries during the same interval produced 240 such editions. Of the 290 editions of these two main works produced between Ramus' death and the outbreak of the Thirty Years War, over 80 per cent were published in Germany and German-speaking Switzerland (*see* fig. 1.1).[5]

This remarkable preponderance was not simply the product of Frankfurt's dominant position within the European book trade, nor even of the shrewd campaign of Ramus' favourite printer, Andreas Wechel, to corner the market of Ramist publication.[6] No sooner, in fact, had Wechel succeeded in outmanoeuvring his competitors in Basle than he began to lose ground to presses in Herborn, Hanau and many other small towns printing to service the needs of newly established Reformed academies and gymnasia there.[7] In order to

---

[5] See especially the table in W. J. Ong, *Ramus, method and the decay of dialogue* (Cambridge, MA, 1958), 296. That Ong's brief commentary on this table (pp. 296–306) remains the most extensive analysis of the mass of material collected in his *Ramus and Talon inventory* (Cambridge, MA, 1958) is an indication of the extent to which German intellectual history in this period has been neglected.

[6] For this view, see Ian Maclean, 'Philosophical books on European markets, 1570–1630: the case of Ramus', in *New perspectives in Renaissance thought: essays in the history of science, education and philosophy in memory of Charles B. Schmitt*, ed. John Henry and Sarah Hutton (London, 1990), 253–63.

[7] In addition to Ong's *Inventory*, see Antonius van der Linde, *Die Nassauer Drucke der Königlichen Landesbibliothek in Wiesbaden*, 2 vols. (Wiesbaden, 1882–7), I, nos. 20, 23, 25, 39, 53, 70, 254, 1303–5, 1540–41, 1605–13, 1780–83, 1840a, 1981, 2095–6, 2103–4, and II, 21 (no. 91); and Josef Benzing, 'Die Hanauer Erstdrucker Wilhelm und Peter Antonius

explain this overwhelming German dominance of Ramist imprints, we need to look not so much at the dynamics of the European textbook trade as at the aims of the Calvinists in Germany and the needs of the academies which they established there.

Viewed from a purely confessional standpoint, their aims are strongly reminiscent of those of their confessional brethren in England. In Germany, as in England, the Reformation appeared to many Calvinists to have stalled in the middle decades of the sixteenth century. Luther, they agreed, had performed a Herculean task in disentangling the central problem of individual salvation from the complex machinery of scholastic theology, canon law and ecclesiastical politics; but so great was his struggle that he had been able to accomplish only the first, most essential stage of it. His reformation of theology still had to be followed by a reformation of worship; and beyond this lay a still greater task: the reformation of life.[8]

Ramism was well adapted to both the theoretical and practical aspects of this agenda. On the one hand, it seemed to offer a means of completing the reformation of theology, of purifying theological education and communication of the last vestiges of scholasticism, human authority and pagan philosophy, and of focusing it still more exclusively on the text of Scripture.[9] On the other hand, Ramist dialectic offered an extremely useful and adaptable tool with which to solve the practical problems at the heart of the reform of popular culture.[10] For such mundane problems as administering a local law court, preparing a popular sermon or running a school, Aristotle's demonstrative logic was of little utility. It could only be applied to a

(1593–1625)', *Archiv für die Geschichte des Buchwesens*, 21 (1980), 1005–26, which includes fourteen Ramist titles not listed by Ong.

8 Bodo Nischan, 'Reformation or deformation? Lutheran and Reformed views of Martin Luther in Brandenburg's "Second Reformation"' in *Pietas et societas*, ed. K. C. Sessions and P. N. Bebb (Knoxville, 1985), 203–14. Paul Münch, 'Volkskultur und Calvinismus. Zur Theorie und Praxis der "reformatio vitae" während der "Zweiten Reformation"', in Schilling (ed.), *Konfessionalisierung*, 291–307.

9 Jürgen Moltmann, 'Zur Bedeutung des Petrus Ramus für Philosophie und Theologie des Calvinismus', *Zeitschrift für Kirchengeschichte*, 68 (1957), 295–318; Wilhelm Neuser, 'Die calvinistischen Ramisten', in *Handbuch der Dogmen- und Theologiegeschichte*, ed. Carl Andresen, 3 vols. (Göttingen, 1980), II, 328–47.

10 This practical advantage has been far less widely noted in the literature. A good example of the extraordinarily heavy emphasis placed on utility in Herborn is discussed in Gustav Adolph Benrath, 'Die theologische Fakultät der Hohen Schule Herborn im Zeitalter der reformierten Orthodoxie (1584–1634)', *Jahrbuch der Hessischen Kirchengeschichtlichen Vereinigung*, 36 (1985), 1–17, esp. 4–8.

limited range of theoretical problems which met a long and stringent series of conditions and therefore (as the Philosopher himself fully recognized) it was excluded from the practical domain of ethics and politics almost completely. What the lawyers, administrators, inspectors, teachers, preachers and pastors needed in order to reform the everyday standards of knowledge, virtue and piety in their communities was rather a far more basic set of practical tools which could be applied to the analysis of any text, to the development and organization of any argument on any subject. In Ramist dialectic they found a basic *organon* well adapted to these needs. Thus, just as puritans and Presbyterians were the chief agents of Ramism in England and Scotland, in Germany it found its strongest support among outspoken advocates of a further Calvinist reformation.

Underlying this basic similarity, however, was a fundamental difference, and this difference had a direct bearing on the capacity of Ramism to prosper and develop. In England, the initiative for further reformation came from outside the inner circles of power. Here the half-way house in need of renovation was the recently established Elizabethan Settlement, the rituals and polity in need of purification were those of the Established church. The episcopal form of church government posed a particularly inescapable point of contention: for the Crown it remained an indispensable tool of centralized government; to the Calvinists it appeared a deplorable vestige of popery. In the empire, however, the situation was quite different. There, ecclesiastical issues had been resolved on a territorial basis. No elaborate hierarchies of bishops and archbishops were needed in order to maintain centralized control over church affairs within these relatively small principalities. Calvinist ecclesiastical polity could therefore be Erastianized in much more subtle ways than was possible in England – and it should be remembered that Thomas Erastus was a professor in Heidelberg and was consulted by the elector when introducing Calvinism into the Palatinate. The secular incentives for adopting such a polity were considerable; for the machinery of Swiss ecclesiastical discipline, once suitably modified, offered these rulers the best available means of transforming the largely intractable populace of their territories into pious, obedient, virtuous, hard-working, self-disciplined and therefore useful members of the church and servants of the state. Far from threatening princely power within these small territories, a subtly

Erastianized Calvinist church polity promised to enhance it.[11] While a second, Calvinist reformation in England was being slowly and painfully driven forward from below, its German equivalent was therefore rapidly implemented from above.

The implications of this contrast for the future of Ramism were immediate: where zeal for a second reformation took on a radical tone, so did the means to achieve it. Whereas an inventory of German Ramists might be mistaken for a roster of leading professors and civil servants, 'the list of Cambridge Ramists', to quote Hugh Kearney, 'reads like a list of the most radical Cambridge Puritans'.[12] While Ramism in Germany remained a useful tool with which to advance the state-sponsored implementation of a second phase of reformation, in Britain it rapidly acquired radical overtones as an instrument with which to break the monopoly of the universities on education, to give to the common man the ability to think for himself and defend his thoughts with confidence. The result is perhaps most clearly evident in the proportion of vernacular editions in the two countries. Of the over 300 editions of Ramist works published in Germany and Switzerland, only two are in German translation. Of the thirty-three editions of Ramus' *Dialectic* published in Britain before 1700, nineteen are in English – more than all those in other vernaculars combined.[13]

This differing relationship to political authority had obvious consequences for the ability of Ramism to establish itself in these two regions. In the Empire, it quickly put down deep institutional roots. In the statutes of the first and most important of the academies founded in order to implement the second reformation in Germany – that which opened in Herborn in 1584 – professors were clearly instructed to teach the fundamental propaedeutic disciplines – grammar, rhetoric and dialectic – in the Ramist method. Such was

---

[11] Georg Schmidt, 'Die "Zweite Reformation" in Gebiet des Wetterauer Grafenvereins. Die Einführung des reformierten Bekentnisses im Spiegel der Modernisierung gräflicher Herrschaftssysteme', in Schilling (ed.), *Konfessionalisierung*, 184–213. The three most important cases are compared and contrasted in Paul Münch, *Zucht und Ordnung. Reformierte Kirchenverfassungen im 16. und 17. Jahrhundert (Nassau-Dillenburg, Kurpfalz, Hessen-Kassel)* (Stuttgart, 1978).

[12] Hugh Kearney, *Scholars and gentlemen: universities and society in pre-industrial Britain 1500–1700* (London, 1971), 61, and in general 46–70; cf. Christopher Hill, *The intellectual origins of the English Revolution* (Oxford, 1965), 31, 56, 270, 291–3.

[13] On vernacular editions in general, see Ong, *Ramus and Talon inventory*, 184–5. The German editions are *ibid.*, nos. 300 and 317. Two English-language editions not listed by Ong are Donald Wing, *Short-title catalogue ... 1641–1700*, 3 vols. (New York, 1945), L432C and L433.

the success of this experiment that it was to be copied, with modifications, almost everywhere that Reformed academies were founded
in Germany, notably at Steinfurt, Bremen, Hanau, Soest and
Zerbst, as well as in a still larger number of gymnasia.[14] In England,
as in Germany, it was almost exclusively at new foundations that
Ramism flourished: in those overseen by Ramus' student, Andrew
Melville, in Scotland; in Trinity College, Dublin; in Gresham
College; and, within the English universities, primarily in Emma-
nuel College, Cambridge, founded in the same year as Herborn.[15]
But not even in these did Ramism enjoy anything resembling the
statutory status bestowed on it in Herborn and her daughter schools:
such Ramist instruction as took place in Cambridge seems to have
been informal and extra-curricular.[16] Only much later, on the
extreme margins of the English-speaking world, was Ramism actually institutionalized to a comparable degree, in Harvard College.

The firm institutionalization of Ramism within German Calvinist
academies dramatically affected its development in another direction of great importance for the subsequent development of
Reformed philosophy. 'In Germany,' as Walter Ong observed over
thirty years ago, 'Ramist method moves into the uppermost
branches of the curriculum with a drive which cannot be matched in
any other country.'[17] Only once Ramist dialectic had become the
basis of instruction and thus the common training of all advanced
students could it profitably be applied to textbooks in the latter
stages of the curriculum. And this is precisely what happened in
Herborn. In the early 1580s, while the opening of the academy was
temporarily postponed by the count of Nassau-Dillenburg's participation in the third Dutch revolt, its professor-elect of philosophy,
Johannes Piscator, systematically emended and republished Ramus'
scholia on grammar, rhetoric, dialectic, physics and metaphysics.
Shortly after the academy opened, Lazarus Schoner added a revised
edition of Ramus' mathematical works. These were soon followed by

[14] Hermann Pixberg, *Der deutsche Calvinismus und die Pädagogik* (Gladbeck, 1964), 72–5, 80–2,
85, 88, 91; Gerhard Menk, *Die Hohe Schule Herborn in ihrer Frühzeit* (Wiesbaden, 1981),
174–92, 203–17.
[15] G. D. Henderson, *The founding of Marischall College Aberdeen* (Aberdeen, 1947), 11–18; John
Durkan and James Kirk, *The University of Glasgow 1451–1577* (Glasgow, 1977), esp. 289–92;
R. G. Cant, *The University of St. Andrews* (rev. edn, Edinburgh and London, 1970), 52–8;
Kearney, *Scholars and gentlemen*, 53–9, 61, 63, 65–70.
[16] Lisa Jardine, 'The place of dialectic teaching in sixteenth-century Cambridge', *Studies in the
Renaissance*, 21 (1974), 31–62.
[17] Ong, *Ramus, method and the decay of dialogue*, 298.

Johannes Althusius' famous Ramist textbooks on ethics, politics and law, and Piscator's complete course of exegetical theology firmly founded on Ramist analysis.[18] The logical culmination of this development was a single, comprehensive, systematically integrated and uniformly organized presentation of the entire encyclopaedia.

A comparison with developments in England is once again instructive. 'Elsewhere,' as Ong reported, 'the Ramist reorganization of the curriculum tends to affect chiefly the rhetoric–dialectic dyad.' Thus, when Howell proposed to illustrate 'how far Ramus's influence spread beyond the boundaries of logic and rhetoric' in England, he could present only a handful of grammars and a few works on arithmetic and geometry, all published between 1581 and 1594.[19] Piscator alone emended and published Ramist textbooks on more disciplines in the three years before the opening of the Herborn academy than are to be found in the entire English Ramist tradition.

Piscator also typifies the next important aspect in the development of this tradition. He was born and educated in Strasbourg, where he absorbed the humanist Aristotelianism characteristic of Sturm's gymnasium there. His university studies took place in Tübingen, where he was particularly impressed with the work of Jakob Schegk, one of the leading Aristotelian exegetes in northern Europe at this time and one of Ramus' most penetrating critics. With such a background, Piscator could not fail to see the serious limitations of Ramist dialectic, and his emendations of Ramus were therefore primarily Aristotelianizations.[20] From the very outset, therefore, Ramist dialectic in Germany was almost always combined with the well-established tradition of humanist Aristotelianism stemming from Philipp Melanchthon to form what was generally known as Philippo-Ramism.[21]

Once again, the English situation presents a marked contrast.

---

[18] The first printing of Piscator's editions are Ong, *Ramus and Talon inventory*, nos. 30, 593, 596, 697, 699; cf. also no. 283. Schöner's work is *ibid.*, no. 686. Cf. Menk, *Herborn*, 25 (n. 20), 32–3, 38, 41, 210. Althusius, *Iuris Romani libri duo: ad leges methodi Rameae conformati: & tabula illustrati* (Basle, 1586, 1589; Herborn, 1588, etc.); *Civilis conversationis libri duo* (Hanau, 1601, etc.); *Politica methodice digesta* (Herborn, 1603, etc.). For Piscator's series of biblical commentaries, published between 1591 and 1621, see van der Linde, *Die Nassauer Drucke*, I, nos. 1327–1408.

[19] W. S. Howell, *Logic and rhetoric in England, 1500–1700* (Princeton, 1956), 245–6.

[20] See Piscator's *Animadversiones in dialecticam P. Rami* (Frankfurt-am-Main, 1580), especially the autobiographical dedicatory epistle; Wilhelm Risse's comments on it in *Die Logik der Neuzeit*, 2 vols. (Stuttgart–Bad Cannstatt, 1964), I, 133, 174–5; and Piscator's intermediary part in the Temple–Digby debate (Ong, *Ramus and Talon inventory*, 506–10).

[21] This is clearly evident in the titles collected in Ong, *Ramus and Talon inventory*, nos. 268ff.

Philosophical instruction in England had stagnated since the Reformation, indeed since the heyday of Oxford logic in the fourteenth century. Only in the final quarter of the sixteenth century was Britain beginning to develop a strong domestic tradition of humanist Aristotelianism such as that which in Germany had been institutionalized for several generations.[22] In such circumstances, Ramist dialectic represented a far more radical break with the established curriculum than in Germany and the prospects of developing some form of compromise were relatively poor. At the same time, the radical political position of English Ramism insulated it from the desire for philosophical and theological reconciliation characteristic of the Rhineland Reformed.[23] Viewed from a continental perspective, English Ramist literature is thus far less conspicuous for its genuine philosophical contributions than for its furious polemics: Everard Digby versus William Temple in the early 1580s; Gabriel Harvey versus Thomas Nashe a decade later. As an aspect of radical ideology with negligible institutional roots, Ramism was also vulnerable to changes in the political climate: by the mid-1590s, when German production was reaching its peak, it was already in retreat even in Cambridge; by 1600 it was a dead letter in Scotland. In the first two decades of the seventeenth century – precisely the years, as we shall see, in which Calvinists in the empire were extending the Philippo-Ramist synthesis to Zabarella and beyond – only four Ramist works were published in Britain, and in only one of these did Ramus' name appear on the title page.[24] Finally, when Ramism began to revive in the 1620s, the old debate between Ramism and Peripateticism, resolved thirty years earlier in Germany, reopened between Richard Montague and John Selden.[25] As a result of this radicalism and its polarization of opinion,

[22] C. B. Schmitt, *John Case and Aristotelianism in Renaissance England* (Kingston and Montreal, 1983), 13–76.
[23] See, most recently, Gustav Adolf Benrath, 'Irenik und Zweite Reformation', in Schilling (ed.), *Konfessionalisierung*, 348–58 and also Benrath's 'Konfessionelle Irenik und Konkordienversuche im 16. und 17. Jahrhundert. Eine Skizze', in *Konfessionalisierung von 16. bis 19. Jahrhundert*, ed. Helmut Baier (Neustadt-an-der-Aisch, 1989), 156–66.
[24] Ong, *Ramus and Talon inventory*, nos. 125, 149, 415; and A. W. Pollard and G. R. Redgrave, *Short-title catalogue of books ... 1475–1640*, 2nd edn, 2 vols. (London, 1976–86), no. 23659.7 (cf. also no. 21106).
[25] For these controversies, see Howell, *Logic and rhetoric in England*, 173–9, 193–202; Ong, *Ramus and Talon inventory*, 506–10; Neal W. Gilbert, *Renaissance concepts of method* (New York, 1960), 200–9; Lisa Jardine, *Francis Bacon: discovery and the art of discourse* (Cambridge, 1974), 59–65, 68–9.

English philosophers played virtually no part in the development of the 'systematic' tradition.[26]

In central Europe, however, confessional imperatives and the needs of the universities soon pressed philosophers beyond this Philippo-Ramist compromise. Even within the German Reformed community Ramism had not been accepted universally. Although its wide practical applicability appealed strongly to the academies, from the loftier vantage point of the universities the advantages of Ramus' logic were much less apparent than its shortcomings. For advanced study in the higher faculties and especially for the complex and subtle reasoning of academic theology, the classificatory logic of Ramus was woefully inadequate. It was for such purposes that Aristotle's demonstrative logic had been adopted in previous centuries and the professors of theology were adamant that their students should not be deprived of the only proper preparation for such studies. When the Elector Palatine proposed to offer Ramus a chair of eloquence in 1570, Zacharius Ursinus, the principal author of the Heidelberg Catechism, and his colleagues objected strenuously, pleading that they could as well teach students to read without letters as to argue without Aristotle.[27] The following year, when Ramus offered to return to a lectureship he had briefly held in Geneva, Theodore Beza declined, stating that it was Geneva's 'sure and established resolution not to diverge from the opinion of Aristotle so much as a hair's-breadth either in teaching logic itself or in expounding the other disciplines'.[28] And, as confessional pressures within the Empire steadily grew in subsequent decades, the theologians of Germany's few fully fledged Reformed universities recognized more clearly than ever before their need for the sharpest possible intellectual weapons in order to defend themselves against polemical assaults from all sides. The results are again clearly

---

[26] Something of this contrast is suggested by Howell's choice of headings for his discussion of the 'systematics'; *Logic and rhetoric in England*, chap. 5: 'Counterreform', section 1: 'Middle ground between contradictions', 282–317.

[27] Ursinus, *Organi Aristotelei libri quinque priores … eiusdem Ursini, de Petri Rami dialectica et rhetorica iudicium, ad illustrissimum principem Fridericum III, electorem palatinum etc., perscriptum anno 1570* (Neustadt, 1586), fols. ✱✱1r–✱✱✱✱1v. Cf. Johann Friedrich Hautz, *Geschichte der Universität Heidelberg*, 2 vols. (Mannheim, 1862–4), II, 57.

[28] *Correspondance de Théodore de Bèze*, ed. Hippolyte Aubert, 16 vols. (Geneva, 1960–), XII, 295 (1 December 1570): '… quod nobis certum ac constitutum sit et in ipsis tradendis logicis, et in caeteris explicandis disciplinis ab Aristotelis sententiam ne tantillum quidem deflectere.' Cf. Charles Waddington, *Ramus. Sa vie, ses écrits et ses opinions* (Paris, 1855), 218–30; Charles Borgeaud, *Histoire de l'Université de Genève* (Geneva, 1900), I, 113 (n. 2).

evident within Ong's *Inventory*. Of the almost 800 editions of Ramus' works listed there, only one was published in Geneva;[29] and although a trickle of Ramist works appeared from such unlikely places as Salamanca and Prague in this period, none ever issued from the active academic presses of Heidelberg, the citadel of Reformed Germany.

The institutionalization of Ramism in the gymnasia and academies of Reformed Germany thus provoked a serious but ultimately fruitful crisis for the universities when, from the late 1580s onwards, an ever-increasing number of students arrived unprepared for the study of systematic theology by a thorough grounding in the more technical sections of Aristotle's *Organon*. In 1599 Bartholomäus Keckermann, a junior lecturer in the divinity school in Heidelberg, summed up a widely held view in blaming Ramus for what he called 'the calamity of our time': namely, 'the fact that those fundamental disciplines, preparatory to all remaining higher learning, [are] now seldom seen among students'.[30] Keckermann perceived this problem especially clearly because he was himself a member of the second generation of the second reformation. He had been schooled in Ramist dialectic in the Reformed gymnasium in Danzig and had only encountered Aristotle during his subsequent university studies in Wittenberg, Leipzig, Altdorf and Heidelberg.[31] With such a background, he was also well placed to find a solution to this problem: a method of exposition that would avoid the serious deficiencies both of the traditional method of teaching philosophy by means of lengthy and disjointed commentaries on Aristotle's archaic and disorganized texts and of Ramus' wilfully oversimplified and tendentious alternative to it. Keckermann's solution was to combine the best features of these two competing logics. The doctrine he expounded was essentially that of Aristotle, but the orderliness, clarity and systematic coherence with which he expounded it were strongly reminiscent of Ramus. The result was a presentation

[29] Ong, *Ramus and Talon inventory*, no. 131: an edition of Talaeus' rhetoric, published in 1602.
[30] Bartholomäus Keckermann, *Opera omnia*, 2 vols. (Geneva and Cologne, 1614), I, 77B–C: 'Illud, benevole Lector, non ignoras, scio, aut negas, ex seculi nostri calamitatibus unam esse, quod fundamentales illae et ad reliquam omnem altiorem cognitionem praeparatoriae disciplinae eos quos possent, aut debebant fructus apud Iuventutem raro ostendant.' Cf. *ibid.*, I, 119B–21H, 126F, 420E–421D.
[31] *Ibid.*, I, 135E, 1769[C–D]; W. H. van Zuylen, *Bartholomäus Keckermann. Sein Leben und Werk* (Leipzig, 1934), 2–5.

of Peripatetic substance in quasi-Ramist form which Keckermann dubbed 'methodical Peripateticism'.

We cannot go into the details of Keckermann's solution here;[32] but three points regarding it are especially germane to the present discussion. In the first place, like Ramism, it was based on a methodological innovation brought to the Reformed community in Germany by a small wave of religious refugees; in this instance, recent Italian converts to Protestantism such as Julius Pacius and Fortunatus Crellius had brought with them the logical writings of their teacher in Padua, the leading Aristotelian commentator, Jacopo Zabarella. Secondly, it was also, like Ramism, based on a system of topics or commonplaces: Keckermann began by deriving clear and succinct statements of Aristotle's positions on key points from his often obscure and convoluted texts; he then carefully arranged these statements in the order in which Aristotle's argument as a whole could most easily be grasped; having done so, he assembled material on each of these points from an impressively wide range of other logical authorities; and finally, he used this material to illustrate, clarify, debate and defend Aristotle's position on each of the points at issue. The result was a method of exposition in which the kind of material previously buried in cumbersome commentaries could be much more clearly organized, easily understood and readily learned. This procedure, thirdly, could also be applied to other disciplines besides logic: between Keckermann's return to his native Danzig in 1602 and his untimely death at less than forty years of age in 1609, he rapidly applied his systematic method of exposition to grammar, rhetoric, metaphysics, physics, ethics, politics, economics, mathematics, astronomy and geography. In fact, Keckermann's method of systematically arranged theses with explanatory commentary – the sum total of which (with his further refinements) he called a *systema* – became the standard form of academic presentation in Germany for a century and more there after.[33]

The success of these works in recasting Peripatetic substance in semi-Ramist form is evident in their enthusiastic reception both in the universities which had refused to abandon Aristotle and in the academies which had embraced Ramus. In Heidelberg, wrote the

---

[32] General expositions of Keckermann's method can be found in the *Opera omnia*, I, 51F–68C, 137G–158B.

[33] Wilhlem Schmidt-Biggemann, *Topica universalis. Eine Modellgeschichte humanistischer und barocker Wissenschaft* (Hamburg, 1983), 92.

consistently anti-Ramist theologian, David Pareus, Keckermann's works were read 'like Sibylline oracles'.[34] The Genevan printers who had contributed so little to the production of Ramus' works printed Keckermann's entire *Opera omnia* in two large folios in 1614.[35] When the Estates of Holland and West Friesland (which had also resoundingly rejected Ramism) decided to designate a single logic textbook as standard for all schools in their provinces, they commissioned the Leiden professor, Franco Burgersdijk, to revise the work of Keckermann.[36] In Oxford a collection of Keckermann's mathematical writings was published as late as 1661.[37] Even the bitterly anti-Calvinist Lutheran universities did not remain untouched by Keckermann's logical writings: in 1617 Jacobus Martini observed from Wittenberg 'that Keckermann's authority is great among many of our own religion as well, and that his *Systema logicum* is in almost every hand'.[38]

These *systemata* appealed no less to the schools and academies in which Ramus had been institutionalized for a generation. In the years after his death, editions of Keckermann's unfinished manuscripts, transcripts of his lectures and abridgements of his more advanced textbooks were published, among others, by Johann-Philipp Pareus, son of the anti-Ramist Palatine theologian and rector of the Casimirianum in Neustadt; Walter Keuchen, rector of the Hanau academy; Jan Turnowski, senior of the Bohemian Brethren (*Unitas fratrum*) in Great Poland and pastor and professor of theology in Thorn; and Petrus Lossius the Younger, professor of

---

[34] '... cuius libri intra breve spatium quasi quaedam sibyllarum oracula publicae prostarent': From Pareus' still unpublished history of Heidelberg, as cited by August Tholuck, *Das akademische Leben des siebzehnten Jahrhunderts*, Zweite Abtheilung: *Die akademische Geschichte der Hohen Schulen*, 2 vols. (Halle, 1854), II, 266.

[35] See above, note 30.

[36] *Franconis Burgersdicii Institutionum libri duo, decreto illust. ac poten. D. D. Ordinum Hollandiae et West-Frisiae, in usum scholarum eiusdem provinciae, ex Aristotelis, Keckermanni, aliorumque praecipiorum logicorum praeceptis recensitis nova methodo ac modo formati, atque editi* (Leiden, 1626), preface. Paul Dibon, *La philosophie néerlandaise au siècle d'or*, I: *L'Enseignement philosophique dans les universités à l'époque précartésienne (1575–1650)* (Paris, Amsterdam, etc., 1954), 99–103, 123–4.

[37] Keckermann, *Systema totius mathematices, hoc est geometriae, opticae, astronomiae, et geographiae publicis praelectionibus anno 1605 in ... Gymnasio Dantiscano propositum* (Oxford, 1661). See Falconer Madan, *Oxford books*, 3 vols. (Oxford, 1895–1931), III, 150–1. On the relatively low esteem for Ramism in Oxford, see most recently James McConica, 'Elizabethan Oxford: the collegiate society', in *The collegiate university*, ed. James McConica [= *The history of the University of Oxford*, vol. III] (Oxford, 1986), 645–732, esp. 699, 713.

[38] Jacobus Martini, *Praelectiones extemporaneae in systema logicum Barth. Keckermanni* (Wittenberg, 1617), fol)(4ʳ: 'videbam, autoritatem Keckermanni apud multos, etiam religioni nostrae addictos, magnam esse, Systemaque hoc Logicum omnium teri manibus'.

Greek in Danzig.[39] In total, the various parts of Keckermann's *Systema logicum* passed through over forty editions between 1599 and 1656, Burgersdijk's revision of it through twelve more, a synopsis of Burgersdijk's text through a further seven printings, and an explication of Burgersdijk's synopsis through yet another seven.[40] By the end of the century, the *fortuna* of Keckermann's logical writings had begun to resemble that of Ramus' *Dialectica* itself.

Given the wide extent of this activity and the confessional and geographical proximity of much of it to Elbing, it is hardly surprising that the circle of Keckermann's admirers in these years should have included the teachers of all of the 'Three Foreigners'. Melchior Lauban, the teacher of Samuel Hartlib, his brother George and their friend, Cyprian Kinner, in Brieg, had previously been prorector and professor of philology in Danzig, where he contributed epigrams to two of Keckermann's writings.[41] In 1617 Keckermann's *Systema rhetoricae* was epitomized by his friend, Johannes Mylius, the rector of the gymnasium in Elbing whom Dury described as his first mentor.[42] And no one fell more deeply under Keckermann's spell than Comenius' teacher in Herborn, Johann Heinrich Alsted.[43]

[39] *Organi Aristotelis analysis aphoristica adumbrata olim a cl. viro Bartholomaeo Keckermanno Dantiscano. Nunc primum ... edita studio et opera Joh. Philippi Parei illustris Scholae Neapolitanae rectoris* (Frankfurt-am-Main, 1614); *Systema grammaticae Hebraeae*, ed. Walter Keuchen (Hanau, [1616 or later]); *Scientiae metaphysicae compendiosum systema; Publicis in Gymnasio Dantiscano praelectionibus adornatum*, ed. J. Turnowski (Hanau, 1609); *Dispositiones orationum, ... annis ab hinc aliquot ... propositum in Gymnasio Dantiscano, a ... Bartholomeo Keckermanno ... : nunc primum ... editum, opera et studio Petri Lossii Dantiscani* (Hanau, 1615).

[40] Burgersdijk, *Institutionum logicarum synopsis* (Leiden, 1632). Adriaan Heereboord, *EPMHNEIA Logica seu Explicatio ... synopsis logicae Burgersdicianae* (Leiden, 1650). See Dibon, *La philosophie néerlandaise*, I, 118, 123–4. For the most important lists of Keckermann's logic writings, see Benzing, 'Wilhelm und Peter Antonius', index refs; *Bibliographia Polska*, ed. Karl Estreicher, 22 vols. (Cracow, 1903–   ), 19, 216–23; *Bibliographica Logica*, ed. Wilhelm Risse, 4 vols. (Hildersheim, 1965–79), I: *Verzeichnis der Druckschriften zur Logik, 1472–1800*, index refs.

[41] The epigrams are in Keckermann, *Disputationes philosophicae, physicae praesertim* (Hanau, 1606), fol.):(5r and Keckermann, *Systematis logici plenioris pars altera* (Hanau, 1609), fol.††7v. On Lauban himself, see Ephriam Praetorius, *Athenae Gedanensis* (Leipzig, 1713), 52–4; *HDC*, 11–12, 384; and Blekastad, *Comenius*, 165, n. 29.

[42] *Bartholomaei Keckermanni systematis rhetorici epitome succincta praeceptorum prope omnium methodo, pro tironibus in Gymnasio Elbingensi adornata a M. Iohanne Mylio Gymnasii Elbingensi rectore* (Hanau, 1611; repr. 1617). Mylius' acquaintance with Keckermann is reported in Joachim Praetorius, *Oratio honori litterarum et memoriae posthumae duorum Gymnasii Elbingensis rectorum Joh. et Mich. Myliorum* (Elbing, 1652): 'id denique etiam assequeretur, ut dignum ipse ille ingens Keckermannus judiceret, a quo disceret'. On his connection with Dury, see Gunnar Westin, *Negotiations about church unity* (Uppsala, 1932), 193; and Blekastad, *Comenius*, 164 (n. 21), 355, 356.

[43] On Comenius' studies in Herborn, see most recently G. Michel, 'Komenskýs Studien in Herborn und ihre Nachwirkungen in seinem Gesamtwerk', in *Comenius. Erkennen – Glauben –*

A large part of Alsted's enormous encyclopaedic labours, in fact, can be viewed as an attempt to extend and complete the pedagogical undertaking inherited from Keckermann after his premature death in 1609. In one of his earliest writings, the *Panacea philosophica* of 1610, Alsted outlined an ambitious encyclopaedic project firmly based on Keckermann's systematic method of exposition, and vowed to complete it.[44] Three years later Alsted culminated the posthumous publication of Keckermann's writings with a two-volume, 3,500-page collection entitled *Systema systematum*: a 'system of systems' which applied the same principles to arranging Keckermann's philosophical work as a whole as those he had applied to organizing works on the individual disciplines and which thus constituted an integrated if still incomplete encyclopaedia of the basic curriculum subjects.[45] And in 1630, after devoting over the course of twenty years a long series of philosophical disputations and introductory textbooks to preliminary treatments of the individual disciplines, Alsted finally published his completed *Encyclopaedia* – the first major publication so called – of two large folio volumes and some 6,000 columns covering thirty-four disciplines: the four philosophical *praecognita,* seven instrumental disciplines, the full range of theoretical and practical philosophy (eighteen disciplines in all), the three higher faculties, an unprecedented systematic treatment of the mechanical arts, and a final collection of thirty-seven *quodlibetica.*[46]

In its disciplinary scope, in the range of philosophical opinions which it collected and attempted to harmonize and in the consistency with which it applied a single set of pedagogical principles to this vast collection of material, Alsted's *Encyclopaedia* went far beyond anything previously attempted within the tradition. An even greater innovation, and one perhaps still more relevant to the methodological eclecticism of Hartlib's 'Baconian' circle described

Handeln, ed. Klaus Schaller (Sankt Augustin, 1985), 11–21; and Gerhard Menk, 'Johann Amos Comenius und die Hohe Schule Herborn', *Acta Comeniana,* 8 (1989), 41–59.
[44] *Panacea philosophica, id est facilis, nova et accurata methodus docendi et discendi universam encyclopaediam, septem sectionibus distincta* (Herborn, 1610). For Keckermann's influence on this work, see especially 13, 34–6.
[45] *Systema systematum clarissimi viri Dn. Bartholomaei Keckermanni, omnia huius autoris opera philosophica uno volumine comprehensa lectori exhibens; idque duobus tomis,* ed. Johann Heinrich Alsted, 2 vols. (Hanau, 1613).
[46] *Cursus philosophici encyclopaedia libris XXVII* (Herborn, 1620). The much-expanded second edition is entitled *Encyclopaedia septem tomis distincta* (Herborn, 1630; facsimile repr., Stuttgart, 1988–90). Reprinted as *Scientiarum omnium encyclopaediae tomus primus [-quartus]* (Lyon, 1649; microfilm edition by the Inter-Documentation Company, Zug, Switzerland).

by Stephen Clucas in the next chapter, was Alsted's attempt to unite the Ramism, Philippo-Ramism and 'methodical Peripateticism' of his major precursors with a still wider variety of logical and pedagogical tools which he collected from the fringes of the Reformed philosophical tradition. To the topical logic of Petrus Ramus, he attempted to join the topical art of memory, despite the fact that his Ramist precursors (like their modern commentators) regarded the latter as antithetical to the former.[47] Alongside Keckermann's 'systematic' method of invention and disposition, Alsted employed the still more mechanical combinatorial logic of the Catalan mystic, Raymund Lull, in spite of Keckermann's explicit disapproval of it.[48] Nor did the extremely unorthodox hermetic doctrines underlying the work of the wandering Neapolitan friar, Giordano Bruno, prevent Alsted from publishing one of his manuscripts, studying, citing and abridging others of his works, and imitating his attempts to combine all the various arts of memory and learning in order to fashion psychological tools of even greater utility and power.[49] Finally, when yet another *novum organum* appeared, this time from England, Alsted was characteristically quick to receive it. The first reference to Bacon yet located in his papers is found in a letter of 1628 to Alsted from his former pupil and future son-in-law, Johann Heinrich Bisterfeld, describing Bacon's unfavourable views on the Lullian *ars magna*. Yet in the final edition of the *Encyclopaedia* published two years later, Alsted appended to his own treatment of history the catalogue of natural histories that concluded the *Instaura-*

---

[47] See especially Alsted's *Artium liberalium, ac facultatum omnium systema mnemonicum*, [= *Systema mnemonicum duplex, pars II*], 2 vols. (Frankfurt-am-Main, 1610). Frances Yates, *The art of memory* (London, 1966), esp. 231–42, 272–4, 276–7, 375–7.

[48] See especially Alsted's *Clavis artis Lullianae* (Strasbourg, 1609) and his edition of *Berhardi de Lavinheta opera omnia, quibus tradidit artis Raymundi Lulli compendiosam explicationem, et eiusdem applicationem* (Cologne, 1612). For Keckermann's criticism, see *Opera omnia*, I, 65C–H, 108A–109G, 424H–427C, 742H.

[49] *Artificium perorandi traditum a Jordano Bruno Nolano-Italo, communicatum a Johanne Henrico Alstedio* (Frankfurt-am-Main, 1612). Synopses of this work are included in Johann Alsted, *Systema mnemonicum duplex. I. Minus* (Frankfurt-am-Main, 1610), 127–36; and Johann Alsted, *Consiliarius academicus et scholasticus ... Accessit consilium de copia rerum et verborum, id est methodo disputandi de omni scibili* (Strasbourg, 1610), 151–65. Cf. Frances Yates, *Giordano Bruno and the hermetic tradition* (London, 1964). Combinations of Lullism with other logics are especially prominent in Alsted's *Panacea philosophica, ... Accessit eiusdem criticus, de infinito harmonico philosophiae Aristotelicae, Lullianae et Rameae* (Herborn, 1610), and *Trigae canonicae, quarum prima est dilucida artis mnemologicae ... explicatio & applicatio. Secunda, est artis Lulliana ... architectura & usus locupletissimus. Tertia, est artis oratoriae novum magisterium, quo continentur utilis introductio ad copiam rerum comparandam per tres rotas sive circulos generis demonstrativi, deliberativi, et iudicialis: itemque ad comparandam copiam verborum per triangulum aliasque figuras* (Frankfurt-am-Main, 1612).

tio magna, recommending it as a series of natural historical common-places within which students should collect material, and thus integrating within the post-Ramist encyclopaedic tradition a germ of so much of the activity of the succeeding era.[50]

Alsted's *Encyclopaedia* thus represents the conceptual and technical culmination of a sixty-year-old pedagogical tradition intimately related to the wider history of German Calvinism as a whole. The roots of that tradition are to be found in the final two decades of the sixteenth century: in the integration of Ramism into a state-sponsored programme of social, political and theological reform; its consequent firm institutionalization in a network of schools and academies founded as Calvinism spread across central Europe; its publication there in the overwhelming majority of contemporary editions; and its subsequent combination with humanist Aris-totelianism and the most recent Italian philosophical developments to create an increasingly flexible and sophisticated pedagogical tool applicable to a wide variety of tasks. The reception of this new pedagogical method throughout a greatly expanded philosophical curriculum in the first decades of the seventeenth century likewise reflects the spread of Calvinism eastwards to such notable courts as the landgraviate of Hesse, the duchy of Brandenburg, seven Silesian principalities and, however briefly, the kingdom of Bohemia. Finally, the *Encyclopaedia* marks the end-point of the tradition in a chronological as well as a teleological sense; for, by the time Alsted's masterwork finally appeared in its definitive edition of 1630, all these political gains had been reversed; and with their loss the institutional foundation of this whole educational enterprise had been drastically undermined. The elector palatine had been defeated, his lands confiscated, his professors dispersed, his great library looted. Bohemia, Moravia and Silesia had begun to feel the full weight of the Habsburg-led Counter-Reformation. Hesse-Marburg had been reclaimed by the Lutherans. Danzig had been lost first to Wittenberg, then to Rome. Hanau had been undermined financially and the age of the Calvinist printers in Frankfurt had come rapidly to an end. Between Bremen in the north and Basle in

---

[50] Hessisches Hauptstaatsarchiv, Wiesbaden, MS 95, 320 II, fol. 180 (Bisterfeld, Graviae in Brabantia, 20/30 November 1628, to Alsted, Herborn): 'Verulamii philosophia illustrio-rem longè artis generalis usum ostendit, quamvis in Augmentis scientiarum in Lullistas graviter invehatur. Dabo operam ut omnia hujus opera Francofurtam mittam.' The passage from *De augmentis scientiarum* referred to is Bacon, *Works*, I, 669; IV, 454. Alsted, *Encyclopaedia* (1630), 2021–2 reproduces Bacon, *Works*, I, 405–10.

the south, Herborn struggled on virtually alone in the heart of Germany throughout the late 1620s, crippled by the Edict of Restitution and other indemnities, exhausted by the haemorrhage to other places of its most talented teachers. The movement that began with the migration of pastors, printers and professors into the Rhineland from all directions ended with their exodus, mainly to the north and west: to the academies of Steinfurt and Bremen, to the young universities of the Dutch provinces, and still further west to England. When Alsted, after having declined numerous invitations to follow them, finally accepted that of Bethlen Gábor to Transylvania, the easternmost outpost of the Reformed world, he was the last major figure to leave. Like Hartlib and Comenius in England, Alsted and Bisterfeld would play a key role in establishing the pedagogical tradition which constitutes the greatest contribution of the subsequent generation of 'Hungarian Puritans' to their national culture.[51] But the academies and universities that they left behind in Germany would never regain the dynamism that had made them, for half a century, the pedagogical pioneers of Reformed Europe.

It is not possible here even to outline the immediate relevance of this tradition to the work of the 'Three Foreigners'. The precise relationship of Alsted's encyclopaedic project to Comenius' pansophic plans, the connection of the longstanding tradition of Reformed irenicism on the continent with Dury's efforts at ecclesiastical reconciliation, and the relations of such other émigrés as Joachim Hübner, Caspar Streso, Cyprian Kinner, Theodore Haak, János Tolnai Dali and even Henry Oldenburg to the tradition we have outlined are a few of the most obvious topics that await research. The following chapter in this volume provides some intriguing indications of central European influence on the methodological eclecticism of Hartlib's English friends. But here we can only conclude by emphasizing the central point: namely, that it is no coincidence that three of the figures most active in, and inspirational for, the scientific, philosophical and educational reform movement of mid-seventeenth-century England should have been central European Reformed refugees. For several generations before Hartlib, Dury and Comenius arrived in England, a network of schools, academies and universities in central Europe had been

[51] R. J. W. Evans, 'Calvinism in east central Europe: Hungary and her neighbours, 1540–1700', in *International Calvinism, 1541–1715*, ed. Menna Prestwich (Oxford, 1985), 167–96, esp. 183, 188.

developing a systematic approach to philosophical pedagogy which, in its novelty, flexibility and utility, was the leader of the Reformed world and second to none in Europe. It was therefore only natural that the destruction of this tradition and dispersal of its principal agents in the first decade of the Thirty Years War should have helped to generate other movements of philosophical innovation and pedagogical reform elsewhere.

CHAPTER 2

In search of 'The True Logick': methodological eclecticism among the 'Baconian reformers'

Stephen Clucas

If we find out not Reason in our owne Reason wee shall never understand or finde out the true logick ...[1]

'A GENEROSITY AND LIBERTY IN ALL OUR STUDIES'

In his *Novum organum* of 1622, Francis Bacon expressed grave doubts about the state of contemporary logic. 'The logic now in use', he declared, 'serves rather to fix and give stability to the errors which have their foundation in commonly received notions than to help the search after truth. So it does more harm than good.'[2] The reformation and amendment of vitiated human knowledge would only be brought about by a radical rethinking of how knowledge is gathered. 'We must begin anew from the very foundations, unless we would revolve forever in a circle with mean and contemptible progress.'[3] Only one 'method of delivery' would suffice, Bacon claimed, and that was 'lead[*ing*] men to the particulars themselves, and their series and order'.[4] Bacon's search for certainty and his desire to shake off the 'idols and false notions which are now in possession of the human understanding'[5] was a mission whole-heartedly embraced by 'the philosophers of the Puritan revolution'. Hartlib's self-appointed role as parliamentary intelligencer and promoter of the advancement of learning took up the philosophical ideals of Bacon's works, augmenting its implicit religious dimensions

---

I would like to thank Dr Howard Hotson of Brasenose College, Oxford, for reading an early version of this chapter and making many helpful and detailed suggestions, and Professor Dagmar Čapková, for her comments on Comenius and the *ars excerpendi*.
[1] *Ephemerides* (1639): (HP 30/4/27A).
[2] *Novum organum*, I, aphorism XII; Bacon, *Works*, IV, 48.
[3] *Novum organum*, I, aphorism XXXI; Bacon, *Works*, IV, 52.
[4] *Novum organum*, I, aphorism XXXVI; Bacon, *Works*, IV, 53.
[5] *Novum organum*, I, aphorism XXXVIII; Bacon, *Works*, IV, 53.

by cross-fertilizing it with a German liberal Calvinist intellectual milieu.[6] Social reformation, religious reformation and the reformation of science, technology and philosophy were inextricably linked. In this context, logic – or method (the 'ordering' of knowledge) – was of paramount importance.

In this chapter I want to examine Hartlib's discussions about logical method, and the nature of reformation in the turbulent years 1639 to 1640. This will demonstrate that the 'Baconian reformers' were operating with a more fluid methodological outlook than this sobriquet implies. It will also reveal some new ways of looking at the intellectual underpinning of the 'puritan revolution', in particular the matrix of continental influences behind some English conceptions of the *Idaea reformationis* in the 1640s.

Although often characterized as a 'Baconian' or a 'Comenian', Hartlib was by no means inflexibly attached to the philosophical outlooks of either Francis Bacon or Jan Amos Comenius despite his efforts to disseminate their works.[7] 'It is not good', Hartlib wrote in his *Ephemerides* of 1639, 'to enslave ones-selfe to any kind of method or meditations.'[8] It was most prudent, he concluded,

to observe a certaine generosity and liberty in all our studys. This will bee found to bee far more profitable. As the overflowings of rivers doe bring in a world of things with them, which they never would have done if they hadde always runne in their wonted channels. Yet some mens wittes have [*so*] bounded themselves within certaine limits, that they can doe nothing.[9]

In the 1630s and 1640s, this 'generosity and liberty' of outlook led Hartlib to consider a wide variety of works on logic, pedagogy, method and systematic encyclopaedism. He attempted to assess their competing claims of comprehensiveness and evaluate their various degrees of utility for the achieving of his reforming objectives. In his Office of Address proposal, written to elicit parliamentary support for an 'intelligencing bureau' on the model of

---

[6] H. R. Trevor-Roper, 'Three foreigners: the philosophers of the puritan revolution', *Religion, the Reformation and social change* (1967; revised 3rd edn, London, 1984), 237–93.

[7] *Ibid.*, 247–51. On the 'systematic Baconian programme' of Hartlib's Agency for Universal Learning, see Webster, 97–9.

[8] On the *Ephemerides*, see Stephen Clucas, 'Samuel Hartlib's *Ephemerides* 1635–59, and the pursuit of scientific and philosophical manuscripts: the religious ethos of an intelligencer', *The Seventeenth Century*, 6 (1991), 33–55.

[9] *Ephemerides* (1639): HP 29/4/21A. Cf. also the opinions of Hartlib's friend, collaborator and researcher, Joachim Hübner, in *Ephemerides* (1639): 'In Meditation a world of thoughts will escape if one binds himself to one Method' (HP 30/4/24A). Cf. 'The binding ones-selfe to any Rule whatsoeuer dose hinder mightily a mans free invention' (HP 30/4/35A).

Théophraste Renaudot's *bureau d'addresse*, Hartlib stressed the need for 'scientificall and demonstrative knowledge', which was like a 'Building wherein the prospective of the glory of God in Christ may appeare to us'.[10] This knowledge was to be prosecuted with 'the Right Frame of Spirit', beginning with a 'full discoverie of the Objects of knowledge'. In this would be encapsulated 'all the partitions of Learning and Sciences' (effectively a Baconian gathering of 'particulars'), and then a 'Reall way to know these objects' would be applied through a logic or method in which such particulars would be ordered and analysed. These could then be referred 'to the manifestation of Christ'.[11] An ordered, logical disposition of knowledge was thus seen as a way towards the truth of Christ. Comenius' *pansophia* also promised an ordered means of comprehending the totality of human knowledge. It was envisaged by Hartlib – and by Comenius himself – in a specifically irenic and millenarian context. 'Certainly God hase some special aime in bringing this notion of a Pansophical learning into the world', Hartlib declared, for it was 'a preparation for that happy promised state of God's church and a forerunner to bring men that blessed and wished for unity and union by stating of all the universal principles aright'.[12] 'The pansophical undertaking is of mighty importance', he wrote elsewhere. 'For what can bee almost greater then to have all knowledge? If it were with the addition to have all love also it were perfection.'[13] It was of such mighty importance, in fact, that Hartlib did not feel confident that it was safe to be entrusted to Comenius alone. Comenius, he thought, was 'very defective in prooving the necessity of [*pansophia*]'. He wanted him to work with the Anglo-German systematic philosopher, Joachim Hübner.[14] Hartlib later added the methodical propositions of the young mathematician John Pell, or *more Pelleana*, to create a 'dream ticket' for the advancement of English science. 'These three', Hartlib wrote, 'are very fit to bee imploied about the Reformation of Learning. The one urges mainly a perfect enumeration of all things. The other is all for that which hase an evident use

---

[10] Webster, 68–9, 76, 375. For Renaudot see H. M. Solomon, *Public welfare, science and propaganda in seventeenth-century France: the innovation of Théophraste Renaudot* (Princeton, 1972). In *Ephemerides* (1640), Hartlib notes the publication of Renaudot's *L'usage et comoditez des Bureaux dans les Provinces*: HP 30/4/64B.

[11] Clucas, 'Hartlib's *Ephemerides*', 34–5.   [12] *Ephemerides* (1639): HP 30/4/11A.

[13] *Ephemerides* (1639): HP 30/4/12A.

[14] *Ephemerides* (1639): HP 30/4/11A. Hübner was researching for Hartlib in the Bodleian Library in the years 1631–42. See R. F. Young, *Comenius in England* (London, 1932), 47.

in vita humanis. The third is all for methodizing and contracting cutting of all verbosities and impertinencies whatsoever. These three being all reduced into one must needes make up a compleat direction.'[15]

Hübner was one of Hartlib's most voluminous correspondents on the subject of logic and method. He was also one of the chief dissenters from the Comenian position in the Hartlib circle. He felt that the publication of Comenius' *Prodromus* and *Didactica* ought to be preceded by 'an *Idaea Reformationis*'.[16] Although the 'reformation of the world will never bee brought to the perfection of its idaea', he suggested, 'yet there is an absolut necessity of the perfectest ideas of it, because ... wee must have a deciding rule that must guide and found our directions'.[17] Hübner was quick to seize on the wider ramifications of Comenius' claims for universalizing and harmonizing knowledge, outside their original pedagogical and educational context. Comenius 'will meddle only with *Reformatio studiorum*', he complained, 'but if those principles bee admitted the *Reformatio Religionis, statuum* etc may be more impartially taken in hand'.[18] Calvinist systematizers and logicians such as Bartholomäus Keckermann and Johannes Piscator had already implanted the seeds of logical scriptural analysis. The German 'systematics' such as Alsted, Polanus and Bisterfeld[19] grafted the sanguine rationalism of these logicians onto the Renaissance traditions of encyclopaedism, mnemonics and *mathesis universalis*[20] and, – with the aid of a growing millenarian fervour – widened the potential (as they saw it) of reforming knowledge.

LOGIC AND THE REFORMATION OF LEARNING

Johannes Piscator characterized logic as 'a general art [*which*] ... can be applied as much to spiritual and divine matters as to human and profane ones'.[21] Comenius' treatment of method in his *Didactica*

---

[15] *Ephemerides* (1639): HP 30/4/5B.   [16] *Ephemerides* (1639): HP 30/4/7B.
[17] *Ephemerides* (1639): HP 30/4/9A.
[18] *Ephemerides* (1639): HP 30/4/6A.
[19] See W. J. Ong, *Ramus, method and the decay of dialogue* (1958; repr. Cambridge, MA, 1983), 297–306; cf. Hotson, this volume, chap. 1.
[20] On the encyclopaedic tradition and *mathesis universalis* see Paolo Rossi, *Clavis universalis: arti della memoria e logica combinatoria dal Lullo a Leibnitz* (Bologna, 1960; repr. Bologna, 1983) and Giovanni Crapulli, *Mathesis universalis: genesi di un'idea nel XVI secolo*, Lessico Intellettuale Europeo II (Rome, 1969).
[21] Johannes Piscator, *Analysis logica epistolarum Pauli ad Romanos* (London, 1591), fol. A6r.

magna, likewise, deals with the *artium methodus* in general terms, before discussing particular applications in natural philosophy (*scientiarum methodus*), ethics (*methodus morum*), language teaching (*linguarum methodus*) and the 'instilling of piety' (*pietatis instillandae methodus*).[22] It is not surprising to find that John Dury was also one of Hartlib's strongest hopes for a 'reformation methodology'. Dury was an admirer of Ramus, who, he said, 'was the first to open men's eyes after Aristotle'.[23] Dury's much-vaunted method was apparently developed with some assistance from Descartes' friend and correspondent, Justinus von Ascher.[24] Dury devised it principally as a tool for scriptural analysis. It was to assist him in his Bible studies and help him frame a universally acceptable dogmatic creed for a united European Protestant church.[25] It was also sought after, however, by Cheney Culpeper as a means of analysing his volumes of chemical commonplaces,[26] and had already been used to analyse a collection of the 'thowghts' of Joseph Webb.[27] In his *Motion tending to the public good* of 1642, Dury described a pansophic enterprise based on a 'universall method of ordering the thoughts',[28] which would apply equally to religion, languages and the sciences, and his method was evidently intended to have such a latitude of applications. Despite entreaties from Hartlib and a number of his correspondents, Dury never printed a treatise outlining his method.[29] There are, however, some fragments relating to it in Hartlib's papers, including a specimen of it as applied to a scriptural topic.[30] It was essentially a means

---

22 J. A. Comenius, *Didactica magna*, ed. F. C. Hultgren (1894; repr. Farnborough, 1968), 149–84.

23 *Ephemerides* (1635): 'post Aristotelem aperuit oculos hominibus' (HP 29/3/15B).

24 *Ephemerides* (1635): 'a rational way of interpreting the sense of the Scriptures which [*Dury*] had fallen of late to set downe ... with Justinus ab Asher. Methodizing his reflexed thoughts and given both Rules and Examples for it' (HP 29/3/14A). On Asher and Dury see *HDC*, 127, 144, 167.

25 J. Dury, 'Methodo investegatoria ad controversias omnes' in his *Irenicorum tractatuum prodromus* (Amsterdam, 1662) and Johann Joachim von Rusdorff's 'Dissertatio Irenica ... considerationi offertur a Joh. Duraeo' (1639), including an 'exegesin logicam et Theologicam' on the 'impediments to concord between the churches' (*HDC*, 308–9).

26 HP 13/128A (Culpeper to Hartlib, 17 February 1645).

27 HP 13/110A (Culpeper to Hartlib, October 1645).

28 *A motion tending to the public good* (London, 1642), 24.

29 *Ephemerides* (1635): HP 29/3/21A; *HDC*, 169; cf. the remark made by Culpeper to Hartlib: 'Mr Durye's Analyticall rule ... yf the world showld loose it by his deathe, he will be thowght to haue buried it' (HP 13/67B).

30 *Specimen speculationis sive meditationis geneticae Dureanae* (HP 24/18/1–30). For a brief outline of the Duraean method see *De usu logicae in analysi et genesi* (HP 24/2/1–8). See also 'Jo: Duraei logica Germanicè', BL Sloane MS 392, fols. 1–121, a treatise on logic written in German.

of systematically reading, referencing, analysing and epitomizing a given corpus. In 1635 Hartlib described the *'singularia'* of Dury's logic, which were: a 'method of invention' (*methodum inventionis*), a method for analysing things and actions (*analysin rerum [et] actionum*), a 'Method applying Theories unto Practise', a 'method of collating or comparing', a 'method of consectarizing' and 'A method of amplification'.[31] Dury's method was probably not terribly original or innovative; Bishop Jewell, for example, told Hartlib that Dury's method of scriptural analysis was 'a peece of his [*own*] method'.[32] Yet Hartlib thought highly enough of it to circulate an outline of Dury's method among logicians of his acquaintance, as can be seen from acknowledgements in manuscript logic treatises in the Hartlib archive.[33] In 1634 Hartlib was convinced that the *'Nova arte Dureana'* and Caspar Streso's *Universalis technologia* – a theological encyclopaedia based on a systematic method of exegesis – would together make a vital contribution to the English reformation.[34] Towards the end of the 1630s, Hartlib was entertaining a larger range of possibilities, although his encouragement of Dury's method did not cease.

The common thread in Hartlib's considerations of logical method can be summed up in the aphoristic pronouncement of Comenius: 'Bonus autem logicus, bonus Philosophus, Politicus, Theologus ... est'[35] – 'the good logician is also a good theologian, politician and philosopher'. But the logic must be a 'true logick' and not that flawed, error-bound idol which Bacon had attacked in his *Novum organum*. In the Hartlibian 'Proposalls towards the Advancement of

[31] *Ephemerides* (1635): HP 29/3/15A.
[32] *Ephemerides* (1641): HP 30/4/71B. Marginal glosses to Dury's *De usu logicae* suggest that he was influenced by the logic of Alsted (see HP 24/2/3A).
[33] See, for example, manuscript logic treatises in HP Bundle 24. The *Methodum tradendae logices* includes this acknowledgement: 'Dn. Duraeus in tractatu quodam m.s. haec habet ...' (HP 24/17/6B). Another piece, the *Vestibulum historicum doctrinae logicae* notes 'Dom. Iohannis Duraei ex manuscripto quodam ... ipsius intimo mihi exhibita ...' (HP 24/16/12A).
[34] See Hartlib's *systemata excerpenda* in *Ephemerides*, (1634): HP 29/2/34B–35A. On the Stresonian method see BL Sloane MS 649, fols. 219–20; *Indicis siue repertorii universalis technologia Stresoniana* (London, 1634); J. Kvačala, *Die pädagogische Reform des Comenius in Deutschland bis zum Ausgange des XVII Jahrhunderts*, Monumenta Germaniae Paedogogica, xxvi, 2 vols. (Berlin, 1903), I, 40–2. Streso's published method in *Technologia theologica recognita contracta et nova duarum concionum* (1641) was dedicated to Hartlib. Its title page is recorded in HP 15/1/15A. Hartlib tried to promote Streso's work in England. He sent one of Streso's treatises, for example, to Joseph Mede in March 1634 for his opinion (which was received in July 1634). See *The works of Joseph Mede* (London, 1677), LXXVI and LXXXV.
[35] HP 35/5/36B. Comenius also cites Boethius' dictum 'aude boetiam dicere Christiana christianorum enim quippe est, vel maxime, irrationabile admittere est'.

Learning',[36] the logic of the universities was attacked as a satanic impediment to knowledge:

Logick or the way of teaching it in the schooles ... [*is*] so farre from the Ende and true use of Rationality, that they even pervert the minde of the Learner from the very aime of reasoning, which is to seeke out truth, & sett it wholly upon the studie of contentious subtilities, habituating it unto a method & pride of contradiction so that it can never afterward apply itselfe unto the demonstrative way of finding out Truth by things foreknown till it hath unlearned all that which in the schooles it hath been taught.[37]

Hartlib himself believed in the existence of a 'true logick', which could only be uncovered by a methodical consideration of all the various logical treatises which had been written. 'If we find out not Reason in our owne Reason', Hartlib judged, 'wee shall never understand or finde out the true logick.'[38] He carefully transcribed Alexander Richardson's 'Notes on the Logick Tables', recording that the author 'dared boldly say' that he had discovered 'the true logicke' which made 'Aristotle's Praedicaments' seem merely 'bubles et toies'.[39] Some of Hartlib's acquaintances believed that logic 'teacheth [*the Christian*] how to prove all the points of religion, overcome all heresyes, and the devills temptations'.[40] Dury, for instance, believed that the Pauline epistles contained a 'spirituall logicke' which could teach the Bible reader 'how to refute to edification'.[41] Others, however, were more sceptical of the benefits of this rational theology. 'I pray all godly young Divines', wrote Walter Welles, 'shall speake not too curiously for logicall method in the scriptures.'[42] One letter in particular – sent to Hartlib from his erudite friend, John Beale – presents a lamentable picture of the religious dangers posed by the serpent logic for the unwitting and overworked university undergraduate:

In my first yeares of logique, I had allmost broken my braine with incessant studyes. I allowed my selfe noe minute of reste. Our very Sabboth ... was taken up with logical or disputative theology. Our dinners and suppers

---

[36] HP 47/2 ('Some Proposalls towards the Advancement of Learning').

[37] HP 47/2/2–3.

[38] *Ephemerides* (1639): HP 30/4/27A.

[39] 'Mr Richerson's notes on the logick tables': HP 24/7/4B. On Richardson, his *Logicians school master* (London, 1629), and the circulation of his notes on Ramus prior to the publication of the second edition in 1657, see W. S. Howell, *Logic and rhetoric in England 1500–1700* (Cambridge, MA, 1956; repr. New York, 1961), 209–10, 275.

[40] *A Christian's philosophy* in the Pell Papers (BL Birch MS 4425, fol. 96r).

[41] HP 9/1/91A (Dury to Hartlib, 13 August 1639).

[42] HP 33/3/1A (Walter Welles to Hartlib, 13 September 1630).

were the times of our sharpest cumbats in sophistry: The spirite of ambition & pride of Victory forct mee to learne by hearte, & promptly all the logicians, old & newe, Protestants & Romanists, Dominicans & Jesuites, briefe or voluminous, That from Germany, Spaine, Italy or France wee could procure. By this inhumane industry my sleepe was allmost taken from mee, & with this wretched spirit of unquietnesse, I got the habite, or Art to direct that short sleepe that I had, about what kind of busines my dreames should bee imployed : which I did most carefully observe, when I was engaged upon compositions in prose or verse.[43]

But this unintentionally humorous account also reveals an interesting slant on the eclectic, interdenominational nature of logic studies. At the same time it presents a vignette of the self-lacerating and guilt-ridden conscience of the puritan scholar. If learning was advanced in 'The spirite of ambition & pride of Victory', it would not promote the 'public good'. Hartlib stressed that knowledge must be useful, methodical, practical and pursued by 'good stewards' in the 'spirit of grace' in 'Union and Communion together through Love' rather than through 'Malice and Ambition'.[44] The importance of 'methodism' or 'systematics' emerged in the context of this ideological – or theological – milieu of communality, congregationalism and intercourse within the public domain. This is certainly the context in which Baconianism (originally conceived in a rather different ideological milieu as 'works for a King' (*opera basilica*) to be performed not by a loving brethren but by efficient servants or functionaries of a priestly 'philosopher-king') rose to a new prominence in the 1630s and 1640s.[45] It is also the context in which Hartlib evaluated the work of the Italian Protestant émigré, Giacomo Aconzio.[46]

ACONTIUS AND JUNGIUS: THE 'TRUE LOGICK', UTILITY AND EXPERIMENTAL METHOD

In his treatise on method, Acontius saw utility as the guiding principle of learning. 'The utility of arts', Acontius wrote, 'consists

---

[43] HP 31/1/50B (John Beale to Hartlib, 17 August 1657).
[44] Clucas, 'Hartlib's *Ephemerides*', 34.
[45] Francis Bacon, *De dignitate et augmentis scientiarum*, in Bacon, *Works*, I, 431–3, 485–6, 491–2. See also the 'Salomon's house' section of *The new Atlantis*, in Bacon, *Works*, III, 144–7.
[46] On Jacobus Acontius (Giacomo Aconzio), see *Dizionario biografico Italiano*, I, 154–9; Paolo Rossi, *Giacomo Aconcio* (Milan, 1952); Charles D. O'Malley, *Jacopo Aconzio* (Rome, 1955) and F. Meli, *Spinoza e due antecedenti italiani dello spinozismo* (Florence, 1934).

not in understanding, but in use.'[47] In its insistence on the orderly concatenation of knowledge in a brief, clear and compendious form, for understanding and for teaching (*contemplandi docendique*), the Acontian method had much in common with the aims of Comenian pansophic encyclopaedism.[48] By Hartlib, Hübner and others, however, it was perceived to have a specific role to play in advancing the English reformation.

'There is a great deal of foppery in Logic', Hübner told Hartlib in 1639, but Acontius was to provide a new start. 'Never hase any body so accurately shewn what order to observe in meditating *in naturalibus* what *in moralibus* etc. as Acontius [*has shown*] in one or two pages.'[49] Elsewhere Hübner criticized Bacon for his 'pompe' in expressing his designs when he 'might have far more simply and profitably delivered all his new observations for reformation of learning'.[50] Acontius on the other hand 'makes Common notions to bee the foundation of Logick, which no body hase done so cleerly heretofore'. Surpassing Bacon in his outline of the 'new logic', Hübner also felt that Acontius surpassed Comenius in identifying the 'true didactic principles'(*vera principia didactica*); 'None hase ... handled them so accurately as hee. O that Comenius had followed them! Whatever he speaks of genus etc they are brought in most accurately and nothing in vaine, and always some special matter in them.'[51] 'The Pansophy premised to an Acontian method will doe wonders, without which also [*the Acontian*] method can never be perfectly practised', suggested another informant.[52] Acontius' idea of method or *ordo* is superior to that of Keckermann, which was 'nothing else but continual definitions and divisions', which operate

---

47 J. Acontius, *De methodo, hoc est, de recta investigandarum tradendarumque scientiarum ratione* (Basle, 1558), 15: 'Nam cum artium utilitas non ex earum cognitione, sed usu constet' (cf. *Satanae strategemata*, II, 78: 'Vtilis doctrina esse non potest, nisi usum habeat aliquem, quod si sola in speculatione sit posita, nullum in actionem emergens, inanis futilisque habenda est'. On the valorization of use and practice in the Hartlib circle, John Beale remarked to Hartlib: 'though wee speake highly of Mathematicall certainty; yet there is noe demonstration so sure, as demonstration of practise' – i.e. orderly method and 'real' knowledge of particulars (BL Add. MS 4384, fol. 94r). Another correspondent said of mathematics: 'if it bee not applied to some noble use in humane life it is a meere vanity' (*Ephemerides* (1640): HP 30/4/46B).

48 Acontius, *De methodo*, 15-16. 49 *Ephemerides* (1639): HP 29/4/22A.

50 *Ephemerides* (1639): HP 30/4/23B.

51 *Ephemerides* (1639): HP 30/4/23B. Cf. *Ephemerides*, (1639): HP 30/4/24B – where Hübner compares Acontius' treatment of the *modum inveniendi communes notiones* to that of Viottus' *De demonstratione* (Paris, 1560).

52 *Ephemerides* (1640): HP 30/4/40A.

STEPHEN CLUCAS

too much within the bounds of the common significations of words. It is this lack of a true sense of method that also hampered the advancement of right religion: 'So it fares with us in divinity. Wee bring our catecheticall and confession tearmes and according to them wee expound the Scriptures.' Acontius taught the 'real part ... of meditation', which would reform religious and scientific knowledge. He ignored the second and third part of logic, which only referred to 'a meere *ars garriendi*'. Instead he focused on the *via analytica*, or the nature of the analysis of given facts. According to this correspondent, Acontius was considered a precursor of the Cartesian method 'observ[*ing*] the same principles which Cartes hase laid down in his booke [*i.e. the 'Discours de la méthode'*] which indeed containes the whole art of reasoning or meditation'.[53] Comenius would be remembered for 'the notion of a Pansophy', Acontius for his framing of the analytic method before 'Verulam, Herbert [*and*] Cartes'.[54] Acontius would remedy the particular deficiencies of both Bacon and Comenius. His status as a logician was particularly eminent among those of Hartlib's circle. It was so exalted, in fact, that Hartlib, Dury and Thomas Goodwin sponsored an English translation of Acontius' *Satanae strategemata* in 1648.[55] This was a work that had been much admired by Ramus. In it, Acontius attacked doctrinal warfare and religious persecution as the source of the decline of Christian religion. He proposed to overcome this by a systematic and methodical understanding of the gospel. His thesis accorded well with John Dury's ecclesiastical mission of negotiating a doctrinal accord among the European Protestant churches. It also reflected the Hartlibian concern to provide a methodological basis for a complete Protestant reformation.[56] In this particular sense, then, Trevor-Roper's 'Country Baconians' emerge more as 'Acontian methodists'. But Bacon is never very far from the Hartli-

[53] *Ephemerides* (1639): HP 30/4/39B. On Acontius as a precursor of Cartesian method see Wilhelm Risse, *Die Logik der Neuzeit*, 2 vols. (Stuttgart and Bad Cannstatt, 1964), I, 262.
[54] The correspondent puts this in an interesting sociological light. Unlike Ramus, Acontius has been forgotten because 'hee [*did*] not dispute [*or*] oppugne some famous adversarie and because hee was not a professor making many disciples therfore hee could make no sect but remains obscure' (*Ephemerides* (1639): HP 30/4/39B).
[55] *Satan's strategems, or the devil's cabinet-council discovered* (London, 1648).
[56] C. D. O'Malley in *Dizionario biografico Italiano*, I, 158. The amenability of Acontius' ideas to English Calvinists – and its promotion by a Cromwellian intelligentsia – is treated by Rossi, *Aconcio*, 111–12 and Meli, *Spinoza e due antecedenti*, 80. On the use of Acontius' doctrine of toleration by Arminians and Socinians see H. R. Trevor-Roper, *Catholics, Anglicans, and puritans: seventeenth-century essays* (London, 1987), 189–90, 192–4, and Rossi, *Aconcio*, 109.

bian agenda. Acontius taught that 'Before wee can bee good logi-
tians wee must furnish ourselves with abundance of experimental
knowledge'; and Hartlib too wanted to see scientists and natural
philosophers who 'had a world of things' discovered through experiments 'brought to a perfection in true reasoning by these Acontian
directions'.[57] Facts alone meant nothing without their 'usefull and
orderly concatenation'.[58] Hartlib swiftly realized that the Acontian
method, while it did not completely usurp the Baconian canon, was
a more concise and clearly expressed manifesto for the prosecution of
an orderly experimental philosophy than Bacon's rather tortuous
descriptions of the inductive method. Like Bacon, Acontius offered a
'real' logic of 'particulars', rather than the verbal sophistries of
scholastic philosophy. Yet Acontius' method seemed to Hartlib and
his colleagues at this time to offer even more than Baconian induction. He was 'better then all the logicians in the world', according to
Hübner.[59] 'Acontius hase taken his *Logica* out of himselfe', Hartlib
wrote. 'If Verulamius had used this method his induction would
have beene far more compendious and rational ... There is a far
nobler use of man's reason then to make inductions only.'[60]
Although claims for logical originality at this time were usually
exaggerated,[61] there was a belief in the possibility of approaching a
perfect or ideal logic. This generated a demand – at whatever cost –
for a 'new logic' which broke radically with the Aristotelian university tradition, and was oriented towards the world of 'facts'. 'Logick
must not bee learned out of other mens Logicke [*such*] as Aristotle
etc,' Hartlib noted, 'but out of ones selfe *beneficio notionum communium.*
Else all is but sophistery.'[62] 'The more particulars and realitys one
knowes the better Logick he will make.'[63]

The following assessment of an array of logical methods, beginning with those of Acontius and Herbert of Cherbury (in *De veritate*),

---

[57] *Ephemerides* (1640): HP 30/4/40A.
[58] See one of Hartlib's Office of Address proposals: HP 47/10/44A–48A.
[59] *Ephemerides* (1639): HP 29/4/21A.
[60] *Ephemerides* (1639): HP 29/4/20B. These nobler uses include being 'able to discerne
centesimas consequentias as accuratly as the first and next to bee lawfully made or inferred'.
[61] On the lack of substantial development of logical concepts in the seventeenth century
before Jungius, see E. J. Ashworth, 'Joachim Jungius (1587–1657) and the logic of
relations', *Archiv für Geschichte der Philosophie*, 49 (1967), 72–85.
[62] *Ephemerides* (1639): HP 30/4/24A. Cf. *Ephemerides* (1639) – 'Herbert and Acontius ... have
given us a true logick, because they have not taken it or exscribed it from others' (HP
30/4/21B).
[63] *Ephemerides* (1639): HP 29/4/20B.

gives us an insight into the new, critical set of demands being formulated by Protestant thinkers in their search for an appropriate intellectual framework:[64]

Herbert et Acontius these 2 have given us a true logick, because they have not taken it or exscribed it from others, but shewn us the way in some measure how wee should find it out in ourselves. O that others would have done so, by this time wee should have had a greater perfection of the use of our reason. Your common *logici* give us but *artem garriendi* and that not fully neither. Keckermann [*is*] to bee preferred before Ramus because hee hase given us more realitys then Ramus, and Alsted more then Keckermann. Where Streso followes himself or his owne reasoning hee hase many choice observations, but as soone as hee undertakes to censure Verulam hee is mightily out, because hee never having seene those experimental *processus* which Verulam for many years was exercised his reason must needes misguide him in such matters.[65]

Reading Hartlib's lists of *desiderata* and memoranda between the years 1635 and 1640, one could extend this list of competing logics beyond Bacon, Ramus, Keckermann, Alsted, Acontius, Herbert and Streso. Henry Reinerus, Johann Bisterfeld, John Pell, John Dury, Franco Burgersdijk, Joachim Hübner ... all had produced logics which Hartlib considered useful or capable of strategic deployment in his search for the 'true logick'.

In 1638, the renowned Hamburg philosopher, Joachim Jungius,[66] sent Hartlib a copy of his newly printed textbook on logic, the *Logica Hamburgensis*, printed for the use of students at the Hamburg gymnasium where he was rector and professor of philosophy and medicine.[67] Hartlib wrote a letter of thanks addressed to Jungius' friend, Johann Adolf Tassius, praising the *Logica* as a contribution towards the achievement of a '*universalem logicum*', which would help 'find out

---

[64] On Herbert and his philosophical writings, see R. D. Bedford, *The defence of truth, Herbert of Cherbury and the seventeenth century* (Manchester, 1979).

[65] *Ephemerides* (1639): HP 30/4/21B.

[66] On Hartlib and Jungius, see my forthcoming article 'Samuel Hartlib and the Hamburg scientific community 1631–1659: a study in intellectual communications'. On Jungius and his works see *DSB*, VII, 193–6. On Jungius' life and thought see esp. G. E. Guhrauer, *Joachim Jungius und sein Zeitalter* (Stuttgart and Tübingen, 1850) and Hans Kangro, *Joachim Jungius' Experimente und Gedanken zur Begründung der Chemie als Wissenschaft: ein Beitrag zur Geistesgeschichte des 17 Jahrhunderts* (Wiesbaden, 1968).

[67] *Logica Hamburgensis hoc est, institutiones logicae in usum scholae Hamburg conscriptae, & sex libris comprehensae autore Joachimio Jungio phil. ac Med.D gymnasii ac scholae rectore. Libri tres priores logicam generalem complexi jam prodeunt* (Hamburg, 1635).

the correct *processum rationis* which was barred from the vulgar masses'.[68] Hartlib's friend John Pell praised Jungius' 'heroic labours' ('*Heroicos* ... *labores*'), while Comenius praised the *Logica Hamburgensis* in glowing terms in the *Reformation of schooles* – a work translated and published by Hartlib in 1642; 'Jungius the *Saxon* ... laboureth to bring the art of Logicke to such perfection, that the truth of propositions may be upheld, and all fallacies avoided, with as much certainty as any of Euclid's Problemes can be demonstrated.'[69] Hartlib himself told Robert Boyle that Jungius was 'one of the best logicians in Germany ... [*who*] conceives if that art were truly understood and applied ... [*all*] real studies ... would flourish more than they have done since the fall of Adam'.[70] Hübner told Hartlib that Jungius' logic had distinct advantages over other methods. 'Descartes, Bisterfeld [*and*] Comenius begin their philosophating *a priori*,' he noted, 'But they will find themselves deceived. Jungius goes more warily and does *a posteriori* not caring so much to teach as first to find out the truth that may not be gainsayed.'[71] He also felt that Jungius' 'analytical method' would obviate the endless circumvention entailed by an exhaustive Baconian collection of particulars, which would 'prevent all'. Jungius' method, he said, 'is not subject to such inconveniencys'.[72] The attractiveness of the Jungian method – as with the Acontian *via analytica* – was its application to the collection of experimental knowledge. Jungius was a practising natural philosopher, working on botany, chemistry, physics, mineralogy and entomology. He was keen to emphasize the application of natural philosophy to scientific procedure. Book IV of the *Logica Hamburgensis*, or *Logicae specialis*, deals especially with the topic of scientific induction and demonstration, and the possibility of deriving canonical or apodictic principles from scientific common notions, on the model of Euclidean mathematical theorems. Jungius called it 'protonoetic philosophy'. It was this side of Jungius' work that Hübner singled out for particular praise. For his part, Hartlib circulated a manuscript manifesto, the *Protonoeticæ philosophiae sciagraphia*, among English scientists in the 1640s.[73]

---

[68] Kvačala, *Pädagogische Reform*, I, 108–11.

[69] J. A. Comenius, *A reformation of schooles* (London, 1642), 28.

[70] Boyle, *Works*, v, 262 (Hartlib to Boyle, 8 May 1654).

[71] *Ephemerides* (1639): HP 30/4/3A.

[72] *Ibid.*   [73] See Clucas, 'Hartlib and the Hamburg scientific community'.

HARRISON'S INDEXING SYSTEM AND THE 'EPITOME
CULTURE' OF THE ENGLISH REFORMATION

One of the many paradoxes of the 'puritan revolution' was that, despite much vocal praise for the 'real', the 'particular' and the 'empirical' as against the verbal, the general and the abstract, the methodological impetus of contemporary thought was much in thrall to words, and particularly to reading. This extended beyond the observable effects such as those of reading and interpreting bibles, and theological or even religio-political tracts, towards the development of new kinds of reading practice as well as new ways of studying and interpreting the written heritage of humanistic culture in Europe. These new 'reading technologies' were of great importance to the Hartlib circle. Hartlib's associates regarded the effective reading and disseminating of ideas as vital to an effective completion of a Protestant reformation. 'The Reformation must not bee begun from schooles', Hartlib wrote in 1639, 'But by true bookes of a solid didactica and Pansophia written in the mother language that every body may bee a schoole unto himself. By this meanes of their own accord every body will come to see the inconveniency of the present constitutions of schooles as likewise meanes how they may bee better contrived and ordered.'[74]

In order to become a 'school to oneself', however, one must be able to make effective and methodical use of individual reading, a concern of humanists from the earliest periods of Italian scholarship onwards. It resulted in the practice of synopsis, excerpting and digesting of reading matter into books of commonplaces, collections of *sententiae*, commentaries, paraphrases and other forms of metatextual paraphenalia. Hartlib's papers are replete with various schemes for improving the effectiveness of reading and communicating ideas – indexes, techniques of digestion, abbreviation and information retrieval, artificial languages and stenography. Acontius had said that method was 'the understanding of something which we wish to conquer and which can teach us how to communicate it to others'.[75] An effective logical method, then, should also include a way of reading designed for effective re-communication. In a series of 'Didactica' on scriptural analysis and theology from the 1630s,

[74] *Ephemerides* (1639): HP 30/4/3в.
[75] *De methodo*, 18: '[*Methodus*] est enim rei alicuius cognitio, quam qui contemplatur, assequi cupit; qui vero docet, aliis impertire nititur'.

Hartlib presents a comprehensive list of various kinds of reading methods that had come to his attention, including the 'Pellian and Reineran analytical reading', the 'Ordered doctrinal reading of Streso', the 'Marginal reading of Dury' and the 'Brinsleyan reading to give popular definitions . . . or descriptions of all'.[76] For different reading tasks, different reading-tools were suggested, sometimes – as in the case of the 'Lectio Richelsono-Stresoniana'[77] – in tandem, or combination with other techniques. 'One Meanes for to teach Children et people to read understandingly', says Hartlib in 1635, 'is to use with them 1. Brinsley's Army of Analytical Questions 2. to observe and teach per praecognitiones Pel's or Brook's Method of construing. [*and*] 3. to aske Questiones Analyticas of Martinius.'[78] As with logic itself, the Hartlibian prescription for 'ordered reading' (which as 'concinnation' is perhaps to be regarded as a form of logic) is eclectic and functionally orientated.

One particular 'reading technology' or 'method' which caught Hartlib's imagination in the period 1639 to 1640 was 'Harrison's booke-invention'.[79] Harrison, a 'good and universal judicious schollar', had devised 'an excellent and the completest and perfect art . . . of *excerpendi*', which, Hartlib felt, went 'far beyond that of [John] Gawden'.[80] The invention – which was a 'passe-port with as much paper vpon it as you please. Vpon [which] there bee slices of paper put on which can bee removed and transposed as one pleases' – was 'an incredible easy compend for quotations', which was praised for its 'Comportibility' and its facility for information-retrie-

---

[76] *Didactica lectionis Scripturae* (HP 22/23/6B): 'Lectio Analytica Pelliana et Reineriana', 'Lectio Concinnatoria doctrinalis Stresoniana', 'Lectio marginalium duræanorum', 'Lectio Brinslejana'. Hartlib speaks of Brinsley's 'lectione puerili' and 'Analyticae quaestiones Brinsleiance' (HP 29/2/59A; HP 29/3/3A) making it clear that this is the educationist John Brinsley the Elder (see next note).

[77] *Didactica Biblica theologia;* (HP 23/23/6A) – a combination of the reading methods of Alexander Richardson and Caspar Streso. Cf. the 'methods' listed for 'Quaestiones Textuales': 'Brukianae. Vechner. Reiner. Brinsley. Martin. Pell'. These were the reading methods of John Brook, Georg Vechner (editor of the 1645 edition of Comenius' *Januae linguarum reseratae vestibulum* and author of *Austeritas Christi* (Leszno, 1640)); see also *J. Slichtingii notae in . . . G. Vechneri concionem quam habuit super initium evangelium Ioannis Lesnae anno 1639* (n.p., 1644), Henry Reiner, John Brinsley the Elder, (author of *The posing of the parts: or, a most plaine and easie way of examining the accidence and grammar by questions and answers* (London, 1630)), the philologist and theologian Matthias Martini and the mathematician John Pell.

[78] *Ephemerides* (1635): HP 29/3/19B.   [79] *Ephemerides* (1640): HP 30/4/46A.

[80] On John Gauden's sermon in support of 'the two great public spirits', Dury and Comenius, see Trevor-Roper, 'Three foreigners', 261–2. The Hartlib archive contains a treatise by Gauden on the divine essence written for Lady Barrington: HP 26/14.

val *avant la lettre*. The device offered 'Mobility to transpose your notions where you will to put in to find presently' through a system of 'allegations by ciphers'.[81] Its main purposes, however, had much in common with the aims of certain logical methods, namely 'to gather ... all the authors, their notions or axioms ... [*and the*] argumentorum of their whole discourses'.[82] It certainly resembled Comenius' *pansophia*[83] as well as Bacon's experimental histories in its 'maine scope' of giving a 'perfect Index upon all authors or a most real and judicious catalogue *materiarum* out of all authors to represent *totum apparatum eruditionis* which is extant in what bookes soever'.[84] In order to create his invention, in fact, Harrison had to write 'a special logick for the art of collecting' and 'mainly hase studied order and this hee calls also contemplation to order exactly every thing'.[85] Hartlib then noted an allusion from Hübner to the effect that Comenius would not go amiss to use this device: 'Nothing', he said, 'is so much capable of exact order as the Pansophia ... [*in which*] wee must presuppose and fetch about many particulars.'[86] In fact, Hartlib concluded, the 'universal index' would 'needes proove a kind of Pansophy'.[87]

Acontius' *De methodo* gave expression to what one could call the 'digest mentality' or 'epitome culture' of the puritan revolution when he said that method should strive for 'the utmost brevity and perspicuity' and 'dispense with all verbosity'.[88] This ethos finds its fullest expression in the systematic reading implied by the Harrison book-invention.[89] 'Harrison observes well that wee make little vse now a days of our reading ... because wee are destitute of ... punctuall collections or references', observed Hartlib. 'Hee hase a

---

[81] *Ephemerides* (1640): HP 30/4/46A, 62A.   [82] *Ephemerides* (1640): HP 30/4/46A.

[83] Hartlib called his 'universal index vpon all authors' an 'opus regium et totius generis humani': *Ephemerides* (1640): HP 30/4/47A. Comenius himself was interested in *ars excerpendi*. This is evident in his 'Mundus possibilis' (*Pansophia*, Gradus I), and 'Pambiblia' (*Pampaedia*, chap. VI); *De rerum humanarum emendatione consultatio catholica*, ed. Academia Scientiarum Bohemoslovaca, 2 vols. (Prague, 1966), I, 195–225, II, 66–83. Comenius and Hartlib were planning a universal record of opinions (*pandogmaticon*) in the 1630s which would have made extensive use of such techniques.

[84] HP 30/4/47A. With Hartlib's characteristic enthusiasm for lost causes, even Harrison's failed systems were of interest 'for it may bee that they may serve some special turne'.

[85] *Ephemerides* (1640): HP 30/4/47A.   [86] *Ephemerides* (1640): HP 30/4/47A.

[87] *Ephemerides* (1640): HP 30/4/47B.

[88] *De methodo*, 15: 'maximam breuitatem cum pari perspicuitate coniungerimus ... in tradendis artibus verbositas omnis fugienda.'

[89] On systematic reading and *methodenlehre* in the Renaissance, see Neal W. Gilbert, *The Renaissance concept of method* (New York, 1960).

way to cut off all superfluitys and impertinencys', he continued. As with the *methodus duraeus* and other forms of logical–scriptural analysis such as the *'more Stresoniano'*[90] it involved a form of logical resuming or abbreviation: 'To the propositions hee gathers the reasons with a *quia* in the end on one side and in the duplicate paper within it is summarily logically expressed'.[91] Hartlib noted similarities with the 'several ways of compendiating ... readings' practised by other scholars, such as Matthias Bernegger who 'lays and spreads so many authors all along ... a long kind of board et *repositorium'*.[92] Pell praised the 'great vse of Indexes' which is 'observed by few'.[93] 'Perfect indexes', he said, would prevent the confusing 'multitudes of lexicons' in language studies, help produce a 'perfect concordance vpon the Bibel and other authors' and provide a 'compend for all sort of knowledge ... already in bookes'. But he prudently tempered these claims, for 'Although by the bare indexes a great vse will bee made ... yet it will be done far more excellently and substantially by those that have read the authors themselves'. Indexes prepared by those unversed in authors may, he warned, be 'raw and incipid'. He also noted that Gemerus' *Catalogus materiarum* or *Pandectae* 'describes the manner of making indexes somewhat like to that of Harrison'.[94] Other correspondents, while appreciating the benefits of indexing, put forward other models. Hübner thought that 'There was never a better device invented for making of indexes then that of Harrison', but that John Gauden's method for 'excerpting of the phrases and sentences goes beyond it'.[95] Another correspondent saw indexing as the *optima methodus studendi*, but recommended Johann Frensheim – friend of Comenius and professor of eloquence and politics at Uppsala – rather than Harrison. He particularly praised his division of non-biblical authors into *'capita* and *versus'*, after the fashion of Isaac Gruterus.[96] Hartlib noted late in 1639 that Mersenne was writing a work in which 'all the sap of scholastic and papist theology' ('succus scholasticae et Papisticae Theologiae') was digested. He anticipated that the 'dispersing and vulgarizing' of Catholic doctrines would 'undermine vnawares all Popery' which through the 'wonderful providence of God' would 'at last ... make it fall to the ground'. On the Protestant side, needless to say, this same

[90] See Clucas, 'Hartlib's *Ephemerides*', 36.   [91] *Ephemerides* (1640): HP 30/4/47B.
[92] *Ibid.*
[93] *Ephemerides* (1640): HP 30/4/55A.   [94] *Ibid.*   [95] *Ephemerides* (1640): HP 30/4/61B.
[96] *Ephemerides* (1640): HP 30/4/63B. On J. C. Frensheim and the Hartlib circle, see *HDC*, 365.

'dispersing and vulgarizing' of doctrines would have the opposite effect, 'exciting of others to contrive a compleat systeme of Practical Divinity that ... all the notions may bee brought together'.[97] Hübner, for example, was committed to reform through digested knowledge. All his notions would be 'express[ed] ... in a most plaine and popular language as [Des]Cartes hase done' and in a 'notional, ordinary way'. The 'Art of meditation', Hübner insisted, was a simple matter 'if one fill himself – by what meanes soever hee can – of a world of matter, then intellectus cannot choose but fall to meditat'.[98] This 'filling' was best performed through digests, by means of which it would become the chief 'meanes of publick reformation et edification'. It was the task of Protestant scholars to increase public knowledge 'by writing and divulging gratis of profitable bookes', a task which Hartlib himself pursued by asking colleagues for lists of *selecti libri*, and asking them to digest them for recirculation. This embracing of the 'epitome' as a way of universalizing knowledge was another area in which the Hartlibian reformers departed from Bacon. He had imagined that Ramus 'merited better a great deal in reviving the good rules of Propositions ... than he did in introducing the canker of Epitomes'.[99] This 'canker' had been wholeheartedly embraced by the puritan intelligentsia of middle Germany, and Anglo-German knowledge brokers such as Hartlib and Hübner did much to establish it in English circles in the 1630s.[100]

HARTLIB AND THE BREMEN CALVINIST LOGICIANS

Other traces of Hartlib's desire to promote learning from the Calvinist milieu of his German correspondence are discernible in the composition of the logic bundles preserved in the Hartlib archive, and from the network of references within some of the manuscript

[97] *Ephemerides* (1640): HP 30/4/62A.   [98] *Ephemerides* (1639): HP 30/4/24B.
[99] Bacon, *Advancement of learning*, II; Bacon, *Works*, III, 407.
[100] On the logical-encyclopaedic milieu of the central European Calvinist diaspora see this volume, chap. 1 and Howard Hotson, 'Johann Heinrich Alsted: encyclopaedism, millenarianism and the Second Reformation in Germany' (D.Phil. thesis, University of Oxford, 1991). On England and its wider relations to continental Calvinist communities, see P. Collinson, 'England and international Calvinism 1558–1640', in *International Calvinism, 1541–1715*, ed. Menna Prestwich (Oxford, 1985), 197–223 and Simon Adams, 'The Protestant cause; religious alliance with the European Calvinist communities as a political issue in England, 1585–1630' (D.Phil. thesis, University of Oxford, 1973).

logic treatises preserved there and the patterns of Hartlib's foreign correspondence itself.[101]

A particularly good example of Hartlib's working within a specific Calvinist milieu is his connection with the logicians of the theology faculty at the Reformed academy in Bremen.[102] The academy there included the English émigré William Ames (Amesius), Johannes Coccejus, Matthias Martinius and Ludwig Crocius.[103] John Dury was closely involved with the Bremen religious community, having the ear of the archbishop and 'his chiefe diuines'.[104] Hartlib's own education at the *Königlichen Gymnasium* of Brieg was under the auspices of the Calvinist rector, Melchior Lauban.[105] It was at this time when, as Wilhelm Risse notes, 'the vocational training of systematic schools ... was developed using the theological logic of congregational puritanism as their basis ... to guarantee the infallibility of theology'.[106] Hartlib's deep interest in the works of Herborn scholars such as Piscator, Alsted, Comenius and Jungius corroborates his lasting interest in fostering Calvinist pedagogical foundations for his English work.[107]

The importance of Bremen as a Reformed centre in the 1630s and

---

[101] I would stress, however, the dangers of generalizing too much from the composition of the extant archive, which is incomplete. One should be wary, I suppose, about drawing inferences from what might conceivably be miscellaneous and disparate remnants of Hartlib's notes.

[102] On Bremen's Calvinists and 'Crypto-Calvinist' Philippists, see Henry J. Cohn, 'The territorial princes in Germany's Second Reformation, 1559–1622', in Prestwich (ed.), *International Calvinism*, 135, 138, 144–5. See also Jürgen Moltmann, *Christoph Pezel und der Kalvinismus in Bremen* (Bremen, 1958). For an overview of the theological issues of the 'Second Reformation' in Germany, see *Die reformierte Konfessionalisierung in Deutschland – Das Problem der 'Zweiten Reformation'*, ed. Heinz Schilling (Gütersloh, 1986).

[103] On Johann Coccejus, see Otto Ritschl, *Dogmengeschichte des Protestantismus. Grundlagen und Grunzge der theologischen Gedanken- und Lehrbildung in der Protestantische Kirchen*, 4 vols. (Leipzig, 1908–27), III, 435–45. On Martinius, see G. Menk, 'Kalvinismus und Pädagogik; Matthias Martinius (1572–1630) und der Einfluss der Hohen Schule Herborn auf J. A. Comenius', *Nassauische Annalen*, 91 (1980), 77–104. On Johann and Ludwig Crocius, see Ritschl, *Dogmengeschichte*, 262ff, and 398–402, 433–5. On Ames see K. L. Sprunger, *The learned Doctor William Ames: Dutch backgrounds of English and American Puritanism* (Chicago and London, 1972); Karl Reuter, *Wilhelm Amesius, der führende Theologe des erwachenden reformierten Pietismus* (Neukirchen Kreis Moers, 1940), and on his logic writings see Howell, *Logic and rhetoric*, 210–12 and Risse, *Logic der Neuzeit*, I, 530–1. For an overview of the sectarian milieu of German pedagogy, see Kristian Jensen, 'Protestant rivalry – metaphysics and rhetoric in Germany c.1590–1620', *Journal of Ecclesiastical History*, 41 (1990), 24–43.

[104] HP 1/29/4A (Dury to Hartlib, Hamburg, 8 March 1640).   [105] *HDC*, 11–12.

[106] Risse, *Logik der Neuzeit*, I, 530–1.

[107] On the Calvinism of Herborn see Gerhard Menk, *Die Hohe Schule Herborn in ihrer Frühzeit. Ein Beitrag zum Hochschulwesen des deutschen Kalvinismus im Zeitalter der Gegenreformation* (Wiesbaden, 1981).

1640s was largely due to the eclipsed fortunes of its neighbours. The
Reformed University of Heidelberg was in the hands of the Habs-
burgs. The University of Marburg had been regained by the
Lutherans in the early 1620s. The leading German Reformed
academies in Herborn and Hanau virtually ceased to function in the
following years. Sheltered from the worst ravages of the Thirty
Years War by its northerly location, Bremen became a centre of
Calvinist intellectual leadership and it became an important port of
call for Calvinist refugees and students from Silesia, Bohemia and
Moravia (including Comenius), on their way to the Netherlands
and the Dutch universities.[108] Bremen's theological standpoint
made it amenable to Dury and Hartlib's liberal Calvinism. It
enjoyed a well-established tradition of moderate, irenical, almost
Melanchthonian Reformed theology. It was hardly surprising that
the Bremen community should be well represented in Hartlib's
correspondence.[109]

Johannes Coccejus (1603–1669), professor of Christian theology
at Bremen, provides a good example.[110] He is represented in the
Hartlib Papers by a manuscript copy of his treatise *De analysi logica
observationes*.[111] Notes about his various theological works appear in
letters of various correspondents at Leiden in the mid-1630s.[112] His
colleague, Ludwig Crocius, corresponded with Hartlib in connection with '*meditationibus logicis*', and theological controversies.[113]
Copies of letters from English bishops to Crocius, and correspondence with Dury, are also preserved in the Hartlib archive.[114] It is
clear from references in the *Ephemerides* that the logical and theo-

[108] See Hans Jessen, '*Hospitium ecclesiae pressae*. Bremen und Schlesien im 16. und 17. Jahrhundert', *Hospitium ecclesiae Forschungen zur bremischen Kirchengeschichte*, 1 (1954), 86–98 and H.
Schmidtmayer, 'Die Bezichungen des Bremer Gymnasium Illustre zu J. A. Comenius und
der mährische Brüdern', *Bremisches Jahrbuch*, 33 (1930).

[109] I would like to stress that I am not positing Bremen as a particularly privileged source of
Hartlibian influence. The itinerant nature of Dury's ecclesiastical tour, and the wide
catchment area of Hartlib's correspondence, both ensure that his archive reflects the
geographical diffusion of the central European Calvinist diaspora. The case of Bremen is a
good example of this broader network of communications (I have considered elsewhere,
for example, his relations with scholars in Hamburg and Gdansk).

[110] See note 103 above, also *Neue Deutsche Biographie*, III, 302–3.   [111] HP 24/12.

[112] e.g. HP 11/1/42 and HP 11/1/59.

[113] See HP 9/1/76, 10/5/1, 11/1/104, 11/1/42 and 11/1/69.

[114] e.g. HP 5/11 (Bishop Morton to Crocius); HP 5/2 (Bishop Hall to Crocius); HP 5/35 and
5/18 (Dury to Crocius). See also HP 1/29/2B (Dury to Hartlib [extracts from letters
1639–1640]): 'Dr Crocius hath writt to me to give his addresse to Bishop davenant and
Bishop Hall to have their judgements of certain passages.'

logical writings of William Ames[115] were also discussed by Hartlib and his friends in the 1630s.[116] This was particularly so following the arrival in England of Ames' Hungarian disciple, Tolnai Dali, who formed a Christian society, the League of Virtue.[117] Another Calvinist-influenced logician whose works are found among Hartlib's bundle of logic treatises is Christoph Scheibler,[118] professor of Greek, logic and metaphysics at the University of Giessen,[119] whose *Liber commentarium topicorum* was printed in Oxford in 1638,[120] and is excerpted in Hartlib's papers under the title *'Canones topici'*.[121] The logic bundles also contain evidence of other influences. The *Artis Lullianae* is represented by an Italian commentary on the *Artis brevis* by Giovanni Battista Homodaeus.[122] This was an approach much discussed by Hartlib correspondents such as Johann Bisterfeld.[123] Bisterfeld's own *Logicum Bisterfeld* was circulated among Hartlib's acquaintances; Hübner felt – unlike Bacon – that Keckermann had

---

115 The *Demonstratio logicae verae* (Leiden, 1632 and Cambridge, 1646) and the *Theses logicae* (Cambridge, 1646).

116 See Hübner, *Ephemerides* (1639): HP 29/4/19B: '[*Ames'*] *Demonstratio Logicae* is not so much of the use of reason as of *Demonstratio Logicae Rameae*, shewing how Ramus used his reason.' See the many references to Ames' works in *Ephemerides* (1634) (e.g. HP 29/2/3B, 29/2/5B, 29/2/6A–B, 29/2/8B, 29/2/19A, 29/2/22B, 29/2/23A, 29/2/37A, 29/2/55A). See also HP 68/3/4 (John Dury to Peter Smart, May 1647) and HP 11/1/69 (Coccejus[?] to Hartlib, 10 May 1635). The most discussed works are Ames' theological writings – *Christianae catecheseos sciagraphia* (Amsterdam, 1635), *De conscientia et eius iure, vel casibus* (Amsterdam, 1631) and *Medulla theologica* (Amsterdam, 1628; repr. London, 1629).

117 Dali appears as a regular source of information in Hartlib's *Ephemerides* for 1634–5 as 'Dominus Tolnaeus'. Most of the entries concern Ames. On Dali's visit to England see Cohn, 'The territorial princes', 184.

118 On Christoph Scheibler (1589–1653) see *Allgemeine deutsche Biographie*, xxx, 700–2; N. Hentger, 'Christoph Scheibler', in *Westfälische Lebensbilder*, 13 (1985), 45–55; Risse, *Logik der Neuzeit*, I, 18, 154, 470–76; J. C. Poggendorff, *Biographisch-Literarisches Handwörterbuch zur Geschichte des Exacten Wissenschaften*, 6 vols. (Amsterdam, 1965), II, col. 782 and Jensen, 'Protestant rivalry', 38.

119 Although Scheibler was a Lutheran, he was educated, like Ludwig Crocius, at the University of Marburg (until it was Calvinized in 1605) and 'played a key role ... in transferring the methodological preoccupations of the Reformed academies and universities into Lutheran Germany' (Hotson, private correspondence).

120 His encyclopaedic *Philosophia compendiosa* (Giessen, 1618), was republished in Oxford in 1657.

121 HP 24/10.

122 'Revolutionum alphabetariarum artis brevis Raymundi Lullij expositio' (HP 24/4/54–92). On the interest of Alsted and Bisterfeld in the combinatorial logic of Lull, see Hotson, 'Encyclopaedism, millenarianism and the Second Reformation', chaps. 5.i, 5.iii, 6.i and 6.vi. Hotson sees this particular synthesis of Lull as characteristic of 'the easternmost members of the German Calvinist diaspora' (private correspondence).

123 Bisterfeld to Hartlib, September 1638 (BL Sloane MS 427, fols. 90–95) – in Kvačala, *Pädogogische Reform*, I, 112–18.

been wrong to criticize Lullism.[124] There are also examples of some home-grown logics: the encyclopaedic *Didactica* of John Brook,[125] a specimen of the Ramist logical analysis of Alexander Richardson,[126] and an epitome of the Acontian method.[127] But a distinct preference for a German Calvinist logical milieu emerges in Hartlib's methodological ruminations. This can be seen from the citation patterns in an unpublished anonymous logic treatise among Hartlib's papers, the *Transformatio specialis doctrinae logicae*. These citations include Alsted's *Logica speciales*,[128] Acontius and the *Artis Lullianae*,[129] Scheibler's *Canones topici*, Keckermann, the universal logic of Johann Bisterfeld and the *De prompta utilium rerum meditatione* of the Bremen theologian, Matthias Martinius.[130] Dating from the late 1630s or early 1640s, this treatise was probably written by a German scholar. However, the author also appears to know the work of Joseph Webb and to have access to Dury's manuscript treatise on scriptural logic as well being very concerned with the usefulness of logical invention for the Protestant church.[131] It is typical of the kind of strategically commissioned tracts that Hartlib was concerned to deploy in England and in sympathetic communities on the continent.

Hartlib's projected membership list for a 'Societas Reformatorum et Correspondency' in 1635 included a number of the logicians already mentioned, notably Bisterfeld, Alsted, Coccejus, Jungius and Caspar Streso.[132] According to Howard Hotson, the persecuted Calvinistic communities of the 'Second Reformation' and the middle-Rhine Calvinist milieu provided a continuous source of

---

[124] *Ephemerides* (1639): HP 30/4/34B: 'Keckermann ineptissimum judicium dedit de Lullo. Fundamentum eius vere excellens si termini tam reales sicuti fingit.'

[125] On Brook's *Didactica*, see HP 22/3, 22/4 ('Praecognita Brookiana dogmatica'), which includes opinions of Brook's works by John Dury and John Pell. See also *Adumbratio brevis eorum quae in linguarum studio hactenus* (BL Sloane MS 649, fols. 285–90). In its stress on the collection of 'praecognita', Brook's work is very much in the tradition of the German Reformed philosophy of Keckermann and Alsted (see Keckermann, *Praecognitorum logicorum tractatus III* (Hanau, 1599) and Alsted, *Philosophia digne restituta: libros quatuor pracognitorum philosophicorum complectens* (Herborn, 1612)).

[126] 'Exemplum analyseos Richersonianae' (HP 24/13).

[127] 'Succincta delineatio rerum in Acontii methodo contentarum' (HP 24/15).

[128] HP 24/16/15B.   [129] HP 24/16/15A.

[130] *De prompta utilium rerum meditatione libri IV* (Bremen, 1614). Martinius was a renowned philologist. His *Lexicon philologicum* (Frankfurt, 1655) was reprinted regularly until the eighteenth century, and he was responsible for a polyglot collection of liturgical epistles and gospels, the *Evangelia et epistolae . . . Graece, Bohemice, Germanice et Latine* (Bremen, 1616).

[131] 'hanc logicam inventionum utilitatem etiam ad Ecclesiam multum emolumenti afferre eiusmodi homines possent' (HP 24/16/16B).

[132] Kvačala, *Pädogogische Reform*, I, 45–6.

irenic and tolerant religious opinions and innovative pedagogical thought.[133] Hartlib and Dury's roles in the educational committees of the Cromwellian commonwealth[134] and in fostering the aims of a harmonizing *pansophia* of religious and scientific knowledge are, in many senses, the inheritors and implementers of this milieu in the English context.[135] The manifestos prepared by Hartlib in his appeals to Parliament were underpinned by a call for the reformation of logic as an academic discipline, a reformation that had long been the concern of Calvinist intellectuals in Europe.

CONCLUSIONS: THE 'DEFECTS' OF THE PANSOPHIC PROJECT, THE FAILURE OF THE 'TRUE LOGICK'

If Hartlib's methodological endeavours for the strengthening of the English Reformation were charged with zealous enthusiasm and idealism, they also constituted a profoundly human and liberal project. It was perhaps a little too liberal and a little too human – not to say fallible – to be true. Hartlib's hopes for a full national implementation of his plans for encyclopaedic learning were never realized. Even within the ranks of his collaborators, many doubts were expressed about the possibilities of achieving a 'universal logic' or *pansophia*. 'The divel will finde one tricke or other to abuse the Pansophia', Hübner predicted, 'And it may bee by gelding as it were the vital parts of it. I meane the religious part of it laboring to make men atheistical.'[136] In many ways the very idea of a perfection in knowledge offended Protestant sensibilities. 'The notion of Pansophy is too proud an attempt', one correspondent concluded, 'For it seemes to take up all and leave nothing to posterity.'[137] Hartlib's correspondents often poured cold water on his warm recommendations of Comenius' encyclopaedic project, stressing the fallibility of the individuals involved. It was 'a great fault in Comenius and others to strive too much for compendiousnes and brevity', com-

---

[133] Howard Hotson, 'Johann Heinrich Alsted and the Second German Reformation' (unpublished seminar paper, Hartlib Papers Project Seminar, University of Sheffield, 3 March 1990). See also Hotson, 'Encyclopaedism, millenarianism and the Second Reformation'.

[134] See Webster, 207–17.

[135] Although it also travels in the reverse direction back into Germany, e.g. the list of items to send to Dr Cimmermann in Hamburg, including 'Artium Duraei', 'Methodus Bisterfeld', 'Generalia Praecepta Brookii', 'Encyclopaedia Puerilis Brukiana 2. Horniana, 3. Pelleana'; Kvačala, *Pädogogische Reform*, I, 46–7.

[136] *Ephemerides* (1639): HP 30/4/5B.   [137] *Ephemerides* (1640): HP 30/4/60B.

plained one of Hartlib's informants, 'wheras some things must of necessity bee handled at large'.[138] Comenius' ideas, said another correspondent, 'requires mighty Credulous men. For hee supposes a world of th[in]gs and takes them for granted. An accurat Philosopher or a Sceptic will never admit of them ... His Synthetical Method which hee follows spoils all. If their bee not a perfect gradation so that but one bee missing all is spoiled'.[139] Hübner attacked the possibility of *pansophia* through a critique of Alsted's histories: 'Many of his canons are most childish containing no direction or reality of notions in them but I know not what at random scribled. Wee have not yet the history of any one Europaean country accuratly and how shall wee write a Pansophy for the whole world?'[140]

It is almost as though Bacon was ultimately given the last laugh at the expense of these exalted ideals of reformation. For the failure of pansophic projects to achieve parliamentary patronage might well be ascribed to *pansophia* affording a proof of Bacon's terse judgement that 'too much method produces iterations and prolixity as well as none at all'.[141]

---

[138] *Ephemerides* (1640): HP 30/4/64B.   [139] *Ephemerides* (1639): HP 30/4/24B.
[140] *Ephemerides* (1639): HP 30/4/2A.
[141] Francis Bacon, 'Preparative towards a natural & experimental history', in Bacon, *Works*, IV, 253.

CHAPTER 3

Comenius and his ideals: escape from the labyrinth

Dagmar Čapková

Jan Amos Komenský (J. A. Comenius) has a portentous reputation in the twentieth century. 'That incomparable Moravian', as his last major biographer in English termed him, has been invoked to support many modern ideals.[1] He has been portrayed as a prophet to the modern Czech fatherland, cited by Masaryk at the inauguration of the first Czechoslovak democratic republic in his famous speech to the nation from the balcony in Wenceslas Square in Prague. Significantly, the same passage from Comenius was also invoked in the same place during the 'velvet revolution' of December 1989 by Václav Havel. In a broader context, Comenius has been hailed as 'the teacher of nations', a kind of elder statesman to UNESCO, which declared 1992 'the year of Comenius'. Had Comenius not argued the case for a framework in which universal human culture could be promoted to further harmony between man and nature, human individuals, communities and states in the world? To educationists, he has long been presented as the 'Galileo of education'. Had he not preached the need for universal, mass education based on a concept of teaching processes which is fundamentally modern? Did he not present education as involving a carefully structured curriculum in which each individual would, to the best of his or her abilities, develop a broad understanding of the world around them and of the organic links between individual phenomena? Did he not stress the importance of visual aids and practical demonstration in teaching? Meanwhile, to historians of science and of ideas, Comenius used to be the visionary who hailed the founding of the Royal Society in London as the model for an advancement of science in his famous treatise *Via lucis* (*The way of light*), published in 1668. In 1992, the 400th anniversary of his birth,

[1] M. Spinka, *J. A. Comenius, that incomparable Moravian* (Chicago, 1943).

the international conference circuit was filled with Comenian com-
memorations across the world. The most prestigious of them all
occurred in Prague under the post-millennial title of 'The heritage
of J. A. Comenius and man's education for the twenty-first
century'.[2]

Heritage and history, however, need to be kept to some degree
distinct. A historian's task is to stress the burden of the past as well as
the heritage for the future; to recover the inconsequentiality of
human experience and, by placing the past in its context, to re-
present it, mistakes, blind alleys and all. In the case of Comenius, it is
true that his career was one of endless endeavour to improve the life
of individuals as well as of society as a whole, a remarkable attempt
to transform the structure of seventeenth-century society into a
peaceful, creative and harmonious community. Yet, like most
utopian writers, Comenius' ideals reflected the complexities and
contradictions of his age. Such complexities and contradictions were
expressive of both his internal conflicts and the external crises of the
Thirty Years War which dominated his mature life.

In some respects, Comenius' intellectual background was rich and
varied but homogeneous. Comenius had been inspired by the
streams of Renaissance European culture, by the patterns and ideals
of Antiquity (such as *paideia* and *humanitas*), as revived by the
humanists. At the same time, he responded to the ideals of Christian
Antiquity. The interrelationship between *fides*, *spes* and *caritas*, the
ideals of the New Testament and the early Christian church (particularly St Augustine) had been given greater prominence during
the Renaissance and Reformation. These ideals were mediated to
Comenius through the Czech Reformation particularly by the
writings of many Neoplatonists. There is no doubt that Comenius
was also inspired by other Neoplatonists such as Cusanus, Paracelsus, Patrizzi, Campanella and Fludd. The mystics, in particular
Boehme and Andreae and the writers of the Rosicrucian movement,
also had a similar harmonizing effect on his thought. In a conver-
gent fashion, and from these various sources, Comenius drew his

---

[2] Other Comenius events and conferences were held in Bratislava, in Uherský Brod (Comenius' native region and the site of the Comenius Museum), Zurich, Paris, Berlin, London,
Amsterdam, Oslo, Göteborg, Uppsala, Montreal, Los Angeles, Palma de Mallorca, Mace-
rata, Torre Pellice, Rome etc., and, tangentially, the conference in Sheffield that has given
rise to this volume.

interests in the old ideal of panharmonia, a Neoplatonic conception of the whole, of the world as an organism in which interrelationships played an important role and mankind is conceived as a microcosm within a macrocosm.[3]

At the same time, Comenius lived through the shattering of the material and moral basis on which this intellectual unity could thrive. The political and religious conflicts of the Thirty Years War began in his country with the unsuccessful struggle of the Czech estates against the house of Habsburg during the years 1618–20. The re-Catholicizing endeavours which took place in the wake of these events in Bohemia afflicted Comenius with persecution (after 1620), and eventually (in 1628) he became an exile. Thereafter he was forced to defend and sustain as best he could the intellectual homologies which he felt had existed in Czech culture before 1620 and which had been so savagely interrupted. It was as a wandering philosopher and theologian, and as a bishop (or senior) of the Czech Unity of Brethren (*unitas fratrum*) in exile, that Comenius attempted to foster and promote the mutually supportive ideals of order, discipline, tolerance and non-violent action, responsibility and a conception of history as the *magistra vitae*, but all within the more hostile, divisive and corrosive climate of the Thirty Years War.

The loss of religious, national and personal freedom was a painful experience for Comenius. The death of his young family, the destruction of his library and the devastation of the landscape of his youth are vividly mirrored in the first two parts of his *Truchlivý* [The mourning].[4] This was the beginning of a more extensive inner conflict for Comenius resulting from his trying to explain, to come to terms with, and to find a way out of the 'labyrinths' of the age. He began to study more systematically the position of man in the world, to balance the grim perception of reality with an awareness of an inner spiritual existence. This gradually took shape in the form of a parallel vision of reality and of utopia in his writings.

The dichotomy between secular chaos, disorder, hatred and selfishness on the one hand, and harmony, love, tolerance, understanding and mutual support on the other was depicted strikingly in his *Labyrint světa a ráj srdce* (*Labyrinth of the World and the Paradise of the Heart*) (1623).[5] He saw the pathway towards harmony leading

---

[3] Comenius, xv/i, 61.   [4] *Ibid.*, iii, 19–101.   [5] *Ibid.*, iii, 267–400.

inward, to inner contemplation which would rid the individual of selfishness and prevent deviation from the road towards perfection. This road would lead eventually towards God as the *centrum securitatis*, once all pride and vanity which bred conflict and mutual misunderstandings had been conquered. This dichotomy became the starting point for Comenius' desire for universal reformation which would itself commence with universal inner spiritual transformation. But the process of transformation could not be divorced from a continual, unending effort to improve and amend what was corrupt and wrong in the world and society at large. So the immense bravura of Comenius' ideals resulted from his attempt to integrate both these aspects – the inner transformation of individual human beings on the one hand and the universal reformation of society on the other. It culminated in his greatest work, the *Consultatio* (General consultation on the reform of human affairs).[6]

The basis of Comenius' thinking lay in his perception of human beings as made in the image of God the creator, and thus endowed with the potential for creative endeavour to perfect (with the grace of God) the world and themselves within it. The potential for perfectibility, however, was never going to be easily realized. Comenius regarded humankind as the most excellent, but also the most complex, changeable and mysterious of creatures.[7] Only by a sustained, lifelong process of overall educative formation would human potential be fully realized. As he put it in the *Didactica magna*: 'Hominem si homo fieri debet formari oportere.'[8]

Comenius' educational endeavours began with encyclopaedic activities and with the reform of Latin studies. His emphasis on overall education gradually caused him to broaden his conceptions to cover elementary education in general as well as more specialized secondary and higher education, until finally (in the *Consultatio*) it embraced adult education and the whole span of human life. As he became more fully aware of the complexities of the advanced civil societies of his day and the conflicts generated within them, Comenius thus came to elaborate a pattern of social reform across all spheres which would be conditioned by a universal lifelong edu-

---

[6] J. A. Comenius, *De rerum humanarum emendatione consultatio catholica*, 2 vols. (Prague, 1966) (henceforth cited as *Consultatio*).

[7] Comenius, xv/1, 39. Comenius, *Consultatio*, I, cols. 594, 918, 930; II, col. 47.

[8] Comenius, xv/1, 67ff.

cational process involving individuals, families, schools, churches, communities and states throughout the world.

All such reforming endeavours came to be predicated on his pansophic vision. Wisdom lay in the three books of Nature (the world around us), Man (the whole personality) and God (the truth revealed in Scripture). *Pansophia* provided the right educative relationship between man and the world, the microcosm and the macrocosm. *Pansophia* was thus a process of universal life-wisdom rather than a fact of universal knowledge. *Pansophia* should integrate intellectual as well as moral and religious activities, pulling together human reason, speech, will, emotions, conscience and endeavour. This ideal of integrating all forms of human thought and activity, practice and *chresis* was different and distinct from the activities of other encyclopaedic thinkers of the seventeenth century. Comenius failed to complete his encyclopaedia, the *Theatrum universitatis rerum* (composed between 1614 and 1627), precisely because his perceptions of the dynamic educative process of pansophy began to render it redundant. Increasingly he saw educative pansophy as the only way of resolving the complex labyrinths of contemporary society.

In his famous *Opera didactica omnia* (1657), the frontispiece to which provides the cover to this volume, Comenius attempted to present the quintessence of his pansophic educational conceptions. As the illustration indicates, Comenius presented the school as the workshop of humanity, the *officina humanitatis*.[9] By *humanitas* he meant the cultivation of everything that makes for man's positive superiority over other animals. Mankind's facility to understand his environment, to develop a right relationship with other human beings and with God, his ability to exploit every possibility and potentiality for improvement of himself and his environment was dependent on this educational and utopian equivalent of Hartlib's Office of Address. In his *Schola pansophica* (1651), Comenius carefully emphasized the interrelationship between the various components, material and spiritual, physical and mental, that went to make up *pansophia*.[10] The *officina humanitatis* meant education for all without discrimination ('*omnes*') in everything of importance for human life ('*omnia*') and in the most complex fashion so that the whole human

[9] Cf. *ibid.*, 77; 80; xv/ii 306ff; xv/iii 195, 263 and 268; Comenius, *Consultatio*, ii, col. 110 etc.
[10] Comenius, xv/iii, 201ff.

being might become educated, both inwardly and outwardly ('*omnino*'). The term *officina* did not mean a mechanic's workshop but rather a place full of well-organized activity, with firmly defined objectives, a series of proper methods, means and assistance, by which mankind would be moulded towards human potential naturally, without violence, as if in play. Schools must be educational environments for the total experience of life. These were themes developed not merely in his *Didactica magna* but also in the *Methodus linguarum*, the *Schola pansophica* and particularly the fourth part of the *Consultatio* (*Pampaedia*). In the latter, he tried to show that rightly conceived relationships between the whole and its parts, between the general and the particular, between the individual and the social, have an epistemological significance as well as a socio-ethical and practical meaning. This led Comenius to stress how potential incompatibles might be harmonized within a common curriculum – general with more specialized education, spontaneity with discipline, fighting for a just cause with the search for peace.

His pansophic conception had already, however, been outlined in his shorter pansophic textbooks, the first of which, *Janua linguarum* [gate of languages], established his European reputation.[11] In a hundred chapters, this textbook presented a compact systematic approach to knowledge of all kinds. Since it was also a language textbook, factual knowledge and language teaching were connected in such a way that it made a practical contribution to the particular pedagogic problems of language training at the time. Although the first edition appeared in Leszno in 1631, its reputation quickly spread. England provides an important case-study of the initial reception of *pansophia* among Europe's intellectual community.

Samuel Hartlib was crucial in the process since it was through his contacts and correspondence that Comenius' work was most substantially circulated in England in the 1630s, and through his efforts that personal communication with Comenius was sustained. According to Comenius himself, two Brethren of the Czech Unity visited Hartlib in the early 1630s to answer his various questions concerning Comenius' work, following the publication of the *Janua linguarum*.[12] Hartlib forwarded a letter to him and thus began their

---

[11] *ODO*, I, 255–302.
[12] J. A. Comenius, *Continuatio admonitionis fraternae* (1669; Stockholm, 1975), 149 (English version); 233 (Latin version).

initial correspondence, much to Comenius' satisfaction since it provided him with an opportunity both to discuss his pansophical projects and to give them a wider hearing.

In some respects, Comenian *pansophia* was not dissimilar from the ideas advanced by Francis Bacon. They both believed that society should be reformed through knowledge and education. They both opposed scholasticism and Aristotelianism. They both believed that schools were too much occupied with words rather than things. Bacon's plans for a 'great instauration' of the sciences through a college of scientific research and the shaping of a well-ordered society commanded Comenius' attention and support. The distinctive Baconianism of many in Hartlib's intellectual circle led them to give Comenius' pansophy a favourable reception. Although specialising in many different branches of knowledge, and despite being divided in their political commitments (they included both moderate and more radical Parliamentarians), they shared a common commitment to reform the Anglican church as well as broader matters such as education as well as economic and cultural life. For many, too, their millenarian beliefs, similar to those of Comenius himself, were also common ground.

They welcomed Comenius' pansophical ideals, recognizing in them a valuable contribution to their own objectives. These included the unification of separate terrains of knowledge and their integration within a reformed curriculum of study.[13] Hartlib's own papers show that he sustained a vast correspondence with scholars in various European countries.[14] Since it was a characteristic of Hartlib's circle of associates that their interests in particular disciplines did not gainsay their involvement in other branches of knowledge, it is not surprising that Comenius' ideals were welcomed by those from a variety of differing backgrounds. Thus the mathematician John Pell, the politician John Pym, the linguist Theodore Haak, the polyhistorian Joachim Hübner and the ecumenist John Dury gave favourable initial responses to Comenius' ideas. The collaborators of Hartlib during Comenius' stay in London in 1641–2 were also broadly welcoming of his ideals – especially Samuel Hartlib himself,

---

[13] BL Add MS 4425 fol 68v: 'It may be Comenius, his Pansophy will save us all a labour.' Cf. D. Čapková, 'The Comenian group in England and Comenius' idea of universal reform', *Acta Comeniana*, 1 (1969), 27.

[14] As indicated in the extracts from the papers cited in, e.g., *HDC*; J. Kvačala, *J.A. Komenského Korrespondence*, 2 vols. (Prague, 1898–1902); J. Kvačala, *Die pädagogische Reform des J. A. Comenius in Deutschland*, 2 vols. (Berlin, 1902).

John Dury, Joachim Hübner and Theodore Haak. Thus, for example, Pell's *Idea matheseos* was considered even by his contemporaries to have much in common with Comenius' plan for *pansophia* although it was mainly intended to indicate the route by which mathematical methods could be improved.[15] Hartlib's ideal of tolerance was also close to that of Comenius' 'longing to do good to all men and to see unity and peace replace the chaos and hatred of seventeenth-century Europe'.[16] Samuel Hartlib and John Dury shared Comenius' zeal for theoretical and practical endeavours in education and science to promote the welfare of mankind. Hartlib supported proposals for change in a variety of spheres similar to those of Comenius. John Dury's ecumenism was close to sentiments expressed by Comenius in, for example, *Cesta pokoje* [the way of peace].

Thanks to Hartlib, Comenius was brought into contact with those who were prepared potentially to collaborate with him in his great endeavours. Joachim Hübner, an exile from Clève, recognised as early as 1636 that the scope of Comenius' work would extend far beyond the reform of education studies. He had been involved in excerpting significant passages from books in the Bodleian Library in Oxford for Hartlib and it was from there that he wrote to him concerning Comenius: 'Und also solche Sachen verheissett quae multorum oculos aperire possunt, ad melius consulendam literarum studiis atque per id Scholis, Ecclesiis, Politiis, totique Mortalium generi.'[17] Comenius' own objective in the course of the 1630s was to elaborate pansophy further in two respects. He wanted to build up a selection of the relevant significant facts of human knowledge in so far as they pertained to Nature, Mankind and God. Secondly he wanted to construct a selection of the important philosophical principles around which the world could be understood. The *Janua linguarum* was intended merely to provide an example of the former. It would serve as one part of the great pansophic work which he planned to advance with Hübner and whose first topic was to be called *'Panhistoria'*. Hübner characterised it as a historical description of the structure of the history of the world.[18]

---

[15] Pamela R. Barnett, *Theodore Haak, F.R.S.* (The Hague, 1962), 37.   [16] *Ibid.*, 12.
[17] Kvačala, *Pädagogische Reform*, I, 69.
[18] Kvačala, *Korrespondence*, I, 61: 'Omnium Particularium a Deo, Angelis, mundo et homine ab initio creationis usque tempora gestorum plena et accurate et filum temporum strictum ubique sequens descriptio'.

The second aspect of *pansophia* (as it was conceived in the great planned work of this period called '*Pansophia*') was to be a kind of metaphysics. But it was unlike the traditional metaphysics of Aristotle in that it did not aim to culminate in a systematic ordering of knowledge. Comenius criticised Aristotle precisely because his metaphysics was incomprehensible and of no practical use.[19] By contrast, Comenius' metaphysics was intended to provide all branches of knowledge with a methodological and philosophical basis, grounded in the worlds of Nature, Man and the Divine Word, whose ontology promised to reveal the common principles, relationships and differences concerning everything, on the basis of which people would learn the truth and how to act in accordance with it.[20]

Comenius outlined his pansophical metaphysics in his *Prodromus pansophiae*. There he expressed his distaste for the separate autonomies of the various sciences and the lack of an integrated approach to the school curriculum. He particularly attacked those theologians who took no account of philosophy, those lawyers who neglected to study the world of nature, and those physicians who ignored the problems of justice, ethics and politics. Comenius wanted the fundamental principles of his metaphysics so evident that no scientific enquiry would operate in isolation from broader human needs. This metaphysics was elaborated in the *Janua rerum* but Comenius continued to develop it throughout the rest of his life. The third part of the *Consultatio* (called the *Pansophia* or *Pentaxia*) contained the elements of the pansophical metaphysics in its first section, called 'Mundus possibilis'.[21]

The goal of integrating the various branches of knowledge and thus providing the basis for a total reform of the education curriculum was readily accepted by Hartlib and his associates. This is why, when Hartlib received the manuscript of the *Prodromus pansophiae*, it was promptly published (without Comenius' authorisation) in Oxford in 1637 as the *Praeludia pansophiae*, and followed by a second, now authorized, version entitled *Prodromus pansophiae*, published in London in 1639. The initial reactions were broadly favourable both

---

[19] Comenius, xv/ii, 18.
[20] *Ibid.*, 40. See also J. Cervenka, 'Problematika Komenského metafyziky' [the problematics of Comenius' metaphysics], *Studia Comeniana et Historica*, 3 (1973), 25–72. This also refers to other literature concerning the methodological significance of pansophical metaphysics. Cf. D. Čapková, 'Neznamý deník Komenského' [the unknown diary of Comenius], *Studia Comeniana et Historica* (supplement), 8–9 (1974), 1–108.
[21] Comenius, *Consultatio*, i, cols. 278–330.

in England and abroad.[22] Tassius wrote from Hamburg of the excitement these ideas had provoked. Mersenne in France reported Descartes' positive commendation. Hartlib, who had acted as distributor to the writings of Comenius in England and elsewhere, entertained the highest expectations and these were shared by several others. John Stoughton, the English millenarian, considered that the pansophy of Comenius, along with Bacon's *Instauratio magna* and Dury's irenic aims, constituted decisive steps towards the coming millennium. Hartlib's correspondents reported that, among many other scholars, Grotius had a high regard for the *Prodromus*. The omens for financial support for Comenius in England and the Netherlands seemed auspicious.

Yet, beyond the initial reactions, there was also dissent. Comenius' proposal had seemed to many, including even Hübner, to have been 'Baconian', especially in its utilitarian aspects.[23] Comenius himself had praised Bacon in the introduction to his *Physicae synopsis* and in the *Prodromus* (along with Campanella and Andreae). He had included citations from his works.[24] But, in fact, Bacon had provided only some of the building-blocks for Comenius' ideals. While Bacon had concentrated on searching for the keys to unlock the secrets of nature, Comenius sought a universal method by which man's relationship with the whole world (including humanity itself) would be transformed. While both Bacon and Comenius stressed that man's learning was synonymous with his abilities to determine things, Bacon interpreted this as action in a particular, utilitarian fashion whereas Comenius interpreted it within a Neoplatonic environment of the homologies between the general and the particular, the realms of ideas and realities. Such homologies were apparent in all Comenius' educational writings. They appeared, for example, in his *Didactic* where, by means of an easy, agreeable, rapid and thorough process of education, mankind might be carried into the loftier realms of the concept of man and his place in the world. They also found their place in his textbook of philosophy and pansophical metaphysics, the *Janua rerum*, which he began to write after completing the *Janua linguarum* and which was designed to contain a selection of general world principles on which to base

[22] D. Čapková, 'The reception given to the *Prodromus pansophiae* and the methodology of Comenius', *Acta Comeniana*, 7 (1987), 37–59.
[23] Kvačala, *Korrespondence*, I, 26–7; and Kvačala *Pädagogische Reform*, 87.
[24] Comenius, xv/II, 36, 41, 44.

particular and individual branches of knowledge. It was precisely this homology that created tensions between Comenius and his English associates.

Thus, when Hübner asked Comenius to elaborate his pansophic method, imagining that it would be 'bisshero so gar Unbekante panharmonia . . . [*sive*] nova inventio de universali complexu',[25] he probably did not fully understand the complexity of what Comenius had in mind. He perhaps conceived that it would be a method resembling Pell's mathematical approach (which he much admired),[26] or Acontius' analytical method, or again Descartes' *Discourse on method* (which Hübner believed could be usefully applied to Comenius' *Janua rerum*, which Comenius was himself considering at that moment as a textbook for pansophical metaphysics). But when Comenius' overarching ideals became clear, Hübner began to have doubts. He was not at all sure whether the three sources of wisdom in *pansophia* (Nature, Man and God) could ever be integrated and subjected to one supreme goal – the unification of man with God. He did not at all accept the way Comenius attempted to apply the principles of pansophy to questions of ethics, as in *Faber fortunae* (1636–7). This extension of *pansophia* beyond the purely intellectual aroused considerable aversion in Oxford.[27]

Hübner also differed from Comenius over the structure of *pansophia*, and the division emerged in his assessment of the *Didactica magna*.[28] His criticism was directed against the connection of educational principles with the philosophy of human life. He was sceptical of the Comenian methodology of 'syncrisis', the third and (to Comenius) vital methodological counterpart of analysis and synthesis, when it came to providing a framework for understanding the world. Hübner was interested in analysis, mainly in the way in which analysis and synthesis determined the content and structure of what was to be included in the pansophical compendium.

Comenius did not ignore all Hübner's critical comments on the *Didactica magna*. He accepted, for example, that he had to enlarge his conception of education beyond the school to embrace education

[25] Kvačala, *Pädagogische Reform*, I, 68, 69, 90.
[26] J. Pell, *De numero et ordine disciplinarum*. Cf. Kvačala, *Pädagogische Reform*, I, 77, 82, 93.
[27] Kvačala, *Korrespondence*, I, 30; Kvačala, *Pädagogische Reform*, I, 91, 100–101.
[28] Kvačala, *Korrespondence*, I, 72–82; Kvačala, *Pädagogische Reform*, I, 141–57; HP 36/5/3–14 (esp. fol. 9); Čapková, "*Prodromus pansophiae*', 46ff;. Čapková, 'The Comenian Group in England', 30ff.

within the family and in society.[29] He agreed that he had to provide advice on how to learn.[30] Yet Comenius never relinquished his basic conception of the relationship between principles of education and the philosophy of human life, and he did not surrender his view of 'syncrisis' as a vital way of comparing the whole and the parts and comparing different parts within a whole, and comparing different but comparable wholes. Through 'syncrisis' Comenius continued to expect to uncover the underlying substantive reality and the fundamental relationships that governed the world. Unlike Hübner, Comenius did not see the *Didactica* as an introduction to pansophy but as pansophy applied to education theory. For his part, although Hübner was finally less than satisfied with Comenian metaphysics and with his *Didactica*, he retained his respect for Comenian ideas of pansophy.[31]

There were also other expressions of dissent which emerged from other quarters. Descartes, of course, provided a critical reaction in his 'Judicium de opere pansophico'.[32] So, too, did various scholars in Germany, notably J. A. Pöhmer and P. Müller. Some, like Hübner and Bisterfeld, concentrated their criticism on Comenian methodology. The sharpest critics remained, however, the theologians. They included the Polish aristocrat, H. Broniewski, a member of the Polish branch of the Unity of Brethren, as well as Lutheran theologians such as J. Botsak and A. Calovius.[33] They detected heresy hidden below the surface of *pansophia*, objecting in particular (with some natural philosophers) to the mingling of human and divine wisdom which it appeared to entail. One anonymous manuscript entitled *Pansophiae librum annotationes*, perhaps reflecting this tradition, is to be found among the Hartlib Papers. Its author has not been identified but it must have been composed some time between 1637 and 1639 because it is clearly responding to the *Praeludia* and does not mention the *Prodromus* of 1639. The manuscript tried to indicate how Comenian pansophy was

[29] This was later incorporated by Comenius in the *Via lucis* (composed in 1641–2 and published in 1668) and the *Consultatio*.
[30] Such advice was later provided in the *Mathetica*, a part of the fifth section of *Pansophia* or *Pantaxia*, that is the third part of the *Consultatio*.
[31] See the details in Čapková, '*Prodromus pansophiae*', 47ff.
[32] See HP 7/96 (published by J. Kvačala in *Analecta Comeniana* (1910)), 14–6ff.; see also the 'Annotatiunculae of J. Broniewski' in HP 7/62/1–6 (published by G. H. Turnbull in *HDC*), 452–5.
[33] HP 7/96.

potentially harmful, full of blasphemy and ultimately unrealizable.[34]

Such criticism may have provided some inspiration to Comenius. He certainly was moved to write an early successful defence of his works in the *Dilucidatio pansophiae* (Leszno, 1638), a first and hitherto unknown edition of which (it was probably the copy he forwarded to Hartlib) has recently been discovered in the British Library.[35] However, although Comenius accepted some criticism, he rebuffed those who denied his fundamental concepts. He continued to consider the place of pansophical metaphysics within the school curriculum and within an overall pattern of universal reformation. He expressed his thoughts in part of his working diary which he despatched to Hartlib in 1646.[36] The attacks of theologians also deflected him from his original purposes and he was forced to defend himself even within his own milieu of the Unity of Brethren.

Opposition from those engaged in developing Cartesian philosophy was harder for Comenius either to ignore or to answer.[37] His Neoplatonic view of the world collided with Descartes' mechanistic approach at every turn. Descartes set man aside from the world as the observer of some great machine. He did not see man and the natural world as an integral unity. Descartes regarded mathematics (or rather, arithmetic and geometry) as the foundation stone of his ideas for the unification of science. He then applied this unified approach to every subject. Mathematical deductions and logical relationships became all-important in a process that reduced complex structures to geometrically conceived relationships from which man

---

[34] I have already analyzed the text in D. Čapková, *Myslitelsko-vychovytelský odkaz J.A. Komenského* [the heritage of J. Comenius – thinker and educator] (Prague, 1987), 98; also in Čapková, '*Prodromus pansophiae*', 51–4.

[35] Comenius scholars have been searching for many years for the first edition of the *Dilucidatio*. It was on my way to the Sheffield conference in July 1992 that I visited the British Library, to be informed by the librarian, Devana Pavlík, that they had recently discovered a rare Comenianum. It turned out to be the missing first edition of the *Dilucidatio*. Further details of the discovery are contained in D. Čapková and D. Pavlík, 'Nález prvního vydání Komenského spisu Conatuum pansophicorum dilucidatio', *Studia Comeniana et Historica*, 23 (1993), 26–34.

[36] This document was discovered as an anonymous text by G. H. Turnbull; subsequently (in 1971) it was identified by D. Čapková and edited. See Čapková, 'Neznamý deník Komenského'; and D. Čapková, 'A "working diary" of J. A. Comenius', *Acta Comeniana*, 4/II (1979), 367–87; Cf. D. Čapková, 'The educational plans of J. A. Comenius in 1646: from a diary sent to English colleagues', *History of Education*, 7 (1978), 95–103.

[37] Čapková, *Myslitelsko-vychovytelský odkaz*, 174ff.

had been abstracted to become merely a rationally observing entity. Time (and the possibility for organic development within it) was subordinated to Cartesian geometrically delineated space. Comenius, on the other hand, based his perceptions on an organically conceived unity of the cosmos, of which man was an integral part. Where Descartes devoted so much thought to space, Comenius concentrated on time. Organic development would only take place in the course of a lifetime. Likewise, the reform of humanity and pansophic method would require time to mature as the variety of approaches – analysis, synthesis and syncrisis – bore fruit in revealing the fundamental relationships of the cosmos. Unlike Descartes and his followers, therefore, Comenius attached a fundamental importance to history. He did not aim to unify the sciences by subjugating them all to one, but rather to link the sciences to all branches of human activity. It was these different emphases that made Comenius, unlike Descartes, a manifestly utopian thinker.

During his visit to England in 1641–2, Comenius found himself consistently broadening the context within which to apply his ideals. The pansophic works he proposed to advance while in London embraced pre-school education, the reform of studies and discussion of broader components of reform as well.[38] Comenius believed that it was essential to understand history and the evolutionary trends of society if universal reformation was to be actively advanced. He was particularly influenced by the perception of the possibilities for advancement through the natural sciences and technology which he had perhaps witnessed while in Hartlib's company. Although much impressed, Comenius also warned prophetically against the dangers of a one-sided approach, reinforcing those fears in the preface to the *Via lucis*, composed when he edited the manuscript for publication in 1668. The overall message of the *Via lucis*, originally written during his stay in London, was that science and education had a social function and that a complete educational environment could only be achieved within the framework of universal reform.[39] He expressed the concept of universality in the *Via lucis* in the proposal for a supreme institution for education and learning, the *collegium lucis*, as a co-ordinating centre for research and the propagation of

[38] These are sketched in the *Elaborandorum operum catalogus* and the *Consultationis brevissima delineatio* in Comenius, XIV, 119–26, 129–36.
[39] *Via lucis* in Comenius, XIV, 281–385.

education. He paid particular attention to the means by which this universal reform could be achieved. Besides universal schools and universal books, he also began to conceive of the possibilities for a universal language.[40] This was to be a language that would be easily learnt and in such a way that people would communicate with one another more easily and precisely and international contacts and co-operation be encouraged. The idea would be carried forward later in *Panglottia*. Indeed many ideas developed in the *Consultatio* originated in the wake of Comenius' visit to London. It was from 1643 onwards that he began to elaborate the basic sevenfold structure of the work.[41] It was these ideas that were reflected in his other writings on school reform whilst he was in Sweden (1642–8), Hungary (1650–4) and the Netherlands (1656–70).

Although the pacification at Münster and Osnabrück brought the Thirty Years War to a close in 1648 it did not bring with it the liberation of Comenius' native country or enable him to return from exile. He retained, therefore, his aspiration that through the universal reconstruction of all society and the establishment of a '*cultura universalis*'[42] (or 'universal, lifelong education of everybody'), national revival would also be accomplished. Such a reconstruction would have to be attempted universally, freely, enthusiastically and courageously, yet unanimously and peacefully.[43]

Where should this reconstruction begin? In the *Consultatio*, Comenius defined those domains 'which contribute to the sublimity of human nature'.[44] The roots of human sublimity lay in the intellect (for investigation), the will (to seek out the good) and the stimulus to activity (which exercises man's versatile faculties). The fruits of these three, the '*tria summa hominum erga*', are philosophy (or the study of wisdom, produced by man's hunger for the truth), religion (or the cultivation and enjoyment of the highest good) and politics (originating from man's eagerness to manage affairs

[40] *Ibid.*, 351–6.
[41] I.e. the seven fundamental parts of *De rerum humanarum emendatione consultatio catholica*, namely: 1) *Panegersia*; 2) *Panaugia*; 3) *Pansophia/Pantaxia* (in eight parts: 'Mundus possibilis', 'Mundus archetypus', 'Mundus angelicus', 'Mundus materialis', 'Mundus artificialis', 'Mundus moralis', 'Mundus spiritualis' and 'Mundus aeternus'); 4) *Pampaedia*; 5) *Panglottia*; 6) *Panorthosia*; 7) *Pannuthesia*.
[42] Comenius, *Consultatio*, ii, col. 4ff.   [43] *Ibid.*, cols. 750–2.
[44] *Ibid.*, i, col. 28. In English cf. A. M. O. Dobbie's translation of *Panegersia* (Shipston-on-Stour, 1990), 10.

effectively in freedom, restoring good order to everyone throughout the polity).[45]

These three domains should be mutually supportive. Philosophy should no more be the *'ancilla theologiae'* (the 'handmaid of theology') but 'its true natural sister; their sister was also politics'.[46] Each of these 'sisters' should support the other and would be rewarded in return. The important principles of the *Consultatio* were 'scire, velle, posse' – 'to know, to will and to be able to act' – and these were to be applied in all the fundamental areas of human activity. Thus, in religion, according to Comenius, faith, hope and charity (*fides, spes, charitas*) were religious and also moral and political categories;[47] they were facets of *scire* (faith conveyed to mankind through God's grace and Christ's sacrifice), *velle* (love, which raised mankind above the animal kingdom and which provided the model for redemption) and *posse* (activity in hope, which ensured that terror and despair could never secure a footing in the labyrinth of human affairs).[48] Politics should always have an ethical basis, seeking to establish and maintain peace and justice in every field of human affairs. Its objective was to will the end of all conflicts and gather the nations together in peaceful coexistence, conscious of the need to recognize fundamental human rights.[49] These objectives were to be practically assisted through the establishment of international institutions such as (besides the *'collegium lucis'*) the *'dicasterium pacis'* (or international 'court of justice') and the *'consistorium oecumenicum'* (or international 'council of churches').[50] Comenius also discussed the best form of government and arrangement of laws.

The detailed dispositions of the seductive utopianism of the *Consultatio* would require much more space to outline than is available here. At the heart of Comenius' thinking lay, however, his conception of man as a creature endowed with free will (*'animal liberae actionis'*).[51] To deny that freedom was to deny the essence of human nature.[52] Yet Comenius recognised that freedom could lead to

[45] Comenius, *Consultatio*, I, col. 30.   [46] *Ibid.*, II, col. 508.
[47] *Ibid.*, I, col. 1031ff; II, col. 514ff.
[48] *Ibid.*, I, col. 1138ff.; col. 1160 ('Spes adversus omnem desperationem anchora firmissima'); II, cols. 517, 520.
[49] *Ibid.*, II, cols. 508–14; 637–58.
[50] *Ibid.*, cols. 539–59; 514. Concerning the best form of social organization, cf. also *Die pädagogik der Mahnrufe des Elias: das Lebenswerk des J. A. Comenius zwischen Politik und Pädagogik*, ed. J. Nováková (Kastellaun, 1978), 192.
[51] Comenius, *Consultatio*, I, col. 547.   [52] *Ibid.*, II, cols. 37, 481, 482..

disorder and anarchy. So individuals must be educated to understand the right use of their free will[53] and this meant engaging the
philosophical, educational, pyschological, ethical, religious and
social forces of *pansophia* and deploying them through the different
contexts of the family, the school, the community, the state, the
church and the whole of human society. The result, when such
forces were rightly deployed and engaged would be what Comenius
describes as '*cultura universalis*', something only fully acquired over a
lifetime of education and experience. The gradual process of its
acquisition in the various 'schools of life'[54] would eventually
produce individuals capable of appreciating, fostering and acting in
accordance with the fundamental virtues[55] of universal culture such
as *prudentia* (prudence), *symbiotica politica* (social interrelationship),
universalitas (universality), *simplicitas* (simplicity) and *spontaneitas*
(spontaneity).[56] Such mature, well-rounded and virtuous individuals could truly be said to have escaped the labyrinths of the age,
and indeed any age.

[53] *Ibid.*, col. 37: 'Arbitrii libertate ut recte utantur Homines.'
[54] I.e. '*Pandidascalia*'. *Ibid.*, col. 84ff.
[55] *Ibid.*, I, col. 918ff.   [56] *Ibid.*, col. 456ff.

Millenarianism and the quest
for religious unity

'The Unchanged Peacemaker'? John Dury and the politics of irenicism in England, 1628–1643

Anthony Milton

Few men were as central to the Hartlib circle as John Dury, and he more than anyone else, perhaps, can be taken to epitomize the ambition of their aims and the magnitude of their failure. Dury aimed at what he called the 'pacification' of the Protestant churches. In an extraordinary career he doggedly pursued this goal of Protestant unity for some fifty years in travels across the length and breadth of Europe, until his death in 1680. As an obsessive irenicist, Dury has received both admiration and ridicule in equal measure, usually according to the commentator's predisposition (or lack of it) towards ecumenism. Yet whether ecumenists (who applaud his high mindedness) or cynics (who ridicule the half-baked naivety of his 'projects for pacification'), scholars have generally agreed in representing Dury (in tones either of admiration or of contempt) as a simple and otherworldly idealist. The contemporaries who failed to offer Dury the support he needed have similarly been regarded as either clear-headed or hard-hearted pragmatists.[1]

This is an analysis that very much reflects Dury's own vision of himself. He presented himself as 'a peacemaker without partiality', whose efforts failed because they were opposed by evil-minded, self-interested, contentious clerics.[2] Ecumenical historians in particular have been prone to take Dury and other professional ecume-

I am very grateful to the members of the Hartlib Papers Project for their assistance on countless trips to Sheffield, to Julia Merritt for her comments on a draft of this article, and to Andrew Thrush for some helpful last-minute checking of references. Earlier versions of this chapter were presented at the Early Modern British History Seminar in Cambridge, at the Hartlib Papers Seminar in Sheffield, and at the Hartlib Conference 'Peace, Unification, and Prosperity', and I am grateful to those present on each occasion for their helpful comments.

[1] Contrast, for example, H. R. Trevor-Roper, *Archbishop Laud 1573–1645* (London, 1940; 3rd edn, London, 1988), 264, with J. M. Batten, *John Dury, advocate of Christian reunion* (Chicago, 1944), 203.
[2] G. Westin, *Brev från John Durie åren 1636–1638*, Kyrkohistorisk Årsskrift: Skrifter Utgivna Av Kyrkohistoriska Föreningen, 1:33 (Uppsala, 1934), 273–4, 275.

nists on their own terms. They have tended to assume the existence of an irenical 'essentialism' in which the association of Christian unity with peace, toleration and ecumenism is presupposed. This 'essentialist' approach has also allowed historians to construct an apostolic succession of moderate, fair-minded people who urged projects for Christian unity, from Erasmus through Cassander and Acontius to Grotius (and, of course, Dury).

Such an approach creates a number of problems. Firstly, it tends to imply that these irenicists were all after the same thing and for the same reasons – as if every attempt to unite different Christian groups was a step towards a truly unified Christendom, and was underpinned by modern principles of religious toleration and comprehension. Secondly, however, the notion of an essentialist ecumenical succession carries the presupposition that a 'true' interest in Christian unity was limited in this period to a small clutch of rationally minded 'Erasmian' figures. In fact, most thinkers of this period accepted that religious unity was a good idea, in the same way that they believed that sin was a bad idea. The problem was, of course, that different people wanted irenicism on different terms, and as implying different consequences. People were usually very much in favour of one form of irenicism, and very much opposed to another. The job of a professional irenicist such as Dury was to convince different groups that a particular reunion scheme was in their interests and would not undermine their own particular understanding of doctrinal orthodoxy.

Different interpretations of irenicism could have direct political implications, making the rhetoric of Christian unity an important tool in the political conflicts of the period. Its ambiguity meant that it could be appealed to both as a shield and as an offensive weapon in religious politics. For example, arguments for Protestant unity might be invoked as a means of preserving a Calvinist status quo and enforcing it upon dissenting elements. Pierre du Moulin thus sought at the Huguenot synod of Tonneins and elsewhere to reinforce his victory over his doctrinal opponent Daniel Tilenus by proposing a permanent association of Reformed churches which would patrol the doctrinal status quo and prevent any individual church embracing non-Calvinist doctrines without the consent of the others. By contrast, ecumenism might also be promoted as offering a means of undermining Calvinist dogmatism by appealing to a broader range of Protestant doctrinal traditions. Thus, when Hugo Grotius found

Arminianism under pressure from Dutch high Calvinists he appealed for a general council of Protestants in order to force his opponents to mellow their hardline Calvinism to the degree necessary to appease the Lutheran churches. Appeals to unity, moderation, and the distinction between 'fundamental' and 'non-fundamental' articles of faith were not, therefore, the shibboleths of liberal-minded tolerationists, but were shared by all sides in the controversies of the period.[3]

The soundness of a particular irenical scheme would often be assessed by contemporaries not so much according to the specific details of the proposal as with respect to the identity and orthodoxy of those who promoted it. Moreover, the ultimate acceptability of an irenical project seems more often to have been determined by which groups it specifically excluded from its irenical provisions. The fact that this was an era of rigid confessionalism need not imply that irenical and ecumenical notions were upheld solely by men reacting against this trend; on the contrary, the two developments could be intimately related. Just as witch-hunting helped to reaffirm the social norms that bound together the wider community, so heresy-hunting helped to emphasize the doctrinal bonds that united the community of orthodox Christians.

This chapter illustrates the politically ambiguous role played by irenical principles in the thinking of a number of different religious groups within the Church of England in the years preceding the Civil War. These groups offered varying support to Dury and his schemes in the first decade of his activities, according to their positive and negative visions of what irenicism should involve. I concentrate on the Church of England because it was this church that Dury believed had a special role to play in his schemes for Protestant unity between Calvinists and Lutherans; but it was a church that also contained some very different ideas about what this unity should entail.[4] This discussion will help to illustrate the flexibility and variety of irenical notions and the part that they had to play in each different religious faction's self-identity.

This analysis should also help to raise broader questions about the

[3] W. B. Patterson, 'James I and the Huguenot synod of Tonneins of 1614', *Harvard Theological Review*, 65 (1972), 241–70; P. Borschberg, 'State and church in the early politico-religious works of Hugo Grotius' (Ph.D. thesis, University of Cambridge, 1990). For this interpretation see especially A. Milton, *Catholic and Reformed. The Roman and Protestant churches in English Protestant thought 1600–1640* (Cambridge University Press, forthcoming), chap. 8.
[4] BL Sloane MS 654, fols. 108v, 121v–122r, 127r, 176r.

mentality of a professional irenicist such as Dury, free from the
stereotype of the naive, idealistic and pacific evangelist which has
often impeded understandings of the work of such ecumenical acti-
vists. If we accept that there was no single 'essentialist' ecumenical
position, and that different irenical schemes would only gain
support according to their willingness to exclude certain groups
from their provisions, then the question of Dury's own consistency
becomes increasingly important. How far in practice, then, did
Dury bend his irenical imperatives to suit the varying theological
winds? The issue of Dury's relative consistency is a particularly
pertinent one, as it was a question that was frequently put to him
during his lifetime, and never more damagingly so than in a tract
written by William Prynne in 1650. Prynne's pamphlet – *The
time-serving Proteus, and ambidexter divine, uncased to the world* – was a
work that accused Dury of having played fast and loose with his
supporters, specifically on the question of Protestant ministerial
orders and forms of ecclesiastical government.[5] Dury, or so it
claimed, had accepted orders in the Church of England despite his
earlier foreign Presbyterian ordination. He had then, it continued,
shifted his political allegiance back to the Presbyterians once more,
only to desert them in their turn for the Independents. In reply,
Dury denied that his foreign ordination had been valid in the first
place and the controversy soon subsided.[6] But was Prynne's charge
merely evidence of a wider inconsistency in Dury's dealings with
different English Protestants?

In fact, Dury can be shown to have consciously tailored his
unification schemes to suit the different audiences for irenicism in
the English Church. As the Church of England fell apart in the late
1630s, Dury was caught between sides, and on the wrong side of
many people's negative image of irenicism. But Dury was to prove
himself an adept 'ambidexter divine' in finding his own way through
the ensuing problems.

The different religious elements with which Dury had to deal in
England during the 1630s may be reduced to three broad groupings,
which can be labelled 'puritan', 'moderate Calvinist episcopalian'
and 'Laudian'.

Dury's first contacts were among puritan divines, who were those

---

[5] W. Prynne, *The time-serving Proteus, and ambidexter divine* (London, 1650).
[6] John Dury, *The unchanged, constant and single-hearted peacemaker* (London, 1650).

who had first urged him to come over to England, and it was these puritan circles who also formed the network of friendships in which Dury's friend Hartlib operated. The letters of William Speed and of Walter Welles to both Dury and Hartlib, which remain among the Hartlib Papers, illustrate how Dury's ideas were propagated among puritan circles in Sussex, Lincolnshire, Bedfordshire, Northampton-shire and Huntingdonshire. The signatories to Dury's *Instrumentum theologorum Anglorum* prepared at this time constitute a roll-call of Caroline puritanism.[7] These puritan divines might be seen as the natural constituency for Dury's work, as they included many figures with whom Dury would later sit in the Westminster Assembly and who would furnish him with donations when he resumed his reunion activities in the 1650s under the Protectorate.

Such support was hardly surprising. These men were the repre-sentatives of what Simon Adams has dubbed 'political puritanism' – the agitation for a confessional foreign policy based on a Protestant alliance with the west European Calvinist communities in order to defeat the forces of popery and restore the Palatinate.[8] As those expressing the greatest concern for the fortunes of international Protestantism, these divines were also the most likely to appreciate the practical benefits to the Calvinist religion if Calvinists and Lutherans could be induced to consider each other as co-religionists in Germany (this would ensure toleration for the Calvinists, who were currently excluded under the terms of the Treaty of Augs-burg). Puritan ecclesiology also naturally favoured this: they tended to view the forces of Protestantism as a supra-national whole, an international community of the godly, united by true doctrine, and forever ranged against the forces of the papal Antichrist. This sort of polarized world view could encourage a disregard for Lutheran errors as long as anti-popery was uppermost in puritan minds. Thus the Lutheran king Gustavus Adolphus received practically universal praise among such divines for his role in opposing Romanist forces in Germany. Also, this heightened sensitivity to the popish threat made men attach all the greater value to Protestant unity in opposing it. Thus, concern for reconciliation with the Lutherans could be emble-matic of sincere Protestantism. At Archbishop Laud's trial, William

---

[7] *HDC*, 128–40; HP 29/2/11B; BL Sloane MS 1465, fol. 2.
[8] Simon Adams, 'The Protestant cause; religious alliance with the European Calvinist communities as a political issue in England, 1585–1630' (D.Phil. thesis, University of Oxford, 1973).

Prynne therefore attempted to demonstrate that the archbishop had impeded Dury's schemes in order to support his more general charge that the archbishop was a crypto-papist. Protestant irenicism was thus in a sense a form of anti-popery.

Nevertheless, what is striking about the 1630s is the fact that Dury does not seem to have kept up regular contacts with puritan groups, despite all his early contacts with them, even though they were still the milieu in which Hartlib moved. Indeed, it was the inertia of these puritans that was Dury's constant complaint during this period. Dury's letters from Sweden in 1636–7 are scathing about the irresoluteness of those puritans who offered excuses for doing nothing towards the project of ecclesiastical pacification.[9]

What were the reasons behind this puritan reticence? It was not simply a matter of inertia or insincerity, although it was always true, as Dury himself admitted, that everybody applauded the idea of unity on the level of theory and were often content to leave it at that. After his first visit to England in 1630 Dury had, of course, tended to concentrate on developing links with the more important English divines in the universities and among the episcopate, as he increasingly emphasized the public role of the Church of England, and of its most prominent representatives, in his activities. But it was not simply a matter of Dury's own neglect. Part of the puritans' passivity may have been inspired by fears of governmental reprisals for implied criticism of the Crown's pro-Spanish foreign policy. Sir Thomas Roe had been aware of the need to counter such fears when he gave his personal reassurance to potential subscribers to the circulated *Instrumentum* (in a letter composed to accompany the document) that they might support Dury 'without offence or scandall eyther to the Church or to the principall gouvernours therin'.[10] But there were other reasons why puritan divines displayed less than complete enthusiasm for Dury's schemes.

In part, the puritans shared (along with most of the English political nation) a deep-seated distrust of the Lutherans for their apparent readiness to side with Rome against the Calvinists (most particularly in the case of Lutheran Saxony). So the puritans were

---

[9] HP 9/1/37B (Dury to Hartlib, Stockholm, 12/22 October 1636); HP 9/1/40A–41B (12/22 October 1636); HP 9/1/44A–45B (21/31 October 1636); HP 9/1/53 (7 January 1637/8). The first and third of these letters were edited and published in G. H. Turnbull, 'Letters written by John Dury in Sweden, 1636–8', *Särtryck ur Kyrkohistorisk Arsskrift* (1949), 204–51, esp. 211–13 and 218–20. See also Lambeth Palace Library (henceforth LPL) MS 2686, fol. 40r.

[10] Westin, *Brev från John Durie*, 106–8; *HDC*, 14; BL Sloane MS 1465.

especially likely to be sensitive to loose talk about possible union with the Lutherans. Puritans were mostly hardline Calvinists, who were likely to be the most unyielding on points of doctrinal orthodoxy, and indeed on those very points of Lutheranism on which conflict had habitually been joined. Considering true doctrine to be essentially constitutive of the church, puritans also tended to regard divine truth as an indivisible whole and any deviation from it as heretical and potentially subversive. Like most English Protestants, puritans believed that Lutheran errors concerning the eucharist and predestination overthrew fundamental articles of faith by direct consequence. When doctrinal purity was everything, and Calvinists felt threatened by the internal heresy of Arminianism, they were unlikely to tolerate the soft-pedalling of doctrinal truth. Outside anti-papal writings (when Protestant unity needed to be emphasized) puritan authors were often outspoken in their condemnation of Lutheran doctrines.

We thus find the ironic situation that those divines who were most enthusiastic for union with the Lutherans on the level of theory were most likely to be those least capable of achieving it in practice. Constant tensions inevitably resulted. For example, Simonds D'Ewes was enraged when Sir Martin Stuteville pointed out the inconsistency of D'Ewes applauding the Lutheran king Gustavus Adolphus for his successes in the Thirty Years War while simultaneously denigrating the doctrines of the Arminians (which Gustavus as a Lutheran presumably shared). Of course, this point was complicated by the fact that Dutch and English Arminians seized on the opportunity to quote Lutheran authors in support of their disputed doctrines, in order to vindicate their own Protestant credentials and wrongfoot their Calvinist opponents.[11]

Dury therefore found himself hampered throughout the 1630s by puritan doubts concerning the doctrinal implications of his search for agreement with the Lutherans. William Speed was warning Dury as early as August 1630 that he might meet with 'some that shall seeme something too scrupulous and averse from this worke', and Speed soon met puritan friends who raised 'very great and strong reasons . . . against such a project'. These 'reasons' included objections that the Lutherans' doctrinal errors were fundamental and maintained obstinately by them (and were therefore by defi-

---

[11] BL Harleian MS 374, fol. 89. See, generally, Milton, *Catholic and Reformed*, chap. 8.

nition heretical), that to conform to Lutheran ceremonies would serve merely to confirm them in their superstition, and more generally that 'our seeking of peace may harden their spirits against the truth'.[12] Puritan alarm and criticism increased whenever Dury moved beyond the enunciation of pacificatory platitudes and started to pursue more tangible doctrinal compromises. In Sweden in 1636, where initial signs had seemed promising, Dury became infuriated with the baleful criticisms of his work made behind his back. Hartlib was typically dutiful in sending these puritan attacks on to his friend, although he sensibly withheld the names of Dury's most passionate puritan critics.[13]

A moderate endorsement of Lutheran errors was feared, as implying a drift towards popery. Indeed, while anti-popery was a valuable force impelling puritans towards Protestant union, it also threatened to upset the same by imposing a straitjacket on Dury's manoeuvres. This point emerged with especial clarity in Dury's correspondence with puritan divines over his negotiations with the Lutherans of Brunswick and Lüneburg in 1640. Here, Dury was forced to adopt a tactically accommodating line towards Roman Catholic sensibilities. The Brunswick officials insisted for political reasons (as they were at that time in league with the emperor) on including in their declaration of support for Dury the stipulation that the negotiations were not intended to make any party against popery.[14]

Now for puritans, of course, this stipulation removed the whole rationale of the exercise. Dury had in the past consistently displayed an awareness of the need to play up the anti-papal aspects of his ecumenical activities in correspondence with puritan divines. Typically, Dury's letter to the puritans Stephen Marshall and Thomas Ball, in 1635, emphasized the need for the unity of Protestants against the forces of the Romish 'man of synne'.[15] Dury was, therefore, fully aware of how bitter a pill the Brunswick declaration would be for his puritan correspondents to swallow. He decided to try to sound them out bit by bit, by proposing the Brunswick stipulation as an unspecified and purely hypothetical situation 'in

---

[12] *HDC*, 133, 137: also 134–5, 139. Note also Thomas Gataker's early scepticism: Bodleian Library, Tanner MS 71, fol. 92.
[13] HP 9/1/37B–38A, 40B–41A, 44A–B; 2/6/12A–14A. See also Westin, *Brev från John Durie*, 273.
[14] HP 6/4/52, 53B.
[15] HP 17/2/2B (Dury to Marshall and Ball). For earlier anti-popery, see also *HDC*, 170; HP 2/2/11A.

case', while also pointedly condemning the motives of 'some [*that*] are moved cheifly to joyne in these thoughts rather in hope that by this meanes Popery will be overthrowne, then for any advantage to religion'. He also cast doubts on 'whether it be a religious act in it selfe to frame a party to oppose popery'.[16]

In reply, however, his puritan ally, Thomas Ball, cast doubt on Dury's motives and entertained 'secret suspicions' that Dury was trying to curry favour with crypto-papists – an apparent reference to Archbishop Laud. It was here that the internal politics of the Church of England served to complicate the reception of Dury's German activities. Whatever Dury's specific schemes, it was his collaboration (however minor) with the government of the Personal Rule that led puritans to suspect Dury's motives when he urged a more moderate line towards Rome, or an indulgence towards Lutheran ceremonies and predestinarian errors. Ball went on to protest stoutly that Dury should not bind himself to anything that would make union useless, or restrain himself from bearing witness against manifest errors and superstitions which subverted the foundations of religion and the sincerity of the Protestant profession. Ball continued, with his thoughts clearly on current developments in England, that it was dangerous to symbolize with papists and heretics in outward things.[17]

Dury's reply to Ball was a carefully crafted epistle – he effectively regained the puritan's confidence in his reunion schemes (as we shall see) by making an implicit condemnation of Laud's policies as inclining towards popery.

Ball's position was not unusual. Other puritans could also blow hot and cold as events and the shape of Dury's reunion programme dictated. The Scots puritan minister, Robert Baillie, for example, was singing the praises of Dury's reunion programme in 1637 and specifically distancing himself from the uneducated masses who might foolishly misinterpret Dury's plans as being a policy to capitulate first to Lutherans and then to papists. Yet in March 1640 Baillie

---

16 HP 6/4/36A–37B (Dury to Thomas Ball, Hamburg, 14 May 1640). Writing to Hartlib, Dury described this letter to Ball as being 'to prepare a way for the communication of the Declarations of those of Brunswic that no preiudice may bee taken therat'. He hoped that the letter might also be shown by Hartlib to others 'whom yow think most prepossessed against Papists to see what they will say of it' (HP 2/2/11A). Note also Dury's anxiety about his readership; HP 2/2/4 (Dury to Hartlib, Hamburg, 8/18 March 1639/40).

17 HP 2/2/22–3 (Dury to Hartlib, Hamburg, 2/12 June 1640); 6/4/54 (Dury to Ball, Hamburg, 14 April 1640).

published a tract in which he levelled precisely this charge against Dury. As in the case of Thomas Ball, the engine behind Baillie's change of heart was the supposed promotion of Dury by Archbishop Laud, and it was the involvement of Dury's work with the religious disputes in England that were to lead to the main crisis of his early career.[18]

Dury had better luck in the 1630s when dealing with the moderate Calvinist episcopalians. As he attempted to put his work on a more public footing, Dury sought to acquire the endorsement of the chief bishops and university professors in the Church of England, whose authority was respected abroad. Sir Thomas Roe provided Dury's initial link with these worthies, although the same Calvinist bishops were also warmly recommended to Dury by puritan divines.[19]

It was these moderate Calvinist episcopalians – men such as Bishops Joseph Hall, Thomas Morton, John Davenant, William Bedell and John Richardson – who became Dury's most dedicated clerical correspondents during the 1630s, and they supported his schemes with far fewer qualms than did the puritans. They provided him with discourses on Protestant unity which he published and translated, with letters of recommendation to continental Calvinist divines, with financial support and with written solutions to particular problems which were noteworthy for their success when deployed. Dury used the writings of Davenant and Bedell to good effect when dealing with the Lutherans of Sweden and Brunswick, for example.[20]

These men had the unambiguously Calvinist, anti-papal credentials that made them enthusiastic proponents of Protestant union – they supported the idea of a confessional English foreign policy, and had scholarly contacts with the high Calvinist divines of the continent – but they combined these with a theological flexibility that was noticeably lacking in Dury's puritan supporters. Their Calvi-

---

[18] Robert Baillie, *Letters and journals*, ed. D. Laing, 2 vols. (Edinburgh, 1841–2), I, 9, 10; Robert Baillie, *Ladensium ΑΥΤΟΚΑΤΑΚΡΙΠΙΙΗ. The Canterburians self-conviction* (Edinburgh, 1640), 31–2. Baillie's later edition of the *Ladensium*, composed after the removal of Laud, saw him shift position towards Dury once more: *Ladensium* (3rd edn, 1641), 32–4. Cf. also his *Letters and journals*, I, 364.

[19] *HDC*, 136, 155, 165.

[20] E.g. Westin, *Brev från John Durie*, 210, 235–6, 275, 323, 325, 332–3; PRO SP 16/269/88; 270/11.

nism was of a more moderate variety – sublapsarian rather than
supralapsarian, tending towards a hypothetical universalism of the
Amyraldian type. At the synod of Dort, Hall and Davenant had
been prominent among the English delegates who, while ensuring
that the Arminians were condemned, had also attempted to ensure
that the emphasis of the canons should be pastoral and edificational,
so that they could disarm potential opponents of orthodox Calvinism. In this way they hoped to ensure both that Calvinists
remained united and that the door was left open to the more
long-term aim of reconciliation with the Lutherans.[21] Their rever-
ent agnosticism on predestinarian issues helped to tempt Lutherans
and to defend the moderate divines of Bremen from their more
rigorously Calvinist opponents; and yet at the same time, the fact
that Ward, Hall and Davenant were still outspoken in their denun-
ciation of Arminian errors helped to reassure their more hardline
Calvinist puritan brethren.[22]

When they dealt with Lutheran errors in their compositions for
Dury, writers such as Davenant managed to remain acceptable both
to Lutherans and committed Calvinists such as Robert Baillie and
John Stoughton.[23] They achieved this by accepting the breadth of
differing views, and adopting a 'lowest common denominator'
approach. Davenant argued that it was quite possible for there to be
unity between churches that believed each other to undermine
important aspects of the faith. Thus Davenant wrote that 'tis not a
thing impossible, nor any way contrary to the duety of good Christians, to entertaine a communion with those Churches which hold
such a doctrine which seemes to us inconsistent with some fundamentall Truth, so that in the meane while they doe expresly believe
& professe that fundamentall Trueth itselfe'. This approach was
more likely to satisfy the preference expressed by Robert Baillie and
others for 'a Syncretisme' rather than 'the extenuating of the
Lutheran errours'. The crucial division that Davenant outlined was

[21] P. Lake, 'Calvinism and the English Church 1570–1635', *Past and Present*, 114 (1987),
    32–76. See also Milton, *Catholic and Reformed*, chap. 8; A. Milton, *The British delegation and the
    synod of Dort* (forthcoming).
[22] On this point see, generally, Milton, *Catholic and Reformed*. For the defence of the Bremen
    divines, see HP 2/2/3A, 8A, 11B, 26A; 5/2/14–19; 5/11/1B–2A; 5/21/3; 9/1/34B; *The works of
    Joseph Hall*, ed. P. Wynter, 10 vols. (Oxford, 1863), X, 235–52.
[23] Baillie, *Letters and journals*, I, 9.

between these churches and the Church of Rome who, by maintaining idolatry, cut herself off from any communion with Christ.[24]

Anti-popery was important to the world view of these divines too, then. Nevertheless, although they were of determinedly anti-papal views and convinced that the pope was Antichrist, these divines were also men who were prepared to allow that Rome was in some sense a true church, and they could be tactically moderate in their approach when the need arose.[25] Dury clearly felt no need to beat the anti-papal drum when writing to them, and in 1640 he sent the declaration of the Brunswick divines on to Bishops Hall and Davenant directly, without any of the anxious correspondence he felt it necessary to use with the puritan Thomas Ball.[26]

The flexibility of these divines offered the best hope for a form of pacification which would be palatable to both moderates and extremists. Towards the end of 1640, Dury finally decided to establish a direct contact between these bishops and the work of the Lutheran syncretist, George Calixtus. It is intriguing to speculate on what might have happened if the bishops had been able to correspond with Calixtus directly.[27] But when Dury sent Calixtus' books on to Bishops Hall and Davenant, he was already too late – the middle position occupied by these divines in the religious politics of Britain had already become untenable under the onslaught of the polarizing forces of puritanism and Laudianism.

The one group of divines from whom Dury received little or no clear support was that associated with Archbishop Laud. In a sense, we might expect them to have been more closely involved in Dury's schemes. For example, they had fewer reservations over Lutheran errors than even the moderate Calvinists. Certainly, there was much in the Lutheran churches that would appeal to Laudian divines. Most importantly, they had retained a form of episcopacy. Moreover, although practices undoubtedly varied, many Lutheran churches also retained at this time a gratifyingly high cere-

[24] 'The opinion of Bishop Davenant', in *Good counsells for the peace of Reformed churches. By some reverend and learned bishops and other divines* (Oxford, 1641), 17–18, 19; Baillie, *Ladensium*, 32. See also A. Milton, 'The Laudians and the Church of Rome c.1625–1640' (Ph.D. thesis, University of Cambridge, 1989), 129.
[25] See Milton, *Catholic and Reformed*.
[26] See HP 5/12/1B–2A (Dury to [Joseph Hall] bishop of Exeter, Hamburg, 12 March 1640).
[27] HP 2/2/43A (Dury to Hartlib, Hamburg, 16 September 1640). It should be noted, however, that Dury was also thinking of putting Calixtus in touch with the notorious Laudian Richard Montagu, even as late as December 1640: HP 6/4/97A (Dury to [Sir Thomas Roe?], 1 December 1640).

monialism. Similarly, Lutheran adiaphoristic doctrines and their anti-Calvinist predestinarian theology were well known and would be welcome to Laudian ears.

However, Laudian divines at this time were most keen to sever connections between the Church of England and the west European Calvinist communities. An increasing anti-Calvinist element is visible in Laudian writings, and an increasing readiness to defend distinctive aspects of the Church of England and her worship without any of the face-saving caveats that normally allowed a defence of the foreign non-episcopalian churches to be sustained. Moreover, the general scope of their ecclesiology did not favour Dury's schemes. One of the vital forces that had held the Calvinist community together had been the conviction that the pope was Antichrist, and that there was a true church of orthodox believers which was in constant warfare with him. But in Laudian ecclesiology there was no room for the separate, orthodox church of 'the more special number of right-believing christians', as Richard Field defined it, from which heretics and schismatics such as Rome were forever excluded. Nor was it accepted that the pope was Antichrist, or Rome Babylon. To the Laudians, Rome was a member of the Catholic Church and essentially on a par with all the Protestant churches. Laud explained that 'the Catholic Universal Church of Christ' has an 'equal existence in all her particulars' (which included Rome). Some of the Laudians, at least, were attempting a notional realignment of the Church of England vis-à-vis the other Protestant churches and feeling their way towards the *via media* of later Anglicanism. Their even-handed approach to the divisions of Christendom was typified by their refusal to communicate in either Roman Catholic or Calvinist churches. I have argued elsewhere that Laudianism was novel and distinctive in its rejection of the reactive aspects of Protestantism, and in the Laudians' determination to see their church's destiny as lying beyond the Protestant/Romanist divisions of the continent.[28]

Of course, if the basic impulse generating a concern for Protestant union was not there, there was yet (by implication) among Laudians a certain sense of remote disinterestedness to the continental divisions over theological dogma, and a doctrinal agnosticism which might in theory encompass Dury's negotiations more easily than the

[28] See Milton, *Catholic and Reformed*, esp. chaps. 8–9.

perspective of hardline Calvinists, as long as the integrity of the
Church of England was not directly involved. Those on the edge of
the Laudian movement, such as Christopher Potter and Joseph
Mede, therefore displayed a benign interest in Dury's schemes,
although this was combined with an unwillingness to become
directly involved.

Archbishop Laud himself enjoyed (if that is the right word) a
decidedly ambivalent relationship with Dury. Laud's primary interests were centred on the problems of the Church of England and the
need to preserve the integrity of her forms of liturgy and government
– and close relations with the continent were generally held by the
Laudians to be one of the means whereby this integrity had been
undermined. It was therefore natural that Laud should insist that
Dury accept re-ordination into the Church of England as a test of his
good faith. While he was prepared to offer Dury verbal support,
Laud also wished to keep out of any reunion negotiations which
might prove a hindrance to the government's foreign policy. That
Laud offered even limited support to a man of Dury's puritan
connections itself bears eloquent witness to the generally felt need to
pay at least lip-service to the ideals of Protestant integration, and
Laud cited his intermittent patronage of Dury at his trial as evidence of his own Protestant credentials.[29]

Yet even introspective Laudians found one form of Protestant
irenicism attractive – the exporting of those liturgical and ecclesiastical forms to which they attached such importance. This was the
great scheme of the Anglican irenicist, Isaac Basire, in the 1650s, but
it is less often noted that this was a style of irenicism with which
Dury himself was happy to conspire when it suited his interests.
When Dury was in Sweden in the years 1636–7, he found the Swedes
involved in a radical reformation of the ecclesiastical structure of the
Church of Sweden, which was intended to include a new ecclesiastical court. Dury suggested that this court might follow the plan of
the Church of England's own Court of High Commission (which
was, of course, the great scourge of Dury's puritan supporters). Laud
was uncommonly delighted with this approach (as Dury must have
known he would be) and arranged for the sending to Sweden of a
detailed description of the constitution of the Church of England,
esteeming this an honour to the English Church and voicing his

[29] William Prynne, *Canterburies doome* (London, 1646), 539.

conviction that this was the right way towards Protestant union.[30] Nothing in the end came of these plans, nor of the hopes for English involvement with Sweden in a north Protestant alliance against the empire, with which plans for ecclesiastical union became inextricably linked.

Nevertheless, Dury also followed basically Laudian emphases in his negotiations with German Lutherans in 1640, when he found that they were eager to receive copies of the Book of Common Prayer and also of the Church of England's book of canons. Until events overtook him, Dury was even imploring Hartlib to send him over copies of the notorious canons of 1640, which were already prompting so much unrest among his puritan supporters in England. However, while Laudian emphases may have helped to make Dury's schemes more appealing to the Lutherans, they also helped to sabotage his negotiations with resentful Dutch Calvinists, and it was the thorny issue of Dury's links with Laudianism and episcopacy that was to make his position increasingly untenable.[31]

As we have seen, Dury's puritan supporters were already looking askance at his links with Laud by the later 1630s. It was soon being alleged that Dury practised a number of specific Laudian innovations, such as bowing at the name of Jesus. As the Scottish troubles developed, Dury became all the more concerned to detach himself from the archbishop. He was anxious to procure the direct support of the king so that it would be clear that his patron was not Laud, since (as Dury explained to his friend) 'the evill which is cast upon ... [Laud] doth every where redound upon me & my worke, by reason of the suspicions of men, which are taken up against him, & all those that seeme to have relation unto him'.[32]

At this stage, though, Dury's puritan links (and especially those of his friend Hartlib) might prove to be as embarrassing and disruptive for him as his connection with the archbishop. In early 1640, printed copies of treatises which Dury unwisely sent to Hartlib from Holland were seized by English officials alert for seditious puritan pamphlets, and it was some time before they were released. Dury became increasingly worried that Hartlib's politically sensitive letters to

---

30 Westin, *Brev från John Durie*, 199, 208, 216–17, 223, 225, 234, 237, 242, 245, 249, 251, 266, 325.

31 HP 2/2/3B–4A (Dury to Robert Baillie, The Hague, 27 January 1640/1); PRO SP 16/311/77, 312/35.

32 HP 2/2/8B (Dury to Hartlib, Hamburg, 20 March 1640); 33B–34A (7 August 1640); 5/12/13–16 (Dury to 'a bishop' (copy), 30 June 1640).

him might be intercepted and was horrified when Hartlib sent him a copy of an anti-Laudian petition from Middlesex in March 1640.[33]

Nevertheless, as the crisis developed Dury struggled in vain to keep his options open by remaining uncommitted to either side. His instinctive response was to remain silent and abroad in order that, as he explained it, he should be 'extra partes, & the more freely mourne for public evills & all the abominations that are committed within Jerusalem'. Cromwell-like, he was determined to wait upon God's Providence.[34]

However, with both sides scrutinizing him for lack of zeal, Dury could not remain aloof. In order to be able effectively to respond to God's Providence, Dury had to retain the confidence of all sides. He was agonizing in August 1640 over how it would be possible for him to continue his activities in such a way 'that none shall take offence at my proceedings, & that I may bee able to iustifie towards every one all that can bee laid unto my charge'.[35] The answer, of course, was that he would have to be duplicitous – and this was best done by assuring each side that he deplored the actions of their opponents. The years 1640–3 thus saw Dury constantly reconstructing himself to suit the changing irenical possibilities, alternately praising and reviling men and institutions according to whichever side's version of Protestant unity he was choosing to adopt.

Thus, when Dury sought to regain the confidence of the puritan Thomas Ball, in June 1640 after their correspondence over the Brunswick declaration, he condemned 'such as now of late began to symbolize in matters of Ceremony with Papists in our Church'. If this was not a clear enough attack on Laud, Dury went still further in offering tacit support for the prayer book rebellion: 'When a ruler of a Church will rather offend all that hee ought to edifye in the trueth then leave off symbolizing with professed adversaries, I cannot excuse him from guiltines nor can I condemne such as stand up for the clearing of theire profession from dangerous collusion with manifest opposites unto the Gospell.' Yet when he wrote to Laud's secretary, William Dell, three months later, thanking Dell for his

---

[33] HP 2/2/10A (Dury to Hartlib, Hamburg, 31 March 1640). See also PRO SP 16/302/63. Hartlib too was sufficiently worried by the possibility of interception to begin to obliterate politically sensitive allusions in Dury's own letters to him, burning out some names, and tearing Dury's signature off the bottom of the letters: e.g. HP 2/2/10A, 16A, 18A, 19A, 20A.
[34] HP 2/2/41A.   [35] HP 2/2/37A (Dury to Hartlib, Hamburg, 28 August 1640).

offer to solicit Laud's financial support for him, Dury averred his firm support for the archbishop and his detestation of his opponents. He added unequivocally that 'you may bee confident that I have seene so much of the partiall & particular wayes of such as stir upp strife and hatred, that I will rather endure the utmost of extremities, then bee accessarie to their guiltynes'.[36]

Dury did not risk entirely repudiating groups until it was clear that he could gain no more from them. Thus he still refused throughout 1640 to oppose Laud explicitly. When he sought to clear himself from the charges made in Robert Baillie's *Canterburians self-conviction* of his involvement in a Laudian-inspired popish plot to reconcile foreign Protestants and the Church of England with Rome, Dury refused to take it upon himself to judge what Laud intended. However, he told the Covenanters firmly and directly that he did not believe that Baillie's book had sufficiently proved its case against the archbishop.[37]

By the end of the year, however, Laud had been impeached by the Commons for high treason and Dury dropped the archbishop hastily as soon as he heard the news. His repudiation of Laud also gave Dury greater freedom to launch into an anti-papal crusade. Dury's pamphlets now combined calls for the convening of an international Protestant synod (in order to distract attention away from internal disputes on church polity) with an increasing and fashionable anti-papal tone. This was all a far cry from his remarks in a letter to Thomas Ball the year before in which Dury had condemned the framing of a party against popery as 'rather a politic then a religious act' and had insisted that the bare affirmation of doctrinal truth was sufficient, making a 'directly professed opposition to Popery & Papists' and other errors unnecessary.[38]

Dury's anti-papal tone grew even more audacious during 1641 and he may well have been involved in the unveiling of an alleged 'popish plot' to the Scots Covenanters in October of the same year, just before the outbreak of the Irish rebellion. This plot to undermine Protestantism, it was claimed, had been masterminded, appropriately enough, by Roman Catholic irenicists, who had sought to

---

[36] HP 6/4/54B (Dury to Thomas Ball, 9 June 1640); HP 6/4/87A–88A (Dury to [William Dell?], 20 October 1640).

[37] HP 2/3/3AB; 6/4/83A–84B, 85.

[38] See John Dury, *A memorial concerning peace ecclesiasticall among Protestants* (London, 1641), 5, 6, 10; also John Dury, *The heads of reasons for which a generall councell of Protestants ought to be called together in England* (London, 1641), 6–7; HP 6/4/36A–37A.

inveigle moderate Protestants into an ecclesiastical pacification
which would split Protestantism and leave the more committed
Protestants defenceless against a papal attack. The unveiler of the
'plot' was coy in his insinuations, and managed to avoid accusing
Laud directly of complicity, but the intention was clearly to provide
an anti-type to the purely Protestant irenical schemes of Dury.[39]

Dury's conversion to a fervent (and fashionable) anti-popery
came at a time when his work was threatening to be shipwrecked on
the controversial issue of church government. The shift to matters of
church discipline as the focal point of religious controversy in
England filled Dury with unease. His whole irenical programme
presupposed that Protestants were only seriously divided in matters
of doctrine – all of which could easily be resolved through a general
agreement on the essentials of the true Christian faith. He was less
equipped to deal with divisions over church discipline.

Dury had not hitherto revealed a commitment to any single form
of church government. Despite, or perhaps because of, the exile that
his father had suffered for his Presbyterian beliefs, Dury had
appeared to be indifferent to such matters. Indeed, he had by his
own account voluntarily sued for an orderly admission to orders in
the Church of England, accepting Laud's encouragement that he be
ordained into the English Church on account of his doubts
regarding the validity of his own earlier ordination, although he

---

[39] *The copy of a letter written to Mr. A. H.* [Alexander Henderson] (London, 1643). This letter to
Henderson, dated 4 October 1641, revealed the existence of a supposed popish plot to the
Scottish Covenanters at a critical juncture in the complex sequence of events in British
politics on the eve of the Irish rebellion. Its authorship, however, remains uncertain. The
grounds adduced for attributing its composition to Dury are: (i) the MS *copy* of the letter
survives in a collection of Dury's correspondence in BL Sloane MS 654 (fols. 199r–208v)
which bears Dury's name (although the name has been partially erased); (ii) the printed
copy of the letter in the Library of Union Theological Seminary bears Dury's autograph
signature (Batten, *Dury*, 86, n. 14 – where Batten takes this fact to confirm Dury's
authorship). However, Dury's signature on the volume more probably represents his
ownership rather than his authorship.

The London bookseller George Thomason attributed the letter to Samuel Hartlib on the
title page of his printed copy (BL E.87 (15)), and the style of the letter would certainly seem
more in tune with Hartlib's preoccupations. The letter's wording and subject matter are
very similar to those of *A faithfull and seasonable advice, or the necessity of a correspondencie for the
advancement of the Protestant cause* (1643) (cf. especially sigs. A2v–A3r). Thomason's copy of
this latter tract was procured, he wrote, 'ex dono Authoris S. Hartlib' (BL E.87 (14)).
Nevertheless, given the letter's subject matter, it seems likely that, even if Hartlib was its
author, he would have sought Dury's approval before sending it to Henderson. Whoever
wrote the letter, its effects on the Covenanters were certainly real enough – see especially
Robert Baillie's *A parallel or briefe comparison of the liturgie with the masse-book* (1641), sigs.
A2v–A3r.

insisted that this did not represent a renunciation of foreign ordination as such.[40] However, by 1638 it was already clear that the
conflicts over church government were likely to hamper Dury's
work. In November of that year a puritan author (whom Dury was
probably correct in identifying as William Twisse) drew up a series
of arguments against Dury's work. Among these he listed the objection that the disagreement of bishops and puritans was wholly
irreconcilable.[41] Moreover, it was becoming apparent that, while
both sides in the conflict might be prepared to support Dury's
broader ecumenical schemes, Episcopalians and Presbyterians
would only ultimately support his work if Dury had in the meantime
displayed his particular loyalty to that specific form of church
government.

Dury's eagerness to avoid conflict on matters of ecclesiastical
discipline led him at first to offer strong support for the endeavours
afoot to negotiate a 'reduced episcopacy' for the Church of England.
In early 1641 he wrote a striking letter to Roe in which he explained
his support for a de-Laudianized episcopacy. Dury insisted that it
was vital that episcopacy should not be abandoned. He believed it to
be both lawful and useful and feared that the necessary prosecution
of the Laudians (of which he now approved) might be allowed to
bring a censure on the office as a whole, thereby committing an
injustice 'to the Pastorall Office & dignity of such as are worthy of
double honour'. Schism and the destruction of all ecclesiastical
government would result if the anti-episcopalian contentions were
allowed to continue; yet Dury could not see how mutual conference
between the different sides would be possible in the prevailing
climate. He therefore proposed to circumvent these problems by
calling for a general council of all Protestants, to take place in
England in 1643. Domestic problems might dwindle when placed in
an international context and in the midst of a suitably irenical
atmosphere.[42]

However, Dury's own contribution to the campaign for a
'reduced episcopacy' soon became a contentious issue in itself. His
lengthy description of the different types of church government

---

[40] Dury, *Unchanged peacemaker*, esp. 11 and 14. See also the account of Dury's interview with
   Laud in *CSPD 1633–4*, preface, xxxv.
[41] HP 2/6/13B–14A (Dury to Hartlib, Hamburg, 30 November 1638).
[42] HP 6/4/103B–104A, 107 (Dury to [Sir Thomas Roe?], copy, Amsterdam, 4/14 January
   1640/1).

available in the foreign Protestant countries, which insisted that all of them recognized the general principle of ministerial imparity, received a hostile response from the formidable Dutch Calvinist divine, Gislebertus Voetius.[43] By late 1641 Dury was finding that he had little room for manoeuvre, complaining that 'I am looked upon with jealous eyes by all parties as siding directly with none', and he accepted with relief the opportunity to go abroad as chaplain to the Princess Mary at The Hague.[44]

Nevertheless, the erosion of the pressurized middle ground during 1642 ultimately made matters easier for Dury. He could now make a more straightforward choice between sides. It was soon clear that his best hopes lay with the Presbyterians and in due course he returned to England and took the Covenant. As usual, however, Dury could only change horses by reviling his previous mount. Just as he had earlier dropped the Laudians for the 'reduced episcopacy' of the moderate Calvinist Episcopalians, so Dury was now required to renounce the latter if he wished to be welcomed into the Presbyterian camp.

The impulse for Dury's final renunciation of episcopacy and conversion to the Covenanter world view came in a letter from the Covenanter Andrew Ramsay, which invited Dury to state his position on matters regarding episcopacy and the Roman church. In reply, Dury eagerly embraced the opportunity to nail his colours to the new mast. He invoked the supposed popish irenical plot first unveiled in 1641 but was more candid than previously in his direct association of the Laudians with a plot to reintroduce popery into England. Dury also gave the plot a new anti-episcopal edge. In contrast to his earlier letter to Roe, where he had insisted on the need to retain episcopacy, Dury now claimed to have been concerned throughout the 1630s that episcopacy bore 'some characters of Antichristianitie', but said that he had been forced to deal with the English bishops merely because they were the king's ecclesiastical representatives. For their part, the bishops had merely pretended to support Dury's reunion schemes the better to disguise their anti-Christian purposes.

After thus renouncing his erstwhile supporters, the moderate Calvinist bishops, Dury now embraced the polarized, apocalyptic

---

[43] HP 5/17/1–2 (Dury to Gijsbert Voet, 31 January 1641/2).
[44] HDC, 331; Batten, Dury, 94–5.

rhetoric of the Covenanters. He proposed that the foundation stone of Protestant unity should be, not some simple Erasmian agreement on the essentials of Christianity, but rather the doctrine that the pope was the Antichrist. This was remarkable, not least because in the 1630s Dury had himself expressed reservations on precisely this score and had favoured in the process an essentially 'spiritual' view of the Antichrist as a generalized force of evil within all men – an interpretation to which he would return in 1650.[45]

Dury thus emerged as a new type of irenicist, better suited to the times. But he still sought to keep his options open – Dury's changes of side were far from over. His acceptance of the Covenant in 1643 was accompanied by a vow in which, with a tortuous series of reservations, Dury insisted that he was not thereby taking sides. By the 1650s, with the revival of his schemes for international Protestant unity, Dury's account of his irenical efforts in the 1630s had restored the 'anti-Christian' bishops to an honourable place. When the monarchy was restored in 1660 Dury had exhausted his supply of allegiances and was forced to depart from England altogether, but this was in spite of the vigour with which he had hastened to disown his erstwhile patron, Cromwell (in tones strikingly similar to his earlier repudiation of Laud).[46]

Even in an age of changing allegiances, John Dury appears, like Marlowe's duke of Kent, as a 'choric weathercock' in the stormy politics of the period, and an explanation is required. Past assessments of Dury which have insisted that he was 'the most zealous, *consistent*, and successful advocate of the union of the churches in the seventeenth century' have often been arrived at by the systematic sanitizing of his letters and writings.[47]

Nevertheless, we should not simply replace the old image of a naive, impractical Dury with the figure of a cynical and pragmatic opportunist. The image of the 'Unchanged Peacemaker', the man free from partiality, was fundamental, not just to Dury's public representation, but also to his own understanding of his mission and

---

[45] BL Sloane MS 654, fol. 220; HP 6/4/2A; K. R. Firth, *The apocalyptic tradition in Reformation Britain 1530–1645* (Oxford, 1979), 243–5.

[46] *A summarie account of Mr Iohn Durys former and latter negotiations* (1657), 2–23; Batten, *Dury*, 100–1, 172.

[47] J. B. Steane, *Marlowe: a critical study* (Cambridge, 1964), 214; Batten, *Dury*, 203 [*my emphasis*]. For examples of such distortions see the bland and selective summaries of the 1641 letter to Henderson in Batten, *Dury*, 86–7, and of Dury's letter to Ramsay in *HDC*, 226.

purpose, and it is vital that we take this image seriously, even if we do not allow it to blind us to the implications of Dury's actions. Dury was obsessed throughout his career with the need to avoid political entanglements, to retain his liberty in order to be free to fulfil God's purpose for him. But this obsession derived in part from the fact that the very nature of Dury's work (as he explained to friends such as Morian who urged against Dury's involvement in political matters) required him constantly to seek public, political authorities to embrace his projects. He was committed to the notion that Protestant unity must be pursued publicly and deplored the fact that he was not entrusted with more specific public authority to negotiate peace.[48]

Dury was therefore a man deeply divided within himself. Determined to seize any opportunity to advance his mission, he was yet at the same time constantly anxious that his spiritual motives were being besmirched by the more secular interests of those who offered him support. Dury was always complaining that he was 'in a prison of relations of state' and deploring 'this whorage into which I am brought' as a result.[49] But as we have seen, Dury was quite capable of picking his way through political minefields, however much he preferred to think of himself as walking in a spiritual sphere far divorced from political calculation. When Dury declared to Thomas Ball that it was essential that one should *not* be wise or subtle and should *not* modify one's actions according to one's hopes, but should simply do God's wishes, he was articulating an ideal that he himself often struggled to follow. Dury declared his passionate determination to avoid 'worldly wisdome' precisely because it was a constant temptation for him. As he explained: 'If I would sette my mind to serve particular endes; I suppose I am not so dull & unexperienced in the world but that I could find a plausible subiect, & if I would professedly chuse a partye I think I could take an opportunitie to steppe in and gette as others doe something for my self.'[50]

As a result of these unresolvable tensions, Dury was throughout his life deeply interested in the formulation of rules of conduct and of vows that would enable him to keep his ideals and his vision to the forefront of his mind and actions. More practically, these were all

---

[48] E.g. HP 9/1/35A (Dury to Hartlib, Stockholm, 26 August [1636]); 45B (11 November [1636]), 80B (Hamburg, 16 April 1637); 81B, 82A (Dury to Sir Thomas Roe, 26 April 1637).
[49] HP 9/1/83A, 85A; cf. fols. 84B, 87A, 71B–72A.
[50] LPL MS 2686, fols. 40v–41r; HP 2/2/22–3.

vows that could also ultimately serve to liberate Dury from earthly obligations. At a basic level, they freed him from any personal responsibility to earthly judges for his conduct. By embracing such a rule, he explained to Ball, he made himself 'free from partiality'.[51]

In the short term, this set of notions could make Dury into a very effective political operator. His determination to liberate himself from political obligations to any party would resurface whenever his association with that party might appear to be impeding his reunion schemes – more often than not, this would be because this particular party was no longer in the political ascendant.[52] Dury's determination to preserve in pristine form his divine obligations thus allowed him to shift allegiances without qualms and, in the process, to heap blame upon his former supporters for the past failures of his reunion schemes. Like Oliver Cromwell, Dury's determination to wait upon God's Providence, allied to his determination to put his divine obligations before all earthly ones, made him a strikingly flexible, and therefore effective, politician. But in the longer term his very flexibility ensured the failure of Dury's reunion schemes. His readiness to find scapegoats amid former allies left him bereft of supporters when the wheel of fortune turned full circle at the Restoration. Dury had once declared to Hartlib in frustrated tones that 'I rather will chuse to be discountenanced and deserted of all men, then loose the content of a freewilling & unrewarded service towards the Church of God'.[53] By the end of his career this wish, at least, had been granted him.

---

51 HP 6/4/54B–55A. Note the accounts of the pact that Dury made with God during his serious illness in Sweden in 1638 – a watershed of Dury's early career – which he saw as freeing him from the influence of Sir Thomas Roe: Westin, *Brev från John Durie*, 347–9; HP 2/2/32A, 9/1/69A. See also 'The vow which J. D. hath made, and the covenant which he doth enter into with God', avowed while he took the National Covenant in 1643: *Harleian Misc.*, VI, 208–12.

52 Needless to say, such a change of allegiance would necessarily be accompanied by an insistence by Dury that he was a man free of all party obligations. See e.g. his taking of the Covenant: *Harleian Misc.*, VI, 208, 211.

53 HP 2/2/22–3.

CHAPTER 5

Hartlib, Dury and the Jews

Richard H. Popkin

John Dury and Samuel Hartlib would have readily seen the hand of providence at work in the intellectual journey that has resulted in this chapter. It was some years ago that I first met Charles Webster. I had been working on the millenarian materials related to my study of Isaac La Peyrère as well as Jewish messianic thought, especially that expressed by Rabbi Menasseh ben Israel. Webster mentioned various important finds he had made in the Hartlib Papers and, not wishing to display my ignorance at the time, I did not ask him what he was referring to. More than a decade later, and by then engaged in a full-scale study of seventeenth-century millenarianism, I read Webster's books which provided me with a context in which to place Hartlib and his circle. This context I was able to explore more fully when, in 1981–2, I had the good fortune to be asked to be William Andrews Clark Professor at UCLA where I had the opportunity to roam freely through the Clark Library's rich resources in English millenarian literature.

By then I had come to realize that Hartlib, Dury and Comenius were key figures in understanding the extraordinary philosemitism that developed in England and Holland towards the middle of the seventeenth century. I was most interested in the role of Jewish thinkers, particularly Menasseh ben Israel, in these developments as well as the relationship between Jewish messianic expectations and Christian millenarianism. John Dury, of course, was closely involved with Menasseh as well as with Rabbi Nathan Shapira of Jerusalem who had visited Amsterdam in 1657. It was clear that I had to see what further materials existed in the Hartlib Papers in Sheffield, and so I finally spent a delightful few days wandering through the material with the aid of what catalogue then existed.

The collection was so rich that I immediately informed others of the importance and significance of the documentation in Sheffield.[1]

The first fruits of this visit emerged in a series of unpublished papers, particularly one given in Leiden in 1985. Sadly, that lecture, and all the notes and transcriptions taken in Sheffield, were stolen in Paris later that year and never recovered. Fortunately, those who had made copies of my copies, or noted my notes, allowed me to reconstruct some of the lost material. But, for better or worse, I was obliged to revisit the Hartlib Papers in Sheffield to reconstitute the research. It turned out to be for the better because I found yet more than I had uncovered the first time.

This material has been assembled alongside the published writings of Dury, Hartlib, Comenius, Menasseh ben Israel and others. It has also been supplemented by the immense collection of Dury papers in Zurich as well as the very large cache of documents concerning the Jewish messianic movement of 1666, also in Zurich. The result has been to enable me to piece together a most unusual picture of the ways in which Christian millenarianism and Jewish messianism interacted from about 1640 onwards in England and the Netherlands.

Shortly before the Long Parliament reassembled in October 1641, Hartlib, Dury and Comenius met in London to determine what was to be done. They were ready to reform everything in preparation for the millennium, the thousand-year reign of Christ on earth. They proposed reforms in education from nursery school to the highest university levels. One of their most important tasks was to bring about the reunion of Jews and Christians, since the conversion of the Jews was reported in the book of Revelation to be the penultimate event before the second coming of Jesus.[2] As a step to bringing this about, Dury and Hartlib made what, for its time, was an extraordinary proposal. They wished to create a college of Jewish studies that would make Christians more aware of what Jews actually believed and practised. This, in turn, would make Christianity 'less offensive' to the Jews. Their objective would be accomplished by publishing Jewish classics both in the originals and in modern

---

[1] Notably, my scholarly collaborator at the time, Professor Jan van den Berg and his then research student, Dr Ernestine van der Wall in the Netherlands as well as Dr David Katz in Israel, whose doctoral dissertation on philosemitism had recently been completed.

[2] Revelation 14.

European languages, by sponsoring lectures on Judaism and Christianity and by making central Christian texts such as the Gospels available in languages the Jews actually read. In the pamphlet of 1642 entitled *Englands thankfulnesse*, Hartlib and Dury offered 'A care to make Christianity lesse offensive, and more known unto the Jews, then now it is, and the Jewish State and Religion as now it standeth more Knowne unto Christians.'[3] From among the Hartlib Papers one can see the development of three more specific plans to advance this objective – a college of Jewish studies, the construction and description of an exact model of Solomon's Temple and the publication of the *Mishna*, with vowels and translated into Spanish and Latin.

The second and third were joint Jewish–Christian projects and took place in the Netherlands. Their importance was believed to be that, since the millennium or the messianic age was just around the corner, the Temple in Jerusalem would have to be reconstructed in exactly the way it had originally stood. And since the Temple was based upon divine measures and constituted a microcosm of the universe, an exact model would be of great value for those preparing for the final stage of human history. The *Mishna* contained the description of what transpired and would transpire in the Temple. Knowledge of the material in the *Mishna* would be of great value to both Jews and Christians in grasping the actual content of Jewish religious practice. Since only a few of the Jews in Amsterdam could read Hebrew without the pointed vowel marks, it would be of great value to them to have the text in this form. For those Jews who did not know Hebrew at all, a Spanish edition would be most helpful. And, for Christians who did not know Hebrew, a Latin edition would serve their needs.[4]

---

[3] John Dury and Samuel Hartlib, *Englands thankfulnesse, or an humble remembrance presented to the committee for religion in the high court of Parliament with thanksgiving for that happy pacification betweene the two kingdomes. By a faithful well-wisher to this church and nation. Wherein are discovered a maine and subtile plot of the pope and his conclave against Protestancy. Their true method and policy how to undermine the same. The best and principal meanes of re-establishing the Palitin house and preserving all Evangelical CHURCHES. As likewise three special Instruments of the publique good in the ways of religion learning and the preparatives for the conversion of the Jewes* (London, 1642). On this, see R. H. Popkin, 'The first college of Jewish studies', *Revue des Etudes Juives*, 143 (1984), 351–64.

[4] On the project to edit and publish the *Mishna*, see R. H. Popkin, 'Some aspects of Jewish–Christian theological interchanges in Holland and England 1640–1700', in *Jewish–Christian relations in the seventeenth century*, ed. J. van der Berg and E. G. E. van der Wall (Dordrecht, 1988), 3–32; and David S. Katz 'The Abendana brothers and the Christian Hebraists of seventeenth-century England', *Journal of Ecclesiastical History*, 40 (1989), 25–52.

These projects bore some resemblance to the activities of Christian Hebraists in the sixteenth century who published Jewish texts with the assistance of Jewish scholars. Many of those texts were specifically designed as conversion devices and included conversionist materials. They were designed to be sold to both Jews and Christians who knew Hebrew.

The Temple model project, we learn, was the joint venture of Rabbi Judah Leon of Middelburg and the leading Dutch Hebraist, the leader of the Collegiants, Adam Boreel, who was a close friend of Dury and Hartlib. The rabbi, like most Dutch Jews of the period, was born and raised a Christian in Iberia and was not a complete master of Hebrew. He also was not wealthy. It seems that Boreel, who then lived in Middelburg, suggested the project to the rabbi and then financed it. In the published description of it, by Rabbi Judah Leon (who soon added Templo to his name), it was said that the model was made *exactly* according to the descriptions in ancient Hebrew texts. The book about it by the rabbi was published in Spanish, Dutch, English and French, and later in German with pictures of the Temple. (He later published another volume with *exact* descriptions of what was in the Temple, the cherubim, ornaments, and so forth.) The model was moved to Amsterdam, where it was put on display in the garden of the rabbi's house, close by the synagogue, where it could be examined by all. It soon became one of the most important tourist sites in Amsterdam. The rabbi tried to donate it to Queen Henrietta Maria of England, the wife of Charles I. Later he took it to England and gave it to Charles II. It has since disappeared.[5]

Once the Temple project was launched, Boreel began the *Mishna* project that was to continue for the next forty years. Rabbi Judah Leon was to insert the vowel markings while Boreel, who was apparently a better Hebraist than the rabbi, would edit the commentaries accompanying the text, adding notes where necessary. What is striking from the Hartlib Papers is that Boreel invited Rabbi Judah Leon to live in his house and dine with him for four years while they collaborated on the project. Boreel learned Spanish and

[5] It apparently still existed in the late eighteenth century and was being displayed in Germany. It is sometimes claimed to be in the possession of the Freemasons. On the Temple project, see A. K. Offenberg, 'Jacob Jehuda Leon (1602–1675) and his model of the Temple', in van der Berg and van der Wall, *Jewish–Christian relations*, 95–115. See also Popkin, 'Some aspects'.

Portuguese so that he could more easily confer with the rabbi about what they were doing, since the rabbi himself knew no Latin.

In the published Hartlib–Worthington letters, there are numerous references to the *Mishna* project.[6] Its first stage was completed in 1646 with the publication of the text which was printed in 4,000 copies. Thereafter, Hartlib, Dury and others attempted to sell hundreds of copies in England, France, Poland and elsewhere, albeit without any success whatsoever. The text, according to a letter of Dury to Hartlib, was such that 'the common sort of Jews might know, what the Constitution of their religion is, and also that the learned sort of Christians upon the same discoveries might be able to deale with them for their conviction'.[7] So the work was supposed to make it possible for Jews to understand Judaism better (and perhaps to see that Christianity was the culmination of Judaism), while making it possible for Christians to understand the fundamentals of the Jewish religion.

Considering the significance attached to the *Mishna* project in the correspondence of Dury and Hartlib, it is surprising that no copy of the *Mishna* edition by Boreel appears to survive. There is, however, in the Rosenthaliana Bibliotheek in Amsterdam a 1646 edition edited by Joseph ben Israel with a preface by Menasseh ben Israel.[8] Dury explained the situation in an undated letter to Hartlib. Boreel told Dury that Rabbi Judah Leon Templo had said that if the *Mishna* were published with the name of a Christian as its editor, the Jews would not accept it. 'And he told me that none but *Menasseh Ben Israel* was fit to have the credit of it, to make it current amongst the Jewes.'[9] In late 1645, two Dutch businessmen (with strong millenarian concerns) contracted with Menasseh ben Israel to publish 4,000 copies in octavo with points (the Hebrew vowel markings) for 2,200 florins. This edition was to be followed by others with larger and smaller formats, from folio to pocket-book, and Latin and Spanish editions were to be prepared. There were to be prefaces by Menasseh and by Templo. Boreel is nowhere mentioned in the contract.[10]

[6] Worthington, I, 242 (Worthington to Hartlib, December 1660); I, 258 (same to same, 1 January 1661); I, 319 (same to same, 3 June 1661).
[7] HP 1/16/12–13 (Dury to Hartlib, n.d.)
[8] I have now located two additional copies of this edition in the Marsh Library in Dublin (which contains the libraries of Bishops Stillingfleet and Marsh).
[9] HP 1/6/13A (n.d., from a document headed 'An extract of a letter from Mr Dury to Mr Hartlib concerning Borrell').
[10] All the details are supplied in Popkin, 'Some aspects'.

Boreel worked until his death in 1661 with Templo and Rabbis Jacob and Isaac Abendana on the Spanish and Latin editions. In 1660, John Worthington told Hartlib that the translations would be of use for Christians 'that hereby might be better instructed to deal with the Jews'. He saw the project as of as great importance as a Latin edition of the Koran.[11] The Spanish translation was apparently completed but never published and the Latin translation was worked on by Rabbi Isaac Abendana for years. It now exists in manuscript in Cambridge where he had been appointed reader in Hebrew. Ralph Cudworth checked the translation for the university, which paid Abendana by the tractate.[12]

In 1649, Dury and Hartlib sought to realize their project for a college of Jewish studies in London. During the years from 1647 to 1649, Hartlib drew up plans for a group of colleges to constitute a federal university of London. One of these would be 'For Conversions or correspondency of Jews and advancement of Oriental Languages and Learning'.[13] Part of their ambitions was directed towards making the 'common sort of Jews' realize the actual constituents of their religion. This, according to Dury, would help them to become Christians. The college would engage in teaching the languages of Judaism and Christianity and publishing their central texts (such as the *Mishna* and the New Testament) in Hebrew. In view of the obvious conversionist plan for the college, it is rather strange that Dury's proposed faculty consisted of three professors: Adam Boreel, then working on the *Mishna* project,[14] Constantine Ravius of Berlin,[15] and Rabbi Menasseh ben Israel. Superficially, it might seem odd that Menasseh would have considered joining such a venture. However, he was constantly having difficulties with the Amsterdam synagogue leadership, partly because of his fraternization with Christians.[16] In an item in the Hartlib Papers, in fact,

---

[11] Worthington, I, 242–3 (Worthington to Hartlib, December 1660). A Spanish manuscript translation of the Koran exists in the collection of the Spanish–Portuguese synagogue, Ets Haim, in Amsterdam.

[12] Katz, 'The Abendana brothers', 41–4.

[13] Charles Webster, *Samuel Hartlib and the advancement of learning* (Cambridge, 1970), 60, and Webster, 233.

[14] At the time (late 1640s), Dury was convinced that Boreel would go on to undertake the Latin translation of the *Mishna* which he also hoped the city of London would help to finance.

[15] Constantine Ravius subsequently purchased Menasseh ben Israel's Hebrew type fonts and took them with him to Sweden to begin Hebrew printing there.

[16] He was, in fact, excommunicated for a short period for insulting one of the leaders of the Synagogue.

Menasseh advises Dury not to write to him care of the synagogue, but rather care of a mutual Protestant friend, since the people at the synagogue were reading his mail.[17] He tried in various ways to find an occupation outside the Jewish community, such as becoming the city of Amsterdam's official Hebrew teacher, or Queen Christina's official editor of a library of Jewish texts, under her sponsorship. Becoming a professor in the college of Jewish studies in London (where no Jews were officially allowed to live) may therefore have seemed one further, possibly attractive, proposition to him. Dury had made clear that the college was only intended for Christian students. In 1649, when the royal land holdings were being confiscated by the government, Dury proposed to Parliament that £1,000 per annum be given to establish a college to study 'oriental tongues and Jewish mysteries'. As Dury explained in a pamphlet published by Hartlib at the time, learning what the Jews knew would help towards their conversion, firstly by showing how the Old and New Testaments are connected, secondly by enabling Christians to communicate with Jews both in terms of knowing their languages and their actual beliefs, and finally by teaching Jews about Christianity. 'The Christian religion doth teach nothing, but that Truth nakedly, which was of old darkly spoken of, and believed by the chief Doctors of the Jews themselves, and from the beginning by *Moses* and the *Prophets*.'[18]

In a letter to Hartlib dated 26 January 1649, Dury sadly reported that because of the troubles in Ireland the funds that he had requested were unfortunately exhausted, so that the proposed college had never materialized. But just when Dury felt that 'God doth seeme to dash all our hopes of settlement here, and doth defeat us of all expectations which wee had to assist public designes and his workes of Jewish Conversion by the Deanes and Chapters revenues, which the Army will swallow up',[19] a new and startling development appeared to indicate that the millennium was close at hand.

---

[17] HP 44/5/3A–4B; cf. E. G. E. van der Wall, 'Three letters by Menasseh ben Israel to John Durie', *Nederlands Archief voor Kerkgeschiedenis*, 65 (1985), 46–62, esp. 59, 62. The originals of these letters are to be found in the Hartlib Papers (HP 44/5).

[18] John Dury, *A seasonable discourse written by Mr. John Dury upon the earnest requests of many, briefly showing these particulars: 1. What the grounds and methode of our reformation ought to be in religion and learning; 2. How even in these times of distraction, the worke may be advanced by the knowledge of oriental tongues and Jewish mysteries. By an agency for advancement of universal learning* (London, 1649).

[19] HP 1/7/1B–2A (Dury to Hartlib, 26 January 1649).

Reports from the Massachusetts Bay colony suggested that the Indians might be Jews, possibly the lost tribes of Israel. A Norfolk minister, Thomas Thorowgood, wrote *Jewes in America, or probabilities that the Indians are of that race* to open up a fund-raising campaign to assist in converting the Indians.[20] Dury was asked to write the preface. This led him to correspond with his friend, Menasseh ben Israel, about a report Menasseh had told him of, concerning a Portuguese explorer, Antonio Montesinos, who had encountered an Indian tribe in the Andes mountains holding a Jewish religious service. Dury's preface is a remarkable millenarian document.[21] He waxed eloquent about the way God's direction of history was emerging in America and how this would lead to the reappearance of the lost tribes of Israel, to their leading the Jews back to the Holy Land from one side of the earth, while the Caraites, the Jews who rejected the Talmud in the ninth century and who were seen by Dury and others as 'Pure' or 'Protestant' Jews, would lead the Jews into Palestine from the other side. This would be followed by the conversion of the Jews, the restoration of Jerusalem, and the millennium.[22]

Dury's agitation about this real sign of the divine course of history led Menasseh to write his most famous work, *The hope of Israel*. Dury and other English millenarians asked Menasseh what the Jewish view was about where the lost tribes of Israel were and when they would reappear. Rather than just answer letter after letter (there are three letters from Menasseh to Dury in the Hartlib Papers), Menasseh wrote his book in Spanish. It was then translated into English, Latin, Hebrew and, later, Dutch. The book became the proof-text of its time for the claim that the messianic age was at hand. Although Menasseh was far more cautious than Dury and only maintained that the evidence, not definitive, indicated that part of a lost tribe was in the Americas and that the final prophecies preceding the onset of the messianic age were being fulfilled, his

---

[20] *Jewes in America, or probabilities that the Americans are of that race. With the removall of some contrary reasonings, and earnest desires for effectuall endeavors to make them Christian. Proposed by T. Thorowgood* (London, 1650).

[21] 'An epistolary discourse of Mr J. Dury to Mr. Thorowgood, concerning his conjecture that the Americans are descended from the Israelites. With the history of a Portugall Jew, Antonie Monterinos, attested by Mennasseh Ben Israel, to the same effect.'

[22] On this, see R. H. Popkin, 'The lost tribes, the Caraites and the English Millenarians', *Journal of Jewish Studies*, 37 (1986), 213–27; and David S. Katz, *Philosemitism and the readmission of the Jews to England, 1603–1655* (Oxford, 1982), chap. 4.

version was seen by Jews and Christians as an authoritative announcement that the end of days was at hand.[23]

Hartlib's papers demonstrate that both Hartlib and Dury were very much involved in the translation of Menasseh's work and in the events thereafter which culminated in Menasseh's trip to England to negotiate with Oliver Cromwell about the readmission of the Jews to England. Dury wrote a preface to the translation dedicated to the Houses of Parliament. The translator, Moses Wall, was a millenarian friend of Hartlib. All that is known about him apart from the fact that he was a friend of John Milton is from Wall's letters to Hartlib.[24] Three editions of the pamplet appeared in 1650, 1651 and 1652, the latter two with an essay by Wall on the need to convert the Jews.

As a result of the excitement caused by Menasseh's book, and the 'realization' that the American Indians were Jews and part of the lost tribes of Israel, the problem of converting the Jews became more immediate. In fact, Dury and Hartlib were convinced this would transpire in 1655 or 1656, that it would take place in England, and then the millennium would commence soon thereafter. Christian efforts to convert the Jews had backfired in Spain and Portugal because the forced conversion policy had only created fake converts, not real Jewish Christians. Following the Reformation, their conversion had not occurred because the Jews had not come in contact with pure, reformed Christians such as those of England. A fanciful work, a pamphlet by one unidentifiable Samuel Brett, reported on a rabbinical council that is supposed to have taken place in Hungary in 1650, where the rabbis had debated about whether the Messiah had already come. Some were almost ready to convert when Roman Catholic priests rushed in and scared them off with their idolatrous behaviour. The moral of the pamphlet was that if the rabbis had been confronted with pure English Christianity they would, of course, have converted.[25]

---

[23] See the introduction in the new edition to Menasseh ben Israel, *The hope of Israel*, ed. Henri Méchoulan and Gérard Nahon (Oxford, 1987).

[24] See R. H. Popkin, 'A note on Moses Wall', in *ibid.*, 165–70. The letters published there are all from the Hartlib Papers (HP 34/4). One of them (HP 34/4/1A; Wall to Hartlib, 18 June 1652) describes Wall's reading of the Brett pamphlet in manuscript and forwarding a copy of it to Hartlib.

[25] Samuel Brett, *A narrative of the proceedings of a great councel of JEWS, assembled in the Plain of Ageda in Hungaria, about 30 leagues distant from Buda, to examine the Scriptures concerning Christ; on the 12th of October 1650* ... (London, 1655).

The Brett pamphlet began to circulate in manuscript in 1651 and Wall sent it to Hartlib. Dury received news about it from the French Reformed minister in London, Jean-Baptiste Stouppe. It was finally published in 1655 and reprinted many times thereafter into the late nineteenth century.[26] The message of the pamphlet was that the Jews had to be brought into contact with English Protestants. Since there were no Jews in the British Isles legally, a movement had to begin to bring them back. They had been expelled by Edward II in 1290. Now was the time to readmit them. A high-level delegation was sent to Amsterdam to try to induce Rabbi Menasseh ben Israel to come to England to discuss the terms of readmission with Cromwell. (Menasseh had appointed himself the agent for the Jewish world and he was the only prominent Jew the English millenarians knew.) Dury stage-managed the discussions with Menasseh and helped the rabbi to draft his *Humble Addresse* to Cromwell, in which he explained that it was necessary to fulfil all of the prophecies before the messianic age would begin. One of the chief prophecies to be fulfilled was that the Jews would be dispersed to the four corners of the world before the Messiah would come. As far as Menasseh could tell they were in most corners, including China, where the Jesuits had just encountered the Chinese Jews, but they were not in England. Hence the readmission was a crucial step to be taken before the messianic age.[27]

Menasseh repeatedly delayed his trip because of strong opposition from the Jewish community of Amsterdam. It was feared that the Dutch government would not like to see one of the Jewish leaders engaging in diplomacy with a foreign power and potential enemy, the British government. What eventually seems to have convinced Menasseh to make the journey does not appear in either Hartlib's or Dury's papers. Menasseh went to Belgium in late 1654 to meet the recently abdicated Queen Christina of Sweden. During that visit, he read for the first time Isaac La Peyrère's *Du Rappel des Juifs*, in which the author predicted that the Jewish Messiah would soon arrive and would join forces with the king of France and lead the Jews back to Jerusalem. Menasseh probably met La Peyrère at this time, as he

---

[26] On this, see R. H. Popkin, 'The fictional Jewish council of 1650: a great English pipe-dream', *Jewish History*, 5 (1991), 7–22. Dury mentions the Brett pamphlet in HP 4/2/5 and 8. The report about it by Stouppe appears in his letter to Dury from Ulrich in Zurich; Staats-Archiv Zurich, Dureana, MS E ii, fol. 457ff.

[27] Katz, *Philosemitism in England*, chap. 5.

was living close to Christina's residence and was trying to negotiate an alliance between her and his patron, the prince of Condé. After reading the book, Menasseh rushed back to Amsterdam where he excitedly told a gathering of Christian millenarians in the house of Dury's schoolmate and friend, Peter Serrarius, that the coming of the Messiah was imminent. This led one of those present to write *Good news for the Jews*, dedicated to Menasseh, to which Menasseh added a brief list of those he knew who were aware that the coming of the Messiah was imminent. The list included two English millenarians.[28]

Menasseh left for England in September 1655. At that time, Dury was on the continent undertaking intelligence work for Cromwell. However, he was kept informed of Menasseh's activities in England by Hartlib. Menasseh met with several people in the Hartlib circle. Adam Boreel came from the Netherlands and had a dinner party where Henry Oldenburg, John Dury's son-in-law and later a secretary to the Royal Society, met with Menasseh and discussed millenarian and messianic expectations. Robert Boyle and his sister, Lady Ranelagh, entertained Menasseh.[29]

The diplomatic climax to Menasseh's visit came firstly with the presentation to Cromwell of a petition for the readmission of the Jews. Then came the appointment of the Whitehall Commission by Cromwell to advise him on the matter. While the Whitehall Commission deliberated in late 1655, Hartlib wrote to Dury to obtain a supporting document in favour of readmitting the Jews. The short essay in Dury's 'A case of conscience' on the question, which has been incorporated into the standard literature on the affair, is in reality a patchwork of two letters from Dury to Hartlib, written specially for public consumption in reply to Hartlib's specific indication as to what points should be addressed.[30] Dury offered positive support for readmission, but was less enthusiastic in these documents than he had been in the past. He even suggested controls that might

[28] R. H. Popkin, 'Menasseh ben Israel and Isaac La Peyrère', *Studia Rosenthaliana*, 8 (1974), 59–63; and R. H. Popkin, *Isaac La Peyrère (1596–1676); his life, work and influence* (Leiden, 1987).

[29] See Katz, *Philosemitism in England*, chap. 6; Celia Roth, *The life of Menasseh ben Israel* (Philadelphia, 1934), chap. 10.

[30] The originals are in the BL collection of Dury letters. *A case of conscience, whether it be lawful to admit Jews into a Christian commonwealth. Written to Samuel Hartlib* (London, 1656) was reprinted in the *Harleian Misc.*, VI, 438–44, along with Henry Jessey's account of what transpired at the Whitehall conference.

be introduced to prevent Jewish misbehaviour, constraints which he had observed in operation at Kassel in Germany where he was resident at that time. Dury's letters came too late to play any role, since, for no apparent reason, the Whitehall Commission abruptly ceased its deliberations on 18 December 1655.

One possible explanation for this sudden cessation, however, appears at the bottom of the composite Dury letter, where he recommended that the Caraites not be readmitted because their readmission would 'fright' the Jews away. We learn from one of Hartlib's letters to Worthington that, at the crucial meeting in December, Boreel had raised the question to parties not named, of whether the Caraites should be readmitted. As I have pointed out elsewhere, the Caraites had recently come to European awareness and were quickly romanticized into pure Jews who had never been corrupted by the rabbinical tradition.[31]

The Caraites were expelled from Jewish communities in the ninth and tenth centuries, but they were as much descendants of the inhabitants of ancient Israel as the rest of the Jewish world. In the seventeenth century, they existed in Lithuania, Turkey, Egypt and the Crimea. A handful of western Europeans had encountered them, mainly in Turkey. J. S. Rittangel, whom Dury had originally wished to appoint to the college of Jewish studies, had lived with them in Constantinople. The Dutch student, Warner, who assembled the important collection of Hebrew manuscripts now at the University of Leiden, bought some of them from Caraites in Constantinople. Isaac Troki, a Caraite leader in Lithuania, wrote a very strong attack on Christianity under the title *The fortification of the faith*, which was circulated in manuscript by the Amsterdam Jews and was considered one of their important justifications for their return to Judaism.[32] Menasseh himself refused to publish any Caraite works when asked by Lithuanian Caraites.

Since their break with Judaism came after the Bible, there is no

---

[31] Worthington, I, 78 (Hartlib to Worthington, 12 December 1655). Dury's comment is at the end of his 'A case of conscience'. On this, see Popkin, 'The lost tribes', 222.

[32] See the presently available edition, translated by Moses Mocatta with an introduction by Trude Weiss-Rosmarin, of Isaac ben Abraham Troki, *Faith Strengthened* (New York, 1970). On the role of this work in the clandestine literature of the seventeenth and eighteenth centuries, see R. H. Popkin, 'The image of the Jew in clandestine literature circa 1700', in *Filosofia e Religione nella Letteratura clandestina Secoli xvii e xviii*, ed. Guido Canziani (Milan, 1994), 13–34. On Troki's place in the development of rationalism in religion, see R. H. Popkin, 'Reason as the rule of faith in Castellio, the early Socinians and the Jews', in *Aequitas, aequalias, auctoritas*, ed. Danièle Letocha (Paris, 1992), 195–203.

guidance in Scripture or even in Josephus as to what to do about them. Although no Caraites are known to have at this time raised the question as to whether they would be allowed to come to England, if the point about readmission was to bring all Jews into contact with pure English Christianity in order to lead to their conversion and then to the onset of the millennium, should this not also apply to the Caraites? Nothing in prior millenarian literature discussed this point. But, or so it seemed to Boreel, the conversion of the Jews, that penultimate step before the millennium, should involve the conversion of all descendants of biblical Jews – the lost-tribe Jews, the people in Jewish communities all over the planet and Caraite Jews. Apparently nobody knew what to answer to Boreel's query. This may well be the reason why the Whitehall deliberations ground to a halt at this juncture.

Dury and Hartlib continued their millenarian activities beyond 1655 despite their lack of positive achievement. By the end of 1656, when the predicted conversion of the Jews had not occurred, Dury became somewhat discouraged; but in the following year he had cause for renewed hope. Dury was back in England when he received a letter from Serrarius informing him of the unexpected visit to Amsterdam of Rabbi Nathan Shapira of Jerusalem.

The rabbi was a fund raiser, visiting Europe each year to gather money for poor Jews in the Holy Land. He usually went to Poland, but because of the Swedish invasion he was unable to follow his usual itinerary and instead he travelled to Germany and the Netherlands. He had written to Menasseh about the terrible plight of the Palestinian Jews and Menasseh actually presented Rabbi Shapira's letter to Cromwell as one of the justifications for readmitting the Jews. After the Amsterdam Sephardic leaders had refused his petition for funds, Rabbi Shapira met the Dutch millenarians who were most sympathetic to his request. There thus began a series of meetings, during which they discovered that he held views that seemed close to their Christian ones.[33] On the basis of what he was told by Serrarius, Dury excitedly published a pamphlet entitled *An information concerning the present state of the Jewish nation in Europe and Judea. Wherein the footsteps of Providence preparing a way for their conver-*

[33] R. H. Popkin, 'Rabbi Nathan Shapira's visit to Amsterdam in 1657', in *Dutch Jewish history*, ed. Joseph Michman and Tirtsah Levie (Jerusalem, 1984), 185–205.

sion to Christ, and for their deliverance from captivity are discovered.[34] The
rabbi had described the terrible conditions that the Jews of Palestine
and Poland were being forced to endure. This convinced Dury that
God was at work, making Jewish life more miserable in order to
hasten the deliverance of the Jews following their conversion. But
even more compelling from Dury's viewpoint were the statements
reportedly coming from Rabbi Shapira about Christianity which
appeared to indicate that the rabbi was almost a Christian already.[35]

When the rabbi was asked for his understanding of Isaiah 53, the
proof-text used by Christians to try to convince Jews that Jesus was
the suffering servant and expected Messiah, Shapira said that in his
view there had been many instances of the Messiah from ancient
times onwards and that Jesus of Nazareth was one of them. Each
time the Messiah appeared, he found mankind so wicked that he did
not stay. Concerning Jesus, Rabbi Shapira was reported as saying
that 'our Forefathers wrongfully put [*him*] to death and that Sin lies
upon us unto this day'. Serrarius told Dury that, when he heard this,
'my bowels were inwardly stirred within me, and it seemed to me
that I did not hear a Jew, but a Christian of no mean understanding,
who did relish the things of the Spirit, and was admitted to the
inward mysteries of our Religion'. On another occasion, the rabbi
commented on the Sermon on the Mount that he thought it was the
fount of all wisdom and that it contained the teachings of the most
pure and ancient rabbis. When Shapira watched the millenarians at
prayer he declared that if there were but ten men so holy in
Jerusalem praying for the coming of the Messiah, he would come
quickly. On the basis of his discussions with the rabbi, Serrarius
asked Dury: 'Is it to be believed that Christ is far distant from a soul
so constituted? or that any such thing can be formed without Christ
in a man? I see Christ in his Spirit, and cannot but love him, and
those that are like him, of which he saith many are at Jerusalem.'[36]

Dury and other English and Dutch millenarians were so enthused

---

[34] Published in London in 1658 by R. W. for Thomas Brewster. This is not included in J. M.
Batten's list of Dury's printed works: J. M. Batten, *John Dury: advocate of Christian reunion*
(Chicago, 1944), 213–22.
[35] What follows is what Serrarius told Dury about Rabbi Shapira's views. I have been told by
a leading Israeli scholar that in unpublished and undatable sermons, Rabbi Shapira made
very un- and even anti-Christian remarks. So far I have not been shown any of these
sermons.
[36] Popkin, 'Rabbi Shapira', 196–7.

about the potential Christianity of the rabbi that they set up a fund-raisIng campaign for his brethren in Palestine. It is the first known case of a Christian venture of this kind for Jews. They collected a large sum of money which was given to the rabbi to take to Jerusalem. Some cynics have suggested that Shapira's philo-Christian views were just a means of securing money from Gentiles. There is no known evidence that this was the case. However, when Rabbi Shapira returned to Jerusalem he was immediately con-demned for taking money from Gentiles and it was only years later that he was posthumously exonerated.[37]

Rabbi Shapira was also used to further another of Dury and Hartlib's philosemitic plans, that of getting the New Testament translated into proper Hebrew. They knew that the existing trans-lation, by Sebastian Munster, was far from perfect. For years they had searched for a means to make a satisfactory version available for Jews. Rabbi Shapira was given a copy of the New Testament and asked to take it to Jerusalem and have it translated. Sadly we know nothing about whether he did anything with the text after he left Amsterdam.[38]

Documents indicate that the millenarians kept in touch with Rabbi Shapira over the next few years. David Katz and I suspect that this link may have something to do with the last philosemitic episode to be discussed here, namely the Jewish messianic movement centred around Sabbatai Zevi of Smyrna. His 'Elijah', Nathan of Gaza, was a student of Rabbi Shapira, and the messianic ferment surrounding him began in the late 1650s and culminated in 1666.[39]

In the late 1650s both Dury and Hartlib were increasingly disillu-sioned. The conversion of the Jews had not occurred and nor had the reunification of the Protestant churches. The reforming Com-monwealth in England was also falling apart without becoming the 'parliament of saints' or ushering in the kingdom of God on earth.

---

[37] This occurred on the grounds that the money he collected from Gentiles went to pay Turkish (Gentile) taxes and was not used by Jews. See David Katz, 'English charity and Jewish qualms: the rescue of the Ashkenazi community of seventeenth-century Jerusalem', in *Jewish history: essays in honour of Chimen Abramsky*, ed. A. Rapoport-Albert and S. J. Zipperstein (London, 1988), 245–66.

[38] It was only in the late eighteenth century that Hebrew copies of the New Testament were issued by conversionist societies in England and Scotland. Dury, Hartlib and others had encouraged translations into American–Indian languages and Turkish as part of their millenarian activities.

[39] On Sabbatai Zevi and his movement, see Gershom Scholem, *Sabbatai Sebi, the mystical messiah* (Princeton, 1973).

Shortly after the Restoration, Hartlib passed away, while Dury lived on to 1680 in enforced exile, accused of being a regicide. This was not before he had tried to remain in England by telling Charles II that he foresaw a divine mission for the restored king, namely that of converting the Jews.[40]

Hartlib's papers tell us little after 1661. The Dureana collection in Zurich and other Dury manuscripts tell us what happened in the following years.[41] Dury continued to travel around Germany, France, the Netherlands and Switzerland in his attempts to unite all the Protestant churches and to fashion a confessional harmonization. From Serrarius he received letters encouraging him with the recent indications that the millennium was not far off. In one of these, from 1664, Serrarius told him of the several prodigies and comets that had been observed and that he, Serrarius, had been in contact with some Jews who told him that a great rabbi reported that there would be enormous changes at the Sublime Porte. When asked for the basis of the report, Serrarius was told that Zion would be restored in 1666 according to some cabbalistic *gematria* calculations. Dury did not have much faith in cabbalistic calculations, but equally he was not in a position to reject what he did not fully comprehend.[42]

By January 1666, Dury had heard from Serrarius that the king of the Jews had arrived. Dury soon had other reports about this from Venice, Frankfurt, Ragusa, Vienna and Corfu, and the news was confirmed by one of the most important Amsterdam Jews, Abraham Peyrera, who had already left for Jerusalem to take part in the messianic age.[43] For his part, Dury was not sceptical about these tidings although he tried to interpret them in a minimalist way. He surmised that the king of the Jews would rule a Jewish kingdom in the Ottoman empire and would be subject to the sultan. More reports reached him, principally from Serrarius, but also from the

---

[40] This appears in Dury's new preface to the 1661 edition of Thorowgood's *Jews in America*. Dury claimed that one of Serrarius' students had had a dream or vision that Charles would be restored and that he would then go on to bring about the conversion of the Jews. See Ernestine van der Wall, 'Prophecy and profit. Nicholas van Rensselaer, Charles II and the conversion of the Jews', *Kerkhistorische opstellan aangeboden aan Prof. dr. J. van den Berg*, ed. C. Augustijn, (Kampen, 1987), 75-87.

[41] The Dureana manuscript collection is six volumes, E II 457a-f in the Staats-Archiv in Zurich.

[42] Staats-Archiv, Zurich, Dureana MS E II 457d, fol. 421.

[43] Dureana MS E II 457e, fol. 747.

French Reformed church in Basle.[44] From Serrarius' letters to Dury the picture is one of growing excitement being generated in Jewish and Christian circles in the Netherlands. Jean de Labadie, we are told, preached to a thousand people about the arrival of the king of the Jews. Jews in Amsterdam were praying and preparing to go to the Holy Land.[45] Dury's response indicates how he tried to make sense of this dénouement – that the Jewish Messiah, and not Jesus, had arrived.[46] Serrarius became the leading western European Christian follower of Sabbatai Zevi. He wrote several pamphlets to alert English millenarians to this new state of affairs. When Sabbatai Zevi turned Muslim in 1667, Serrarius still accepted him as the Messiah and told Henry Oldenburg that this just showed that God acted in mysterious ways. Serrarius seems to have convinced Comenius about Sabbatai Zevi; and Serrarius actually died en route to meet his Messiah in the Near East in 1669.[47]

In this tumultuous period Dury was much more cautious. He entertained various possibilities, such as that Sabbatai Zevi was the king of the Jews in the Ottoman empire; a local potentate, that he was the Jewish Messiah sent to show Christians how evil they were, how undeserving of *their* expected Messiah. After Sabbatai Zevi's conversion to Islam, Dury decided that the state of Christianity was in too much conflict and disorder to embrace the hope of Israel.[48]

Further research is needed to find out how long the Sabbatai Zevi episode affected Christian millenarians. We do know that even after Sabbatai Zevi's messianic claims were rejected by many leading rabbis and after his conversion, he still had a strong Jewish following, especially in Amsterdam.[49] It would be interesting to find out if the (by then) underground Jewish support for Sabbatai Zevi carried over to radical Christian groups as well. It was not long afterwards that another Jewish messianic movement began, this time centred

---

[44] *Ibid.*, fol.747v. On all of this, see R. H. Popkin, 'Two unused sources about Sabbatai Zevi and his effect on European communities', in Michman and Levie, *Dutch Jewish history*, II, esp. 70–1, and R. H. Popkin, 'The end of the career of a great 17th century millenarian: John Dury', *Pietismus und Neuzeit*, 14 (1988), 203–20.

[45] Dureana, MS E II 457, fols. 995–7.

[46] Dureana, MS E II 457e, fols. 747–8, 1167, 1179–83.

[47] On this, see Michael McKeon, 'Sabbatai Zevi in England', *Association of Jewish Studies Review*, I (1976), 131–69; and Ernestine van der Wall, *De Mystieke Chiliast Petrus Serrarius (1600–1669) en zijn Wereld* (Leiden, 1987).

[48] Dureana, MS E II 457e, fol. 1167.

[49] Yosef Kaplan, *From Christianity to Judaism. The story of Isaac Orobio de Castro* (Oxford, 1989), chap. 8.

around a Dane, Oliger Pauli, and led by an Amsterdam rabbi, Moses Germanus, who had converted to Judaism.[50]

The Dury Papers indicate that he became increasingly sad and disillusioned in the 1670s. His plans for church reunification were rejected by various religious groups. He was denounced as a Socinian and a heretic. He settled in Kassel and there wrote his last major work on the interpretation of the book of Revelation by itself, published in 1674. In this work, Dury disowned historical prophetic predictions. He said that most of the predictions had been fulfilled by now, but that God had not given us any way of calculating when the remaining ones would take place. It was for God alone to decide when these would happen.[51] Then Dury went on to internalize millennial expectations. They could be realized in ourselves, spiritually, until such time as God himself made them occur in history. Dury, who had devoted his life to pursuit of the millennium actively and energetically in the political history of time, abdicated the task in this late work, written just a few years before his death.[52]

The philosemitism that is revealed in Hartlib's and Dury's papers was a major political, social and religious force during the period 1640–70. It was central for those who saw actual history as the unfolding of the divine plan laid out in the books of Daniel and Revelation. This would be merely a curiosity, as it is in present-day America, where fundamentalist preachers interpret everything from the emergence of the state of Israel, the Cold War, the collapse of the Soviet Union, the Gulf War and the Los Angeles riots as part of the scenario laid out in biblical prophecies, were it not for the fact that people such as Dury and Hartlib and their collaborators were very influential in English and Dutch affairs during this period. Their philosemitic aspirations came to naught because God did not cooperate by converting the Jews or sending Jesus back to earth. Yet this is not to gainsay the enormous energy dispensed on these ventures and witnessed in the papers of Hartlib and Dury. There may, however, have been some more lasting legacies. Christians and

---

50 On Oliger Pauli and Moses Germanus, see Hans Joachim Schoeps, *Philosemitismus im Barok* (Tübingen, 1952), 67–81.

51 Dury, *Touchant l'Intelligence de l'Apocalypse par l'Apocalypse mesme comme toute l'Ecriture Ste. doit estre entendue raisonablement* (n.p. [probably Kassel], 1674). I have only been able to locate two copies of this work, one at the Herzog August Bibliothek at Wolfenbüttel, the other at the Marsh Library in Dublin.

52 On this, see Popkin, 'The end of the career of a great 17th century millenarian', esp. 211–18.

Jews were brought into contact with one another on almost equal terms, joint intellectual ventures were fostered, similarities and differences in beliefs were conjointly explored. The tolerance towards Jews that developed first in the Netherlands and then in the American colonies and in England probably emerges in part from the millenarian philosemitism of various Christian groups. It helped to produce a world in which there could be mutual respect, first between Christians and Jews, and then between Christians and non-Christians in general. This, in part, resulted from the realization by Christian millenarians such as Dury that they could not force the millennium to come into being; that it was up to God to decide when and where this would happen and that it was God who would bring about the conversion of the Jews. So, finally, there was not much left for philosemitic millenarians of the period to do besides individual spiritual and moral improvement. A century later, at the time of the American and French Revolutions, they would once more become active politically in their enduring quest to bring about the millennium through reforms, through benign efforts to unite Jews and Christians and even to rebuild the Holy Land, efforts still going on among Christian Zionists.

CHAPTER 6

Millenarianism and the new science: the case of Robert Boyle

Malcolm Oster

Ever since Charles Webster's explicit association of puritan religious eschatology and Baconian utilitarian science in *The great instauration* there has been renewed interest in the impact of religious expectation on the advance of the new science. However, the specifically millenarian–utilitarian tradition of puritans such as Hartlib, Dury and Haak, which Webster had rightly found significant, was soon extended by Margaret Jacob to embrace Anglican millenarianism of a latitudinarian hue in the natural philosophy of the later seventeenth century.[1] In reaction, a decade ago John Henry, in his work on the Catholic Blackloist mechanical philosophy and eschatology of Kenelm Digby and his mentor, Thomas White, legitimately challenged their use of millenarian expectation. Henry argued that rather than longing for a political utopia under a thousand-year rule of the saints on earth, 'most natural philosophers in the period were anticipating the Day of Judgement when all social and political aspirations would be *suspended* once and for all'.[2]

With this debate in mind, I want to look again at some of these issues through examining a key figure in both the advance of the new science and the Hartlib circle, the chemist and physiologist Robert Boyle. Given the prominence that James Jacob gave to Boyle's 'millenarianism', I believe we need to consider again whether Boyle was particularly influenced by these decades of apocalyptic and millennial speculation and whether his own position was discernible.[3]

---

[1] Webster, esp. chap. 1; Margaret C. Jacob, 'Millenarianism and science in the late seventeenth century', *Journal of the History of Ideas*, 37 (1976), 335–41. See also Christopher Hill, *The intellectual origins of the English Revolution* (Oxford, 1965).

[2] J. Henry, 'Atomism and eschatology: Catholicism and natural philosophy in the Interregnum', *British Journal for the History of Science*, 15 (1982), 211–13, 234–6.

[3] James Jacob, 'Boyle's circle in the Protectorate: Revelation, politics and the millennium', *Journal of the History of Ideas*, 38 (1977), 131–40; James Jacob, *Robert Boyle and the English Revolution* (New York, 1977), 118–32.

During the middle years of that crucial decade of the 1640s, Boyle had returned from the continent and taken up residence at the Stalbridge estate in Dorset, where he patiently worked his way through the composition of an ethical treatise, 'The aretology'.[4] While he was to complain to both his elder sister, Lady Ranelagh, and his former tutor, Isaac Marcombes, of the inordinate expenditure of time and energy devoted to its construction, he appeared implicitly to recognize the unavoidable necessity of disciplined industry and time involved in projects where knowledge might be acquired.[5] As he noted in 'The aretology': 'Knoledg has, Generatio Longa, Fruitio Breuis; tho A long Generation, yet but A short Fruition: it is so long in the Purchasing, that it seldome coms to the Enjoying. For we lern with labor, and by Peece-meal; and ... (as Hippocrates has it) ... one half of a man's life is spent to instruct the other.'[6] Boyle was soon to appreciate this truism for both moral and experimental knowledge.

Similarly, the example of the Pythagoreans was brought into play by Boyle in an untitled discourse of the later 1640s on what is elsewhere raised as his 'doctrine of thinking'.[7] The Pythagoreans provide that exceptional example and cautionary warning which the rest of mankind has rarely heeded. Progress has been painfully slow but, Boyle implied, thanks to a destined minority (which possibly includes himself?), there is now a quickening of knowledge before the final conflagration: 'Had all men been as carelesse of Thinking as most men are, the world might til it's Dotage haue ... embrac't the Errors of it's Infancy; and for a More Cleare liht of things [we] might haue stayd till the last great Fire.'[8] In an essay on animal suffering from the same period, Boyle again linked this consciousness of new knowledge with eschatology through those who now increasingly argued 'That Beasts do participate of Reason ... in this more inquisite & discerning Age'. Indeed, he had even been informed 'by one of the ablest & famousest Diuines our Age can boast ... that in the Greate Renouation at the Last Day / of all things / [the] Beasts also shall receaue & be preferr'd to a more exalted Nature'.[9]

[4] Royal Society, Boyle Commonplace Book, 195 of which 192 appears a draft. This is now transcribed and published along with other early Boyle compositions in *The early essays and ethics of Robert Boyle*, ed. John T. Harwood (Carbondale, 1991), 1–141.
[5] Boyle, *Works*, I, xxx, xxxiv.   [6] Harwood (ed.), *Early essays*, 9.   [7] *Ibid.*, 185–202.
[8] *Ibid.*, 186.
[9] Malcolm Oster, '"The Beame of Diuinity": animal suffering in the early thought of Robert Boyle', *British Journal for the History of Science*, 22 (1989), 151–79 (173, lines 25–36).

As I have suggested, one of the pervasive characteristics of millenarian as opposed to general apocalyptic speculation is the more
specific expectation adopted in predicting a particular configur-
ation of literal political transformations of the earth, and this was
usually in conformity with predictions from Revelation, John's
Epistles and Daniel. This was also likely to entail a more confident
tone in elucidating the meaning of present events. Yet in one of
Boyle's early comments on the question of deciphering the precise
sacred meaning of events, both private and public, one detects a
distinct reluctance to follow that disposition: 'That though in afflic-
tions, especially national or publick calamities, God oftentimes
seems to make no distinction betwixt the objects of his compassion,
and those of his fury, indiscriminately involving them in the same
destiny; yet his prescience and intentions make a vast difference,
where his inflictions do not seem to make any.'[10] I have tried to show
elsewhere that even by the late 1650s, no specific political alternative to the Protectorate was being actively promoted or anticipated by Boyle and that prevailing notions of providence placed
constraints on partisan political ambitions as they could work
against God's intentions. Indeed, the relative lack of success of
Hartlib's group which Boyle still actively associated with, despite his
immersion in Oxford science after 1656, pointed to the need for
continued vigilance and confidence in the inscrutability of providential intent.[11]

In similar vein, in *Style of the Scriptures* (*c*.1648), while alluding to
the problem of abstruse texts in the formulation of doctrine, Boyle
commented 'that perhaps some mysteries are so obscure, that they
are reserved to the illumination and blazes of the last and universal
fire'. The suggestion that the Last Judgement will be the means by
which God will make His intentions more transparent is given
added weight by Boyle's additional observation regarding the
obscure texts of Revelation: 'There are divers prophetical passages
in the Revelation, which we know as little the use, as meaning of,
which yet doubtlesly our posterity will not find barren.'[12]

During the time he was composing his *Style of the Scriptures*, Boyle

---

[10] Boyle, *Works*, I, 258 – *Seraphic love* (*c*.1648).
[11] Malcolm Oster, 'Virtue, providence, and political neutralism: Robert Boyle and Interregnum politics', in *Robert Boyle reconsidered*, ed. Michael Hunter (Cambridge, 1994), 19–36.
[12] Boyle, *Works*, II, 267, 278. Boyle argues further on that divine justice requires that 'the
whole world shall one day perish by fire' (*ibid.*, 312).

wrote some revealing letters to his friend and neighbour, John Mallet, in late 1651 and early 1652. In his first letter, Boyle affirmed his enthusiasm for learning the Hebrew tongue and recounted a meeting between a 'learned Amsterdam' Jew who had arrived in London (doubtless his acquaintance, Menasseh ben Israel), and 'Some new Pretenders to the Gift of Tongues'.[13] Boyle underlines the rabbi's attempt to explain to one of their group that his 'Gibberish' was not Hebrew but 'replyes the Fanaticke ... my Hebrew is better & Ancienter then Your's, for I speake the Hebrew that Adam spoake in the Garden'.[14] Moving on to developments at Westminster which may procure the advance of 'Publicke Intelligence', Boyle revealed that 'I do with Some confidence expect a Revolution, whereby Diuinity will be much Looser, & Reall Philosophy flourish beyond men's Hopes'.[15] The probable meaning of these words is an expectation of a new reformation of learning, the early signs of which are already evident in the new science. There need be no reference to any imminent millennial social order here, close to the heart of the 'Fanaticke' perhaps, but rather the reasonable and reformist pursuit of true religion and natural philosophy. This hope of Boyle would have been in accordance with the *instauratio magna* of Bacon, the *pansophia* of Comenius and Hartlib and the irenicism of Dury. Bacon, in particular, integrated the prophecy of Daniel 12 into his philosophical programme to provide it with an apocalyptic colouring rather than a millennial eschatology.[16]

In his further letter to Mallet in 1652, after dealing with advances in both husbandry and divinity, Boyle echoed similar sentiments: 'For the Criticall Productions of these last Yeares make me not

[13] BL Harley MS 7003, fols. 179v–180r, November 1651. Boyle had visited Menasseh ben Israel in the spring of 1648, 'the greatest Rabbi of this Age' (Boyle, *Works*, IV, 375). Boyle also mentions him in *Works*, II, 280, 301; V, 183. Menasseh (1604–57) was a petitioner to Cromwell for readmission of the Jews into England. For further discussion of Menasseh ben Israel, see chap. 5, this volume and D. Katz, *Philosemitism and the readmission of the Jews to England, 1603–1655* (Oxford, 1982). Boyle had already consulted Jews to learn more about their religion, in Florence in 1642. See R. E. W. Maddison, *The life of the Honourable Robert Boyle* (London, 1969), 35.

[14] BL Harley MS 7003, fol. 180v.

[15] *Ibid.* Jacob insists in 'Boyle's circle in the Protectorate' (133) that Boyle's words indicate an 'imminent' expectation but there is little direct evidence for this. Cf. J. Jacob and M. Jacob, 'The Anglican origins of modern science: the metaphysical foundations of the Whig constitution', *Isis*, 71 (1980), 251–67, where the reformist 'Anglican millenarianism' of Boyle and others is contrasted with sectarian revolutionary aims (253, 259). Shapin and Schaffer follow Jacob in *Leviathan and the air-pump: Hobbes, Boyle, and the experimental life* (Princeton, 1985), 304.

[16] Webster, 21, 23.

unapt to expect, that the Scripture Should be more illustrated within these ten Yeares, then it was formerly in as many Ages'.[17] This flowering of learning could, in principle, proceed into an indefinite future for Boyle in so far as the Last Judgement had no known date, though other evidence will indicate he may well have pondered on the closeness of its arrival. Thus, Charles Webster's comment on the ramifications of puritan science in the context of millennial transformation can equally be used to explain the motivation of amillennial natural philosophy. As Webster argued: 'There was little point in engaging ... into long term scientific investigations at a time when the thousand-year rule of the saints was expected to begin in the near future.'[18] There is little doubt that Boyle's decision to take up residence in Oxford in late 1655 was indeed to engage in long-term scientific investigation, given the investment of time, wealth, physical apparatus and assistants that he was to employ during his period there.

The theological unease felt in the Anglican hierarchy over millennialists is perfectly captured in Boyle's favourite mentor on meditation, Bishop Joseph Hall, whose *The arte of divine meditation* (1607) had provided a model for Boyle's *Occasional reflections* (1665), written during the Stalbridge years.[19] Hall opens his work, *The revelation unrevealed* (1650), by commending Boyle's pastor at Geneva, Jean Diodati, whom Boyle heard preach intermittently for over four years during his Grand Tour. As regards Revelation, Diodati 'grants that there are some parts of this Book still reserved under God's secret Seal; the explication whereof is utterly uncertain'.[20] Hall disclaims any personal concern with millennial tenets for his own faith, but is annoyed at those who throw off 'scripture and ordinances' by supposing Christ's reign to have started, or who read into every misfortune of the church 'severall stages of their Saviour's approach', as well as those who 'applaud themselves in their imminent ... glory' while denying it 'but for qualified persons only'.[21] Yet this hardly prevents Hall, in keeping with other

---

[17] BL Add. MS 32093, fol. 293 (2/12 March 1652). Boyle's links with Mallet in husbandry and divinity are detailed in Oster, '"Beame of Diuinity"', 161.

[18] Webster, 517.

[19] Boyle shows his debt to Hall in the preface to the *Reflections* in Boyle, *Works*, II, 327, 332, 333. However, this does not mean he adopted other positions of Hall without qualification, such as Hall's long-standing support for divine episcopacy, shared by Bishop George Downame, who emphasized continuity with Roman antecedents.

[20] Joseph Hall, *The Revelation unrevealed* (London, 1650), 2–3.   [21] *Ibid.*, 8–9

exponents of more traditional eschatology, in being persuaded as an article of faith 'that the coming of our Saviour is neer at hand; and that before that great Day God hath decreed, and will yet effect a more happy and flourishing condition of his Church here on earth'.[22] Hall only allows for a gathering in of the Gentiles, the conversion of the Jews and the final pouring out of grace upon believers in the last days, while going on to outline the great variety of constructions that can be placed upon texts such as Daniel 12 and Revelation 20 – with Diodati again cited as a source for caution in approaching their interpretation.[23] Hall spends the second half of the book in listing the paradoxes and confusions that result from a thousand-year rule of the saints, which include the establishment of a worldly kingdom, a double judgement and resurrection, the saints meddling in earthly affairs while both mortal and sinless, and the wicked able to wage war during the reign. The essential message of Hall, as for most Anglicans and puritans of his stamp, is that a careful examination of the Scriptures in historical context, a sentiment close to Boyle's preoccupations in these years, reveals the spiritual nature of God's kingdom.[24]

A particularly difficult piece of evidence in assessing Boyle's position is an undated letter sent to him while he was in Ireland in the early 1650s from his elder sister, Lady Ranelagh.[25] She reported accounts that Hartlib had received from Germany where 'their very waters are turned into blood', and from 'our northern parts' news of a vision of a perfect rainbow in 'pure blue' in the midst of a black cloud with warriors at each end, the 'party at the east end' finally victorious.[26] She continued:

These being set for signs and for seasons, do hereby signify something; though I think he that would dare to affirm in particular what, might be as like to mistake as hit right; but we have a sure word, that tells us, all this old frame of heaven and earth must pass, and a new one be set up in its place, and then your expectation of seven years will be abundantly answered and exceeded; but whether it will come within the years, I dare no more say than I do know; on this methinks I am sure of, that it is a brave thing to be one of those, that shall lift up their heads with joy in expectation of a

[22] Ibid., 10.   [23] Ibid., 17, 21, 44, 64.

[24] Ibid., 109–230. The Anglican thinker Jeremy Taylor, in his The liberty of prophesying (London, 1648), provides a similar approach.

[25] Boyle, Works, VI, 532–4. The letter opens with 'Since your going into Ireland ...' which dates it after June 1652 and before July 1654, when he returned.

[26] Ibid., 534.

present redemption, when all these ruins and confusions shall be upon the earth.[27]

Clearly, one cannot be certain that it is Boyle alone who has provided this prediction or that she has understood Boyle correctly, but even allowing for this, the short, specific time span of seven years is quite unlike the usual type of calculation used in millennial speculation. The sources that Boyle could have drawn on include either some unorthodox prophetic framework, or a mathematical science such as astrology or numerology, both of which, it has to be said, are largely out of character.[28] Perhaps Boyle was looking forward to the mid-1650s and the conversion of the Jews widely expected at that juncture. In support of this possibility, one finds Boyle commending his friend, the poet Abraham Cowley, who had underlined in the preface to his *Poems* (1656) his belief in the conversion of the Jews and a complete reformation of the literary arts preceding the return of Christ.[29] On the other hand, the distinctly non-committal and open-ended hope of Lady Ranelagh for a new heaven and earth to emerge out of a period of tribulation for believers may point to a conservative reading of John's Revelation on her part.

The ambiguity of much relevant material extends to another significant figure close to Boyle, Henry Oldenburg, the future first secretary of the Royal Society. For example, there is a collection of notes among the Boyle papers in Oldenburg's hand, dating from the late summer and autumn of 1655, of sermons preached by leading figures among the Fifth Monarchy Men, such as John Simpson and Cornet Day, at Allhallows Church, London.[30] However, the dating suggests that it was most unlikely that Boyle knew Oldenburg well enough at that time to send him there to assess the threat of a sect who had now come to view Cromwell's creation of the Protectorate and peace with the Dutch as treachery against God and a sign of the

---

[27] *Ibid.*

[28] Jacob assumes the letter proves the millenarianism of Boyle and Lady Ranelagh. See Jacob, 'Boyle's circle in the Protectorate', 133. B. Teague also assumes Boyle is millenarian, though in his case only until the Restoration. See B. Teague, 'The origins of Robert Boyle's philosophy' (Ph.D. thesis, University of Cambridge, 1971), 97–112. I am grateful to Howard Hotson (Brasenose College, Oxford), who is familiar with both English and continental millenarianism, for helping me make sense of the letter and its possible contexts.

[29] Boyle extols Cowley's *Davideis* as the poetry of the new age: Boyle, *Works*, II, 249.

[30] Royal Society, Boyle Papers, 43, fols. 290–7.

millennium.[31] Similarly, Oldenburg's letter on millenarian theories
to Menasseh ben Israel in 1657 is neutral in tone and his comment in
a letter to Hartlib of 12 September 1658, 'It is not unlike, that a sore
persecution hangs yet over the Protestant Churches, before the
destruction of AntiChrist', may still indicate a more traditional
position.[32] If the use of 'AntiChrist' is seen to affirm Oldenburg's
millenarianism, it should then be noted that Boyle, Oldenburg's
virtual patron by the late 1650s, never appears to use that term
theologically in his work or correspondence, much less identify it
with Rome.

Again, James Jacob's insistence that the extracts Oldenburg
copied and saved of his correspondence with Lady Ranelagh in 1656
and 1657 prove her millenarianism is unfounded. Indeed, the manuscript in question largely reinforces Jacob's own observation that she
and Oldenburg shared the widely held view that 'England in the
1650s stood poised for the fulfilment of the Reformation in what
would amount to a new heaven and earth'.[33]

More recent evidence regarding Oldenburg's role in purveying
apocalyptic and more specifically millenarian ideas contained in
papers formerly owned by Thomas Birch has been cited by
Hunter.[34] Most of the material dates from 1666, when a new
Messiah, Sabbatai Zevi, who signalled for many prophetic followers
the conversion of the Jews and the end of the world, was at large in
the Near East. Oldenburg's report on the French millenarian, Jean
Labadie, who was known to have arrived in Amsterdam in July
1666, together with two further letters from Amsterdam in Oldenburg's hand with more news of the impact of Zevi on the Jewish
community of Amsterdam, at least shows how involved the Royal
Society's secretary was in disseminating this sort of information.[35]
But as Hunter rightly points out, it remains uncertain whether
Oldenberg himself was caught up positively in an expectation of a
millennium or just recording information. However, it is not part of

---

[31] Jacob in 'Boyle's circle in the Protectorate' (137–8) only discusses the notes in the context
of competing political visions.

[32] Oldenburg, I, 124, 180. Noted in Michael Hunter, 'Promoting the new science: Henry
Oldenburg and the early Royal Society', *History of Science*, 26 (1988), 165–81 (esp. 178–9).
The essay is also reprinted in Michael Hunter, *Establishing the new science: the experience of the
early Royal Society* (Woodbridge, 1989), 245–60.

[33] Jacob, 'Boyle's circle in the Protectorate', 136. The extracts in Royal Society, Boyle Papers,
MS 1, notably fols. 190v–191v, conform to the expectations of Dury in Hartlib Papers,
Bundle 1.

[34] Hunter, 'Promoting the new science', 176–81.   [35] *Ibid.*, 177–8.

my argument to suggest that significant figures close to Boyle such as Lady Ranelagh and Oldenburg did not entertain millenarian ideas or even positively hold them themselves; rather, it is that the evidence remains far more ambiguous than has been allowed for and that, in particular, Boyle had his own considered views on these issues.

Among the Hartlib papers can be found a letter dated April 1659 from Benjamin Worsley, another figure from Boyle's early years, to, it seems, Lady Ranelagh. The letter further illustrates continued expectancy of great change which Worsley convinces himself is near at hand.[36] Though the republican regime of Richard Cromwell was in dire trouble, Worsley indicated that he had sent regards to the republican leader, Sir Henry Vane, and reminded his correspondent:

Therefore though for a while and a very small while the people of ye Lord may bee under some discouragemt from the power at present of Lordly, and wicked men – yet their hope shall suddenly increase, their Confidence shall bee raysed ... the Lord shall appeare as hee hath promised (I say 66) ... seeing the time appointed is short, very short, even at hand ... And to consider, that of all and every part of this there shall be no end but it shall endure without any change, cessation, alteration or diminution for ever and ever.[37]

Again, the emphasis is on spiritual transformation, which will endure as a heavenly bliss rather than the limited duration of any millennial reign. We do know from Birch's *Life of Boyle* that Boyle in the same year attended a meeting where Vane preached, and interrupted him to correct his interpretation of Daniel 12:2, in order 'that the sense of the scriptures might not be depraved', an indication of Boyle's stance towards prophetic assertion and the seriousness with which he dealt with scriptural meaning.[38]

It has to be said that Samuel Hartlib – another figure close to Boyle – grew increasingly circumspect by the mid-1650s with regard to the millennial enthusiasm he had earlier espoused. One wonders whether Boyle ever intimated in personal conversations his more prudent eschatology, given the virtual absence of the question in

[36] HP 33/2/13A–14B (copy letter from Worsley to [Lady Ranelagh?], Dublin, 20/30 April 1659).
[37] HP 33/2/13A–13B. The reference to 'I say 66' in the fourth line was probably incorrectly transcribed from the name Isaiah.
[38] Boyle, *Works*, I, cxl.

any of his private correspondence with Hartlib. By March 1656, Hartlib had written to John Worthington, master of Jesus College, Cambridge, not only distancing himself, unsurprisingly, from the Fifth Monarchy millenarians, but the position in general. He noted: 'Both the forain and domestick world begin [*to be*] more & more divided about this grand point, De Felicitate Ultimi Saeculi ... the French divine Amirault hath written a Treatise on purpose against all kind of Millenaries [*which*] is looked upon by many as unanswerable ... Pontificem Romanum esse Magnum illum Antichristum is more in my apprehension than a probable truth.'[39] Similarly, in a letter to Worthington in December 1660, Hartlib threw further doubt on the very question of the significance of Jewish conversion for eschatology. Challenging the authority of the puritan divine William Ames, Hartlib was probably expressing a personal disappointment that the conversion had not yet happened as much as prudence in the changed political landscape in which he now found himself:

By the adjoined Letter of Mr. Boreel's to Mr. D[*ury*] you will see how he methodizes the great affairs of God's kingdom. The world may not expect any great happiness before the conversion of the Jews be first accomplished. But many tell me that Mr. Lightfoot can find no such truth revealed nor promised, either in the Holy records, or in any of the Jewish writers. Till it be known what grounds he doth alledge, we can oppose the authority of the late learned Dr. Ames, who professed to his dying day the conversion of the Jews to be a most liquid scriptural truth, but could not approve of any of the Millenary tenets.[40]

Though Boyle was quite probably associated with the publication of *A discourse concerning liberty of conscience* (1661) by his friend and colleague, Sir Peter Pett, at the Restoration, the motive was not only the fear of a 'vindictive retaliation' by the restored clergy and the search for a broadly based church, as Burnet affirmed in Boyle's funeral sermon. The *Discourse* also underlined that, quite apart from Pett's more immediate secular concerns, the criteria for toleration hinged as much on how far the Anglican establishment could accept the contingent character of what they termed heresy, as sectaries could demonstrate their commitment to keep religious and civil peace. Boyle's knowledge of the early church may well have been

---

[39] Worthington, I, 80 (Hartlib to Worthington, 10/20 March 1656).
[40] *Ibid.*, 249–50 (Hartlib to Worthington, 17/27 December 1660). Ames' eschatology would not have escaped Boyle's notice in all probability.

employed by Pett to provide grounds for extending toleration even to the sect of Fifth Monarchy Men:

Those who professe the belief of a fifth Monarchy, that is, of Christ's Reigning personally on the Earth a thousand yeares, and draw no consequences from thence about their duty in promoting that fifth Kingdom, by being active in dethroning any Magistrates, or divesting Bishops and Ministers of their places, because they are said to be of the fourth, may not for that opinion be liable to any punishment. For as ill uses as this opinion hath been put to in our dayes, it was believed by almost all the Fathers of the Church before the first Nicene Councell.

It should be pointed out that these sentiments remain very similar to those expressed by Boyle in correspondence of the mid-1640s to Lady Ranelagh and Isaac Marcombes where, to the latter, Boyle characterized the flood of sectary opinion as largely 'new editions of old errors', that rub alongside those that are 'glimpses ... of obscure or formerly concealed truths'. This was part of Boyle's longstanding belief that certainty, particularly religious certainty, was prone to error without an appropriate framing of 'Rules & Maximes upon the Axioms of People acknowledg'd skillful in their owne Professions, when neither our Reason noe experience persuade us to the contrary'.[41]

In conclusion, the evidence presented here makes it more probable that Boyle's apocalyptic eschatology belonged to a perception closer to the Protestant mainstream than was typical of most natural philosophers and virtuosi he associated with, though natural philosophy took on a particular significance within that eschatology. Boyle could perceive himself as one of God's instruments in bringing about a new 'Revolution' in both science and divinity before the final transformation of a new heaven and a new earth. He had cause to think that this might be close at hand, a sentiment shared by others in the Hartlib circle. However, it was essentially a spiritual rather than political vision and therefore we can take Jacob's description as it stands, without its allusion to Boyle's material interests, as a change that 'would be in the nature of an intellectual, moral, and spiritual reformation, a reform of conduct and not of

[41] Gilbert Burnet, *A sermon preached at the funeral of the Honourable Robert Boyle* (London, 1692), 27 and in Boyle, *Works*, I, cxli; Pett, *A discourse* (1660), 9–10; Boyle to Marcombes, 22 October 1646 (Boyle, *Works*, I, xxxii–xxxiii); Royal Society, Boyle Papers, 7, fol. 285r; 'Daily Reflection' in *Early essays*, 230.

institutions'.[42] Indeed, the very idea of a political Utopia, though close to the heart of Hartlib, was not really part of Boyle's disposition, which rather centred on the notion 'that Vertu is the Cement of humane society'.[43] Similarly, it is doubtful that Boyle embraced the Restoration with a specific political agenda for the advancement of the mechanical philosophy beyond the desire for strong central government and a broadly based irenic church.

It is, of course, perfectly legitimate to conjecture that millennial beliefs were secretly held by Boyle, much as his alchemical beliefs largely were, perhaps expressed in private correspondence which was subsequently destroyed. After all, one only needs to be reminded of Boyle's puritan friend, Richard Baxter, studying Revelation secretly in prison in 1686 while a Roman Catholic ruled England or Newton's secretive studies on the same book, to recognize how aware Boyle must have been 'of the damaging effect upon less tutored minds of such speculations'.[44] Among the Boyle Papers, for example, can be found notes almost certainly written in the later part of Boyle's life by one of his assistants, Hugh Greg, on the meaning of various numbers in the book of Revelation as predicting the overthrow of Rome.[45] It does not, with its elaborate number calculations, reflect the personal commitment of Boyle, but it may at least indicate that Boyle continued to be alert to millennial speculation. However, my suggestion has been that the temper of Boyle's understanding of knowledge, opinion and belief pointed towards a different vision in which Christianized atomism and the advancement of learning provided the appropriate historical ciphers for his religious eschatology.

[42] Jacob, 'Boyle's circle in the Protectorate', 137.   [43] *Early essays*, 146.
[44] William Lamont, *Richard Baxter and the millennium* (London, 1979), 15.
[45] Royal Society, Boyle Papers, 3, fols. 98–9.

PART II

The communication of knowledge
Secrecy vs. openness

Closed and open languages: Samuel Hartlib's involvement with cryptology and universal languages

Gerhard F. Strasser

Besides the larger and interrelated subjects that engaged Samuel Hartlib, such as education and the advancement of learning, his involvement with cryptology and universal languages may not appear so self-evidently relevant to his other interests or of such transcendant importance. Nonetheless, the vicissitudes of communication in war-torn Europe and in the England of the Civil War provided reason enough for members of the widespread European intellectual community such as Hartlib and his correspondents to resort to various means of 'closed' communication and concealment in parts of their letters. By the same token, it was this very group of scholars who – in their efforts to bring about peace and unification in the different religious factions – seriously considered the development of a truly open, dogmatically neutral means of (written) communication. I shall here attempt to outline some of the most important systems of both kinds of communication that were available to scholars such as Hartlib around the middle of the seventeenth century. In so doing, I intend to show that the 'art of cryptology' is closely associated with attempts at creating a *lingua universalis*. 'The arts of cryptology' was the expression used by the seventeenth-century authority on the subject, Gustavus Selenus (alias Duke August the Younger of Brunswick-Lüneburg),[1] in his 1624 *Cryptomenytices et cryptographiae libri IX*.[2] Although cryptology had always appealed to scholars trained in mathematical and combinatorial skills, men such as Johannes Trithemius, Athanasius Kircher, or John Wilkins – to name only a few – enjoyed a linguistic

---

[1] Gustavus Selenus is correctly identified as the author of this work in Hartlib's papers (HP 8/47). Gustavus Selenus is tentatively identified as Duke August who, together with Juan Caramuel (another major seventeenth-century writer on cryptological and mathematical-combinatorial matters), was supposedly the only one to have elucidated the 'thirty-one spirits' in the *Steganographia* of Johannes Trithemius.

[2] *Praefatio* (Lüneburg, 1624), fols. a5r–a6v, as well as 3–5, 6–8.

awareness that enabled them to use cryptological elements in their efforts to create new means of universal communication.[3]

It should not come as a surprise that Hartlib either owned a copy of Duke August's *Cryptomenytices* or had easy access to one, and certainly he was familiar with its cryptological contents. In a letter sent from Paris on 8 October 1655, Etienne Polier, a Swiss citizen and political informant, offered to provide Hartlib with inside information on the French court. Such communication, he added, would necessarily have to be carried out in cipher and he inquired whether Hartlib wanted him to use one of Hartlib's own ciphers, one of Polier's, or one taken from the book of Selenus (as Polier referred to the author), 'qui en a traitté en Maistre'.[4] In the dedication to Emperor Ferdinand II, Duke August (alias Selenus) had stressed the practical use of his compendium, which offered numerous systems and choices to the knowledgeable user – an aspect the duke had not emphasized in the body of his work, however, partly because he feared 'misuses' by men such as Polier.[5] The preface explained that the duke had originally only planned an elucidation and illustration of the *Steganographia* of the German abbot, Johannes Trithemius (1462–1516), but that this task had soon revealed the need for a systematic analysis of the entire field of cryptology.

In his *Steganographia*, which was written around 1500 but not published until 1606 since it was suspected of black magic, Trithemius suggested that some of the cryptological schemes he had devised could also be used for the opposite purpose, namely universal communication.[6] During the sixteenth century, therefore, a number of highly coveted manuscript copies of this work circulated in the scholarly world. John Dee, for example, owned one. At the threshold of modern cryptology, Trithemius covered up simple

---

[3] This chapter is based in part on my book, *Lingua universalis: Kryptologie und Theorie der Universalsprachen im 16. und 17. Jahrhundert*, Wolfenbütteler Forschungen 38 (Wiesbaden, 1988), esp. on chap. 1A, 29–63.

[4] HP 7/118/1B. I am indebted to Professor Leonard Forster, Cambridge, for this reference. See also Gerhard F. Strasser, 'Geheimschrift', *Sammler – Fürst – Gelehrter: Herzog August zu Braunschweig und Lüneburg 1579–1666* (Wolfenbüttel, 1979), 181–91, here 190.

[5] Duke August, *Cryptomenytices*, fol. a6v. See also Gerhard F. Strasser, 'The noblest cryptologist; Duke August the Younger of Brunswick-Lüneburg (Gustavus Selenus) and his cryptological activities', *Cryptologia: A Quarterly Journal Devoted to All Aspects of Cryptology*, 7 (1983), 193–217, esp. on 206.

[6] *Steganographia. Hoc est: ars per occultam scripturam animi sui voluntatem absentibus aperiendi certa . . . Praefixa est huic operi sua clavis* (Frankfurt, 1606).

vowel–consonant substitutions through a great number of 'magic' formulas in which only certain letters of the incantations and conjurations signified the meaning, while the other letters were nulls.[7] The third part of the incomplete *Steganographia*, however, defies interpretation,[8] and this portion has long been considered the abbot's abortive attempt to write a treatise on magic under the guise of cryptology.[9] It seems that this third part most interested Hartlib.

In 1508, Trithemius drafted the manuscript of his *Polygraphia*, which was published in 1518, two years after his death, and thus became the first printed book on cryptology. True to the meaning of 'multifold writing' implied in its title, Trithemius' polygraphic system consists of lists of words paired up with each of the twenty-four plain-text letters of his alphabet. These lists contain words from the same group, such as nouns, verbs, adjectives, adverbs; the author selected them so carefully that the correspondences for the letters – when taken from consecutive lists – yield an acceptable cipher-text, namely a rather inconspicuous prayer. (This is the reason for calling the system the 'Ave Maria' cipher.) The selection of the letter in each list or table is determined by the respective letter in the plain-text, as is seen when we look at the top lines of the first four columns of Book 1 of the *Polygraphia*:

a Deus	a clemens	a creans	a celos
b Creator	b clementissimus	b regens	b celestia
c Conditor	c pius	c conseruans	c supercelestia
d Opifex	d pijssimus	d moderans	d mundum[10]

If, for example, the name *abbas Trithemius* at the beginning of a secret message had to be enciphered, DEUS would have to be selected from the first column, CLEMENTISSIMUS from the second, then REGENS and CELOS, and so forth. These words, taken together, yield the beginning of a Latin prayer: DEUS CLEMENTISSIMUS REGENS CELOS [MANIFESTET OPTANTIBUS LUCEM SERAPHICAM / *CUM OMNIBUS* / DILEC-

---

[7] David Kahn called them 'nonsense words' in his standard work, *The codebreakers: the story of secret writing* (New York, 1967), 130–2. See also Strasser, 'The noblest cryptologist', 203.

[8] It is no longer the 'polygraphic' system planned in 1499 and indeed executed by Trithemius in his second cryptological work, the *Polygraphiae libri sex* (Basle, 1518).

[9] For a discussion of recent views on this third book and further references, see Strasser, *Lingua universalis*, 42–4. For a discussion of this third book in Hartlib's correspondence, see note 1.

[10] Trithemius, *Polygraphia*, fol. A1r–A1v. See also Strasser, *Lingua universalis*, 44–6.

TIS / *SUIS IN* / PERPETUUM / *AMEN* / ...]¹¹ Trithemius' polygraphic method was indeed used to transmit a message successfully from Constantinople to Venice, as Blaise de Vigenère, himself the author of a major sixteenth-century treatise on cryptology, reported.¹²

Apart from the first two books with variations on the 'Ave Maria' cipher, Trithemius' *Polygraphia* contains the first printed polyalphabetic substitution table or tableau (*see* fig. 7.1). The publication of this famous square table is one of the milestones in the history of cryptology, and enabled German cryptologists finally to catch up with their counterparts in Italy and France. With its sixteenth-century modifications by Giovanni Battista della Porta and Blaise de Vigenère, the tableau established itself as a standard item in cryptology and would have been one of the methods considered by Hartlib in his own cryptologic enterprises.

For the purposes of this analysis, it is important to look at the *Clavis polygraphiae* bound in with the 1518 edition. In this key, Trithemius gave a number of reasons for the value and safety of his polygraphic system. It is here that we encounter anew what Trithemius had devised as early as 1499: hidden in this polygraphic invention, Trithemius suggested, was the potential use of the method for purposes of 'universal' – and not secret – communication. A person not versed in Latin could use the lists drawn up in Books I or II to write, read, speak and understand this language (albeit within the limits of these lists, the abbot added) – and all that in a few days or even hours.¹³ It is clear how Trithemius conceived of such universal communication with the help of his Latin tables: as long as sender and recipient of a message possessed the same word-lists, anyone speaking only German, French or Dutch could 'transform' a message into a Latin prayer text and openly send it to his correspondent – who in turn could 'reconstruct' this text and recreate the original message. It is this principle of transmission via a neutral language or medium – be it Latin or a mathematical number sequence, as would be suggested in the seventeenth century – that was to become one of the two bases for the development of universal languages 150 years after its invention

¹¹ Various connectors – such as prepositions, pronouns or adverbs – are printed vertically to the right of a number of columns to provide the syntactical framework. To highlight them here, they are printed in italics between slashes.
¹² *Traicté des chiffres, ou secretes manieres d'escrire* (Paris, 1586), fol. 183r–183v.
¹³ *Clavis polygraphiae* (separately paginated), fol. BIV.

Recta transpositionis tabula.

a	b	c	d	e	f	g	h	i	k	l	m	n	o	p	q	r	s	t	u	x	y	z	w	
b	c	d	e	f	g	h	i	k	l	m	n	o	p	q	r	s	t	u	x	y	z	w	a	
c	d	e	f	g	h	i	k	l	m	n	o	p	q	r	s	t	u	x	y	z	w	a	b	
d	e	f	g	h	i	k	l	m	n	o	p	q	r	s	t	u	x	y	z	w	a	b	c	
e	f	g	h	i	k	l	m	n	o	p	q	r	s	t	u	x	y	z	w	a	b	c	d	
f	g	h	i	k	l	m	n	o	p	q	r	s	t	u	x	y	z	w	a	b	c	d	e	
g	h	i	k	l	m	n	o	p	q	r	s	t	u	x	y	z	w	a	b	c	d	e	f	
h	i	k	l	m	n	o	p	q	r	s	t	u	x	y	z	w	a	b	c	d	e	f	g	
i	k	l	m	n	o	p	q	r	s	t	u	x	y	z	w	a	b	c	d	e	f	g	h	
k	l	m	n	o	p	q	r	s	t	u	x	y	z	w	a	b	c	d	e	f	g	h	i	
l	m	n	o	p	q	r	s	t	u	x	y	z	w	a	b	c	d	e	f	g	h	i	k	
m	n	o	p	q	r	s	t	u	x	y	z	w	a	b	c	d	e	f	g	h	i	k	l	
n	o	p	q	r	s	t	u	x	y	z	w	a	b	c	d	e	f	g	h	i	k	l	m	
o	p	q	r	s	t	u	x	y	z	w	a	b	c	d	e	f	g	h	i	k	l	m	n	
p	q	r	s	t	u	x	y	z	w	a	b	c	d	e	f	g	h	i	k	l	m	n	o	
q	r	s	t	u	x	y	z	w	a	b	c	d	e	f	g	h	i	k	l	m	n	o	p	
r	s	t	u	x	y	z	w	a	b	c	d	e	f	g	h	i	k	l	m	n	o	p	q	
s	t	u	x	y	z	w	a	b	c	d	e	f	g	h	i	k	l	m	n	o	p	q	r	
t	u	x	y	z	w	a	b	c	d	e	f	g	h	i	k	l	m	n	o	p	q	r	s	
u	x	y	z	w	a	b	c	d	e	f	g	h	i	k	l	m	n	o	p	q	r	s	t	
x	y	z	w	a	b	c	d	e	f	g	h	i	k	l	m	n	o	p	q	r	s	t	u	
y	z	w	a	b	c	d	e	f	g	h	i	k	l	m	n	o	p	q	r	s	t	u	x	
z	w	a	b	c	d	e	f	g	h	i	k	l	m	n	o	p	q	r	s	t	u	x	y	
w	a	b	c	d	e	f	g	h	i	k	l	m	n	o	p	q	r	s	t	u	x	y	z	

In hac tabula literarū canonica fiue recta tot ex uno & ufuali noftro latinarum literarum ipfarum per mutationem feu tranfpofitione habes alphabeta, quot in ea per totum funt monogrammata, uidelicet quater & uigefies quatuor & uiginti, quæ faciunt in numero D.lxxvi. ac per to tide multiplicata, paulo efficiunt minus q̄ quatuordecem milia.

o ij

Figure 7.1 Polyalphabetic substitution table or tableau taken from Johannes Trithemius' *Polygraphia libri sex* (Basle, 1518) [reproduced with permission of the Herzog-August Bibliothek, Wolfenbüttel]

by Trithemius.

Towards the end of the sixteenth century, the earliest information on the Chinese and Japanese languages and their writing systems became available, and acquainted Europeans with the notion of a direct correspondence between the sign and the 'thing' it symbolized. In his 1605 work, *Of the proficience and advancement of learning*, Francis Bacon expressed these ideas as follows: 'It is the use of China and the kingdoms of the high Levant to write in Characters Real, which express neither letters nor words in gross, but Things or Notions; insomuch as countries and provinces, which understand not one another's language, can nevertheless read one another's writings, because the characters are accepted more generally than the languages do extend.'[14] In the 1623 expanded Latin version (*De dignitate et augmentis scientiarum*), Bacon reiterated his ideas and stated: 'Any book written in characters of this kind can be read off by each nation in their own language.'[15] These were seminal statements which influenced language reformers throughout the seventeenth century. At the same time the expanded version contained Bacon's famous 'biliteral cipher', which is still known in cryptological handbooks. Bacon claimed to have invented this cipher in his youth in Paris and managed to express all letters of the alphabet by means of A and B only; plain-text a becomes AAAAA, b AAAAB, c AAABA and so on.[16]

While these various considerations were important in preparing the groundwork for a discussion of universal languages, the most serious reason for the creation of such a tool was the gradual demise of Latin as the undisputed *lingua universalis*. The causes for the retrenchment of Latin are manifold; in England, for example, the use of the vernacular was no longer part of an evolutionary process, as Vivian Salmon has shown, but was strongly advocated by the puritans, who systematically opposed the teaching and use of the 'Popish tongue'.[17] This was one of the reasons for the surprising support the universal language idea received in mid-seventeenth-

---

[14] Bacon, *Works*, III, 399-400. This passage is printed almost verbatim in John Wilkins' early cryptological work, *Mercury, or the secret and swift messenger: shewing how a man may with privacy and speed communicate his thoughts to a friend at any distance* (London, 1641), 106-7.
[15] Bacon, *Works*, IV, 439-40.
[16] Bacon, *Works*, IV, 445ff. See also Johann Ludwig Klüber, *Kryptographik: Lehrbuch der Geheimschreibkunst* (Tübingen, 1809), 122-7.
[17] Introduction to *The works of Francis Lodwick. A study of his writings in the intellectual context of the seventeenth century*, ed. Vivian Salmon (London, 1972), 46-8.

Figure 7.2 Francis Godwin's musical cipher of the name of *Gonsales*, the protagonist of *The man in the moone*

century England. Samuel Hartlib has to be considered a catalyst in these endeavours since he was responsible for bringing Jan Amos Comenius to England.

Two prime examples of the interrelation between cryptology and universal languages based on mathematical-combinatorial (and not philosophical) systems can be found in England in the early half of the century. The first is Francis Godwin's musical language in his utopian novel, *The man in the moone*, published posthumously in 1638. As early as 1620–1, Godwin and his son, Thomas, had submitted to King James I a design 'for conveying Intelligence into Besieged Towns and Fortresses, and Receiving Answers therefrom'.[18] The court was not interested in their proposal and in 1629 the material was recast in the more extensive, but not necessarily clearer, *Nuncius inanimatus*.[19]

Six years after Godwin's death, the novel *The man in the moone: or a discourse of a voyage thither*, purportedly written 'by Domingo Gonsales / The speedy Messenger', finally appeared. And for the first time, Godwin's cryptological knowledge was being used in the creation of a cipher-like means of universal communication, more precisely a musical cipher. Gonsales described his 'lunatique language' in terms of the tonal values of the Chinese language and showed how his own name could be written in the musical notation of this language (*see* fig. 7.2).

[18] PRO SP 14/210/11; quoted by H. Neville Davis, 'Bishop Godwin's "Lunatique Language"', *Journal of the Warburg and Courtauld Institutes*, 30 (1967), 296–316.

[19] An English translation by Thomas Smith appeared in 1657, reprinted in '*The man in the moone' and 'Nuncius inanimatus'*, ed. Grant McColley (Northampton, MA, 1937), 49–67. In the *Nuncius*, Godwin refers to carrier pigeons as well as smoke, fire and acoustical signals that can relay information over great distances and in a very short time by means of chains of sending and receiving stations.

It seems that the printers of the later editions saw little value in this and a subsequent example; both were corrupted in the 1657 edition and omitted in all following ones.

John Wilkins was not so dismissive. He studied the two notations of the 1638 text, realized that both tonal quality and quantity were needed to determine the letter value of each note, and devised the entire alphabet for his 1641 handbook of cryptology, *Mercury: or, the secret and swift messenger: shewing how a man may with privacy and speed communicate his thoughts to a friend at any distance.* The subtitle of this, the third of Wilkins' books aimed at popularizing science, indicates the thrust of the work. In it, the author discussed methods of secret communication, although he was aware of the potential misuse of his material – but then, he felt that 'if all those useful inventions that are liable to abuse, should therefore be concealed, there is not any art or science which might be lawfully profest'.[20]

Wilkins introduced the alphabet based on Godwin's suggestions by stating: 'The lunary inhabitants . . . have continued the letters of the alphabet upon the notes after some such order as this:'[21]

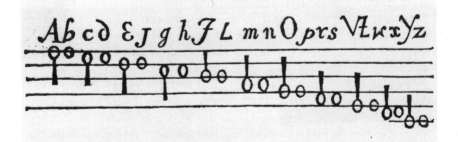

Figure 7.3 John Wilkins' 'musical alphabet' in his 1641 *Mercury: or, the secret and swift messenger*

He then commented on the cipher-like character of this notation and engaged in the thought of actually reversing the cryptological character of this means of communication by using the notes as a

[20] *Mercury: or, the secret and swift messenger*, accessible in: *The mathematical and philosophical works of the Right Rev. John Wilkins*, 2 vols. (London, 1970), II, 87.
[21] Wilkins, *Mathematical works*, II, 73–5 and chap. 17: 'Concerning a language that may consist only of tunes and musical notes, without any articulate sounds.' In the alphabet reproduced from the 1641 edition of the *Mercury*, the letters J and F are reversed.

'universal character': 'But now if these inarticulate sounds be contrived for the expression, not of words and letters, but of things and notions (as was before explained, concerning the universal character), then might there be such a general language, as should be equally speakable by all people and nations . . .'.[22]

John Wilkins gives us the best seventeenth-century example of the use of a cryptological device for the reverse purpose, namely universal communication. Chapter thirteen of his *Mercury* contains a rather erudite discussion of what, in 1641, he considered a 'universal character'. It should not come as a surprise that the sources from which he drew his inspiration comprised most of the standard handbooks of cryptology. This chapter-long excursion from cryptology to universal communication formed the basis for Wilkins' lifelong preoccupation with the idea of a universal language, although he ultimately abandoned the mathematical-combinatorial system in favour of a philosophically based universal language.[23]

The publication of Wilkins' *Mercury* occurred in the same year in which, after a ten-year correspondence, Samuel Hartlib finally managed to bring Comenius to England. During this stay, which lasted into mid-1642, Comenius and the Hartlib circle discussed the foundation of a universal college and the creation of a universal tongue, one of the college's preconditions. Comenius' parting gift to his English friends, the draft of his *Via lucis*, may well have contained his definition of a universal language as it appeared in the printed version of 1668.[24] The seed of these ideas continued to bring forth language projects; in 1647, Hartlib supported the publication of Francis Lodwick's first proposal for a universal character entitled *A common writing*.[25] Hartlib's diaries and correspondence are full of references to language projects in England and on the continent during this period. Early in 1657, Cave Beck published *The*

---

[22] *Ibid.* The reference to the previous discussion was to chap. 13: 'Concerning an universal character, that may be legible to all nations and languages. The benefit and possibility of this.'

[23] This topic has recently been treated by Werner Hüllen in *Their manner of discourse: Nachdenken über Sprache im Umkreis der Royal Society* (Tübingen, 1989), in particular in the chapter entitled 'Über Konzepte von Universalsprachen', 148–94.

[24] Chap. 19: 'Lingvae universalis ratio', also chap. 21; now accessible in Comenius, xiv, 281–370.

[25] The subtitle identifies the project in the Trithemius succession: *Whereby two, although not understanding one the others language, yet by the helpe thereof, may communicate their minds one to another*; reprinted on 166–202 of Salmon, *The works of Francis Lodwick*.

universal character, by which all the nations of the world may understand one anothers conceptions, reading out of one common writing their own mother tongues (London, 1657), the first viable language project to appear in England.[26] This universal character, as the author stated in his introduction, could certainly also be used 'for secret Writing, [*for*] it is the most common Character whereby men indeavour to hide their Conceptions from an intercepting hand'.[27] Shortly after the appearance of Beck's mathematical-combinatorial work, George Dalgarno, who in 1661 published the first philosophically based universal language scheme, *Ars signorum* (London, 1661), invited the public to subscribe to his entirely different work and wrote to Hartlib on 20 April 1657: 'As for my own judgement if it can be taken for impartial, I find [*Beck's universal character*] nothing else, but an enigmatical way of writing the English language.'[28]

Hartlib saw the *Ars signorum* and he was aware of Wilkins' preparatory work on his essay – which, however, did not appear until 1668, when Wilkins was finally able to publish *An essay towards a real character, and a philosophical language* (London, 1668). This 457-page folio, dedicated to the newly founded Royal Society – of which Wilkins was secretary – completely departed from his 1641 notions of a universal language and character as they were suggested by his cryptological research. The 1668 work relied on a complete reclassification of all 'things and notions', devised a 'Natural Grammar', and finally translated this into a system of universal writing that Wilkins called 'Real Character', which led to his universal – and philosophically, not cryptologically, based – language.

In closing, I would like to reiterate that John Wilkins is the prime example of a seventeenth-century scholar engaged in the business of devising a universal language who progressed from the mathematical-combinatorial systems derived from cryptology to an entirely new concept of universal communication, a system based on the reclassification of all knowledge along philosophical lines. Francis Bacon had provided a first impetus for this reorientation, but the main discussion of this philosophical 'langue universelle'

---

[26] A French version, *Le Charactère Universel*, appeared prior to the English one. See Salmon, *The works of Francis Lodwick*, 17–19, 130–1 and her article, 'Cave Beck: a seventeenth-century Ipswich schoolmaster and his "Universal Character"', *Proceedings of the Suffolk Institute of Archaeology*, 33 (1976), 285–98.

[27] Beck, *The universal character*, fol. B1v.

[28] BL Sloane MS 4377, fol. 148v, quoted by Mary M. Slaughter, *Universal languages and scientific taxonomy in the seventeenth century* (Cambridge, London, New York, 1982), 121.

began with a letter that René Descartes sent to his fellow scholar, Marin Mersenne, on 20 November 1629, in which he proposed such a reordering of all human notions by beginning with the 'idées simples' and building an entire philosophical system upon them. It was Wilkins who finally accomplished this reclassification, greatly aided by friends such as John Ray, responsible for the botanical 'tables', or Samuel Pepys, then working in the Naval Office, who wrote in his diary that he had provided Wilkins with 'some of [his] tables of navall matters, the names of rigging and the timbers about a ship'.[29]

---

[29] *The diary of Samuel Pepys*, ed. R. C. Latham and W. Matthews, 11 vols. (London, 1970–83), VI, 148 (1666).

CHAPTER 8

Language as the product and mediator of knowledge: the concept of J. A. Comenius

Jana Přívratská and Vladimír Přívratský

Jan Amos Komenský (Comenius) has become identified in the public mind mostly as the reformer of education whose ideas were deeply rooted in generalizations arrived at on the basis of his empirical experiences as a teacher. His ideas comprised implicitly, on the one hand, a psychological approach as well as a critical analysis of contemporary methods of education. On the other hand, they reflected his pansophical and panorthotical goal: to provide every human individual with an appropriate education.

His extensive published works (over 200 titles) cover, nevertheless, many fields of human knowledge and spheres of human activity. One of the issues he addressed throughout his life was that of language. The fields of his interest in this issue were multifarious, e.g. the lexical and syntactical aspects of language, etymology, proverbs, lexicography, exactitude of expression, oral forms of speech, differing capacities of expression in particular languages, the mother tongue, foreign languages, universal language and, at the most general, the relationships between speech, thought and reality. He carried out investigations that would, in a later generation, have been regarded as comparative linguistics. He also, among his many other interests in linguistic matters, analyzed individual languages with the aim of evaluating them according to general linguistic criteria.

The breadth of his language interests is unusual and remarkable. It attracts the attention of specialists in general linguistics as well as those in etymology, comparative linguistics, pedagogy, psychology, philosophy, the history of ideas, and the like, including those engaged in the historiography of linguistics. Many studies have been undertaken to analyze this cultural heritage, each from a specific point of view.[1] They therefore obviously pay less attention to the interrelationships between individual themes. The integrated nature of Comenius' thinking on language is, however, the most rewarding aspect to study because, in turn, it gives breadth and a more decisive significance to the specific studies that language specialists undertake in their different spheres of interest.

Whether we approach Comenius' opinions on language for the purely philological, pedagogical–linguistic or socio-linguistic aspects of his conclusions we find, in fact, that Comenius based his patterns of thought on unified general principles of philosophy and methodology. This approach to language by Comenius means that it is conceived not as a vast mosaic, a summary of partial conclusions, but as a system of related elements, each integrated to his methodological and philosophical view of the world.

The basic location for the question of language in Comenius' thought is provided by the basic philosophical triad: *res – mens – lingua*. This triad defines the framework within which Comenius developed a profuse system of interrelationships and dependencies. His methodological approach consisted, first and foremost, of analogy, parallelism and syncrisis – i.e. a comparative method. This methodological apparatus was intended to identify the optimal solutions in keeping with the axiomatic demands of a universal panharmony. In keeping with this apparatus, the basic triad was transformed into the derived triads: *mens – lingua – manus*; *ratio – oratio – operatio*; *sapere – agere – loqui*, each one conforming to, and reinforcing, the different aspects of the relationship and its dynamics under investigation.

From the point of view of methodology (including the problems of language), Comenius' 'Triertium catholicum' is particularly interesting.[2] The preface provides a diagrammatic representation of the

---

[1] V. T. Miškovská-Kozáková, 'Comenius on lexical symbolism in an artificial language', *Philosophy*, 27 (1962), 238–44; K. Horálek, 'Zur Sprachphilosophie Comenius', *Acta Comeniana*, 1 (1969), 175–8; V. Skalička, 'Probleme der Panglottie', *Acta Comeniana*, 1 (1969), 179–81; G. B. Craemer, *Sprache und Sprachbildung in der Sicht des Comenius* (Tübingen, 1977); J. Caravolas, *Le Gutenberg de la didacographie ou Coménius et l'enseignement des langues* (Montreal, 1984); B. Aschbach-Schnitker, 'Introductory essay' in John Wilkins, *Mercury or the secret and swift messenger*, ed. Achim Eschbach (Amsterdam and Philadelphia, 1984); G. A. Padley, *Grammatical theory in western Europe, 1500–1700; trends in vernacular grammar*, 2 vols. (Cambridge, 1985–9); O. Pombo, *Leibniz and the problem of a universal language* (Münster, 1987); L. Formigari, *Language and experience in seventeenth-century British philosophy* (Amsterdam and Philadelphia, 1988); W. Hüllen, '*Their Manner of Discourse*'. *Nachdenken über Sprache im Umkreis der Royal Society* (Tübingen, 1989).

[2] 'Sapientiae primae usus Triertium catholicum appellandus' (*Comenius*, XVIII, 237–365).

entities *mens – lingua – manus* which he was studying. Although his
attention was mainly devoted in this treatise towards the relationships between work, speech and thought, what Comenius presents in
the preface is a tetrad, the fourth component of which is objective
reality (*res*). All the interrelationships of this tetrad are presented.
The parallel arrangement of the text of the 'Triertium' itself may
seem naive, mechanistic and over–simplifying of the phenomena it is
concerned to investigate. More detailed analysis, however, reveals
that this is a linear representation of the three basic entities and their
relationship to objective reality, and that Comenius is here displaying his sense for the relationships of the parts to the whole. Comenius
was aware of the stratified, polydimensional nature of the interrelationships between the elements in the triad *ratio – oratio – operatio*.
We may imagine his thought construction looking rather like this:

$$ratio \text{———} oratio \text{———} operatio$$
$$\diagdown \qquad\qquad\qquad \diagup$$
$$\longleftarrow (res) \text{– – – – – – –} (res/opus) \longrightarrow$$

Res/opus, the outcome of the process of thinking, speaking and acting
is, according to Comenius, qualitatively different and of a higher
order than the former *res*. This newly formed *res* then, in its turn,
affects the mind and senses, is newly communicated by speech and is
itself finally expressed in a higher, practical form. This process is
constantly being repeated in an upward spiral. The dialectic results
in movement. This methodological approach of Comenius in the
field of language means that it does not deprive language of its
dynamic aspects, of the possibilities for constant adaptation and
change. This plays an important role in his ideas on the function of
universal language, formed not as an end in itself, but determined
fully by the needs of a society undergoing reform.

   In order to be able to fulfil the tasks Comenius ascribes to
language in his vision of a new society, mankind has to be fully
prepared. For this reason, Comenius stressed two areas of necessary
endeavour: the cultivation of language itself; and the pedagogical
aspects of the acquisition of a knowledge of language. By these two
means alone could the requirements for an adequate verbal expression of the 'world of things' be met and the demanding social
function of language in Comenius' emendatory conception of
human society be realized. It is in this framework alone that
Comenius' linguistic activities become fully comprehensible.

Comenius' efforts in the field of language are closely related to his conviction that mankind is capable of acquiring knowledge and that, on the basis of that knowledge, he is obliged consciously to form his character in such a way that it brings into harmony his activity with the world he is living in and learning about. The degree to which this happens depends on man's self-reflection, which consequently depends on the quality of man's character. This is why Comenius stresses that the specifically human attribute of language requires conscious individual human application.

The process of knowledge acquisition which came about from relating the human phenomenon to reality and its results had to be embodied and communicated in language. This process was, however, the only way in which mankind would confront the challenges that face him. Comenius longed to reform the world, and it is precisely in this perspective that his justifications for the significance and role of language emerge.

Comenius was profoundly convinced that language, albeit a divine gift, was dependent upon human cultivation for its quality and social effectiveness. He saw the origin, existence and functioning of language as linked to man's nature as a social being. It was thus integral to his nature and accompanied him throughout his life. From the viewpoint of language, human life begins with '*nihil sermonis*' and ends with '*omnia sermonis*'.[3] Without the help of others, without society, mankind would never progress beyond that first stage – for speech does not develop spontaneously, as Comenius demonstrated by the example of 'children fostered by wolves'.[4] Without society, man would remain '*nihil*'. Thus, in terms of language, Comenius expressed the social character of human life. All stages between '*nihil*' and '*omnia sermonis*' are, in fact, dependent on the education process. This means that '*omnia sermonis*' is the final outcome of education in language as a social process. The quality of speech, however, does not reflect the level of general knowledge that had previously been achieved and, therefore, Comenius inevitably focuses on revealing the principles by which language is controlled and speech performed, because this is fundamental to the acquisition and communication of knowledge. It is thus man's duty to foster his own language skills.

For scholars in the history of linguistics, however, Comenius has

---

[3] *Ibid.*, 256.   [4] *Didactica magna*, in *ODO*, chap. 6, para. 6, cols. 35–6.

become known as the proponent of universal language. This activity corresponds to similar efforts in the same direction by his contemporaries and, since it has already been extensively analysed elsewhere, we need not discuss it in detail here.[5] We need only mention here that, contrary to many of his contemporaries, Comenius did not lose sight of man as the user of a new, artificial language. He thus refused the temptation to reduce the linguistic problems of the relationship between language and knowledge to the level of mathematical logic, and recognized that a language had to be simple and easy to learn as well as comprehensive, accurate and clear, above all capable of communicating overall knowledge. These criteria applied not merely to a newly formed, ideal language, albeit created by those whom Comenius regarded as the best scholars, but also to all extant, living languages.

Our analysis of the main trends in Comenius' thought on language suggests that he had a theory of language. One of the most exacting demands of linguistic theory is to analyze and describe the transition of a linguistic system from one stage to another, and Comenius does not evade the issue.[6] An ideal linguistic theory would include a set of theorems that would allow us to forecast the way a given linguistic system would change and react.[7] Comenius' conception fails to match this ideal, but then so does all known linguistic theory. To meet it would require a knowledge of all relevant external circumstances affecting linguistic development. In a general sense, though, the transition of language from one stage to another can be viewed synchronically or diachronically, and both approaches are to be found in Comenius. He concentrated on the dialectical tension between language and reality. He remarked, for instance, that two people speaking the same language about the same subject may use their common language differently. Comenius realized that language reflects continuous reality by dissociating discrete elements that are associated by the subject with a variety of objects, processes, and so on. He rightly perceived that these elements are meaningful, and that the speaker passes on his message by linking these meaningful elements of language in a sequence

---

[5] J. Přívratská, 'Panglottia – the universal reform of language', *Acta Comeniana*, 5 (1983), 133–42; V. T. Miškovská-Kozáková, 'Comenius' linguistic theory and experiment', *Acta Comeniana*, 4/2 (1979), 291–319.

[6] See his *Panglottia*, the fifth part of *De rerum humanarum emendatione consultatio catholica* (henceforth *Consultatio*), 2 vols. (Prague, 1966), II, cols. 147–204.

[7] V. Krupa, *Jednota a variabilita jazyka* (Bratislava, 1980), 18.

which can report on events, states of affairs, and so on. This may be why he suggested in his diary that one should seek parallel entities by analysing language.[8] In this way, discrete elements of speech create a reflected analogue of the fragment of reality under discussion. For, as Comenius put it: 'Speech mirrors things; speech ... is not concerned with nothing in particular, but with things, the images of which the speaker carries in his mind, which he clothes in words and hands on to the mind of his listener.'[9]

The diachronic level of consideration of the transition from one language system to another over time is constantly present throughout *Panglottia*, representing both Comenius' perception of language as a human product and also as the product of a long historical evolution. From the general linguistic point of view we might describe the creation of a universal language by Comenius as the ultimately irreversible diachronic transformation deliberately carried out by man himself. It might also be seen as only possible when there is sufficient understanding of the function and laws governing synchronic transformations and their relations within language seen as a diachronistic phenomenon. In this way, language becomes a product of the realization of human knowledge.

A further intriguing series of questions, sometimes elaborated in great detail by Comenius and in other places only cautiously touched on, concerns the future epistemological function of language. Superficially Comenius seems to find himself in a state of insoluble conflict. On the one hand, he believed in the existence of a complete or absolute (as it were) system of acquired knowledge of things, the essential requirement for an absolutely equivalent expression of these things in verbal terms. On the other hand, Comenius' firm conviction was that the human mind was capable of infinite understanding, that it was never content with the known but sought further revelation of the divine mysteries, a revelation which he believed was man's God-given right.

Yet was this in fact an insoluble conflict? Perhaps it would be better to consider that he approached the matter at two levels, both of which intertwined and mutually conditioned his writings concerning the formation of a universal language and the social function of language. For the new universal language to fulfil gradually

[8] D. Čapková, *Neznámý deník Komenského*, supplement to *Studia Comeniana et historica*, 8–9 (1974), 1–108.
[9] *Methodus linguarum novissima*, in *ODO*, Part 2, chap. 4, para. 3.

all the requirements set by Comenius – that is, for it to be objective, harmonious, philosophical – it must be based on maximum knowledge of the material and the spiritual world, of all its aspects and its interrelations. Such a language can only be elaborated, according to Comenius, on the basis of the necessary knowledge of linguistic laws. This new artificial language would be natural, something which Comenius appreciated as its great advantage, because it would offer a conscious reflection of the observed qualities and laws of things. It follows that this conscious reflection of reality, material and spiritual, would be dependent on the highest possible degree of knowledge. There was a direct correlation: the higher the degree of our knowledge, the more fruitful would become our efforts to understand the qualities of relations in all things and their place in the hierarchy of creation; and the deeper we understand the significance of the underlying relationships, the better we shall become at the scientific construction of a universal language. Since, however, the world is in constant flux, and things (in the widest sense of the term) are constantly in contact, changing and influencing one another, this must also apply in the sphere of language. Language should become such that it can reflect exactly and to the maximum extent the quality and quantity of the things it expresses, including the changes that may take place. Indeed Comenius makes further demands: this new language should express the reasons for change, reasons which, when fed back, could further promote knowledge. Thus this second level of Comenius' thought is not concerned with the immediate future but the distant prospect of humanity. The apparent conflict becomes a functionally inevitable one which reveals the distinction between the immediate goals and the longer-term aims of Comenius.

Seen in this light, Comenius' practical attempt to elaborate a universal language – the *Novae harmonicae linguae tentamen primum*[10] – was clearly conditioned by the possibilities of his time, entirely typical of the period. Yet his idea that true scientific knowledge was the necessary prerequisite for man to have a right to intervene so fundamentally in his means of communication still persists.

Once the new universal language acquired the qualities that Comenius insisted it must, it would no longer be an artificial language (as we understand it today) but an adaptable and viable

---

[10] Comenius, *Consultatio*, II, cols. 189–204.

means of human communication which faithfully expressed reality. This conception comes closer to our present idea of language as a system of relative stability, expressing both assimilatory (conservative) tendencies and accommodatory tendencies, allowing the system to change and evolve according to the needs of society. In spite of its apparent rigidity and static absolute state, which (as we have suggested) were formal and derived from the European metaphysical and philosophical way of thinking, the conception of universal language held by Comenius was essentially dynamic, for it included and assumed diachronical changes, constant regeneration and restoration of the linguistic system in interaction with the process of acquiring knowledge. That was the kind of language he sought, but he did not arrive at a solution. And since it was unthinkable to him to lower his standards, he got no further than the experimental stage.

Although demanding the maximum correspondence between language and the reality it describes, Comenius did not identify reality (*res*) and its structure with language and the structure of the corresponding utterance. He understood that reality, thought and language are not identical, but that they exist in certain mutual relationships. This made it possible for him to approach language together with thought, against the background of the process of acquisition of knowledge. 'Speech is born of thought, and thought is provoked by things. Thought is the image of those things we have in mind, and speech is the image of those thoughts which pass through our minds.'[11] Comenius developed the theme again in this fashion:

Things have no extrinsic laws; they are what they are, and are ruled by their own laws. The concepts the mind forms are ruled both by themselves and by the objects of thought, the latter in the first place, and the former secondarily. Since these concepts are the image of things, they are bound to keep close to their model, just as my reflection in a mirror not only reflects my shape and colour, but my gestures as well. The concepts of the mind, however, must also be aware of their identity, so as not to interfere with other concepts, not to blur them, not to merge with them. Ultimately, words must take into account three things: the object, the concept, and their own existence.[12]

---

[11] *Methodus linguarum novissima*, in *ODO*, Part 2, chap. 2, para. 4.
[12] *Ibid.*, chap. 2, para 13.

From the perspective of his endeavour to solve all the problems of language, Comenius' work may be characterized as a continuous search for the optimal solution directed by the demands and pre-requisites that we have outlined. This effort was spread over an appreciable length of time, was of quite a specific nature and comprised his best work in terms of its scholarly, intellectual and creative ambitions. Yet it was the decade of the 1640s that was of primary importance when it came to the formation of Comenius' linguistic concepts. Firstly there was his masterpiece, the *Methodus linguarum novissima*, one of the manuscript versions of which is among the most valuable materials in Hartlib's papers.[13] In this treatise, Comenius tackles a whole range of problems, beginning with what would now be termed general linguistic points of departure, before taking up the topic of what is now known as comparative linguistics and then dealing with the theoretical issues of methodical patterns in language instruction (teaching and learning), a section where Comenius includes psychological and psycho-social insights. This treatise was undoubtedly stimulated by Comenius' need to come to terms with the relationship between the level of linguistic knowledge and its integration into the methods of modern language instruction.

The *Methodus linguarum* was completed in 1646 and published two years later. By this date, Comenius was working intensively on a set of language textbooks for Swedish schools and managing to bring to fruition his years of pedagogical experience. Moreover, at the same time he started to collect materials for an even more ambitious undertaking – that of the *Panglottia*. This should be regarded as the culmination of his endeavours in the area of linguistics.

In spite of the fact that this period did not give rise to any universal language projects (excluding the schemes for universal writing) it is evident that for Comenius and the development of his ideas on language, the 1640s were most significant. It was towards the middle of the decade that the close co-operation between Comenius and his student Cyprian Kinner began. Their interest in the principles of maximum correspondence between language and reality led them to utilize Aristotelian taxonomy with an intention to create a system of comprehensive language based on an encyclopaedic arrangement of things and notions.[14] We should be more aware of

---

[13] HP 35/5/1–180.
[14] M. M. Slaughter, *Universal languages and scientific taxonomy in the seventeenth century* (Cambridge, 1982).

the collaboration between Comenius and Kinner than of their methodological contradictions. More could be learnt from the Kinneriana among Hartlib's papers about their sense of common purpose. Those engaged in Comenius studies believe that these archives will carry forward our understanding of the relationship of Comenius with English planners of language and (as may very well be the case) Comenius' influence in their movement.

Some recent literature, contrary to its antecedents, tries to interpret this movement as something that arose *sui generis*, recognizing minimal inspiration from outside England.[15] The international dimension of the Hartlib Papers, however, demonstrates the mutual contacts that existed at every turn and the flow of information 'from' and 'into' England.

It is not difficult to imagine that, during his stay in London, Comenius may well have established direct contacts with those engaged in the field of language unification in England. Both before and after his visit to England, Comenius continued to correspond with Hartlib, who paid a great deal of attention to, and supported, those in England who were interested in the subject. The real possibility of Comenius' relations with English thinkers on language is of significance for interpreting his own approach to language issues. There is good historical justification for uniting Comenius' linguistic endeavours and the indigenous language-planners in England. We may suppose that the persistent attempt in England to create a real system of universal writing and, later, a universal system of language led Comenius to the conclusion that it was 'technically' possible to form such a new, philosophical means of communication.

It is interesting that, despite this background, there were only a few attempts to create a universal language in England as compared to the more numerous efforts to generate a real character. This may well be due to the probability that they originated with authors who came in contact with external impulses to a great extent and were influenced by them. These stimuli may well have been communicated or mediated by Comenius himself since his interests in this respect were identical to those of the English reformers, namely to solve the semantic tasks of the new science as the prerequisite of the advancement of learning.

---

[15] V. Salmon, *The study of language in seventeenth-century England* (Amsterdam, 1979).

Comenius insisted, however, on the projection of the results that would be achieved onto society because only in this context would they be meaningful. This is why, for Comenius, there was not only a relationship between language and thought but also between language and social activity, including work.

It was not long after his visit to England that Comenius began working on the *Panglottia*.[16] No doubt he was still under the influence of the discussions of the English attempts to create a universal language instrument capable of mirroring human perception of the world to a considerable degree and corresponding, above all, to the development of the natural sciences. The atmosphere was one of a lively interest in shorthand writing, in solving the relationships between language and knowledge, and in attempts to create universal script and language – all of which might be perceived as topics that would help him to meet his pansophical concept of the arrangement of human society as expressed in the *Via lucis*, composed in England in 1641–2.[17]

Beyond these attempts to solve the semantic problems of the new science, Comenius had a loftier aim. He was profoundly convinced that knowledge could not be limited to the perception of natural phenomena but comprised an understanding of human society, including human affairs. So the social function of language meant that society, having such an instrument, capable of precise and comprehensive expression of knowledge, at its disposal, should be capable of using it for its own emendation. This complex knowledge should serve as the basis for the perfect, socially functional vehicle of communication.

This dimension of Comenius' concept of knowledge is the reason why, many years later, he added a preface to the first edition of the *Via lucis*, published in 1668, addressed to the newly established Royal Society of London which called their urgent attention to the real sense of acquiring knowledge of the world: 'Vos igitur in Naturalibus Veritatis Mystae, eja rem strenue, agite! Ne semper a vana, manca, superficiaria, falsa, sine utilitate, subtili, Philosophia, genus Humanum ludificetur, efficite.'[18] At the same time, however,

---

[16] A. Patera, *Jana Amosa Komenského korrespondence* (Prague, 1892), 97 (Comenius to Louis de Geer, 8/18 April 1645) and 135 (Comenius to Hartlib, 12 June 1647).

[17] It was published later, in Amsterdam, in 1668.

[18] *Via lucis*, trans. E. T. Campagnac (Liverpool and London, 1938), 22: 'We bid you, then, who are priests in the realm of nature, to press on your labours with all vigour. See to it that mankind is not for ever marked by a Philosophy empty, superficial, false, uselessly vain.'

Comenius claims that 'non satis erit Rerum EXTRA NOS Scrutinia instituisse, majora etiam quaerenda erunt omnino: Veritas nempe rerum INTRA NOS, et Veritas regni Dei AD NOS. Quae si ignoramus, etiamsi mille Mundi extra nos sint, et nos intelligamus omnes, possideamusque cum suis thesauris omnes, nihil nobis proderit'.[19]

Comenius believed that language would be of a higher quality if improved consciously by man on the basis of a deep understanding of nature and human affairs. Such a language would be capable of communicating human knowledge effectively and thus of forming prerequisites for the advancement of learning. This advancement, in a mutually reinforcing process, would cause the further improvement of language. Knowledge and language, in Comenius' thought, represent an open, two-in-one, synergetic system, and one that is in a state of constant development.

---

[19] *Ibid.*, 25: 'We shall not be content to have set up inquiries into things without us; our search must be directed to objects altogether greater: for the Truth of things is within us and the Truth of the Kingdom of God is for us. If we have no knowledge of that Truth, even though there be a thousand worlds outside us and we understand them all and take possession of them all with all their treasures, yet it will profit us nothing.'

Authorship and ownership

CHAPTER 9

Milton among the monopolists: Areopagitica, intellectual property and the Hartlib circle

Kevin Dunn

In *Eikonoklastes*, Milton states: 'Human right commands that every author should have the property of his own work reserved to him after death as well as living.'[1] This sentence has attracted a good deal of critical attention because it appears to contain at least two notions that disturb the conventional chronologies of the history of ideas.[2] The first, which remains at the level of implication, is that the right to property inheres in a man's labour. The notion is surprising, of course, because it was written so long before Locke, in his *Second treatise of government* (1690), articulated his well-known theory that property has its origin and justification in human use and labour. The second notion, much more boldly asserted, is that a text is a thing that can be owned and that its author is its proper owner. Such a sense of ownership, as distinct from the very limited seventeenth-century sense of owning a 'copy', has generally been considered by historians of copyright and authorship to have been a product of the eighteenth century. It was made possible by the Copyright Act of 1709 (9 Anne, cap. 19), but not fully expounded until the case of *Millar* v. *Taylor* in 1769. As these historians are quick to note, however, the legal history of copyright is by no means coterminous with the history of publishing practice or of the arguments for and against that practice.

In order to pursue the question of authorial property itself,

---

[1] *Eikonoklastes* was first published in 1649 but the sentence in question was one of the numerous additions of the second edition of 1650. See *CPW*, III, 365.
[2] See, in particular, Richard Helgerson, 'Milton reads the king's book: print, performance, and the making of a bourgeois idol', *Criticism*, 29 (1987), 1–25; and Elisabeth M. Magnus, 'Originality and plagiarism in *Areopagitica* and *Eikonoklastes*', *English Literary Renaissance*, 21 (1991), 87–101. For a more general analysis of the history of intellectual property and authorship, see Martha Woodmansee, 'The genius and copyright: economic and legal conditions of the emergence of the "author"', *Eighteenth-Century Studies*, 17 (1983–4), 425–48; and Mark Rose, 'The author as proprietor: *Donaldson* v. *Becket* and the genealogy of modern authorship', *Representations*, 23 (1988), 51–85.

however, one must begin with the more rudimentary assumption on which notions of intellectual property are based, namely that information is, in fact, a commodity. I want to examine this assumption, which Milton works within yet challenges, by placing it in the context of the ideology of information, as epitomized in the writings of Samuel Hartlib and his associates.[3] This circle of puritans espoused free trade, an uncensored flow of ideas and the disinterested performance of public works. Such notions had been percolating in England in one form or another at least since the Commonwealth men of the mid-sixteenth century and are common in mercantilist literature, for instance, in the first decades of the seventeenth century.[4] But it was Hartlib (following Bacon, Comenius and others) who made the most concerted effort to institutionalize these notions, most notably in the Office of Address.

In this context, a seemingly anachronistic question of intellectual property opens out into the broader cultural issue of whether the market-place could constitute itself as a truly public institution, or only serve as a conduit for furthering private interests. The Hartlibians viewed the market with a steady fascination, yet ultimately felt the need for some intervening model of social and political incorporation. This cultural problematic translates into a number of important questions for the issues of textuality to be addressed here. First, are texts properly profit-bearing objects and are their authors the proper recipients of that profit? Much more importantly, will the market-place allow texts, momentarily 'de-monopolized' by the chaos of civil war, to exist without a reincorporation that separates them from their authors; that is, does hierarchy always reassert itself as a new form of incorporation? Finally, can the state itself become a means of avoiding incorporation; is there a body politic or social corpus to which the textual corpus can resort without authorial alienation? After examining these questions in the works of Hartlib and his associates, I will conclude with a brief look at Milton's *Areopagitica* as a meditation on these same concerns.

---

[3] Milton dedicated *Of education* to Hartlib and carried on a sporadic correspondence with him and other members of his circle. I am not suggesting, however, that Milton could be considered a 'Hartlibian'. The distance between the two men can be measured in the gap between Hartlib's Comenian ideas about education and the old-fashioned humanist pedagogy that dominates *Of education*.

[4] For the ideas and activities of the Commonwealth men, see Arthur B. Ferguson, *The articulate citizen and the English Renaissance* (Durham, NC, 1965).

THE 'TRADE IN KNOWLEDGE'

Perhaps the best-known manifesto of the Hartlib circle is Gabriel Plattes' *A description of the famous kingdome of Macaria* (1641), which treats the issue of whether knowledge is a commodity in its very self-presentation as a 'brief and pithy' redaction of More's *Utopia* and Bacon's *New Atlantis*, a puritan Utopia stripped of all humanist ornament, trimmed down to its unambiguous and utilitarian core.[5] The dialogue opens with a 'Traveller' meeting a 'Schollar' in the Royal Exchange and asking him: 'But what doe you heare in the Exchange; I conceive you trade in knowledge, and here is no place to traffick for it; neither in the book of rates is there any imposition upon such commodities: so that you have no great business either here or at the Custome-house. Come let us goe into the fields.'[6]

Plattes implies that information, the stuff of the 'intelligencing' traveller, bears at best an analogical relationship to the commodities at the Exchange and that its free passage, unencumbered by the custom-house, makes it the superior partner in this analogy ('it bee worth all the merchandize in the kingdome'). The two men retire to 'Moore fields' (Moorfields), the quasi-rural place of retired thoughts, to discuss in detachment the ideal state of Macaria, recently visited by the traveller. By the end of the pamphlet, however, once the traveller has sketched a society in which every department of government pertains either to production or to trade, the relationship between knowledge and the market-place has become less clearly metaphorical. The traveller asks: 'Well, doe you know any man that hath any secrets, or good experiments? I will give him gold for them, or others as good in exchange.'[7] Perhaps equally significant is the change of venue for their next meeting; the traveller suggests a meeting 'next Munday at the Exchange', trading the pretence of rural retirement at Moorfields for the mercantile bustle at the heart of the city. Yet if Plattes' interlocutors appear to have 'commodified' knowledge, they also give a backward glance at more 'rural' – humanist – models of knowledge, models that serve as a check on the market's drive towards privatized profits.

This ambivalence is built into the very structure of the Office of Address. The Office was to have served as a combination patent

---

[5] The text is that of *Samuel Hartlib and the advancement of learning*, ed. Charles Webster (Cambridge, 1970), 80.
[6] *Ibid.*   [7] *Ibid.*, 89.

office, employment agency, commodities exchange, spiritual counselling centre and public library. It was, in short, a clearing-house of information, and not just economic information. Its founders divided the agency into two 'Branches'. 'The Office of Bodily Addresses', or 'the Addresse of *Accomodations*', was created 'to Meddle with al Outward Things', namely goods and services, while 'the Office of Spirituall Addresses', or 'The Addresse of *Communications*', existed 'to meddle with all Inward things', including not only what we would call 'Spirituall' matters but also inventions and other 'Wayes whereby [*men*] may be helpfull one to another'.[8] Thus the Office of Address simultaneously analogizes knowledge and movable goods and attempts to enforce a difference between the two, to maintain the analogy as analogy and not to suggest an identity. In enforcing this difference, it reinforces the distinction made by its tutelary spirit, Bacon, who feared nothing more than premature profit taking from his new method. In the *New Atlantis*, he describes the 'Merchants of Light', who leave the scientific Utopia of Bensalem to 'maintain a trade, not for gold, silver, or jewels; nor for silks; nor for spices; nor any other commodity of matter; but only for God's first creature, which was light: to have light (I say) of the growth of all parts of the world'.[9] Bacon's merchants do, in fact, carry 'commodity of matter', but only to trade for 'God's first creature'. They remain resolutely uninterested in monetary profit.

Yet while enforcing Bacon's distinction, Hartlib is much more ready to test the waters that separate the two halves of the analogy than is his predecessor. In a prefatory epistle to a work of Cressy Dymock, Hartlib writes: 'It is nothing but the Narrownes of our Spirits that makes us miserable; for if our Hearts were enlarged beyond our selves, and opened to lay hold of the Advantages which God doth offer, whereby we may become joyntly serviceable unto one another in Publicke Concernments; we could not be without Lucriferous Employments for our selves; nor Unfruitful to our neighbours.'[10] The Latin original of 'Lucriferous' – *luciferum*, or 'lucre bearing' – is so uncommon that Hartlib's word seems likely to

---

[8] Samuel Hartlib, *A briefe discourse concerning the accomplishment of our reformation* (London, 1647), 42.

[9] Bacon, *Works*, III, 146–7.

[10] Cressy Dymock, *An essay for advancement of husbandry-learning: or propositions for the errecting colledge of husbandry* (London, 1651).

have been formed on a punning analogy to 'luciferous', 'light bearing', a Baconian key word. Criticizing those who would turn prematurely to profit taking, for instance, Bacon writes in the Preface to the *Instauratio magna*, 'fructifera (inquam) experimenta, non lucifera, quaesivit'.[11] The *Oxford English dictionary* first records 'lucriferous' in 1648, in William Petty's *Advice ... to Mr. Samuel Hartlib*, and the brief life of this semantic unit coincides entirely with the efforts of Petty, Hartlib, Dury and others to identify more fully the Baconian project of scientific collaboration in the public interest with economic theories that private enrichment could serve the public good.

THE 'BENEFIT OF MUTUALL COMMUNICATION'

These efforts are intimately connected with new notions of the body politic. John Dury states the ideological credo of his associates when he says: 'It is evident that the benefit of Mutuall Communication in good things is the Chief fruit of all Society.'[12] Such an ideology requires the rewriting of older notions of the state in which information was hierarchically distributed and controlled. In a series of letters to Sir Cheney Culpeper, published by Hartlib in 1642 under the title *A motion tending to the publick good of this age, and of posteritie*, Dury states again his faith in the salubrious effect of freely exchanged information, speaking of 'the liberty of publique communication of the best things, which in the kingdome of God must alwaies bee inviolably observed'.[13] Dury, who was to be responsible for the religious undertakings of the Office of Communications, formulates his description of the *res publica* in such a way that, despite the theological framework, one can still sense the new idea, pre-dating Hobbes' *Leviathan*, that the public good is, in fact, a composite of the good of each private citizen and, concomitantly, that public discourse can and should be constituted out of discrete acts of private speech: 'A Publique good', he writes, 'is nothing else but the universall private good of every one in the life of God', and

---

11 Bacon, *Works*, I, 128 (trans. IV, 17: 'it [*that is, previous scientific experimentation*] has sought, I say, experiments of Fruit, not experiments of Light').
12 John Dury, *Considerations tending to the happy accomplishment of Englands Reformation* (London, 1647), 41.
13 Cited in Webster (ed.), *Samuel Hartlib*, 107–8.

'none can procure this good to others, farre lesse to all, that doth not seeke it for himselfe, and in some measure purchase it.'[14]

Dury articulates this description of the public good in the face of, and in reaction to, the system of patents and monopolies that had largely outgrown its intended purpose of stimulating native industry and turned into a tool of the patronage system. An Act of 1624 had curtailed the granting of monopolies to individuals, but a loophole allowed them to towns and 'corporations, companies or fellowships, of any art, trade, occupation or mystery or to any companies or societies of merchants'.[15] Not surprisingly, monopolists were able to use incorporation to evade the restrictions on individual monopolies. Culpeper voiced scepticism to Dury concerning the feasibility of the Office of Address, and the source of his scepticism was his anticipation of virulent opposition from 'monopolizing corporations'.[16] Culpeper, perhaps rightly, questions whether the figure of embodiment behind the notion of incorporation is capable of being broadened beyond the authorative corpus of the monopoly. He sees incorporation as a kind of inclusion that serves only to exclude. In other words, the Office of Address arises in part as a reaction to what might be seen as a fear of the private, a fear that any scheme for the public good is capable of being 'embodied' in a private venture. The rhetoric of the Hartlib coterie, therefore, directs itself towards reversing the valence of the terms, acknowledging the primacy of private concerns to the merchant, but arguing that if these concerns are not allowed to be prematurely 'incorporated', they will *ipso facto* produce public profit. This reversal of valence has, I would argue, profound significance for the way authorship and intellectual property are depicted. By refusing the conflation of public and private in the monopolizing corporation and by positing instead a system of private acts that benefit the larger public, the Hartlibians grant information a value as a commodity, publicly open yet privately owned.

Such a system, I suggest, is also implicit in the way Hartlib, Dury and others presented their texts as authored. Not only were the books of this group of men very often communally written, with one man producing a draft and another revising and supplementing the text, they were even more often presented to the public in a way

[14] *Ibid.*
[15] Quoted by Charles Wilson, *England's apprenticeship 1603–1763*, 2nd edn (London, 1984), 102.
[16] Webster, 68–9.

seemingly designed to baffle modern scholars. When not published entirely anonymously, they were quite often printed with a letter signed by Hartlib, or simply published under Hartlib's name even though he was not the chief writer. In effect, the name 'Hartlib' becomes a clear example of Michel Foucault's 'author function', a label identifying a particular ideologically identifiable product. In 'Hartlib', authoring has been all but severed from writing. If knowledge has been commodified, its ownership has still not been localized in the labour of the writer.[17]

The ideological difficulties attending authorship and intellectual property for the public-spirited puritan are crystallized in the front matter to William Potter's important economic treatise *The key of wealth* (1650).[18] Potter was not, strictly speaking, a member of the Hartlib circle.[19] Nonetheless, he shared most of the group's presuppositions about the relationship of private and public spheres. In *The key of wealth*, he argues that by increasing the money supply, everyone in the Commonwealth could be encouraged to spend more and that the increased circulation of capital would bring more goods into the hands of rich and poor alike. He articulates this seventeenth-century trickle-down theory in terms of the ancient fable of the body politic, famous from Menenius' speech in *Coriolanus*, but now radically altered with the times:

As in the Body Natural, no Member can subsist by itself, without both serving the whole Body, and receiving (as reward of such publique service) a competent nourishment from it; So in the Body Politique, no Artificer or Trades-man can accommodate himself, with all things necessary to a comfortable subsistence, by his Industry in any one Calling, without transmitting the overplus of the fruits of his endeavors therein, to other the [*sic*] Members of the said Body Politique, and from them receiving instead

---

17 Many of the works were published at Hartlib's expense, and as he dissipated his estate disseminating the ideology of the puritan instauration, he became less and less able to aid the artisanal writers who were grouped under the author-function 'Hartlib'. Gabriel Plattes, for example, the writer of *Macaria*, died impoverished and homeless in the streets of London, Hartlib having been unsuccessful in arranging a parliamentary annuity for the inventor. For the vexed question of the authorship of the Hartlib circle's publications, see Charles Webster, 'The authorship and significance of *Macaria*', in *The intellectual revolution of the seventeenth century*, ed. Charles Webster (London, 1974), 373: 'Indeed the precise attribution of authorship was of little concern to Hartlib's tightly-knit community of reformers. In the interest of the rapid diffusion of information, identities were usually suppressed in their writings.'

18 W. Potter, *The key of wealth; or a new way for improving trade* (London, 1650).

19 Potter worked with Henry Robinson as 'registrar of debentures on "the act for the sale of late king's lands"' (*DNB*); but his ideas for the development of these lands into efficient plantations were disputed by, among others, Hartlib and Cressy Dymock.

thereof, a proportionable reflex of the surplusage of their labours and commodities.[20]

Potter imagines a social corpus that looks very different from the traditional body politic. The stomach that enriches the rest of the body with its 'surplusage' no longer represents the aristocracy, as in Menenius' speech, but rather the 'Artificer or Trades-man' who, in seeing to his own 'comfortable subsistence' transmits 'the overplus of the fruits of his endeavors' to the other members of society. And although the merchant seems to have a pre-eminent position here, unlike the classical body politic, this one shows a remarkable homogeneity of tissue. Theoretically, at least, the circulation of goods would seem to have had a radically democratizing effect on the hierarchical body of classical political theory.[21]

Potter's actual proposal, his 'key to wealth', is a scheme that depends on replacing the old hierarchical ligatures binding the body politic and economic with new contractual relations whose forms he describes in very Hartlibian rhetoric. Anticipating the advent of banknotes in England by some one hundred years, he observes that money is nothing but 'an Evidence or Testimony, to signifie how far forth men (by their joynt Agreement . . .) are Indebted'. It is a 'publique Obligation' rather than an inherent value in the coin that gives it usefulness. The key, then, that Potter advertises appears to be a scheme to substitute coins of base metals for those of precious specie, creating a coinage that, because based on purely contractual value, possessed worth that could not be clipped, trimmed or otherwise debased – an important quality at a time when even copper coins were routinely weighed by merchants rather than accepted at face value. The effect of this contractual relation, of course, is to enforce a Hobbesian 'public'; all transactions are meaningful only in relation to a publicly agreed set of values.

Like many other puritans, Potter suggests a tentative association of Parliament with this new social body that can ratify contractual valuation of coinage. Yet there is a canker in this democratized paradise and this reflects the ambivalence toward the market-place that is to be seen in Hartlib's attitudes as well. For the most intriguing element of Potter's quite intriguing argument is that he

---

[20] Potter, *Key of wealth*, 2.

[21] For the political implications of the metaphor of circulation in the seventeenth century, see also the debate on Harvey's politics between Gweneth Whitteridge and Christopher Hill in Webster (ed.), *Intellectual revolution*, 182–96.

witholds the very 'key' that his title promises. 'I have yet', he tells Parliament, '... concealed one principal Adjunct, the ignorance of which, will make fruitless the endeavours of any, that without further direction, should either here or in any other part of the world, undertake this practice.'[22] He never, in fact, reveals that this 'principal Adjunct' is the new system of coinage, describing only the effect of increased circulation. Although he makes some noises about the value of this secret to the Commonwealth, one suspects that he reveals the real source of his concealment when he goes on to write: 'And although upon publication thereof, I conceive it not necesary, to seek any Priviledge, Pattent, Broad-seal or the like, as other Authors upon such occasions (in reference to the satisfaction of their manifold expences of time, pains, trouble, charges and hazard, which in such interprises are not usually small) apprehend they have just cause to do.'[23] Here we see how new modes of incorporation provided models of intellectual property that were, at the very best, unclear. Potter is loath to mar the discourse of public service with the 'Priviledge' of the monopolist, especially when that privilege has the monarchist associations of the 'Broad-seal' of the King's chancellor. He is, however, very worried about the possible piracy of his 'manifold expences'. He thus tells Parliament that he trusts they will 'interpose' their 'Authority' if anyone attempts to profit from his labours. Yet if the old model of monopoly was ideologically unavailable to him, the new social corpus provided no recognizable protection for the author from private 'incorporations' of ideas. It is never clear to the reader, and perhaps not to Potter himself, what would be the form any parliamentary interposition between an author or entrepreneur and a voraciously imitative market would take. Therefore, in case Parliament failed to fulfil the role assigned to it, Potter chose to occult the very thing promised in his title, the 'key' to wealth.

Potter's scheme and his suppressing of that scheme echo each other in their paradoxical nature. Just as this 'publique Obligation' may be privately owned (in fact, can exist only as a function of that private ownership), so Potter's discourse of the public good – he signs himself as one 'Who is as much desirous, as unworthy to be publikely useful' – can and must come into being as the result of 'private' articulations. Since Potter's whole scheme depends on a

[22] Epistle Dedicatory. [23] *Ibid.*

universally enriching circulation, he cannot appeal to the hated model of the monopoly, where money and goods are not circulated but merely exchanged in a hierarchically determined ritual. At the same time, however, he must mark his ideas as his own and he does this by withholding them, an act that both creates ownership and (with any luck) raises the price of the goods.

In a similar fashion, even the Office of Address, my model for the free flow of information, maintains a system of occlusions at its very heart. It was, after all, never conceived of as anything other than an organ of state – so that, like the Royal Exchange itself, it bore only an analogous and even metaphorical relation to the markets of Smithfield, for example, which lay beyond the city walls and largely beyond governmental supervision. And Dury describes both branches of the Office as possessing, alongside the public registers of commodities, a 'secret' register, by which the agent in charge may 'communicate ... to whomsoever he should think fit and expedient'.[24] The Office, therefore, shows itself as an incompletely democratized form of Bacon's House of Salomon, a version in which the aristocratic Brethren distribute information to people and state alike, but according to their discretion. In the end, Potter's dilemma, like Hartlib's, is the ambivalence about the mercantile, an ambivalence that also haunts Milton in *Areopagitica*.

MILTON AND THE MONOPOLISTS

Milton's famous comments on authorial rights in *Areopagitica* (1644) place him squarely in the middle of the issues debated by the Hartlibians. He is, however, everywhere more suspicious of incorporation. Perhaps as much as it is an argument against censorship itself, *Areopagitica* is a critique of the form that censorship takes, namely, that of an incorporated monopoly invested in the hands of the Stationers' Company, the guild of printers and publishers. He remains, therefore, deeply distrustful of even an analogical linking between knowledge and commodities. 'Truth and understanding', he says,

are not such wares as to be monopoliz'd and traded in by tickets and statutes, and standards. We must not think to make a staple commodity of all the knowledge in the Land, to mark and license it like our broad cloth

24 Dury, *Considerations*, 130–2.

and our wooll packs. What is it but a servitude like that impos'd by the Philistims, not to be allow'd the sharpning of our own axes and coulters, but we must repair from all quarters to twenty licencing forges.[25]

A 'staple' commodity, of course, was one on which a person or corporation held a royal monopoly. The injustice of such a system for Milton is figured in the 'twenty licencing forges', which represent the presses of the twenty master printers allowed under the Star Chamber decree of 1637. Like the Philistine prohibition of Israel's forges, the Star Chamber decree was designed to curtail polemical tools, but beating figurative swords into figurative ploughshares, Milton sees the prohibition as the unnatural interposition of the monopolists between a labourer and his work.[26]

The monopolist and the monopolizing corporation, then, stand behind *Areopagitica*'s fundamental ambivalence towards the market-place. Everything about the ideological drift of the tract, with its master metaphor of collation – the production of truth through the public editorial process of comparing texts – suggests the salubrious effect produced by the free circulation of what Milton calls 'our richest Marchandize, Truth'.[27] Yet he consistently represents the merchant as a figure of contempt, 'addicted to his pleasure and to his profits', finding religion the only 'mystery' he cannot master.[28] When he praises Spenser for teaching the futility of a 'fugitive and cloister'd vertue', Milton chooses as his example Guyon in the Cave of Mammon – like Christianity, textuality must be proved in a place of peril, the market-place. In fact, Milton's famous error of placing the Palmer with Guyon during this episode may reflect his sense that Mammon represents a much greater temptation than even Spenser makes him. Thus, in his conclusion, Milton is quite specific in his placement of blame. Citing with approbation the 1642 decree of the House of Commons that licensed only by stipulating that the 'name

---

[25] *CPW*, ii, 535–6.
[26] For an illuminating look at *Areopagitica* in the context of Milton's subsequent career as a censor, see Abbe Blum, 'The author's authority: *Areopagitica* and the labour of licensing', in *Re-membering Milton*, ed. Margaret W. Ferguson and Mary Nyquist (London, 1988), 74–96.
[27] *CPW*, ii, 548.
[28] *Ibid.*, 544. Christopher Kendrick points to just this ambivalence in his brilliant account of *Areopagitica* and the market-place: 'The essential argument of the treatise is for the free circulation of ideas ... But Truth's entrance into the commodity form is an ambivalent one: the whole tract, beginning with the defense of books, might be read as a protest against the commodification of human activity' (Christopher Kendrick, *Milton: a study in ideology and form* (New York, 1986), 40).

and consent of the Author' be attached to any printing, he sees the hand of the Stationers' Company in the undermining of that order:

> And how it ['*hypocrisy*'] got the upper hand of your precedent Order so well constituted before, if we may believe those men whose profession gives them cause to enquire most, it may be doubted there was in it the fraud of some old *patentees* and *monopolizers* in the trade of bookselling; who under pretense of the poor in their Company not to be defrauded, and the just retaining of each man his severall copy, which God forbid should be gainsaid, brought divers glosing colours to the House, which were indeed but colours, and serving to no end except it be to exercise a superiority over their neighbours, men who do not therefore labour in an honest profession to which learning is indetted, that they should be made other mens vassals . . . But of these *Sophisms* and *Elenchs* of marchandize I skill not.[29]

Not only is the Stationers' Company an incorporated monopoly controlling all printing, it is one with great inequities between its members, inequities exploited by the wealthier members as a 'pretense . . . not to be defrauded'. Milton does not trust the corporation not to produce another hierarchy like the one it replaced. The new lords of 'marchandize' convert 'labour in an honest profession' to vassalage. Milton's implicit accusation that the monopolizing corporations constitute a new feudal order recalls the objection of Coke and others to monopoly on the grounds that it impinges upon the 'liberty and freedom of the subject'.[30] In the words of Sir Edwin Sandys: 'All free subjects are born inheritable, as to their land, so also to the free exercise of their industry, in those trades whereto they apply themselves.'[31] Moreover, Parliament, the hope of Hartlib's circle, proves guilty by association in Milton's reasoning. Although he addresses the tract to them as one who wishes to 'advance the publick good',[32] it is clear from his guarded tones that Milton does not see Parliament as an adequate representation of a fully public social corpus; in fact, it seems doubtful that he even believes in the possibility of an integrated body politic that is not coercive and privatized.[33]

---

[29] *CPW*, II, 570.

[30] Joan Thirsk, *Economic policy and projects: the development of a consumer society in early modern England* (Oxford, 1978), 100. Coke was the principal sponsor of the 1621 legislation against monopolies; although this bill failed to pass, it stood behind the successful legislation of 1624.

[31] *Seventeenth-century economic documents*, ed. Joan Thirsk and J. P. Cooper (Oxford, 1972), 437.

[32] *CPW*, II, 486.

[33] Only two years earlier, in *An apology against a pamphlet* (1642), Milton had celebrated his status as 'a member incorporate' (*CPW*, I, 871) in the puritan cause. But this corpus must

Thus while the economics of free circulation is in perfect keeping with his social epistemology of 'collation', he makes only tentative steps toward applying this new ideology to his picture of Truth and to his notion of authorial property. Yet if Milton is not asserting that an author has a right to perpetual monetary profit from a text, he is not abandoning the field to the Stationers' Company, merely refusing to contest the question of profit. His moment of solidarity with the poorer printers recalls the analogy of the Philistines to the licensers, suggesting the alienation of the worker from the field worked. It is Milton's belief that the Stationers' Company was attempting arbitrarily to patch together authors' labour into the monolith of a licensing monopoly; and it is this belief, I would argue, that stands behind the particular relish with which he describes the hewing and strewing of the 'mangl'd body' of Truth. Milton associates the body of Truth with that of Christ and claims that after the resurrection Truth was rapidly dismembered. To attempt to reassemble her body too soon, he argues, is to attempt to circumvent history: 'We have not yet found them all [*the limbs of Truth*], Lords and Commons, nor ever shall doe, till her Masters second comming; he shall bring together every joynt and member, and shall mould them into an immortall feature of lovelines and perfection.'[34] Until the Apocalypse, therefore, all attempts at incorporation remain arbitrary exertions of authority, and his sudden apostrophizing of Parliament emphasizes how thoroughgoing he intends his assault on incorporation to be. Stationer, prelate and Parliament alike are engaged in the artificial project of creating 'the forc't and outward union of cold, and neutrall, and inwardly divided minds'.[35]

What remains to the followers of Truth is to do 'obsequies to the torn body of our martyr'd Saint'[36] and to pursue the individual lost limbs. While the 'homogeneal' body of Truth cannot be fully reconstituted until the Apocalypse, Milton nonetheless applauds the surgical practice of 'closing up truth to truth as we find it',[37] as long as that practice makes no pretence to be totalizing. Yet when he attempts to articulate metaphorically the relationship between an author and his text, it becomes clear that he will have some difficulty distinguishing the two surgical procedures. Amid the welter of figures adduced, there emerges a tendency to see the text as, if not

still have seemed marginalized enough in Milton's mind not to have threatened to become hierarchical itself.

[34] *CPW*, ii, 549.   [35] *Ibid.*, 551.   [36] *Ibid.*, 550.   [37] *Ibid.*, 551.

consubstantial with, nonetheless in a bodily relation to the author. 'For Books are not absolutely dead things, but doe contain a potencie of life in them to be as active as that soule was whose progeny they are; nay they do preserve as in a violl the purest efficacie and extraction of that living intellect that bred them.'[38] Milton hesitates here over whether he will grant books the autonomy – however limited – of a child, or instead see them as mere receptacles, both alchemical and sepulchral, of the author's essence. The direction in which he revises his figure is significant in light of the quotation with which I began, arrogating proprietary rights to the author even after his death. And this direction is reaffirmed a few sentences later when he calls the book the 'imbalm'd' spirit of the author, the 'season'd life of man preserv'd and stor'd up in Books'.[39] Milton, like so many literary historians that follow, regards the book as pickled author.

Areopagitica, then, can be seen to be a competition over modes of embodiment. In attempting to constitute the book as a bodily extension of the author, distinct from the Frankenstein monster sewn up prematurely by the Stationers' Company with parts missing which had been removed by licensing, Milton unwittingly but perhaps necessarily reconstitutes the monstrous image in his language of 'seasoning' and 'imbalming'. Yet by locating the significance of a work in the author's body rather than in any larger corporeal figure, Milton, in effect, lays the groundwork of authorial individualism necessary for a notion of authorial property. His pronouncements imply a conception of texts with clear moments of origination in an enunciating subject, a subject that could at least theoretically claim proprietary rights over that text, at the same time that the text takes its value from its free circulation in the market-place – a text, that is, that can be owned without being embalmed.

Returning to the opening quotation from Milton's *Eikonoklastes*, one can see that, strikingly modern as this sentence appears, it is, within the context of Milton's argument, an afterthought at best. It comes from what is in many ways the crowning glory of his attack on *Eikon basilike*,[40] namely his revelation that a prayer presented

---

[38] *Ibid.*, 492.   [39] *Ibid.*, 493.

[40] The effectiveness of Milton's critique can be judged by the fact that the prayer was dropped from most editions of *Eikon basilike* during the 1650s. Also telling is the contention, beginning with Thomas Wagstaff in 1693 and continuing into this century, that Milton

as Charles' utterance on the scaffold was, in fact, a nearly word-for-word repetition of Pamela's prayer from Sidney's *Arcadia*.[41] Milton's primary objection to this prayer, however, is not its lack of literary originality but its lack of decorum: the king introduces a pagan prayer from 'the vain amatorious Poem of Sr. Philip Sidneys *Arcadia*'[42] into avowedly Christian orisons. Only after many pages does he pause to add: 'But leaving what might justly be offensive to God, it was a trespass also more then usual against human right.'[43] Why, one might ask, this sudden afterthought in defence of the 'amatorious' Sidney, in an argument censoring discursive promiscuity?

Although Milton charges that Charles errs in being unable to invent unpremeditated prayer and compounds his sin by choosing a prayer from a pagan cultural corpus, he is ultimately less concerned with Charles' artistic poverty than with the insidiousness of his incorporation. Charles is like that 'most cruel Tyrant', Andronicus Comnenus, who 'by continual study' of Paul's Epistles 'so incorporated the phrase & stile of that transcendent Apostle into all his familiar Letters, that the imitation seem'd to vie with the Original'.[44] Milton is not worried about unauthorized (or even unacknowledged) quotation *per se*, and he is certainly not defending the rights of Sidney's descendants to profit from his writings. What worries him is a very particular mode of appropriation, a textual incorporation in which the corpus in question is alienated from the body of the author and reinscribed into a hierarchy that turns that writing to its own, decontextualized, dehistoricized purposes. *Eikon basilike* becomes the monstrous, stitched-together text Milton had feared and decried in *Areopagitica*.

In this context, Milton's cry for authorial rights to texts begins to sound not so much like a radical call for a 'possessive individualism' of intellectual property, but like a humanist critique of travestied *imitatio*. The threat to the integrity of an author's text does not come only from above, from feudalistic attempts to appropriate what is properly the product of a marketable labour. *Eikonoklastes* is notably virulent in its attacks on 'the vulgar sort'[45] who were the readers of

actually conspired to have the prayer added to *Eikon basilike* in order to unload his devastating exposé. See *CPW*, III, 152ff. for the history of this theory.
[41] One of the great ironies behind Milton's charge of plagiarism is that he seems to have known that *Eikon basilike* was largely a forgery, but chose to accept it as authentic in order to facilitate his attack on the recently executed king.
[42] *CPW*, III, 362.   [43] *Ibid.*, 364–5.   [44] *Ibid.*, 361.   [45] *Ibid.*, 348.

Eikon basilike. And it is the taste of these readers that produced 'the lip-work of every Prelatical Liturgist, clapt together, and quilted out of Scripture phrase, with as much ease, and as little need of Christian diligence, or judgement, as belongs to the compiling of any ord'nary and salable peece of English Divinity, that the Shops value'.[46] It is the market itself that threatens to separate an author from his work, to render that work unrecognizable as pastiche or anthology. Thus, the quotation with which I began may not be so much an articulation of an idea whose time was yet to come as a reflection of a conception of authorship that was passing from the scene, a conception of a world of privileged textuality, a world in which authorship was constructed not by the audience in the market-place, but by the collation of texts in the writer's study.

[46] *Ibid.*, 360.

CHAPTER 10

George Starkey and the selling of secrets

William R. Newman

George Starkey, otherwise known as Stirk, was born in Bermuda in 1628 and died in London in 1665.[1] After receiving an AB from Harvard in 1646 and an AM shortly thereafter, he emigrated to London, where he became a prominent iatrochemist.[2] In the 1640s, Starkey had made a favourable impression upon Robert Child and Richard Leader in New England. Hence, when he arrived in London in November 1650, he was well placed to become a member of the circle of savants gathering around Samuel Hartlib. Indeed, Hartlib's *Ephemerides* for early 1650 relays a report from Leader about 'one Stirke or Starkie' who is 'of a most rare and incomparable universal Witt'.[3] On 11 December 1650 Hartlib met Starkey for the first time, and the latter immediately assumed a central place in Hartlib's goals for chemistry.[4]

While a member of Hartlib's entourage, Starkey circulated a number of influential alchemical treatises under the assumed title of 'Eirenaeus Philalethes'. As I have shown elsewhere, the most famous of these, the *Introitus apertus ad occlusum regis palatium*, was surely written by Starkey himself, between 1651 and 1654/5.[5] Entries in

[1] The following chapter is a slightly altered extract from my forthcoming book on George Starkey – *Gehennical fire: the lives of George Starkey, an American alchemist in the scientific revolution* (Harvard University Press).

[2] Some of the more significant pieces written about Starkey are the following: George Lyman Kittredge, 'Dr. Robert Child the remonstrant', *Transactions of the Colonial Society of Massachusetts*, 21 (1919), 1–146; George Turnbull, 'George Stirk, philosopher by fire', *Transactions of the Colonial Society of Massachusetts*, 38 (1947–51), 219–51; Ronald Sterne Wilkinson, 'George Starkey, physician and alchemist', *Ambix*, 11 (1963), 121–52; Harold Jantz, 'America's first cosmopolitan', *Proceedings of the Massachusetts Historical Society*, 84 (1972), 3–25; William Newman, 'Prophecy and alchemy: the origin of Eirenaeus Philalethes', *Ambix*, 37 (1990), 97–115.

[3] *Ephemerides* (1650): HP 28/1/57A; see R. S. Wilkinson, 'The Hartlib Papers and seventeenth-century chemistry, Part II', *Ambix*, 17 (1970), 86, n. 7.

[4] *Ephemerides* (11 December 1650): HP 28/1/80A; see Wilkinson, 'Hartlib Papers', 87, n. 12.

[5] Newman, 'Prophecy and alchemy', 102–6.

the *Ephemerides* and other Hartlib documents make it clear that Starkey concocted an elaborate fiction about a supposed New England adept who gave him some 'philosophical mercury' capable of transmuting mercury into precious metals. Starkey claimed that the Philalethes manuscripts were really by this adept, and that he had been entrusted with them as a faithful friend.[6] He circulated these manuscripts to Hartlib, Friedrich Clodius, Robert Boyle and others; there is no evidence that any of them disbelieved his story of the New England adept. The *Introitus*, published posthumously in 1667, has acquired subsequent fame as perhaps the favourite alchemical text of Isaac Newton.[7]

Starkey's *persona* of 'Eirenaeus Philalethes' was not merely a pseudonym in the usual sense, intended to conceal the author's identity. Starkey revelled in creating facts about his adept's life: indeed, he was so ingenious and persistent in this that he inspired others to do the same. Thus Kenelm Digby told the German physician, Cardilucius, the impossible story that he had been visited by 'Eirenaeus Philalethes' when he was imprisoned in England during the 1640s,[8] and rumours were still circulating in the 1680s that the

---

[6] *Ibid.*, 100–1, where the pertinent literature is cited.

[7] Among Newton's alchemical productions one finds the *Index chemicus*, a systematic topical index of his alchemical readings that went through several redactions spanning the 1680s. In its final form, the *Index chemicus* extends to over 100 pages and contains 879 headings. What is most valuable about this document is that it allows us a means of judging which alchemical authors Newton considered most important. Richard Westfall has performed a valuable service by enumerating the references to each author's works for the forty-six longest entries in the *Index*, so that one can arrive at a quantitative figure for each author listed. If one adds up the entries in which 'Eirenaeus Philalethes' appears, one will find 302 references. Since Michael Maier, the next most cited author, gets 140 references, one can quickly arrive at a rough measure of the esteem in which Newton held Philalethes. See Richard Westfall, 'Isaac Newton's Index chemicus', *Ambix*, 22 (1975), 174–85, esp. 178, 182–5.

[8] George Lyman Kittredge, who discovered Cardilucius' relation, translated part of it for his proposed monograph on Starkey. His translation is found in Box 1, Folder 2 of his Starkey notes in the Harvard Archives. I reproduce it here, having checked it against the German (Johann Hiskias Cardilucius, *Magnalia medico-chymica* (Nuremberg, 1676), 298–300):

But I felt scruples about printing it [*the* Introitus apertus], for its unheard-of clearness made me think that it was meant only to circulate in manuscript among some well-disposed lovers of the art as a shining lantern in the dark laboratories – one to pass it along to another for copying. Accordingly, as soon as I obtained it, I presented it to the great and world-renowned Hermetic philosopher, Earl Digby, who was glad to have it copied. He had known about the tract before. Indeed he related circumstantially that he was well acquainted with the author. Once, he told me, when the so-called Protector Cromwell had thrown him into prison as a Royalist, this author visited him and offered to supply his necessities with money or otherwise; the Earl assured him that by God's blessing he had means in abundance and lacked nothing but liberty, which, indeed, he later obtained by God's help. The author departed on his travels. The Earl also told me the real name of the author,

adept was alive and well in the West Indies – long after Starkey's death in 1665.[9] Starkey's adept even acquired a personality of his own: Michael Hunter has unearthed a sheet in the Robert Boyle Papers in which Boyle goes so far as to rebut the arguments of 'Philalethes' for maintaining alchemical secrecy.[10] And in his *Historical account of a degradation of gold* (1678), Boyle refers disapprovingly to furtive 'Philalethists'. On these occasions, Boyle used Philalethes as the embodiment of the jealous occultist, propping up an acquisitive secrecy with sophistical arguments.

The creation of Starkey's fictive adept throws a rather lurid light on his character. Was Starkey simply a compulsive liar, or do his bizarre actions have some other explanation? I wish here to illuminate Starkey's puzzling character by considering his attitude towards the partial or total concealment of facts. I shall argue that Starkey, despite all appearances to the contrary, was not suffering from the pathology of an Odysseus, but that his concealment of the truth was due to the convergence of three factors. The most obvious of these was the need for Starkey, as a metallurgist and inventor of drugs, dyes and perfumes, to retain his processes as trade secrets. Yet this alone, I argue, cannot account for his obsession with secrecy. On the one hand, his adoption of the epistemology of Joan Baptista van

---

which I have forgotten, and he added that my manuscript was free from errors, except that 'anno aetatis meae vigesimo tertio' was a mistake for 'trigesimo tertio' ... Since, however, in the course of time Herr Langius published this tract in Latin, and I found, on consulting my manuscript, that some errors (trifling as to words, but of such a character as to reverse the meaning completely in the main point of the treatise) had made their way into his copy, I have long wished that this might be rectified by some one. Since up to date this has not been done, I have finally taken it upon myself not merely to correct the tract according to the manuscript, but also to translate it anew into German, following the very words and meaning of the author, according to the assurance I received from Earl Digby, at rest with God, to whom the author was well known.

Digby was imprisoned by Parliament between 1642 and 1643 and subsequently banished. He returned to England in 1649 and was immediately banished again. In 1654 he returned again, at that time in Cromwell's good graces. He left in 1655, to travel through parts of Europe including France and Germany, returning to England in 1660 (*DNB*). The only time that fits with Cardilucius' remarks, therefore, is the period 1642–3, when Digby was indeed imprisoned 'as a Royalist'. It is interesting that Digby wanted to modify the text of the *Introitus* in order to bring the age of Philalethes into conformity with that of his supposed visitor.

9 Johann Otto de Helbig, *Judicium de Duumviris Hermeticis Foederatis* (Jena, 1683), 42: 'Licet amicus quidam Londini, cum nuper in Anglia essem, suam de Philaletha suspicionem, & quod sub Imperio Britannico, in Insula quadam Anglicana adhuc viveret, mihi dixerit.'
10 Michael Hunter, 'Alchemy, magic and moralism in the thought of Robert Boyle', *British Journal for the History of Science*, 23 (1990), 407, n. 70. The document is found in Royal Society, Boyle Papers 19, fols. 187v–188r.

Helmont and of more traditional alchemists led him to view his chemical discoveries as divinely sanctioned revelations, fit for him alone. On the other hand, the social exigencies imposed by his immigration were such as to make the portrayal of himself as a master of secrets a useful strategy for dealing with such luminaries as Robert Boyle.

In May 1651, Starkey was persuaded by John Dury to send a letter of introduction to Johann Morian, a corresponding associate of Hartlib, then living outside Amsterdam. In the letter, Starkey described himself as a 'silent explorer of art and nature', who 'seeks truth, not fame', and who has 'no secrets for sale'. Despite the fact that he had no *venalia … secreta*, Starkey certainly did have secrets aplenty, for the letter is largely a description of the 'philosophical mercury' needed to transmute metals. Here, as elsewhere, Starkey put the emphasis on his role as 'discoverer' rather than 'vendor' of secrets. Why was Starkey so eager to downplay the sale of chemical secrets in the atmosphere of the Hartlib circle, with its incessant praise of lucriferous knowledge? Part of the answer lies in Starkey's means of acquiring his arcane knowledge.

There are at least two recorded instances in which Starkey believed that he had acquired his secret knowledge of nature from dreams. The first occurred in New England, where he had been perusing Lazarus Zetzner's *Theatrum chemicum* when sleep came upon him. As Hartlib reports: 'Hee falling asleep in the reading of it Hee was bidden to arise and looke out such a place in it that speakes of the true Philosophical fire, which accordingly hee did, and turned to the very place and sleeping in the darke yet underlined it which hee hath to shew to this day.'[11]

Thus we find Starkey falling asleep and being requested by an unnamed inhabitant of his dream to look up a crucial passage in Zetzner on the 'philosophical fire'. The revelatory character of this passage is clear, but a far more dramatic case may be found in a letter written by Starkey to Boyle on 26 January 1651/2. Here Starkey describes how, late one night, he had exhausted himself in his search for the alkahest. He fell asleep with his head on his arm, and a deep sleep came upon him. As he says:

Behold! I seemed intent on my work, and a man appeared, entering the laboratory, at whose arrival I was stupefied. But he greeted me and said

[11] *Ephemerides* (1651): HP 28/2/4B–5A; see Wilkinson, 'Hartlib Papers', 87.

'May God support your labours.' When I heard this, realizing that he had mentioned God, I asked who he was, and he responded that he was my Eugenius; I asked whether there were such creatures. He responded that there were ... Finally I asked him what the alkahest of Paracelsus and Helmont was, and he responded that they used salt, sulphur, and an alkalized body, and though this response was more obscure than Paracelsus himself, yet with the response an ineffable light entered my mind, so that I fully understood. Marvelling at this, I said to him, 'Behold! Your words are veiled, as it were by fog, and yet they are fundamentally true.' He said 'This is so necessarily, for the things said by one's Eugenius are all certain [*scientifica*], while those just said by me are the truest of all.'[12]

In this episode, Starkey's dream involves a visitation from his 'good genius', or tutelary spirit, whose presence was already implied in the former dream. The spirit reveals the secret of the alkahest to Starkey, and this revelation is accompanied by instant comprehension. As the spirit relates, such certain comprehension is the necessary consequence of revelation. It is clear from other remarks in this letter that Starkey considered the direct source of his inspiration to be divine. Thus he tells Boyle: 'I know well enough what the alkahest is, and I have gathered it both from Paracelsus and from the effects of Helmont, but I have penetrated into the fabric of the thing with the aid of the Father of Lights Himself.'[13]

Now one might certainly propose that Starkey was merely trying to impress his intended patron here by giving his own discoveries a divine cachet. Such an argument, however, cannot be advanced for Starkey's laboratory journals, which contain his recipes and failures and were not intended for circulation. Thus he reports on 20 March 1656 that 'God has revealed the whole Arcanum of the liquor alkahest to me: let there be eternal sanctification, honor, and glory

12 Royal Society, Boyle Letters, fol. 133r: 'Et ecce videbar negotio intentus, apparuitque homo laboratorium intrans, ad cujus adventum stupui, is vero salutavit me dixitque, Succedat Deus tuos labores. Quod cum audissem, mente recollecta quod Deum nominasset, rogavi quis esset, qui respondit, se Eugenium meum, rogavi an tales essent creaturae. Respondit quod sic, multaque alia interrogabam quae taedio essent recensere, tandem rogavi quidnam esset Paracelsi et Helmontis Alcahest, deditque responsum usi sunt sale sulphure, et corpore Alcalito, et licet hoc responsum sit obscurius Paracelso ipso, tamen cum responso intravit mentem lux ineffabilis, adeo ut plenissime intelligerem, quod ego admiratus dixi illi, ecce tua verba sunt admodum caligine tecta, et tamen fundamentaliter sint vera. Dixit sic opportet esse nam quae ab Eugenio dicuntur, omnia sunt scientifica, Haec autem quae dixi sunt longe verissima' (Starkey to Boyle, 26 January 1651/2).
13 Royal Society, Boyle Letters, fol. 133r: 'Sat novi quid sit Alkahest, idque tam ex Paracelso quam Helmonte in effectis collegi, at a Patre Luminum rei ipsius fabricam impetravi' (Starkey to Boyle, 26 January 1651/2).

to Him'.[14] And in another, undated entry, he states that 'God has communicated the whole secret of volatilizing alkali's to me'.[15] This entry is followed by a long recipe involving salt of tartar and turpentine.

It is evident that Starkey is drawing here on an old tradition of viewing alchemical knowledge as the province of the elect. In the thirteenth century, the *Summa perfectionis* of pseudo-Geber had asserted that the philosophers' stone was a *donum dei*, which God 'extends to and withdraws from whom He wishes'.[16] More significant than this, perhaps, is the fact that J. B. van Helmont, Starkey's hero, wrote extensively in defence of divinely revealed knowledge. Starkey translated a long section of van Helmont's *Ortus medicinae* on this very subject. In the extant part of Starkey's translation, van Helmont uses traditional faculty psychology to distinguish between 'reason' and 'intellect': only the latter can lead to true 'understanding' in van Helmont's vocabulary.[17] Indeed, discursive reason was the fruit of the knowledge of good and evil, acquired after man's creation. It does not form an intrinsic part of the human soul. Intellect, on the other hand, which purveys the immediate knowledge of things, is eternal, forming an integral part of both God and the soul. As van Helmont put it:

But I beleeve that the Almighty alone, is the only way, truth, life, & light, both of things living and al things else, not Reason. And therefore it behoves our mind to be intellectual, not rational, if it hold forth the immediate Image of God. This Paradox wil be very necessary to be unfolded, before wee enter upon the search of al things knowable, but most Especially of such things which are Adepta.[18]

As the passage implies, van Helmont believed that true knowledge of the things attained by the *adepti* can only come from intellect and this must be dispensed by the Almighty. After this passage, van Helmont proceeds to offer an elaborate defence of scientific knowledge acquired by dreams and visions, even recounting a number of dream sequences in detail. Van Helmont speaks of these as 'intellectual visions'. They are accompanied by a sensation of brilliant

[14] BL Sloane MS 3750, fol. 19v: 'Bristolii Martii 20 1655/6 Deus integrum liquoris Alchahest Arcanum mihi propalavit cui aeterna sit sanctificatio, honor & gloria' (Starkey).
[15] BL Sloane MS 2682, fol. 89r: 'Deus mihi integrum Alcalium volatizandorum secretum communicavit' (Starkey).
[16] William Newman, *The Summa perfectionis of pseudo-Geber* (Leiden, 1991), 785.
[17] BL Sloane MS 3708, fol. 95r.
[18] Van Helmont, in Starkey's translation, BL Sloane MS 3708, fol. 95r.

light, and van Helmont uses this as indirect evidence that they descend from 'the Father of Lights' himself. It is clear that these dreams and their defence form the *locus classicus* for Starkey's belief that his secrets were divinely inspired.

To Starkey, there was a secret behind the alkahest, a '*Gordian-Knot* that puzzles' most 'doting fond Alchemists', namely 'the Mystery of *spiritual Love*'. This secret was 'our hidden Name, our *Diploma*, our Mystery incommunicable, but the Gift of GOD, [*given*] to whom, and when he pleaseth'.[19] The acquisition of this secret required a 'mental man', not just any 'fond' alchemist.[20] As he says in the posthumous *Liquor alchahest*: 'Only a true mental man will intellectually apprehend, and intuitively behold, with the clear sight of the Soul or mind.'[21] This is an obvious allusion to the Helmontian theory of illumination which has just been outlined. The word 'mental' reflects the Latin *mens* or 'mind', the faculty of the soul believed by van Helmont to receive a genuine knowledge of nature. In order to be an adept, one had also to be such a mental man.

Starkey thus genuinely believed himself to be a recipient of divine intelligence; his natural secrets were the immediate gifts of a godly largesse. This belief formed the primary justification for his many comments about natural secrets made to members of the Hartlib circle. Boyle, who was also a follower of van Helmont, cannot have been untouched by Starkey's appeal to this oneiric epistemology.[22] Michael Hunter has unearthed clear evidence of Boyle's belief that the philosophers' stone could be a supernatural gift, and that it could even operate on the supercelestial realm.[23] Let us now consider Starkey's earliest extant letter to Boyle, written in the spring of 1651. This letter contains Starkey's 'key into antimony', a recipe for making an amalgam of mercury, antimony and silver. The product was supposed to be a 'philosophical mercury' in which gold would 'melt like ice in warm water' and undergo a series of changes leading to the great transmutative agent – the elixir or philosophers' stone.

[19] Starkey, *Pyrotechny* (London, 1658), 143–4.
[20] Starkey, *Natures explication* (London, 1657), 91.
[21] Starkey, *Liquor alchahest* (London, 1675), 35. See also Eirenaeus Philalethes, *Ripley reviv'd* (London, 1678), 112: 'Now Faith, and a kindled Desire in the Soul is that extatical Passion which attracts the whole Phaenomena of Nature. This is the Dignity of a Mental Man.'
[22] The degree of Boyle's indebtedness to van Helmont is even now little appreciated. For a recent reassessment thereof, see Antonio Clericuzio, 'A redefinition of Boyle's chemistry and corpuscular philosophy', *Annals of Science*, 47 (1990), 561–89.
[23] Hunter, 'Alchemy', 387–410.

The following passage, preserved only in a German translation, shows that Starkey considered himself to be giving Boyle a secret of the highest value. The passage has hitherto escaped detailed attention but it is fundamental in determining Starkey's early relation to Robert Boyle:

Thus, your Honour, you have the right key to this cabinet, which I have worked seven years to unlock; my opening of the same has been candid and simple, and this because I hold you for an honourable and sincere man, who uses intellect in the investigation of nature; hence I have not been dark or allegorical in words or types of speech; rather I wish to be understood literally ...

Your Honour, I communicate these things to you and intrust them to you on your soul as it were in a sealed chest: this is why I have not before urged you to silence – because I believe it is inborn in you that you can keep silent. I avoid the selling of nature's secrets and for this reason alone is Glauber so antithetical to me, and this causes Graaf and his sponge Farrar to slander me so viciously.

I have never suffered want, but should it happen, I would still not sell the slightest secret to Farrar: but where I find that someone is worthy of it, there I will allow myself to be generous.

To speak plainly, I esteem no man for his rank, for I honour God, and even if you possess excellence and dominion, I still possess such secrets as please me more than any wealth whatsoever. And since I have come thus far, I wish to say with the poet – 'Sicelides Musae paulo majora canamus'.[24]

In this passage, Starkey immediately asserts the importance of his revelation, calling it a 'key' which took seven years to discover. He explains that he has chosen to reveal the key without obfuscation because Boyle is 'honourable and sincere'. Then, tacitly calling on Boyle's well-known admiration for van Helmont, Starkey lauds him as one 'who uses intellect in the investigation of nature'. In other words, Starkey wishes to imply that Boyle too has adopted the Helmontian preference for intellect over reason.

It is for this reason, Starkey continues, that he has entrusted his secrets to Boyle. Understanding the true nature of acquiring secrets of nature, Boyle can be trusted not to divulge them, especially not for a price. Starkey adds that for his own part, he would never sell his secrets for money, and that this venal practice is what makes Glauber so detestable to him. The final lines of the passage perhaps offer the most interest. Here the provincial immigrant is moved to inform Boyle, soon to be one of the richest men in England, that he

[24] *Dr. Georg Starkeys chymie* (Nuremberg, 1722), 448–9, my translation.

esteems 'no man for his rank ... and even if you possess excellence and dominion, I still possess such secrets as please me more than any wealth whatsoever'.

Up to this point, I have tried to unravel Starkey's justification for his attitude towards the divulging of natural secrets. These are, as it were, the result of a compact between him and the 'Father of Lights'. Let us now consider Starkey's use of these Helmontian doctrines in manipulating his relationship with Boyle. We know from the 'Philalethes' writings that Starkey was willing to package the beliefs he actually held in such a way as to maximize his own benefit from them. This can clearly be seen in the case of the *Introitus apertus*, where Starkey intentionally concentrates on topics close to the interests of those in the Hartlib circle. The *Introitus* contains several long prophetical passages where Starkey announces the coming of the Paracelsian *Elias artista*, and the imminent revelation of natural secrets by God Himself. In the meantime, Philalethes says, the *Introitus* offers a succession of hints to those who are intelligent and pious, so that they may acquire limitless wealth and the ability to heal without end. Given that Starkey portrayed himself as the intermediary between Philalethes and those of Hartlib's acquaintance, that he wrote the *Introitus* while an active associate of the group, and that he even circulated the manuscript to its members, it seems self-evident that he tailored it to their particular set of interests. This does not require us to assume that Starkey disbelieved the prophetical doctrines expressed in the *Introitus* any more than it implies his distrust of the antimonial preparations described therein.

A similar manipulation is going on in Starkey's letters to Boyle in the spring of 1651. This can be seen more clearly if we examine that part of the 1651 letter that has survived in English. We must cite Starkey *in extenso* once again:

Some Gentlemen sollicite me to follow extractions of gold and silver out of antimony and iron, among whom Mr Worsley an ingenious Gentleman did much perswade. To this an argum[en]t did move not a little respecting the suddaine profit that might accrue by it, to which the ill dealing of some with whom I had dealing betweene England and New England seemed inforcingly to invite (al the bills that I brought to the Value of 150^{lb} being protested). yet I Considering that first my way of extraction of gold & silver being not done by violent heats fluxes waters or the like, but in a more philosophick way, viz of volatilizing the body & after Congealing it, required no Charge to speake of much less partners, & in a thing which I Could Command as a Master, I would not work as an Amanuensis, Nor yet would I in such a way of lucre prostrate so great a secret as I judged the mercury of antimony to be.[25]

So we find Benjamin Worsley and other unnamed gentlemen attempting to convince Starkey that he should take part in a joint venture to exploit his process of 'extracting' gold and silver from antimony and iron. Starkey relates that his increasing debt made this a temptation, but that he declined the offer. Once again we find him hesitating to trade nature's secrets for lucre. But at this point a further element becomes apparent, namely Starkey's unwillingness to act as a servant of others when he can be his own master.

The same idea is elaborated a few lines later, when he tells Boyle that he is unwilling 'to imbrace a life (in Exchange of a studious search of Natures mysteryes) which might be Compared with that of a Milhorse running round in a wheele today, that I may doe the same tomorrow'.[26] Starkey immediately reveals that it is not only the distribution of secrets to the unworthy that bothers him, but the fact that Worsley's plan will relegate him to the status of a mill-horse, plodding along at the same process with no end in sight. The emphasis here, as in the use of the 'amanuensis' metaphor, is on servitude. Instead of being his own master, Starkey feared that the acceptance of capital from an outside source would turn him into a mere wage earner.

Let us now reconsider the remarks made in the German portion of the 1651 letter. After telling Boyle that he detested the sale of nature's secrets, Starkey then said – at first sight rather gratuitously – that he valued no man 'for his rank', and that all of Boyle's wealth was of less consequence to him than his own secrets. Yet we now see that these comments were far from gratuitous. By placing his secrets in antithesis to Boyle's vast wealth, Starkey was attempting to inflate his significance as an alchemist in order to offset his low social and economic standing. Starkey was attempting to establish his secrets as a sort of commodity equivalent in value to Boyle's assets. I say 'sort of commodity' because there can be no doubt that Starkey himself would have been horrified and insulted by such an imputation. And yet Starkey's secrets were subject to the same laws that he thought to cover other objects of exchange. Starkey knew, for example, that his secrets would decline in value as they became more widely available: this is what he meant, in part, when he wrote of 'prostrating'

[25] William Newman, 'Newton's clavis as Starkey's key', *Isis*, 78 (1987), 571–2.   [26] *Ibid.*

his antimonial secret 'in a way of lucre' while referring to Worsley's proposal. He adopted the principle that such 'vulgarization' led to price devaluation in a number of instances. In a letter to Boyle dated 16 January 1651, Starkey recounts his attempts to sell his perfumes to a perfume dealer. Despite the fact that the distributor has no money to pay him, he acquiesces to the pleas of the former to resist supplying another perfumer. Starkey gives the following reason for his action: 'With only one seller, and he of good note and fame ... the thing will be rarer and of greater estimation ... Otherwise when many have the same and sell it, there will be a trade-war [*certamen*] that will attract many buyers, and therefore one will sell to another at a lower price.'[27] The wide distribution or 'vulgarization' of a product thus devalues it. A similar idea is expressed in *The reformed commonwealth of bees* (1655), where Starkey notes that the best way to reduce wine consumption in England would be to increase domestic production. This would make the product more widely available and cheaper. In Starkey's words: 'If it were once become (as its easily so to be made) a domestick Commodity, no man then would want it for his necessary use, and by the reason of its commonnesse, the price of it would be brought farre lower, and by consequence the request it finds among the sipping Gallants of our time would abate.'[28]

Returning to the German letter of 1651, we see that Starkey was in a peculiar predicament. He hoped to use his secrets as a commodity in exchange for Boyle's material support of his research. Yet he ran thereby the risk of 'prostrating' or devaluing his arcana by vulgarizing them. Moreover, he refused to become a 'mill-horse' or 'amanuensis'. Starkey wanted to set the agenda for his own research, not carry out someone else's research projects.

The delicacy of Starkey's position is quite clear. Boyle, as Steven Shapin has emphasized, continually employed 'laborants' or 'operators' to man his laboratories.[29] Although some of these were quite

---

[27] Royal Society, Boyle Letters, fol. 132r: 'uno solo haec Aromata vendente, eoque notae ac famae bonae ... res et rarior, et majoris aestimationis Erit ... prout aliter cum plures idem habent, venduntque, certamen erit, quis plurimos Emptores alliciet, ideoque unus alio minoris vendet et per consequens adulterabit, sic tandem vilius fiet, minorisque pretii' (Starkey to Boyle, 16 January 1651/2).

[28] *The reformed commonwealth of bees* (London, 1655), 19.

[29] Steven Shapin, 'The invisible technician', *American Scientist*, 77 (1989), 554–63; Steven Shapin, 'The house of experiment in seventeenth-century England', *Isis*, 79 (1988), 373–404; Steven Shapin, 'Pump and circumstance: Robert Boyle's literary technology', *Social Studies of Science*, 14 (1984), 481–520. Professor Shapin has kindly sent me a draft

successful, such as Peter Sthael or Ambrose Godfrey Hanckwitz, they in fact occupied the position of labourer rather than researcher. As it happens, we have an opinion on such paid exploiters of chemistry in the words of Benjamin Worsley himself. In a letter to Samuel Hartlib (written before 28 February 1653/4), Worsley expresses his disenchantment with chemistry thus: 'For the truth is, I have laid all considerations in chemistry aside, as things not reaching much above common laborants, or strong-water distillers, unless we can arrive at this key, clearly and perfectly to know, how to open, ferment, putrify, corrupt and destroy (if we please) any mineral, or metal.'[30] Worsley's scorn for 'common laborants' and 'distillers' stems from the fact that they lack 'the key' to open and operate on metals. 'In this', Worsley states, 'both principally and only, I conceive [chemical] learning, judgment, or wisdom to consist.'[31] Without such a secret, Worsley continues, chemical preparations are 'not much to be valued'.[32]

Now it is precisely such a key as Worsley describes for arriving at the 'anatomy of metals' that Starkey thought he had discovered and transmitted to Boyle in 1651. As Worsley's letter makes clear, it was this key that distinguishes a true chemical philosopher from a mere 'laborant' or operator. Starkey was acutely aware of this fact, and we know that he was engaged in processes for making perfumes, dyes and ardent waters during the period in which he was corresponding with Boyle. He therefore ran the risk of being viewed as a mere artisan unless his preparations could be shown to proceed from such a key as Worsley describes. Needless to say, a key of this nature would make up one of the natural secrets that Starkey would refuse to sell.

It is also known that Starkey was being supported by Boyle from late 1651 (if not earlier) and through 1652, when the two of them were busily preparing a copper compound known as *ens veneris*. In one letter, Starkey thanked Boyle for the monstrous pie that his benefactor had sent him and, in *George Starkey's pill vindicated*, referred to the fact that he prepared the *ens veneris* 'for' Boyle.[33] Boyle himself, in a critical passage, stated that he provided 'the requisites

chapter from his forthcoming book, *A social history of truth: gentility, civility, and credibility in seventeenth century english science.*

[30] Boyle, *Works*, VI, 79.   [31] *Ibid.*   [32] *Ibid.*

[33] For the *artocreas ingens*, see Royal Society, Boyle Letters, fols. 131r–132r, *in margin* (Starkey to Boyle, 16 January 1651/2). For Boyle's support of the *ens veneris* project, see *George Starkey's pill vindicated*, 11.

to the work'. In these endeavours, Starkey must have felt himself perilously close to becoming Boyle's 'operator', since he appears to have carried out most if not all of the manual labour. Indeed, Starkey was so assiduous in pursuing the objective of isolating the essence of copper that he temporarily poisoned himself, putting the whole project into jeopardy.

Boyle's own comments relating the history of the *ens veneris* affair are worth further examination in this context. According to Boyle, he and Starkey – whom he calls 'an industrious chymist' – were reading van Helmont one day when it occurred to them that the mysterious stone of 'Butler' might be prepared 'by destroying (as far as we could by calcination) the body of copper, and then subliming it with sal armoniack'.[34] The two chemists then decided to begin the process with a vitriol (copper sulphate), since the 'body of *Venus* seems less locked up in good vitriol, than its metalline form'.[35] These remarks are followed by some comments that throw a rare shaft of light on the precise relationship between Boyle and Starkey:

But the person I discoursed with, seeming somewhat diffident of this process, by his unwillingness to attempt it, I desired, and easily persuaded him, at least to put himself to the trouble of trying it with the requisites to the work, which I undertook to provide, being at that time unable to prosecute it my self, for want of a fit furnace in the place where I then chanced to lodge.[36]

Here we have Boyle placing Starkey effectively in the classic role of operator or 'laborant'. His own contribution was primarily that of providing the capital and deciding the experiment to be carried out. Starkey, however, was 'diffident of this process' and at first unwilling to attempt it. Yet we know from Starkey's notebooks that his enthusiasm for experiment was virtually limitless. His diffidence certainly did not arise from inexperience or laziness. It is surely more probable that Starkey's reticence stemmed from objections of the sort that he had made to Boyle himself only a few months before, in regard to Worsley's proposal. If so, Starkey was here trying zealously to retain his own sovereignty while, at the same time, also attempting in a determined fashion to keep the close confidence of Boyle. His strategy of avoiding the sale of secrets had suc-

[34] Boyle, *Works*, II, 215.   [35] *Ibid.*, 216.   [36] *Ibid.*

ceeded, since he was preparing this one for no monetary reward, but only at the risk of his becoming Boyle's unpaid 'operator'.[37]

Starkey's Helmontian theory of knowledge thus combined with his own concerns about his social and economic status to make him fundamentally wary of disbursing his chemical secrets. Although Starkey's individual recipes had a real economic value and were therefore worth keeping covert as trade secrets, they had additional worth as tools for maintaining prestige and as tokens of God's esteem for the alchemist.

How, then, was Starkey able to sell any alchemical product, given the powerful forces enjoining him to secrecy? It may come as a surprise to learn now that Starkey considered the majority of chemical products to be *venalia*. In his 1651 letter to Morian, for example, Starkey referred to his 'aromatic oils' as 'highly saleable' (*venalia bene*). Moreover, he claimed to 'know the secret of extracting the same in a five times greater quantity' than that known to 'the vulgar', thus making his process quite lucrative.[38] A product became unsaleable only when it acquired the status of a 'key' – meaning above all the 'philosophical mercury' that could supposedly transmute metals, or that 'universal dissolvent', the Helmontian alkahest. Yet even in the case of his 'aromatic oils', Starkey claimed that his great yields result from 'a secret fermentation' unknown to 'vulgar distillers'.[39] This 'secret fermentation' too had surely acquired the status of a 'key'; but since the product, namely

---

[37] The fact that Starkey was unpaid may seem to violate the essence of the master–operator relationship, which Shapin has defined as follows: 'Thus the seventeenth-century technician can be defined by his remuneratively engaged status, his dependence upon the commands of his master, and the ascription to him of, at most, skill rather than knowledgeability about the operations he was paid to carry out.' Boyle was surely drawing on Starkey for more than mere technical expertise, but his later description of the experiment is at pains to depict Starkey as a mere 'industrious chymist', rather than a theorist. Thus Boyle's narration of the project effectively portrays Starkey as a laboratory technician carrying out Boyle's plan to replicate the Helmontian *lapis Butleri*. Hence two of Shapin's three criteria are easily met, leaving only the absence of remuneration. It is clear, however, that Boyle was supporting Starkey's efforts by payment in kind, if not *in specie*. Hence Starkey's reference to the *ingens artocreas*, literally a 'huge pie' sent to him by Boyle (Royal Society, Boyle Letters, fols. 131r–132r, *in margin* (Starkey to Boyle, 16 January 1651/2)).

[38] HP 17/7/2: 'si nimirum venalia bene forent olea aromatica, rosacea, Ligni Rhodii aut id genus alia, novi secretum extrahendi eadem quintuplo majori quantitate quam vulgo parantur' (George Starkey to Johann Morian, 30 May 1651).

[39] HP 17/7/2: 'olea item longe polliceor meliora, (per secretam puta fermentationem impetrata,) quae surdo auscultant distillatoribus vulgaribus, apud quos olea non digesta prius simplicium cruditate (quod sane fermentum nostrum (valde secretum) praestat) forsan etiam (oleo amygdalino admisto) adulterata, venundantur' (Starkey to Morian, 30 May 1651).

perfumes, could not be used to perform other marvels of nature, it was thus definitely a marketable process. A 'key', therefore, was any product or principle that had the ability to 'unlock' or reveal *further* secrets of nature. If a product such as Starkey's perfumes was to be considered a 'trade secret', in the sense that no one else was able to manufacture it, then the key to its manufacture might be described as a second-order secret.[40] Such a key had to be hidden from the rabble lest its accessibility make further revelations available to them. Part of Starkey's horror at such revelation derives from the fact that a key, as soon as its abilities were fully known to 'the vulgar', would by that fact alone cease to reveal further secrets. By definition, then, it would lose its power to open nature's 'closet', and so would cease to be a key.[41]

Considerable light is thrown on the relationship of 'keys' to ordinary secrets by Starkey's two letters on insects addressed to Hartlib and published in *The reformed commonwealth of bees* (1655). These letters are remarkable not only for the natural philosophy therein expressed, but also for the light that they shed on his involvement in industry. The first letter opened with a prophetic appeal to an imminent time *'when Ingenuities of all kind shall more and more flourish'* and *'the envy of Artists shall cease'*.[42] In a vein reminiscent of the *Introitus apertus*, Starkey asserted that God uses the envy of alchemists to 'keep obscured, that which he in his justice judges the ungrateful world at present unworthy of'.[43] Nonetheless, there were men who were willing to impart their secrets to those who were *'daily searchers into the secrets of nature'*; by such means knowledge might be advanced.

Starkey proceeded to provide some 'hints', as he called them, about such matters as the production of *aqua vitae* from unmalted peas and grain, the manufacture of dyes from insects, and of course, bee-keeping. By his own confession, he had not *'been ... very free in this thing'*.[44] The reader of Starkey's first letter was irritated by this discretion and Starkey began the second with a response to the

---

[40] Starkey, *Natures explication*, 216; here Starkey uses the Paracelsian term *arcana* for a type of alchemical medicament. In describing the process by which such 'secrets' are produced, he can therefore call them the 'True keys of arcanas'. In BL Sloane MS 3750 Starkey also repeatedly refers to individual drugs as *arcana* or 'secrets'.

[41] Starkey, *Natures explication*, 322. Here Starkey speaks of 'a Key by which you may enter the Closet of the most noble vegetable'.

[42] *Reformed commonwealth of bees*, 16.   [43] *Ibid.*   [44] *Ibid.*, 30.

'Admonitory Annotations' of the recipient.[45] In a defensive tone, Starkey replied to his critic:

[*Your*] first Answer (so it is called) doth seem to desire in that Epistle an open candidness, and a candid openness: in that I conceive I was not only open, but also plain, and I doe not know what I should have added, as to the matter proposed, and not have exceeded the bounds of an Epistle, and therefore I really intended what I said, and did conceive my apertnesse a candid Testimony of my intentions.

Having thus reaffirmed his goodwill, Starkey then elaborated a little, saying that he had intended to write like a traveller, who gives a summary report without all the details. He did not give his discoveries in the form of recipes, as his correspondent evidently wanted, because he feared that he might arouse anger by inadvertently leaving out a crucial detail. In more colourful language, he continued: 'My meaning is, that in as much as those Experiments were not so reiterated, as a Tanners making his liquor, I could not possibly throw the Receipts into the mouth of every one that could but gape. For what I try in a gallon, if I should prescribe in that quantity, My receipt would be contemptible.'[46] Here Starkey openly admitted that his major concern was the dissemination of his hard-earned secrets to those who can 'but gape'. The result of this misplaced generosity would be that his recipes would become contemptible. Their value would be diminished by vulgarization. Therefore, as Starkey said, rather than casting his pearls before swine, he chose only to 'hint to the ingenuous'. After giving a relation of 'things fecible ... both possibly and easie in nature ... I added the Meanes or Key, both for the one and other, namely, by reiterated fermentation, and so writing, I wrote to such, who in some measure understood Philosophy'.[47]

Despite his resolution to 'leave every man to his own Ingeny', Starkey proceeded to give a number of detailed procedures in the second letter on insects.[48] He describes a method of 'graduating the tinctures' or dyes to be obtained from insects, for example, by first

---

[45] *Ibid.*, 32. As Timothy Raylor has pointed out to me, Starkey's correspondent may have been Sir Cheney Culpeper rather than Hartlib. This is perhaps supported by the fact that the Hartlib Papers contain a note by Culpeper on Starkey's method of feeding bees with molasses: HP 55/3 – as printed in Wilkinson, 'Hartlib Papers', 106, n. 126. On the compilation of *The reformed commonwealth*, see Timothy Raylor, 'Samuel Hartlib and the commonwealth of bees', in *Culture and cultivation in early modern England: writing and the land*, ed. Michael Leslie and Timothy Raylor (Leicester, 1992), 91–129.
[46] *Reformed commonwealth of bees*, 34.   [47] *Ibid.*   [48] *Ibid.*, 35.

breeding a type of worm from an infusion of redweed. Employing what he calls his 'usuall Encheiria', he allows the worm to metamorphose into a fly.[49] The fly, once killed, represents 'the tincture of the Concrete whence it was produced', but since the original pigment has been '*graduated* beyond its own nature', it 'leaveth its dye in grain'.[50] By using such an 'animantative fermentation', Starkey claimed that he could produce a dye no 'whit inferior' to cochineal.[51] The process could even be extended by successively sealing up the flies produced by putrefaction and letting them die too. When the vessel was then reopened, a new worm would be generated, and from it a new fly. By this means, Starkey claimed, one might produce ever more graduated 'tinctures' or dyes.[52]

As in the earlier case of distillation without malting, Starkey evidently resorted to the 'Key' of fermentation. In concluding the process, he reported that he had desired merely 'to give hints of what rare secrets are in Nature attainable'. Starkey was here evidently willing to describe his processes in detail but with the clear implication that such procedures would only work for someone who understood the 'philosophicall key'. The key to fermentation is only vaguely hinted at in *The reformed commonwealth of bees*. Starkey's strategy was clearly to stimulate his reader's interest while retaining his own rights to his secrets. These secrets were no doubt lucrative, and so Starkey had every reason to keep them closely guarded. At the same time, as we have already seen, Starkey sincerely believed that such operative keys were secrets revealed to him by God Himself. Hence it was only right that they should redound to his profit rather than become the property of those who could but gape. Such secrets might also be used as a means of exchange with other sincere searchers into nature, such as Boyle. This was also to be permitted but only so long as no money changed hands. It was only when the likes of Farrar 'came gaping' that Starkey's wrath was aroused, and after that regrettable person had offered him £5,000 for his 'key into antimony' – tantamount to his secret of extracting precious metals therefrom – Starkey would no longer show him 'the least familiarity'.[53]

[49] *Ibid.*, 38   [50] *Ibid.*, 25.   [51] *Ibid.*, 25–6, 39.

[52] *Ibid.*, 26. The same series of spontaneous generation followed by intentional corruption and the birth of a new insect is laid out in Starkey's letter to Hartlib on insects: BL Sloane MS 427, fol. 86r.

[53] Newman, 'Clavis', 572. 'Farrar' might be the Richard Farrar who wrote an epitaph for Sir Kenelm Digby, printed in John F. Fulton, *Sir Kenelm Digby* (New York, 1937), 28. This

Starkey's attitude towards the concealment of knowledge cannot be reduced to a simple case of desiring to retain trade secrets any more than it can be accounted for by the excuses given in the *Introitus*. Though he was acutely aware of the devaluation of products resulting from their ease of accessibility, Starkey had additional motives for portraying himself as a 'silent searcher into nature's secrets'. His abhorrence of Glauber and Farrar as sellers of secrets was closely linked in his mind with the notion of base vulgarization for profit. This was the realm of 'operators' and 'laborants' rather than researchers such as himself. Such was the message that Starkey was trying to broadcast to Hartlib and Morian, but above all to his patron, Robert Boyle. And yet, despite these transparent efforts at publicity and the still-greater publicity stunt implicit in his creation of 'Eirenaeus Philalethes', there can be little doubt that Starkey's own personal identity demanded that he be true to his image of the Helmontian adept as one who was worthy of a divinely inspired intellectual understanding. But the clear bifurcation between 'adepts' on the one hand and a rabble that 'could but gape' on the other suggests the underlying antinomianism of Starkey's vision. The adept – and there can be no doubt that Starkey believed himself at times to be one – was held to a higher law, and that law did not preclude the elaborate mystification of a Philalethes.

appears to be the 'Dr Farrar' to whom the following recipe is ascribed in Royal Society, Boyle Papers 29, fols. 136r–139r: '*Volatile salt of [tartar], or fixed [spiritus vini], to dissolve [sol] Docr Farrar*' (courtesy of Dr Michael Hunter). The same recipe is found in MS 2124 of the Wellcome Institute (193), again with the attribution to Dr Farrar. This collection, and the recipes found clustered around fols. 136r–139r of Boyle Papers 29, are very similar – indeed often identical – to those occurring in the *Choice collection of rare chymical secrets* made by George Hartman from Digby's manuscripts and published in London in 1682. In the printed work, Richard Farrar and the Dr Farrar of the recipe can be identified as one, by comparing A4v, A5r and 234.

PART III

The improvement of nature and society
Natural philosophies

Benjamin Worsley: engineering for universal reform from the Invisible College to the Navigation Act

Charles Webster

Benjamin Worsley (1618–77) belongs to the class of individuals who possess evident historical importance, yet invite neglect. Worsley's name occurs in many associations, both during the Interregnum and after the Restoration, when his authority was respected on a wide range of questions. He was recognized as an agent of innovation in the fields of economics, colonial affairs and experimental science. Yet he played a somewhat shadowy role. He possessed pretensions as a scientist, but was not a member of the Royal Society. His vocation was medicine and he was known in his later career as Dr Worsley, yet he seems to have possessed no medical degree, probably no degree of any kind, and was not associated with the London College of Physicians. He published virtually nothing. All of this obscurity resulted in his omission from the original edition of the *Dictionary of national biography*.

It must be admitted that Worsley was not always fortunate in his choice of projects. His shortcomings over the Irish survey resulted in scathing attacks from the formidable William Petty, sufficient to damage Worsley's reputation permanently. Characteristically, the chronicler of Petty's Down Survey describes Worsley as 'médicastre sans clientèle'.[1] Of course, Petty himself embarked on some bizarre and unsuccessful ventures, and few leaders of the Royal Society are immune from criticism on this score. Consequently it would be a mistake to write Worsley out of the story of Baconian reform on the basis of the judgement of his jealous competitors. Although the evidence relating to Worsley's contribution is scattered among the archives, even the material located in the Hartlib Papers, which forms the basis for the present chapter, is sufficient to indicate that

---

[1] Y. M. Goblet, *La transformation de la Géographie Politique de l'Irlande au XVIIe siècle dans les cartes et essais anthropogéographiques de Sir William Petty*, 2 vols. (Paris, 1930), I, 215.

Worsley played a leading and constructive role in the reform movements of the Interregnum. This point will be illustrated with particular reference to the early career of Worsley, concentrating on the
period between 1645 and 1651, when an interconnected series of
events led Worsley from his ill-fated saltpetre project to political
importance as a prime mover of the Navigation Act of 1651.

The essential details of Worsley's career are provided in a self-
justificatory autobiographical note addressed to Lady Clarendon in
1661 and, therefore, exaggerating his political neutrality.[2] However,
in most respects Worsley's account is consistent with other evidence.
His career apparently began in Ireland, when in 1640 he went into
the service of the earl of Strafford. He reports that his main work was
establishing a hospital for the wounded of the Irish rebellion and
that he was given the salary of an army physician. The documentary
evidence suggests that he was employed as surgeon-general. The
autobiographical note mentions that he joined Trinity College,
Dublin and obtained a degree, whereas the records show only that
in 1643 he was admitted at the age of twenty-five, and that he was
an eldest son, born and educated in London, which enables us to fix
his approximate date of birth as 1618. Even if he was not a graduate,
it is evident that Worsley was well educated and linguistically
competent.

The autobiographical note suggests that Worsley sought to distance himself from the troubles by travelling to the Low Countries
where, after a false start, he eventually arrived in 1647 and
remained until after the death of Charles I. In fact Worsley returned
from Ireland to London where he established his reputation as a
technical expert and became central to the activities of the Hartlib
circle.

The death of Gabriel Plattes in the winter of 1644/5 had removed
Hartlib's main source of technical advice. Also it had become
increasingly clear that Plattes was impeded by his lack of formal
education, and Hartlib's expectations of rescuing posthumous publications from the remaining manuscripts of the technician were soon

---

[2] Bodleian Library, Clarendon MS 75, fols. 300–1 (Worsley to Lady Clarendon, November
1661). A convenient summary of biographical evidence is provided in J. B. Whitmore, 'Dr.
Worsley being dead', *Notes and Queries*, 185 (1943), 123–8; supplemented by C. Webster,
'Benjamin Worsley', *DNB – missing persons* (Oxford, 1993), 732–3. See also G. E. Aylmer,
The state's servants. The civil service of the English Republic 1649–1660 (London, 1973), 270–2,
416–17.

abandoned. Worsley emerged as an able substitute, enjoying the advantages of youth, education and ingenuity.

Apparently Worsley's first patron in London was Sir John Temple, who was master of the rolls in Ireland until his suspension in 1643. In London he took the parliamentary side and published, in 1646, an account of the Irish rebellion which inflamed popular opinion against the Irish. The first substantial evidence of Worsley's encounter with Hartlib derives from the latter's correspondence with Sir Cheney Culpeper, the well-connected Kent parliamentarian. The first contact between Worsley and Hartlib seems to have been made by the summer of 1645. By the autumn of that year Worsley was frequently mentioned and his intimacy with many members of Hartlib's circle was evident by the spring of 1646.[3]

Worsley came on the scene at an opportune moment, when Hartlib was developing his ideas on the Office of Address, alternatively called his 'College' in the correspondence of this period. Central to Hartlib's idea of a collegiate organization devoted to the advancement of learning was the task of promoting 'ingenuities'.[4] The appeal of Hartlib's scheme to influential patrons depended on its function as a source of inventions and other intelligence useful to the state. Worsley seemed like a helpful asset to the Office of Address, while the Office provided Worsley with influential political and entrepreneurial contacts, as well as access to Hartlib's intelligence on the activities of rival inventors, not only in Britain but also on the continent.

At the time of Worsley's introduction to the Office of Address, Hartlib and Culpeper were corresponding about the residual papers of Plattes, about the promotion of the work of the sixteenth-century innovator Palissy, and about the translation of the recently published works of J. B. van Helmont. They were assessing prospects for inventions by Barton, Joiner, Harrison, le Pruvost, Webb and Wheeler. The main topics under consideration were perpetual motion, and techniques and principles of ploughing. There was particular enthusiasm for the possibility of the growth of seedlings by planting seeds with a coating of fertilizer, especially saltpetre. This idea of 'philosophical dung' or 'quintessential dung' was perhaps responsible for attracting Worsley's interest in the production and

[3] HP Bundle 13.   [4] Webster, 67–77.

utilization of saltpetre, which was already in great demand because of its place as a necessary ingredient of gunpowder.[5]

In the context of the above profusion of ingenuity, Worsley was described by Culpeper as one of the actors on the 'brave centre and stage' of activities in London.[6] The Culpeper–Hartlib correspondence suggests rapid disillusionment with the work of most of the English inventors. Optimistic early reports on them were not confirmed. Of the Englishmen, apart from Worsley, only William Wheeler seemed to offer tangible benefits, but Wheeler was notoriously egocentric and not altogether trusted or reliable. The immigrant Peter le Pruvost was also reputable, but he was unwilling to stay in England because of the absence of guaranteed recompense or secure patronage.

Worsley was co-operative, reliable and more in tune with the ethos of Hartlib and Dury than was the case with Plattes. Great excitement was evoked by Worsley's saltpetre project, which seemed practicable and was supported by well-informed technical memoranda consistent with the principles of Paracelsian chemistry. Worsley seemed to have evolved a simple method for generating a widely useful product, offering the opportunity to replace traditional and inconvenient methods of production and reduce dependence on expensive imports.

Because it could not be advanced 'without the interest as well as the activity of a State', the saltpetre project was seized upon by Culpeper and Hartlib as providing justification for a publicly funded and state-patronized Office of Address. In March 1646 a committee of aldermen examined Worsley's scheme and, on the basis of their support, the saltpetre project was considered by both the House of Commons and the House of Lords in the autumn of 1646.[7] By this stage Worsley's credentials as an inventor and servant of the public interest were firmly established and before the flaws in this proposal were discovered, he had diversified his activities and

---

[5] HP 13/109A–112A and HP 13/279A–282B (Culpeper to Hartlib [Autumn and probably December 1645]). The first dated letter mentioning Worsley is 31 October 1645 (HP 13/115A–116B). Worsley's writings on saltpetre are discussed in Webster, 377–80.

[6] HP 13/279A–282B (Culpeper to Hartlib, n.d. [probably December 1645]).

[7] *Commons Journal*, v, 686 (7 October 1646); *Lords Journal*, VIII, 573–4 (21 November 1646). See also various letters from Culpeper to Hartlib in HP Bundle 13; HP 13/123A–124B (27 November 1645); HP 13/277A–278A (n.d. [early December 1645]); HP 13/125A–126B (12 January 1645/6); HP 13/127A–128B (17 February 1645/6); HP 13/131 (23 February [1645/6]).

located alternative means of establishing a reputation. It should be remembered that simultaneously William Petty was easing his path to preferment with the double-writing instrument, an invention for which he made extravagant claims, but which was soon lost sight of, once it had impressed his patrons.

From the outset Worsley was attracted by the broader purposes of the Office of Address. Culpeper suggested that this 'colledge' was likely to make its impact by the slow accretion of improvements, discoveries and 'well-principled indeavors'.[8] Culpeper recognized the opportunity for this venture to link the irenic activities of Dury with the secular work of Hartlib. The ideal arrangement was a college situated in London, associated with a correspondency for the advancement of ecclesiastical peace, human learning and ingenuities. Thus, in the autumn of 1645 Culpeper was advocating a college containing an 'invisible' dimension formed by its correspondents.[9] If it were judged perverse to link the spiritual and secular correspondences, Culpeper pointed out that only by increasing the fruits of the earth would humans come to live according to the simplicity of the patriarchs. Then God would be glorified throughout the whole world, which he took as representing Worsley's general aim. Therefore Culpeper encouraged Hartlib to opt firmly for extending the remit of his college to embrace universal objects, including exploitation of the 'sea of ingenuities'. This view received direct support from Worsley, who wrote enthusiastically about the college and advised that it should be guided by 'humble feare' and that its discoveries should be used only according to the aims of the reformation to which they subscribed.[10]

The letters cited above are also instructive for indicating the circle of patronage upon which the promoters of the Office of Address depended. Of course, there was no sharp line between promoters and patrons, as indicated by Culpeper, who was both architect and political sponsor. New recruits such as Worsley and Petty clearly joined the inner circle of correspondents and pamphleteers, which consisted of Culpeper, Dury and Hartlib. Culpeper's letters written between the autumn of 1645 and the spring of 1646 also gave prominence to an outer circle of sponsors. He mentioned supportive

8 HP 13/279A (Culpeper to Hartlib, n.d. [December 1645]).
9 HP 13/117A–118B (Culpeper to Hartlib, 5 November 1645).
10 HP 13/295B (Culpeper to Hartlib, December 1645) and HP 13/223A (Worsley to Culpeper, undated excerpt from a letter [probably 1648]).

contacts with such influential figures as Sir Robert Honywood, his wife, Lady Frances Honywood, John Milton, Hugh Peter, Henry Robinson, Lady Katherine Ranelagh, John Sadler, Walter Strickland, Sir Henry Vane the younger and Thomas Westrow. This group was linked politically and by ties of neighbourhood and family relationship. For instance, Culpeper, Honywood and Westrow had strong links with Kent; Lady Honywood was the sister of Vane; and Lady Ranelagh was the niece of Mrs Dury and the patron of Milton.

Culpeper's letters of this period also display a noticeable increase in political and religious radicalism, and point to a rift with the Presbyterians. He applauded the 'democraticall growing spirits' while attacking as locusts the 'Papall, Episcopall, Presbiterall' parties. It seemed to Culpeper as if the general speeding up of events was a prelude to the fall of Babylon and Antichrist. The wider patronage circle reflected precisely the same bias, as a result of which they came to exercise increasing political influence with the growing consolidation of the power of the Independents. This political trend increased the positive response to Hartlib's schemes and, as noted below, it was vital to the success of Worsley when he returned from the Netherlands in 1649.[11]

An important confidant of the Hartlib circle was Katherine, Lady Ranelagh, the elder sister of Robert Boyle. There is no evidence that Boyle himself was familiar with the early proposals for the Office of Address.[12] This is scarcely surprising because, when the Office of Address was devised, Boyle was only eighteen and just settling down in England after returning from the continent. However, the increasing involvement of Hartlib's group with the experimental sciences, especially chemistry, added to the potential interest for Boyle. In December 1645 Culpeper reported that his own involvement in chemistry extended back for twenty years and in the same letter gave a summary of his ideas on generation in the context of discussion of Worsley's saltpetre project.[13] Some months later Culpeper responded enthusiastically when Hartlib obtained a manuscript copy of an unpublished work by Johann Rudolph Glauber,

[11] HP 13/129A–130A (Westrow to Culpeper, 20 February 1646/7) reports that Cromwell's support for the idea of a foreign correspondency had been obtained; this was enclosed with HP 13/167A–168B (Culpeper to Hartlib, 1 March 1646/7).
[12] R. E. W. Maddison, *The life of the Honourable Robert Boyle* (London, 1969), 57–88.
[13] HP 13/109A–112A (Culpeper to Hartlib, [Autumn 1645]).

probably his *Furni novi philosophici*, which established itself as the standard work on techniques of distillation. In a later letter Culpeper sought Worsley's opinion on his 'Chymicall philosophy'.[14] William Petty, who was first mentioned by Culpeper in March 1647, was soon directed to translate Glauber, but in the event manuscript translations were produced by others, including both Culpeper and Worsley.[15] The first published translation was produced in 1651 by John French, another associate of the Hartlib circle.

The contact between the young Robert Boyle and the Hartlib circle was not long delayed. Boyle immediately became one of Hartlib's most active supporters and a keen advocate of the Office of Address. In a letter to Hartlib, probably dating from the spring of 1647, Boyle wrote effusively about his wish to contribute to 'that college, whereof God has made you hitherto the midwife and nurse'.[16]

Boyle's earliest letters to Hartlib, written in the spring of 1647, make no reference to Worsley, but they mention John Hall of Cambridge, whose association with the Office of Address had also just commenced, and who was translating utopian works on behalf of Hartlib. In December 1646, soon after his acquaintance with Hartlib, Hall asked to be introduced to Milton and Worsley, and soon he was engaged in active correspondence with the latter.[17] In February 1647 a particularly notable exchange between them took place on the question of 'whether the Scripture be an adequate Judge of Physical Controversies', Worsley producing much the longer contribution to the debate.[18] Hall soon extended his network of contacts to Boyle, whom he described as breathing 'an high and Aethereall Genius'. His letters of April 1647 mention both Boyle and Worsley in the context of 'our utopian Academy', which may well represent a reference to the Invisible College.

As I have argued elsewhere, Worsley devised the Invisible College as a means of keeping in touch with correspondents who were likely

14 HP 13/147 (Culpeper to Hartlib, 1 October 1646); HP 13/196A–197B (Culpeper to Hartlib, 20 October 1647).
15 HP 13/166 (Culpeper to Hartlib, 16 February 1646/7) and 13/167A–168B (Culpeper to Hartlib, 1 March 1646/7); HP 13/196A–197B (20 October 1647).
16 Boyle, *Works*, I, xlvi. Boyle's first dated letter to Hartlib is from 19 March 1647.
17 HP 60/14/3A–4B (Hall to Hartlib, 17 December [1646]).
18 HP 36/6/1A (Hall to Worsley, 5 February 1646/7) and HP 36/6/3A–6B (Worsley to Hall, 16 February 1646/7).

to meet only infrequently in London.[19] Worsley's closest associate in
this venture was Robert Boyle, whose letters provide the only direct
references to the Invisible College. After his return from a tour of
Europe, Boyle settled at Stalbridge in Dorset, which left the young,
cosmopolitan intellectual somewhat isolated. No doubt his link with
Worsley occurred through Lady Ranelagh. Worsley would have
seemed an ideal person to assist with Boyle's growing interest in
experimental philosophy and the applied arts. The contact between
Boyle and Worsley seems to date from 1646. Certainly by November
1646, the date of Boyle's first recorded letter to Worsley, they were
friends. Boyle, who was only nineteen at the time, evidently looked
upon Worsley as a mentor, and a similar impression is conveyed by a
second letter written in February 1647, just before Worsley's departure for the Netherlands.[20] Significantly, the first letter opened with
congratulations on the grant of parliamentary support for the saltpetre project. These letters were primarily concerned with practical
matters, particularly horticulture and chemistry. But it was also
apparent that Boyle was in sympathy with Worsley's wider aspirations. Indeed, Boyle directed at Worsley some of the most extravagant expressions of admiration ever recorded in his writings.

This enthusiasm was reflected in accounts of the Invisible College
given by Boyle to his correspondents Isaac Marcombes and Francis
Tallents. He explained to Marcombes that his group was concerned
with 'natural philosophy, the mathematics, and husbandry, according to the principles of our new philosophical college, that values no
knowledge, but that it hath a tendency to use'.[21] To his Cambridge
tutor, Francis Tallents, Boyle underlined their emancipation from
scholasticism and 'narrow-mindedness'. They were willing to learn
from the 'meanest, so he can but plead reason for his opinion', and
they were guided by 'charity', or 'universal good-will', taking 'the
whole body of mankind for their care'.[22]

Boyle's continuing high regard for Worsley was perhaps reflected
in a letter from Lady Ranelagh alluding to 'one of your own
fraternity, who thinks himself in the highest class of your philosophi-

[19] C. Webster, 'New light on the Invisible College', *Transactions of the Royal Historical Society*,
24 (1974), 19–42; Webster, 57–67.
[20] Boyle, *Works*, VI, 40–1, 39–40 (Boyle to Worsley, *c.* 21 November 1646 and February
1646/7).
[21] *Ibid.*, I, xxx (Boyle to Marcombes, 22 October 1646).
[22] *Ibid.*, xxxiv–xxxv (Boyle to Tallents, 20 February 1646/7).

cal Society'.[23] Boyle's involvement with the Invisible College might be dismissed as a *jeu d'esprit*, or a reflection of uncritical youthful enthusiasm, but it also served a more serious and permanently important purpose. It established guidelines for Boyle's scientific mission, from which he never actively departed. Experimental philosophy was justified on the basis of its wider social, ethical and religious purpose. Boyle's insatiable curiosity about empirical phenomena and his commitment to exhaustive experimentation were motivated by these higher objectives. Given the apprenticeship of the Invisible College, there was no risk that Boyle would degenerate into the idle curiosity of the Restoration virtuosi. More than any other personal influence, Benjamin Worsley was responsible for establishing the deep spiritual motivation and broad horizons of Boyle's scientific activities.

One immediate effect of the Invisible College exercise was to arouse Boyle's interests in the activities of Samuel Hartlib. Their first contacts in March 1647 related to Hartlib's sponsorship of translations of utopian tracts. These tracts by Andreae and Campanella described ideal communities and intellectual fraternities which would have appealed to the Invisible College. Very quickly Boyle became alerted to the Office of Address. His letter seeking advice about progress with the Office of Address offered in return some information for Hartlib about the Invisible College.[24] This seems to have been Hartlib's introduction to the Invisible College.

Worsley's capacity to relate mundane technical activity to the sphere of universal values is illustrated by the unpublished tract 'Proffits humbly presented to this kingdome'. Although no author is given, the tract relates closely to other writings by Worsley and it arguably represents one of the earlier statements of his political and economic programme. Although 'Proffits humbly presented' contains themes developed more extensively in writings produced in 1649, I favour an earlier dating on account of (a) the primacy given to the saltpetre project, the credibility of which was in doubt by 1649; (b) emphasis on improvements in husbandry of the kind under discussion in 1646; (c) frequent reference to the welfare of the 'Kingdom', which was replaced by 'commonwealth' in his later writings; (d) no direct evidence of the benefit of his Dutch experi-

---

[23] *Ibid.*, xxxvi–xxxvii (Lady Ranelagh to Boyle, 3 June 1647).
[24] *Ibid.* xl (Boyle to Hartlib, 8 May 1647).

ence; (e) finally, no special mention of the American colonies, which were the predominant concern of his 1649 writings. Consequently 'Proffits humbly presented' may well date from 1647, the period when the Invisible College was one of his primary concerns. From the starting point of the saltpetre project, 'Proffits humbly presented' urged the broad potentiality of technical innovation. Optimization of production and economic diversification required systematic development of the colonies. Crucially, the benefits of such planning and development would be lost unless more effective regulation of trade with the colonies was introduced. Without such regulation the wealth of the nation would drain away and the imperial pretensions of Britain would be jeopardized. On the other hand, Worsley offered the prospects of growing economic and political strength, given the pursuance of active policies in the field of trade and plantations. Indeed, Britain might become the 'judge and Umpire of al Christian differences'. With respect to specific programmes, a prosperous Britain would be able to undertake the propagation of the Gospel throughout the world, the reform of education, the advancement of learning, the conversion of the Jews and the reconciliation of the Protestant churches.[25] Although primarily a technical and economic tract, 'Proffits humbly presented' gives an insight into Worsley's broader and, indeed, utopian aspirations. It is quite likely that similar ideals were appealing to the Invisible College. Such an ambitious framework would help to explain the evident intensity of the young Robert Boyle's commitment to this project.

'Proffits humbly presented' possesses a wider relevance, because it provides an insight into the ideology of the parliamentarian intelligentsia. The idea of inseparable connection between elementary innovations designed to assist the poor and the wider framework of international trade and colonial policy was consistent with economic thinking that had been developing since the 1620s. 'Proffits humbly presented' added the apocalyptic and pansophic inspiration which was an influential motivation within the parliamentarian coalition and which was developed with particular force within the Hartlib circle. The synthesis of sound practical advice, economic advantage, altruism, imperialism and messianic uto-

---

[25] 'Proffits humbly presented to this kingdome', HP 15/2/61. For the full text, Webster, 539–46.

pianism represented by the Invisible College pointed towards the programme that was taken up by the politicians, entrepreneurs and religious idealists who gained the ascendancy in 1649 and were faced with establishing the legitimacy of the newly founded republic.

Probably in late February 1647, without any particular explanation, Worsley abandoned his promising career in London for an extended visit to the Netherlands. But his decision should not occasion surprise. Perhaps Worsley realized that substantial support for the Office of Address was not likely to be forthcoming in the short term. Such pessimism turned out to be fully justified. It is evident from 'Proffits humbly presented' and other economic tracts of that period that the Netherlands was regarded as a main trading competitor, many of whose practices deserved to be investigated and evaluated. Hartlib had many contacts in the Low Countries and was keen to obtain information about the activities of inventors, especially the chemist, Glauber. Consequently it was entirely appropriate that Worsley should pursue his long-term intention to work in the Netherlands. It is likely that he was specifically commissioned to convey intelligence to Hartlib and also he may have been acting as an agent of Parliament. Of course, Worsley retained his links in England through correspondence and by contact with a stream of English visitors, including Robert Boyle, who spent about two months in the Netherlands in 1648.

Worsley's departure created some difficulties for Hartlib because it removed the latter's main technical adviser, but William Petty seemed to be an able substitute. Petty first emerges in Hartlib's correspondence at precisely the time of Worsley's departure. Hartlib described Petty as 'not altogether a very dear Worsley, but ... a most rare and exact anatomist, and excelling in all intellectual and mechanical learning'.[26]

Worsley rapidly established himself in the Netherlands, and he travelled widely. His main patrons were leading members of the English community such as Sir William Boswell, Sir Charles Herbert, and Sir Robert Honywood and his wife. An especially

---

[26] Boyle, *Works*, vi, 76 (Hartlib to Boyle, 16 November 1647). Attitudes to Petty fluctuated. For instance, in June 1647, Culpeper criticized Petty and Wheeler for being mercenary, whereas in December he expressed unreserved admiration and called for public encouragement of his inventions; HP 13/180A–181B (Culpeper to Hartlib, 18 June 1647) and HP 13/206A–207B (Culpeper to Hartlib, 22 December 1647).

important contact was Walter Strickland, Parliament's envoy in
the Netherlands, who was to play a leading part in promoting Worsley's Virginia project. It will be recalled that Boswell had known
Francis Bacon and was in possession of many of Bacon's manuscripts. Indeed, these may have been among the manuscripts that
he showed to Worsley on the latter's visit to The Hague.[27] Intellectuals already associated with Hartlib, such as Adam Boreel,
F. M. van Helmont, Johann Morian and Menasseh ben Israel, provided other important points of contact.

Evidence from many parts of Hartlib's papers shows that
Worsley set about collecting intelligence on an extensive scale. He
reported that 'I gave myselfe out, to bee a man curious in novelties,
especially in matters of Art, and Invention; and in all companies,
putting in seasonable Interrogatories of this nature, and taking
occasion to view their saw-mills and other mills, to see what light
would come of itselfe'.[28] His correspondence relayed information on
practices and improvements in such areas as agriculture, horticulture, distillation, mining and refining of ores, mills, drainage engineering, lens-making and the improvement of microscopes and telescopes.

He reported on the activities of local inventors such as Glauber,
Fromanteel, Kuffeler, le Pruvost and Wheeler, as well as on such
figures as Hevelius in Danzig, Hobbes in Paris and Johann Wiesel
in Augsburg. All of this effort impressed Worsley's English correspondents. Typically, Culpeper expressed his admiration for 'the
trade of soe much ingenuity and knowledge'.[29] Much of Worsley's
energy was absorbed in specific technical missions, such as attempting to discover whether the mills devised by Wheeler were likely to
yield a return to the many patrons who had invested in his work.

On the whole, the evidence relating to Worsley's visit to the
Netherlands suggests a remarkable degree of continuity with his
preoccupations in London. Much time was occupied on deliberat-
ing over the same inventions and inventors, the continuing efforts
to translate Glauber, further elaboration of aspects of chemistry
relevant to the saltpetre project and the uphill task of securing
public patronage for the Office of Address. This latter problem provided a setback to plans for attracting le Pruvost back to England,

---

[27] HP 36/8/1A–5B (Worsley to Hartlib, 4/14 February 1648).   [28] HP 36/8/1A.
[29] HP 13/196A–197B (Culpeper to Hartlib, 20 October 1647).

a possibility that Worsley was urged to keep open on behalf of the Hartlib circle.

During his stay in the Netherlands, Worsley produced a series of informative letters and short tracts on topical subjects, of which 'Proffits humbly presented' constitutes an outstanding example. Some of these writings cannot be traced: for instance, the tract entitled 'The interest of the people' from 1647 or his paper on eclectic philosophy sent to Boyle in 1648.[30] His letters collectively constitute important evidence for the consolidation of the influence of Baconian experimental philosophy. Indeed, if produced by members of the Royal Society, they might well have attracted considerable interest. As it is, the letters of Worsley pre-date the Baconian wisdom of the Royal Society, such as Sprat's celebrated *History*, by nearly twenty years.

Typically, Worsley recognized the potentialities of the microscope and took an active interest in the improvement of lens grinding and microscope design. The observations he recorded show that he was a practical microscopist, recording phenomena that later attracted the attention of Hooke and Power. Worsley reported that he 'received more pleasure and satisfaction at spare hours by looking at small and minute bodies in these glasses, than almost from anything'. He argued that microscopy provided an avenue to certainty of knowledge in areas that were rife with speculation. He insisted that knowledge must be immediately deduced from, or built upon 'Reall, and certayne experiments, and those so many, as to make an infallible universall'. His aim was 'to discover to the world this little Atlantis, or unknowne part of the Creation hitherto not well lookd after by Any'. He believed that the microscope would reveal the immensity of the wisdom of God and prove that nothing happened by chance.

The microscope confirmed his addiction to 'experimental learning', to the extent that he had 'abdicated much reading of Books, vulgare received Traditions, and common or school opinions'. His wider aim was to undertake a systematic natural history, which would contribute a body of knowledge, not only 'certaine, or reall, but useful'.[31] The above sentiments must echo Worsley's early communications with Boyle, which caused the latter to commit

---

[30] HP 13/202A–203B (Culpeper to Hartlib, 10 November 1647); 13/237A–238B (Culpeper to Hartlib, 16 August 1648); 13/243 (same to same, [19?] August 1648).
[31] HP 8/27/5A (Worsley to Hartlib, 27 June 1648).

himself to 'furtherance of your great design, and the enabling you to do for the great world, what the chairman of physicians has done for the little, publish a discourse *de usu partium*'.[32]

Worsley detected a parallel between enlightened science and religion. In the case of divine knowledge, he acknowledged 'none to be the necessary Rule of fayth but what the spiritt of God hath sett doune plainely, in symple, and univocal tearmes, and easy to the understanding of any'. Accordingly he argued that the essentials of religion could be distilled into a 'few particulars' which would enable free communication among those infused with the spirit of God.[33] This approach has affinities with Dury's irenicism or latitudinarianism, but in practice Worsley was drifting way beyond the limits of tolerance of the major denominations, into the territory inhabited by the Quakers and other enthusiasts.

By the summer of 1649, Worsley's visit to the Netherlands was bringing diminishing returns and he was facing increasing financial difficulties. The Office of Address remained a distant prospect. In desperation, long after all the desirable posts had been filled by academics loyal to Parliament, Hartlib and Dury solicited appointments in Oxford. Culpeper lamented that they would be 'buried in Oxforde', and that this would remove them 'from that stage which is moste proper for that publique trade in ingenuity, which you desire to put into motion'.[34] The Oxford plan was abandoned and no realistic alternative emerged until Worsley took up the issue towards the end of his stay in Ireland, almost a decade later.

Like some other innovators such as le Pruvost, Worsley turned his attention to the possibility of a career in the colonies. Through Hartlib he was well informed about affairs in the American colonies, particularly from John Winthrop junior, governor of Connecticut, who was an authoritative source on colonial technology. Worsley was also informed by Hartlib about the learned American physician, Robert Child, who was also an expert on agriculture. Child then visited Worsley in the Netherlands. Child introduced Hartlib to his fellow-American chemist and alchemist, George Starkey, whom Child described as an inventor of furnaces whose abilities equalled those of Glauber. Hartlib relied on Worsley for assessment

---

[32] Boyle, *Works*, VI, 40 (Boyle to Worsley *c*. 21 November 1646).
[33] HP 8/27/1A–9A (Worsley to Hartlib, 27 June 1648).
[34] HP 13/258A–259B (Culpeper to Hartlib, 22 July 1649).

of the extravagant claims and eccentric behaviour of the extraordinary Starkey.

Undoubtedly conversations with Child increased Worsley's curiosity about the American colonies. America and the West Indies
seemed an ideal location for the development of the kind of model
plantations he had envisaged in 'Proffits humbly presented'. The
superior climate and ample natural resources of America offered a
source of cheap raw materials and other commodities which might
constitute a major asset to the wealth of the nation, provided
regulations were introduced to ensure 'Our Nation receiving the
Whole benefitt both of the Commodities it selfe and monopolizing
also the trading of them into their owne hands'.[35] 'Proffits humbly
presented' lamented that Britain experienced adverse trading relations with its competitors, but Worsley's ideas for improving this
situation were mainly indirect. He placed the main emphasis on the
encouragement of innovation, diversification of trading contacts,
the building up of the merchant fleets and the greater protection of
shipping.

A long series of letters and memoranda, impressive in their intensity and quality and communicating a sense of great urgency, all
written in the space of a few weeks during July and August 1649,
evolved a more radical approach to Britain's trading problems.

The occasion for a more draconian approach to economic policy
stemmed from the flagrant opposition to Parliament in some of the
American colonies and many of the islands of the West Indies. The
worst example was Virginia, which represented a particularly
serious problem because of the economic importance of this colony.
Worsley was consulted on this crisis and was persuaded by his
English correspondents to elaborate his ideas. His first review of this
problem seems to have been sent to John Sadler, a prominent
London lawyer, an MP and member of the Council of State, who
had been one of the first public defenders of Neoplatonism at
Cambridge. Sadler was, of course, an associate of Hartlib.

In reporting to Dury on his contacts with Sadler, Worsley briefly
elaborated his plan for Virginia. He realized that le Pruvost was
more expert on some technical issues, but Worsley argued that his
own broader programme was more relevant in the circumstances.
He regarded the colony as an ideal location for development of a

[35] 'Proffits humbly presented', in Webster, 542.

model plantation and for application of his long-standing ideas on
the encouragement of trade and industry, the reform of education
and the civilizing of the indigenous inhabitants. There was no
shortage of commodities which might be produced in abundance in
Virginia; he specified aniseed, sweet fennel, liquorice, rice, almonds,
raisins, figs, olives, cotton, cork oak and oak galls. Such development
was expected to benefit the British economy in the many ways
already explained in 'Proffits humbly presented'.

Worsley believed that the expertise and capital to support such
development was readily available, but the regime in power was
odious from both the political and religious perspectives. Therefore,
a necessary condition for the realization of his economic objects was
the removal of the governor and the replacement of the government
of Virginia, reinforced by control of ships and their passengers to
prevent the infiltration of delinquents, and by wider measures to
protect the security of trade. Worsley proposed that the parliamentary authorities should appoint commissioners in London to
supervise reform in Virginia.[36]

In response to spontaneous expressions of interest from Hartlib's
circle and influential politicians, Worsley further elaborated his
ideas, increasingly emphasizing that success of his propositions
depended on rigid control of shipping with Virginia, in the first
instance to secure the political loyalty of all those entering the
colony, but also to obtain a strict monopoly of trade. Worsley
calculated that £5,000 each year would be gained from tobacco
duty alone if this trade were limited to English vessels. The possibility of direct, tangible benefits on this scale was undoubtedly an
attraction both to politicians and merchants in London. Of course,
they were capable of thinking of such measures for themselves, but
Worsley emerged as a spokesman able to draft proposals in a form
suitable for impressing the legislators.[37]

By mid-August 1649, Worsley had refined his ideas concerning
the statutory control of Virginia. At one stage he proposed four
commissioners, with Hartlib as their secretary. Shortly afterwards
he envisaged himself acting as secretary and Hartlib was not again

---

[36] HP 33/2/18A (Worsley to Dury, 27 July 1649).

[37] HP 33/2/3 (Worsley to Dury, 17/27 August 1649). See also 'A memorandum of the
Virginia plantation' (HP 61/5); 'Further animadversions about Virginia' (HP 61/6); and
'Letter to Mr Strickland' (HP 61/8).

mentioned in this capacity.[38] Worsley emphasized that wealthy undertakers were standing by to set up a major operation in Virginia, but he insisted that they would not consider investing in this scheme unless Parliament fulfilled the investors' demands concerning political and economic regulation. He also made this action a condition for his own further participation and return to London.[39]

Worsley's audacious demands produced a rapid and favourable response. In London, his case was pressed by a miscellaneous coalition comprising the Hartlib circle, entrepreneurs and politicians. Worsley's scheme appealed to the altruism and reformist instincts of the Hartlib circle, the self-interests of those willing to invest in speculative ventures, and politicians concerned with the perilous state of the economy, eager to detect additional sources of revenue and fearful of the repercussions of the continuing political recalcitrance of Virginia and its allies.

It is instructive that every one of the names mentioned above as supporting the Office of Address scheme in 1646 re-emerges in 1649 as a backer of Worsley's Virginia project. In 1649 they enjoyed inestimably greater authority. Vane, Sadler and Westrow were influential MPs and the first two were members of the Council of State. Milton was Latin secretary to the Council of State. Strickland, as mentioned above, was envoy to the Netherlands. Hugh Peter and Henry Robinson were recognized as authorities on economic and political affairs.

Prompt response by Parliament to the Virginia proposals contrasted with the lethargy shown earlier over the Office of Address. An important difference was made by the existence of the Council of State formed in 1649. The Hartlib circle enjoyed firm support on the Council of State and energies on behalf of Worsley were exercised from that direction. Dury assured Worsley that the Council of State was taking the lead and that Parliament would follow. In July 1649, he mentioned that Sadler was a confirmed supporter and that Milton, John Trenchard and John Bradshaw, the lord president of the Council, 'all relish the Motion exceeding well'.[40] Trenchard was the father-in-law of Sadler, and an influential Dorset MP. Although

[38] HP 33/2/1–2 (Worsley to Hartlib, 3/13 August 1649); HP 33/2/3–4 (Worsley to Dury, 17/27 August 1649).
[39] HP 33/2/3–4 (Worsley to Dury, 17/27 August 1649).
[40] HP 1/2/9 (Dury to [Worsley], 30 July 1649).

Bradshaw has been appropriately described as a 'humourless medio-
crity', his goodwill was a real asset.[41] In subsequent letters, Dury
recorded support from other politicians ranging from William
Lenthall, speaker of the House of Commons, to the rising London
common councillor, Richard Hill. Worsley's list of possible commissioners (Thomas Andrews, Nicholas Corsellis, Maurice Thomson,
William Pennoyer and Martin Noell) gives some indication of
merchants willing to participate in the scheme.[42]

The papers relating to the Virginia project are infused with a
mood of confidence rarely present in Hartlib's papers. Dury
appealed to Worsley as 'a man of life and action, and of a very
public Spirit' to return to Britain and apply himself to ingenuities.[43]
In correspondence among Worsley's parliamentary supporters,
Strickland passed on the relevant memoranda to Vane, mentioning
that Worsley was 'most Active in framing this new modell and
Animates it'. Worsley was 'exceedingly Able for Any Imployment,
Being of very high parts, both naturall and Acquired and I have
heard in particular for the improving of all Things which may be for
Trade and manufacture'.[44] On this basis, Strickland followed Sadler
in recommending Worsley for the post of secretary to the Virginia
commissioners.

Given this substantial degree of support from influential quarters,
Worsley returned to England by the Christmas of 1650. As in so
many of the Hartlib initiatives, the initial burst of enthusiasm was
dissipated without decisive action being taken. However, on this
occasion the momentum was not entirely lost. Indeed Worsley's
efforts were partly responsible for a larger success than he anticipated when, in August 1650, Parliament established a council or
commission for advancing and regulating trade, with Worsley as its
secretary, with the substantial salary of £200.[45] Samuel Hartlib
junior was taken on as clerk to this committee. Furthermore, of the
fifteen commissioners, no fewer than four (Culpeper, Honywood,
Thomson and Vane) were directly involved with Worsley's Virginia

[41] Aylmer, *The state's servants*, 22.
[42] HP 33/2/1–2 (Worsley to Hartlib, 3/13 August 1649); HP 33/2/20–1.
[43] HP 1/2/12–13 (Dury to [Worsley], 8 August 1649).
[44] HP 61/9 (Strickland to Vane, c. September 1649).
[45] The letters of Henry More to Hartlib in HP Bundle 18 establish that Worsley had decided
to return to England some time between the beginning of November and Christmas 1649.
Firth & Rait, II, 403–6 ('An Act for the advancing and regulating of the trade of this
Commonwealth', 1 August 1650).

project. The instructions setting out the work of the council of trade constitute an obvious agenda, but they also probably reflect the bias of Worsley himself and would have reflected the ideas of other economists such as Hugh Peter, Henry Robinson or Thomas Violet, as well as the interloping merchants, since they were distinctly unfriendly towards corporate interests. The final instruction seems particularly to reflect the aims of the Virginia memoranda:

Twelfthly, They are to take into their consideration the English Plantations in America or elsewhere, and to advise how those plantations may be best managed, and made most useful for this Commonwealth; and how the Commodities thereof may be so multiplied and improved, as (if it be possible) those Plantations alone may supply the Commonwealth of England with whatsoever it necessarily wants.[46]

The council of trade lasted until the end of 1651, during which time it produced some fifteen reports and intervened on a wide variety of issues. Because relatively little detailed evidence exists relating to its deliberations, the precise role of Worsley is difficult to establish. However, it is clear that the council's most important interventions in the field of trade were consistent with Worsley's programme. Significantly, the first important result of the work of the council was the Act prohibiting trade with Virginia and the royalist enclaves in the West Indies.[47] This Act was primarily concerned with cutting off trade with the rebels, but it included the important extension that 'the Parliament doth forbid and prohibit all Ships of any Forein Nation whatsoever, to come to, or Trade in, or Traffique with any of the English Plantations in America, or any Islands, Ports or places thereof, which are planted by, and in possession of the People of this Commonwealth' without licence granted by Parliament or the Council of State.[48] Consequently, this Act represented the implementation of the main regulatory principle of Worsley's Virginia scheme, without reference to his wider economic objectives, which were no doubt expected to follow after the effective suppression of disorder. As Brenner concludes, this Act, 'ostensibly passed as a wartime response to the colonies which had revolted against the new Commonwealth regime, actually aimed at permanent closing of the entire English Empire in the Americas to

---

[46] Firth & Rait, II, 405.   [47] 'An Act prohibiting trade', 3 October 1650, *Ibid.*, 425–9.
[48] *Ibid.*, 427.

all foreign commerce'.[49] Because the 1650 Act reflected the priorities
laid down by Worsley for the implementation of his Virginia
scheme, it is not unreasonable to regard it as the work of the
consortium of interests which coalesced for the purpose of promoting
the Virginia project, and which was able to exercise effective influence owing to its ascendancy on the Council of State.

The above Act was supplanted by the Navigation Act of 1651,
about which an enormous literature has accumulated, including
much discussion of the question of authorship.[50] One of the few
direct sources of evidence is Worsley's testimony that 'I was the first
sollicitour for the Act for the incouragement of navigation, and putt
the first fyle to it, and after writt the Advocate in defence of it'.[51] A
similar claim was made by Thomas Violet and, of course, it must be
recognized that the powers of the draughtsmen were circumscribed
by compromises effected between their political and entrepreneurial
superiors. Therefore, Worsley's individual role at this advanced
level of political action was likely to be limited. It is not intended to
add to the debate over the sources of the 1651 Act, but clearly the
papers relating to the Virginia project in 1649 constitute an important relevant source, which has so far been overlooked by the various
protagonists. These documents provide a particularly revealing
insight into the dynamics between the various interest groups which
contributed to the formation of policy. Not surprisingly, ambitious
politicians such as Vane or prosperous merchants such as Andrews
exercised a major degree of influence, but it is also clear that
altruistic reformers and technical experts such as Hartlib, Dury and
Worsley were playing a significant constructive role and were recog-

[49] R. Brenner, 'The Civil War politics of London's merchant community', *Past and Present*, 58
(1973), 53–107, esp. 103.
[50] For representative opinions on the Navigation Acts, see C. M. Andrews, *British committees,
commissions, and councils of trade and plantations* (Baltimore, 1908), 24–48; J. A. Williamson,
Cambridge history of the British empire (Cambridge, 1929), I, 215–18; L. A. Harper, *The
English navigation laws* (New York, 1939); C. Wilson, *Profit and power: a study of England and
the Dutch wars* (London, 1957), 48–60; C. Wilson, *England's apprenticeship* (London, 1965),
61–4; R. W. K. Hinton, *Eastland trade and the Common Weal of England in the seventeenth century*
(London, 1959), 90–4 (Hinton reprints Worsley's *Advocate* and *Free ports*); J. E. Farnell,
'The Navigation Acts, the First Dutch War and the London merchant companies',
Economic History Review, 16 (1963/4), 439–54; J. P. Cooper, 'Social and economic policies
under the Commonwealth', in *The Interregnum: the quest for settlement 1646–1660*, ed. G. E.
Aylmer (London, 1972), 121–42; Brenner, 'Civil War politics'; R. M. Bliss, *Revolution and
empire. English politics in the American colonies in the seventeenth century* (Manchester, 1990).
[51] Bodleian Library, Clarendon MS 75, fols. 300–1 (see note 2 above). Worsley, *The advocate*
(London, 1652).

nized as essential for purposes of legitimization by their more powerful associates.

It has been suggested above that the coalition of forces involved in
the Virginia project was influential in the council of trade and in
framing the 1650 Act. It is therefore tempting to speculate that a
similar coalition played an active part in the negotiations over the
1651 Act, although clearly the compromises that Worsley and his
allies were obliged to make in 1650 were extracted from them to an
even greater degree in 1651.

In important respects, the Navigation Act of 1651 represented a
step back from the provisions of the 1650 Act and a departure from
the ideas of Worsley on regulation because it allowed direct exports
from the colonies to other countries, even in foreign ships, while
allowing imports direct from other countries to the colonies in
English ships, or in ships of the countries producing these commodities. Also, like its 1650 precursor, the 1651 Act was not concerned
with Worsley's wider economic objectives. Consequently, although
the Navigation Act is regarded as a turning point in policy and
important because of its part in provoking war with the Dutch, it
represented only a limited fulfilment of Worsley's general programme. He himself was left campaigning on other issues, especially
on free ports, which fell within the remit of the council of trade and
evoked his second publication, the pamphlet *Free ports* (1651), but in
this case no action was forthcoming because of the impossibility of
reconciling the conflicting corporate interests.[52] The council of
trade's impact on other issues was even less decisive. Consequently,
Worsley may well have been pleased when, in 1652, a new opportunity for preferment emerged and he was given an opportunity to
exercise his talents in Ireland.[53]

In some circles there has been a tendency to regard the work of
Hartlib and his friends as somewhat insubstantial. They were con-
signed to the sidelines of history. This tendency has now been
corrected. Nevertheless, the influence exercised by figures such as
Beale, Culpeper or Worsley is only slowly becoming appreciated.
Such assessments are by no means straightforward. They involve

---

[52] Worsley, *Free ports. The nature and necessity of them stated* (London, 1652).

[53] T. C. Barnard, *Cromwellian Ireland* (Oxford, 1975), 214–44. Apparently, Worsley was on the
verge of taking up an appointment in Ireland in 1647 when he was confirmed as surgeon-
general to the army in Ireland – *Commons Journal*, v, 247 (16 July 1647).

reliance on archival sources and they raise points of difficult judgement upon which categorical conclusions are rarely possible. The
above survey of a brief period in Worsley's early career illustrates
many of these difficulties. This review should demonstrate that it is
possible to piece together many fragments of evidence to construct a
continuous account of intellectual development. Thereby Worsley
emerges from the shadows and appears on an equal plane with his
more prestigious contemporaries. Worsley was recognized as possessing genuine expertise and knowledge across a broad front. His
particular ability to connect the particulars of ingenuity with a
general theory of society assured him a position of leadership. The
many expressions of admiration from shrewd observers quoted
above indicate the high stature attained by Worsley during the Civil
War and early years of the Interregnum.

His part in the Invisible College, the Office of Address and
especially as a speculator and draughtsman on economic and
colonial policy should themselves be sufficient to secure Worsley's
permanent reputation. He emerges as one of the leading proponents
of Baconian experimental philosophy and of mercantilist economic
policy of the mid-seventeenth century. His longer-term influence
was secured through impact on the thinking of Robert Boyle, or in
the less definable area of the development of organized activity in
the field of experimental science.

Arguably, 1651 represents the summit of Worsley's influence.
However, despite the failures of the saltpetre project and the Irish
survey, his level of constructive activity was maintained and he
continued to command respect, even after the Restoration necessi-
tated a lower public profile.

Worsley continued to espouse the cause of universal reform and he
retained the confidence of his closest associates in these ambitious
objectives. For instance, in 1658, he argued that the public resources
for the advancement of learning needed to 'be managed entirely
among ourselves, who understand the aimes, hearts, lives, ends,
principles and spirits one of another. I mean yourselfe [*Hartlib*], Mr.
Durye, Mr. Boyle, Mr Sadler'.[54] Such references suggest that the
unity of outlook secured in the context of the Invisible College and
early phase of the Office of Address was maintained until the eve of
the Restoration.

[54] HP 47/3/2A (Worsley to Hartlib, 26 May 1658).

The Royal Society largely eliminated Worsley's opportunity to pursue scientific projects, but his advice as an economist remained important. Under the patronage of Shaftesbury, he gradually came to exercise almost the level of influence enjoyed in 1651, and was the architect of the councils of trade and plantations established under Charles II, which duly reinforced the policies advocated by Worsley under the Republic.[55] In recognition of Worsley's continuing authority, Petty indirectly sought his advice on his Irish affairs and was forced to admit that 'Hee is a person of very good qualification . . . and yet very capable to judge aright if hee pleases'.[56] Any such praise from a deadly enemy suggests that there might well be some justification for the rehabilitation of Benjamin Worsley.

---

[55] Andrews, *British committees*; R. P. Bieber, 'The British plantation councils of 1670–4', *English Historical Review*, 40 (1925), 93–106; W. Letwin, *The origins of scientific economics* (London, 1963); K. H. D. Haley, *The first earl of Shaftesbury* (Oxford, 1968), 255–60, 284, 289–90; J. C. Sainty, *Officials of the Board of Trade 1660–1870* (London, 1974).
[56] Bowood House MS 19, fols. 72–3 (Petty to Tomkins, 7 December 1672).

CHAPTER 12

New light on Benjamin Worsley's natural philosophy

Antonio Clericuzio

In 1692 – one year after Robert Boyle's death – John Locke sent to press *The general history of the air*, a book that contained many of Boyle's observations, a number of papers and letters written by different authors and a variety of Locke's notes selected from the years 1666 to 1683.[1] Boyle had been collecting the material for nearly twenty-five years, but never edited it. As its full title made clear, *The general history of the air* was only 'designed and begun' by Robert Boyle.[2]

Among the papers published in *The general history of the air* was an anonymous letter to Samuel Hartlib dealing with astrology. This undated letter is, in fact, a short tract on the influences of planets on the earth and on human bodies. Since the eighteenth century the letter has been regarded as the most solid evidence for Boyle's early commitment to astrology. Some passages of it were quoted by Ephraim Chambers in the *Cyclopaedia* (article 'Astrology') to support the view that natural astrology – as opposed to judicial astrology – had been a respectable component of natural philosophy.[3] Chambers' statement and the passage of the letter he had quoted also occurred in Diderot and D'Alembert's *Encyclopédie* under the heading 'Astrologie', where there was also an analogous positive evaluation of Boyle's 'natural' astrology.[4] Modern scholars have regarded this letter as proof that Boyle adopted a 'moderate' position on astrology. Hence, under the aegis of Robert Boyle, the astrological letter to Hartlib became the symbol of the kind of

---

[1] *The general history of the air* (London, 1692).
[2] Locke's letter to Boyle of 21 October 1691 contains information on the manuscript of *The general history of the air* and on Locke's editorial work: *The correspondence of John Locke*, ed. E. S. De Beer, 8 vols. (Oxford, 1976–89), IV, 320–2.
[3] E. Chambers, *Cyclopaedia, or an universal dictionary of arts and sciences* (London, 1728).
[4] *Encyclopédie ou dictionnaire raisonné des sciences, des arts et des métiers*, 17 vols. (Paris, 1751–75).

legitimate and respectable 'scientific' astrology that flourished in mid-seventeenth-century England.[5]

More recently, the letter has attracted the particular attentions of Patrick Curry. By studying it in relation to Boyle's manuscripts on astrology and to the Hartlib circle's astrological studies, he has argued that it contains Boyle's fullest statement on astrology.[6] However, an investigation of documents contained in the Hartlib Papers has thrown new light on the astrological letter and, in turn, on Benjamin Worsley's natural philosophy.

AN ANONYMOUS LETTER

Among the Hartlib Papers there are a remarkable number of papers and letters dealing with astrology. Most of these were either written by Benjamin Worsley or contain references to him.[7] Worsley's letters to Hartlib in 1657 contain references to a 'Physico-Astrologicall Letter' and to a *'Problema Physico-Astrologicum'*. Two versions of the *'Problema'* survive: one in English, the other in Latin.[8]

Worsley enclosed the *'Problema'* in a letter to Hartlib of 14 October 1657. In it he also stated that he had forwarded to him his 'Physico-Astrologicall Letter' three months previously, and that it should be communicated to Nicholas Mercator, Thomas Streete and, as he put it, to 'our friends & correspondents from Oxford'.[9] Worsley was evidently anxious to know the comments of those who had received it: 'And indeed I should be willing to answer any objections, clear scruples or receive myselfe any information from learned persons about that subject which I begin to see more & more necessary if any man will pretend to a degree of natural knowledge.'[10]

In addition, he asked Hartlib to send the 'Astrologicall Letter'

[5] M. E. Bowden, 'The Scientific revolution in astrology: the English reformers, 1558–1686' (Ph.D. thesis, Yale University, 1974), 202–10; B. Capp, *Astrology and the popular press* (London and Boston, 1979), 189.

[6] P. Curry, 'The decline of astrology in early modern England (1642–1800)' (Ph.D. thesis, University of London, 1986); P. Curry, 'Saving astrology in Restoration England', in *Astrology, science and society*, ed. P. Curry (Bury St Edmunds, 1987), 245–59; P. Curry, *Prophecy and power* (Princeton, 1989), 62–3.

[7] C. Webster, *From Paracelsus to Newton. Magic and the making of modern science* (Cambridge, 1982), 33, 45.

[8] HP 42/1/16A–17B; 26/59/1A–2B. A translation of the Latin text is in P. Curry, 'Decline of astrology', 258–61.

[9] HP 42/1/9A. On Streete, see Capp, *Popular press*, 333.   [10] HP 42/1/9A.

and the '*Problema*' to Elias Ashmole, whose judgements upon them he very much desired. In due course, Worsley received from Hartlib the opinions of the 'Oxford Professors' on the 'Physico-Astrologicall Letter'. As may be seen from Worsley's reply to Hartlib of 20 October 1657, the Oxford professors did not like the hypotheses it advanced.[11] However, Worsley's reaction to their disapproval betrayed no resentment. Although he complained that 'our University Professors are resolved to stand to the doctrines & Traditions of their Fathers, without further doubt or question', Worsley enclosed his own comments on the controversial subject, which, in fact, stressed the hypothetical character of his theories. He maintained that he did not draw apodictic conclusions as to planetary influences on earthly affairs; he merely wanted to promote further investigations into such influences. From Worsley's letter to Hartlib of 20 October, we also learn that the 'Astrologicall Letter' was translated into Latin by Mercator in order to be circulated among continental scholars – Hübner, Hevelius and Jungius, in particular, were mentioned.[12] Hartlib had evidently forwarded Worsley's letter to Mercator promptly as, according to a letter of 29 September 1657 from Mercator, he wrote that he was engaged in the translation of Worsley's 'elegant and judicious' discourse. From Mercator we learn that Worsley wanted to have his own name removed from the astrological letter.[13]

These documents make it possible to identify Worsley's 'Physico-Astrologicall Letter', quoted in the correspondence of Hartlib, with an anonymous letter surviving in two versions: in English and in Latin. Both are amanuensis' copies, undated and unsigned. The authorship is, however, revealed by a note on the top of the Latin version which reads: 'Exemplar literarum Benjamini Worslaei ad Samuelem Hartlibium.'[14]

Remarkably, this letter turns out to be none other than the astrological epistle published in Boyle's *The general history of air* and generally attributed to him. There is no doubt that Boyle was one of the recipients of the astrological letter since this is attested to by what Worsley wrote to Boyle on 14 October 1657: 'If you thought that large letter worth the communication to our learned friend with

---

[11] HP 42/12/10A. On Elias Ashmole's astrology see Curry, *Prophecy and power*, 35–43.
[12] HP 42/1/10A.
[13] HP 65/1/77A. Mercator also translated Worsley's *Problema*, see HP 56/1/86A–86B.
[14] HP 42/1/18.

you there at Oxford, I would be glad to receive something, that might offer a further occasion of discussion and debate, being no way tied to this or that opinion or expression.'[15] Hartlib's reference to Worsley's astrological tract – contained in a letter to Boyle of 8 December 1657 – confirms that Boyle was well acquainted with Worsley's astrological letter: 'Mr Worsley is expecting still some engagement upon his physico-astrologicall letter.'[16] Boyle evidently kept his friend's letter and included it in the miscellaneous material which he had sought to publish as the *History of air*. When Locke was editing *The general history of the air*, he was probably not aware of the authorship of the anonymous astrological letter to Hartlib that he had found among the papers and letters which Boyle had intended to publish. In this fashion, Worsley's astrological tract was incorporated in Boyle's work and, as a result, Boyle has commonly been regarded as its author.

CELESTIAL INFLUENCES: WORSLEY AND BOYLE

I doubt if the reattribution of the astrological letter to Worsley entails a dramatic revision of our interpretation of Boyle's views of astrology. The fact that Boyle included it among the material for *The general history of the air* shows that he saw his friend's discourse as a valid contribution to the study of the 'hidden qualities' of air. Boyle had paid special attention to the effects of celestial influences on the atmosphere, claiming that some of the qualities of air, as well as its chemical properties, might originate from unknown corpuscles coming from celestial bodies.[17] In the *Suspicions about the hidden qualities of the air* (1674) he maintained that 'the Sun and Planets (to say nothing of the fixt Stars) may have influences here below distinct from their Heat and Light'.[18] Moreover, in the tract *Of celestial magnets* (published as an appendix to *Suspicions*) Boyle asserted that the spots on the sun, as well as the moon and her place in the zodiac, may have consequential effects on the air.[19] Boyle's interest in what

---

[15] Boyle, *Works*, VI, 636.   [16] *Ibid.*, 97.

[17] See *Tracts written by the Honourable Robert Boyle about the cosmicall qualities of things* ... (Oxford, 1671), 4–5; Boyle, *Works*, III, 316–17. On celestial influences see J. D. North, 'Celestial influence – the major premiss of astrology', in *Astrologi hallucinati. Stars and the end of the world in Luther's time*, ed. P. Zambelli (Berlin and New York, 1986), 45–100.

[18] Robert Boyle, *Tracts containing suspicions about the hidden qualities of the air* (London, 1674), 4; Boyle, *Works*, IV, 85.

[19] *Tracts containing suspicions*, 59; Boyle, *Works*, IV, 98.

he called 'celestial magnets' was spurred on by Henry Oldenburg's letters of 1659 informing Boyle about some French chemists (namely Jacques de Nuysement and Henri de Rochas) and their theories on the spirit of the world as well as the ways to capture it.[20]

If the attribution of the astrological letter to Worsley does not modify the view that Boyle integrated astrology into the body of natural philosophy, it certainly has important consequences for our understanding of Worsley's natural philosphy, of his position in the Hartlib circle and his role in the intellectual career of Robert Boyle.

Patrick Curry has described the astrological letter as a typical example of the Hartlib circle's programme to reform astrology along Baconian lines.[21] He considered it to be a development of Francis Bacon's views and this is, in fact, confirmed by Worsley's initial statement that condensation and rarefaction are the two fundamental movements in nature. For in his *Historia densi et rari* Bacon had provided a detailed investigation of the phenomena of rarefaction and condensation and related them to the motions of the spirits.[22] Bacon interpreted spirits as air, fire, interstellar ether and celestial fire, and conceived them as the 'substance of planets'.[23] The idea that astral effluvia act on the spirits contained in natural bodies, as well as on those in human bodies, was an integral part of Paracelsian cosmology, as exemplified by Peter Severinus' *Idea medicinae philosophicae* (Basle, 1571) and by Oswald Crollius' *Basilica chymica* (Frankfurt, 1609). This view of spirit had wide circulation in the seventeenth century and played a central part in natural philosophy and medicine.[24] Worsley's position was evidently a development of Paracelsian ideas. He asserted that, since our spirits were aeriferrous, etherial and luminous substances they were best suited to receive, and thus to be impressed by, the specific lights coming from planets and their concomitant virtues and tinctures. Worsley put special emphasis on the role of spirits in natural bodies: he called them 'the only principles of energy, power, force

[20] See A. Clericuzio, 'The internal laboratory. The chemical reinterpretation of medical spirits in England (1650–1680)', in *Alchemy and chemistry in the Renaissance and early modern times*, ed. P. M. Rattansi and A. Clericuzio, forthcoming.
[21] Curry, *Prophecy and power*, 59–64.   [22] Bacon, *Works*, II, 227–305.
[23] See G. Rees, 'Francis Bacon and "Spiritus Vitalis"', in *Spiritus. IV Colloquio Internazionale del Lessico Intellettuale Europeo*, ed. M. L. Bianchi and M. Fattori (Rome, 1984), 269.
[24] D.P. Walker, 'Francis Bacon and "Spiritus"', in *Science, medicine and society in the Renaissance*, ed. A. G. Debus (New York, 1972), 121–30; A. Clericuzio, '"Spiritus Vitalis". Studio sulle teorie fisiologiche da Fernel a Boyle', *Nouvelles de la République des Lettres*, 9 (1988), 33–84.

and life, in all bodies wherein they are, and the immediate causes through which all alteration comes to the body themselves'.[25] In the astrological letter Worsley also adopted the Paracelsian theory that stars and planets were endowed with activity and life.[26] The light of the sun, according to Worsley, does not merely illuminate the planets, but, as he put it, 'through the power, virtue, and activity it hath, doth also raise, excite and awaken and stir up the several properties and dispositions, that are in those ... bodies'. This is what happens with the earth, which is not only illuminated by the sun, but, according to Worsley, has its own 'magnetical planetary virtue' fermented by the power of the sun.[27] Worsley's account of the role of the sun and of its light is taken almost verbatim from Jean d'Espagnet's *Enchiridion phisicae restitutae*, a work that was extolled by Samuel Hartlib in his *Ephemerides* of 1651. As Betty Dobbs has argued, it was also one of the sources for Newton's alchemy.[28] In the *Enchiridion* the following statement is to be found:

The [*second*] universal Agent is that same light; not so immediately issuing from the Fountain [*i.e. the sun*], but reflected from solid bodies, inlightened by it ... ; because the light of the Sun bearing upon those bodies, gives a motion to their dispositions and faculties, and alters them, and diffuseth their several and different virtues by the reflection of its rays ... ; by those rays, as by so many conveyances, are the various effects of several bodies dispersed every where for the benefit and Harmony of Nature, which are called by us influences.[29]

According to d'Espagnet, the power of the sun is diffused throughout the universe. In the process, it excites the virtues of celestial bodies and supplies our globe with seeds, or seminal principles which are responsible for the generation of all natural bodies.[30] Like d'Espagnet, Worsley asserted that the sun had the power

25 *General history of the air*, 74; Boyle, *Works*, v, 641.
26 On Paracelsus' cosmology and astrology see W. Pagel, *Paracelsus, an introduction to philosophical medicine in the era of Renaissance* (Basle, 1958), 65–72, 117–21. See also K. Goldammer, *Paracelsus in neuen Horizonten* (Vienna, 1986), 250–87; and G. Zanier, *L'espressione e l'immagine. Introduzione a Paracelso* (Trieste, 1988).
27 *General history of the air*, 75; Boyle, *Works*, v, 641.
28 On Jean d'Espagnet (1564–1637) see J. Ferguson, *Bibliotheca Chemica*, 2 vols. (Glasgow, 1906), I, 248–50; Hartlib, *Ephemerides* (1651): HP 28/2/25A; B. J. T. Dobbs, *The foundations of Newton's alchemy* (Cambridge, 1975), 37–9.
29 This and the following quotations are taken from the English edition, *Enchyridion physicae restitutae: or a summary of physics recovered* (London, 1651), 60. The date and the place of the first edition (in Latin) of the *Enchiridion* are still uncertain: Ferguson suggests Paris, 1608. I have not seen this edition.
30 d'Espagnet, *Enchiridion*, 124.

to stir up and to draw into the air the 'seminal dispositions, odours and ferments' (both benign and malignant) normally lodged in the bowels of the earth.[31] As Worsley himself stated, the letter to Hartlib was not intended as an apology for astrology. Its aim was rather to stimulate the study of planetary influences in order to improve medicine, natural philosophy, husbandry and gardening. Worsley's outlook is clearly formulated in his letter to Hartlib of 14 October 1657, where he claimed that only those who achieve universal learning can 'apprehend things rightly, lineally & originally'.[32] Accordingly, he warned that the study of astrology, if it were pursued as an end in itself, would never afford real knowledge, but merely ignorance and superstition. Likewise, for Worsley, those who study medicine and chemistry separately 'shall always be in a labyrint, & in a thick wood'.[33] In a typically Paracelsian and Comenian fashion, Worsley pointed out that astrology, alchemy, medicine and theology were strictly connected. It is not surprising that Worsley's views were not accepted by those Oxford professors who in 1654 had rejected John Webster's proposal for a reform of the university curricula which, in fact, had been based on analogous ideas.[34]

The moon's influence on the earth was the subject of Worsley's 'Problema Physico-Astrologicum', which, like the astrological letter to Hartlib, was translated into Latin by Mercator.[35] In this short tract – which was closely linked to the 'Physico-Astrologicall Letter' – Worsley maintained that the virtues and powers of the celestial bodies were reinforced by the mediation of the moon. This was the premiss of Worsley's enquiry which attempted to establish the moment 'when the Moone is most dignified, dispos'd or assisted to poure out her influence upon us'.[36] The remaining part of the 'Problema' contained a series of queries as to which of the celestial signs were best fitted to increase the power of the moon on the earth. Worsley's 'Problema' was not particularly original. The belief in the influence of the moon on the earth was widely accepted, even by those who firmly rejected judicial astrology. Nonetheless, Worsley

---

[31] General history of the air, 75; Boyle, Works, v, 641. The notions of semina, odour and ferment played a central role in van Helmont's natural philosopy; see W. Pagel, Joan Baptista van Helmont: reformer of science and medicine (Cambridge, 1982).
[32] HP 42/1/7A–8A.   [33] Ibid.
[34] See A. G. Debus, Science and education in the seventeenth century: the Webster–Ward debate (London, 1970).
[35] HP 56/1/87A (Mercator to Hartlib, 24 November 1657).   [36] HP 42/1/16B.

held out no hope that his '*Problema*' would attract any support from Oxford. On 20 October, six days after despatching his '*Problema*' to Hartlib, he wrote once more: 'But the first Discourse, receiving noe better entertainement, that Probleme I sent you in my last I therefore desire, may bee wholly suppressed, unless it bee to Mr Sadler, to Street, or Mr Beale as I writt to you before; or to Mr Sparrow & Ashmole, but noe more to Oxford, for they do not understand it.'[37]

THE 'ASTROLOGICALL LETTER' AND THE HARTLIB CIRCLE

It is highly likely that Worsley was stimulated to write his astrological letters and tracts by the posthumous publication of Robert Child's 'Answer to the animadversor', which appeared in the third edition of *Samuel Hartlib his legacie* (1655).[38] Child flatly declared that the common belief that the position of the sun and the moon at the time of sowing could affect the harvest was mere folly.[39] He went on to state that astrology was neither demonstrable *a priori*, nor *a posteriori*: the notions upon which it was based were not demonstrated, while the calculations very often disproved the predictions. The only influence of the stars and planets he would accept was simply that of light. Child's ultimate reason for rejecting astrology was, in fact, his belief in the infinite power of God. As a consequence of God's infinite power, he asserted the infinity of the universe and the infinity of worlds. On the other hand, he firmly stated that speculations about the interactions between the parts of the universe, as well as predictions such as those formulated by astrologers, were not allowed to 'the narrow capacity of frail mans intellect'.[40]

Child's harsh attack on astrology was not echoed by other members of the Hartlib circle. It is, however, likely that it prompted Worsley to articulate his position on the subject and to communicate it to a wider public. Among the members of the Hartlib circle, Worsley singled out John Beale as 'a Person of much Reason, Judgement, Integrity, Candor ... a solid and universall Schollar', whose comments on both the 'Astrologicall Letter' and the '*Prob-*

---

[37] HP 42/1/12A. For John Sadler (1615–74), master of Magdalene College, Cambridge and author of astrological and other tracts, see *DNB*. For John Sparrow (1615–65), the translator of Jacob Boehme's works into English, see *DNB*.

[38] See *HDC*, 98. On Child see G. H. Turnbull, 'Robert Child', in *Transactions of the Colonial Society of Massachusetts*, 38 (1959), 21–53.

[39] *Samuel Hartlib his legacy* (3rd edn, London, 1655), 160.   [40] *Ibid.*, 161.

244   ANTONIO CLERICUZIO

lema' he was anxious to receive from Hartlib.[41] John Beale's comments on Worsley's 'Astrologicall Letter' were generally positive. Beale's warm support for Worsley's astrological doctrines becomes of still greater interest when one considers that in a letter of 21 June 1657, Beale had launched a vehement attack on the judicial astrology of William Lilly and Nicholas Culpeper, which he censured as 'abominable and unfit to be tolerated by a Christian Magistrate'.[42] Beale's observations on Worsley's astrological tracts are contained in a letter to Hartlib of 15 September 1657, which reads: 'The more I read Dr Worsleys discourse of the Planets & Thermometer the better I like it, but I am fitter to encourage others of better capacityes ... to undertake the prosecution of all due experiments.' Yet Beale was more cautious than Worsley when it came to planetary influences. As he pointed out, 'wee oftentimes call those Influences planetary, which are but the operations of our ... globe'.[43] Worsley's astrological letter prompted Beale to articulate some general reflections on astrology, conceiving it as part of the *prisca theologia*: 'And I am of this Heresy, That Astrology is a most serious affayre, if it were handled with ancient sanctity, as I conceive & find anciently recorded, That the holy Patriarchs did doe.'[44]

John Beale restated his favourable outlook of Worsley's astrological tract in a letter to Hartlib of 14 December 1657, where he maintained that he never saw astrology more fully demonstrated than by Worsley. On the other hand, he regretted that the letter had not received due consideration in Oxford. It is apparent that Worsley's astrological letter and the short astrological '*Problema*' had a strong impact on the Hartlib circle. At least three prominent members of the Hartlib circle, namely Mercator, Beale and Boyle, explicitly supported Worsley's astrological views. Moreover, Worsley's letter stimulated Beale's interests in astro-metereology and prompted Boyle's researches into the hidden qualities of air, into celestial effluvia, as well as into the technology of thermometers and barometers.[45] It is apparent that some of Boyle's subsequent studies of – as he called them – 'weather glasses' stem from Worsley's letter.

[41] HP 42/1/9A (14 October 1657).
[42] HP 25/5/21A. Attacks on Lilly's astrology are discussed in D. Parker, *Familiar to all. William Lilly and astrology in the seventeenth century* (London, 1975), 183. On Nicholas Culpeper and astrology see Capp, *Popular press*, 206–8.
[43] HP 31/1/56B. (Beale to Hartlib, 15 September 1657).   [44] *Ibid.*
[45] On Beale's astro-meteorology, see Capp, *Popular press*, 189. On seventeenth-century barometers see W. E. K. Middleton, *The history of barometers* (Baltimore, 1964), 55–80.

Besides formulating his theories on celestial influences, Worsley's letter gave practical instructions to observe, and possibly to quantify, their effects on the air. In order to achieve this ambitious aim, Worsley prescribed two tasks: (a) to establish a more detailed theory of planets; and (b) to investigate the effects of the planetary influences on the air and on the weather by means of a series of accurate observations. The latter was what Worsley set out to do in the second part of the astrological letter. He aimed at improving both the instruments (i.e. thermometers or weather glasses) and the techniques of observation – which he found rather defective and unserviceable for his purposes. Worsley, whose skills in the field of scientific instruments are attested by his papers and letters, suggested some devices to produce more sophisticated weather glasses: firstly, he tried to establish the best proportion between the diameter of the tube and that of the head of the weather glass (which he found to be 1:16 or 1:24); secondly, he suggested having the cylinder divided into at least 360 parts, in order to discover not only the small, but also the more sudden changes of the weather; thirdly, he examined the liquors to be used in the weather glasses, in connection with their affinity with the air. The experimental techniques were of no lesser moment for Worsley. He suggested using weather glasses of different dimensions and filled with different liquors in the same place, as well as identical instruments in different places.[46]

Worsley's observations on the weather glasses and on the experiments to be performed with them prompted Robert Boyle to question (in *The experimental history of cold*, 1665) the accuracy of the investigations made with ordinary weather glasses and to recommend the use of hermetically sealed ones. Boyle believed that some corpuscles contained in the air could affect the behaviour of the substances filling the weather glass. These corpuscles could even pass through the glass and, accordingly, affect the motion of the liquors contained in weather glasses, even in the hermetically sealed ones. As evidence for this, Boyle reported that in Orthelius' commentary on Michael Sendivogius' *Novum lumen*, he had found mention of a liquor distilled from bismuth. This liquor, according to Boyle, 'will swell in the glass it is kept in, not only manifestly, but very considerably at the full Moon; and shrink at the new Moon'. Boyle concluded that 'which wonder being admitted, may not only

---

[46] *General history of the air*, 77–9; Boyle, *Works*, v, 643–4.

countenance what we were saying, but hint some other very strange things in Nature'.[47] As this passage shows, Boyle's views of celestial influences were very close to Worsley's. Worsley's letter testifies to the strict links unifying astrology, chemistry and medicine in the mid-seventeenth century. Paracelsian and Comenian ideals of universal learning were shared by Beale and by the young Robert Boyle. It is, however, evident that the impact of Worsley's letter on Boyle was not confined to his early career. Boyle developed the views contained in his friend's letter of 1657 in the following decades and incorporated it in *The general history of air*. Yet his compliance with Worsley's request to have his own name removed from the letter has prevented Worsley from being recognized as one of the most prominent advocates of natural astrology.

[47] *New experiments and observations touching cold, or, an experimental history of cold* (London, 1665), 62–3; Boyle, *Works*, IV, 496.

CHAPTER 13

'These 2 hundred years not the like published as Gellibrand has done de Magnete': the Hartlib circle and magnetic philosophy

Stephen Pumfrey

When Charles Webster first brought the importance of Samuel Hartlib's circle and papers before a wide audience, he began by noting 'that the invention of printing and of gunpowder, and particularly the voyages of discovery, seemed to herald a revival of learning which was thoroughly consistent with [*their*] envisaged utopian paradise'. The voyages of discovery were made possible by the magnetic compass needle which, like the other two inventions, was of special significance to the sixteenth and early seventeenth centuries. While it can hardly be claimed that discussion of magnetic navigation and philosophy was a dominant topic in Hartlib's circle when compared with that of education reforms or agricultural projects, the evidence presented in this chapter suggests that members invested knowledge of the magnetic needle with a prominent, almost emblematic significance.

This possibility is raised by Hartlib's extraordinary praise of a minor tract, published in 1635 by the Gresham College professor of astronomy, Henry Gellibrand, entitled a *Discourse mathematicall on the variation of the magnetic needle*.[1] In his *Ephemerides* for that year, Hartlib penned everyone's dream review: 'These 2 hund[*red*] y[*ears*] not the like published as Gellibrand has done de Magnete.'

Hartlib's judgement first strikes one as an absurd exaggeration. As with Francis Bacon's own famous dismissal of William Gilbert's work, hindsight has not been kind to Baconians' assessments of seventeenth-century science.[2] Yet Hartlib's eulogy provides a problem to be solved and an invitation to explore the significance of

[1] Henry Gellibrand, *A discourse mathematicall on the variation of the magnetic needle* (London, 1635); Webster, 1.

[2] *Ephemerides* (1635): HP 29/3/20B. The entry was printed in Webster, 358, n. 82, although it was not associated with Gellibrand's *Discourse*. It was discussed in my doctoral thesis 'William Gilbert's magnetic philosophy, 1580–1684: the creation and dissolution of a discipline' (University of London, 1987), chap. 5.

practical magnetic philosophy in his world. Having done so, we shall still conclude that his judgement was flawed. But the exercise of placing Gellibrand's work in the context of the broader concerns of Hartlib's circle will afford us some insights into the social and religious meanings attached to magnetic philosophy in the period.

Some of the reasons why Hartlib's circle should have been attracted to the magnetic needle in their pursuit of 'peace, unification and prosperity' are obvious and follow from the revolution in navigation it had brought about. Prior to the development in late medieval Europe of the mariner's compass and the techniques of magnetic navigation, maritime voyages were generally limited to coast-hugging routes. Pilots worked from local knowledge or from portolan charts which allowed a vessel's position to be found in relation to prominent land features. Of course, techniques of astronomical navigation, using the position of the noonday sun or the stars, were well known, but they could not be employed in cloudy conditions and were of very limited accuracy in rough seas. They could confirm a bearing and give a more or less approximate indication of latitude, but were of no practical use for determining longitude. For the centuries either side of Hartlib's life, to find longitude at sea remained the prize sought by navigators and offered by state authorities. Positional uncertainties kept oceanic navigation a risky business for navigators, navies and the new merchant adventurers alike.

It was Spanish and Portuguese navigators who exploited the new compass technology in the late fifteenth century during their explorations of the Far East and the extraordinary 'New World' of America. Indeed the demarcation line of the 1494 Treaty of Tordesillas, by which the pope divided the new worlds into equal Spanish and Portuguese hemispheres was (supposedly) that of a prime magnetic meridian.[3] After the Reformation of the sixteenth century, voyages backed by Protestant states were forced either to search for non-existent northern passages or to run the gauntlet of Iberian naval might. But despite the religio-political and technical obstacles, trans-oceanic magnetic navigation to the new worlds had become routine in early seventeenth-century England.

---

[3] See R. H. Major, *The life of Prince Henry, surnamed the Navigator, and its results* (1868; repr., London, 1967), 423.

To contemporaries, the compass seemed to have effected profound economic, ethnological and intellectual revolutions, and it offered real possibilities for a new world order of peace, unification and prosperity. Prosperity had evidently come to the Spanish and Portuguese from their establishment of empires, extraction of gold, silver and other raw materials, and from their command of massively increased volumes of trade. North Atlantic nations, including Scotland with its abortive Darien project, sought similar routes of expansion. Unification had manifestly occurred in a geographical sense – the world had been circumnavigated, its previously unknown lands and peoples documented, and continents brought into communication. This kind of unification was not, of course, the same as unification through peace. As well as wars of trade and imperial expansion, the navigational revolution also extended inter–confessional rivalries throughout the world. On the Catholic side, the Society of Jesus was founded with the explicit aim of bringing Catholicism to new peoples in order to replace the souls lost to Protestantism. Consequently, Jesuit colleges included training in magnetic navigation. But Reformed apologists also urged upon the numerically inferior Protestant peoples a similar policy of spreading true religion through colonial expansion. It thus became part of the standard rhetoric of promoters of navigational innovations, especially of magnetic schemes, to signal their utility for the sure expansion of spiritual and temporal kingdoms through enhanced nautical prowess.[4]

Of many texts that presented the magnetic compass as a cultural transformer, one of the most widely read was that of the French humanist, Jean Bodin. Because of the magnet, he wrote, 'our contemporaries every year sail around the world with their sea-crossings and have colonised, so to speak, a new world. Not only has a profitable commerce derived therefrom ... but men have linked themselves to one another and marvellously participate in the universal republic as if they formed the same city'.[5] Early Stuart navigators might have been more familiar with the instrument maker Robert Norman's more insular sentiments, expressed in his

---

[4] See for example Edward Wright, *Certaine errors in navigation* (1599; 2nd edn, London, 1610), 8; Guillaume de Nautonnier, Sieur de Castelfranc, *Mecometrie de l'eymant cest a dire la maniere de mesurer les longitudes par le moyen de l'eymant* ('Venes', 1603), 'Au lecteur', 1.

[5] J. Bodin, 'Methodus ad facilem historiarum cognitionem' in *Oeuvres philosophiques de J. Bodin*, ed. P. Mesnard (Paris, 1951), 227–8.

work on the compass needle. 'Wee being secluded and divided from the rest of the world, are notwithstanding as it wer Citizens of the world, walking through everie corner, and round about the same, and injoying all the commodities of the wor[l]d.'[6] And the confessional benefits were still being advocated in 1690 by John Edwards, who noted that

by the help of this Invention we have the Advantage of propagating the Gospel, and spreading the saving Knowledg [sic] of the True God, and of his Son Jesus Christ throughout the World. The Improvement of Navigation may be serviceable to this great and excellent End; yea, we hope it is partly so already, the New Voyages and Discoveries being a happy Introduction to the Conversion of the Gentiles.[7]

Although the England in which Hartlib began his exile in 1625 had been comparatively late to develop expertise of oceanic navigation, the previous fifty years had witnessed a dramatic rise in competence, initially through the literal pirating of Iberian knowledge. Later there were indigenous developments made in London's thriving maritime community by practitioners such as William Borough, and Edward Wright, whose Certaine errors in navigation of 1599, revised by him in 1610, remained the high point of English navigation for decades. The new military and, especially, economic importance to England of mathematical and magnetic navigation was mirrored in the numerous formal and informal lectureships financed by companies of, or individual, adventurers. By the early seventeenth century, as Iberian schools declined, these London networks supported what English commentators could justifiably believe to be the best science of navigation, and certainly the best science of magnetic navigation in the world. A major reason for English pre-eminence was the superb tradition of research and instruction established since 1597 at the private Gresham College, by the successive mathematics professors, Henry Briggs, Edmund Gunter, Samuel Foster and, since January 1626/7, Henry Gellibrand.[8]

[6] Robert Norman, The newe attractive, containyng a short discourse of the magnes ... (London, 1581), 'Epistle Dedicatorie'.

[7] John Edwards, A demonstration of the existence and providence of God ..., 2 vols. (London, 1690), II, 624, cited in Roy S. Wolper, 'The rhetoric of gunpowder and the idea of progress', Journal of the History of Ideas, 31 (1970), 589–98, esp. 596ff.

[8] Wright, Certaine errors; for English workers see E. G. R. Taylor, The mathematical practitioners of Tudor and Stuart England (Cambridge, 1954); for Gresham College see F. R. Johnson, 'Gresham College: Precursor of the Royal Society', Journal of the History of Ideas, 1 (1940), 413–38.

Gellibrand was born into a learned, clerical London family in 1597. Henry Briggs, who later became his patron, had just become the first professor of geometry at the new Gresham College. Gellibrand took his BA from Trinity College, Oxford in 1619 (and later an MA), and became a friend of Briggs, who had moved, also in 1619, from London's Gresham chair to Oxford's Savilian chair of geometry. Gellibrand's interest in mathematics led him to leave an ecclesiastical career for mathematics and in 1627, with Briggs' patronage, he succeeded the deceased Edmund Gunter as the Gresham professor of astronomy. Briggs continued to advance Gellibrand's reputation from beyond the grave, having bequeathed him his unfinished *Trigonometria Britannica*, which Gellibrand completed and published in 1633.[9]

One of Gellibrand's primary duties as the Gresham professor of astronomy was, of course, the advance of navigation. It was the subject of his second publication, which received more general attention, being an 'Appendix concerning Longitude' contributed to *The strange and dangerous voyage of Captaine Thomas James* ...[10] This frequently reprinted work recounted a celebrated rendezvous in mid-Arctic in 1631 of two English ships, converging on the basis of magnetic compass measurements. This was possible because navigators, in determining their courses, had to allow for and keep records of the variation of magnetic needles from true north. In the high latitudes sailed by the English, variations were large and differed from place to place. Since its endorsement by Edward Wright and William Gilbert, English practitioners had explored the possibility of using these patterns of variation to determine latitude and longitude. Such considerations had formed part of Gellibrand's advisory brief concerning the James voyage.

Although magnetic variation was difficult to determine, hard to explain, and seemed to follow no regular pattern, there was obviously a principle underlying magnetic longitude schemes. Indeed it was universally acknowledged that variation always remained the same in the same place – universally acknowledged, that is, until

---

9 See John Ward, *The lives of the professors of Gresham College* (London 1740; repr., New York, 1967), 81–5; *DNB*, 'Gellibrand, Henry (1597–1636)'.

10 See D. W. Waters, *The art of navigation in Elizabethan and early Stuart times* (London, 1958), 288, 499; Thomas James, *The strange and dangerous voyage of Captaine Thomas James in his intended discovery of the Northwest Passage into the South Sea ... With an appendix concerning longitude by H[enry] G[ellibrand] ... With an advise concerning the philosophye of these late discoveryes by W[illiam] W[atts]* (London, 1633).

Gellibrand published in 1635 his *Discourse mathematicall on the variation of the magnetic needle*. The bones of this short tract were logarithmic calculations proving that Gellibrand's determination of the variation in London in 1634 was some two degrees less than that of his predecessor, Edmund Gunter, in 1622. Uniquely able to believe that the earlier measurement was reliable, Gellibrand concluded that the variation really had decreased and that the even larger figures recorded by Elizabethans such as Borough were not errors, as had previously been assumed, but further evidence 'that the variation is accompanied with a variation'.[11]

Although Gellibrand's claim was startling and was later (thanks to promotion by Hartlib's circle) to elicit international discussion, there were few immediate responses even in England. None matched Hartlib's effusiveness. How was it, then, that a significant but small advance in magnetic philosophy (as seen by others) became transformed into a prodigious discovery for Hartlib's circle? To answer the question, this chapter investigates the context to Hartlib's remark and it does so in three sections of successively increasing generality. Firstly, it shows how Gellibrand's magnetic work fitted the practical interests of Hartlib's early circle. Secondly, it follows the contrasting response as Hartlib's allies thrust it upon Marin Mersenne's continental circle. This demonstrates that, while the correspondence was sustained by a superficially shared interest in magnetism, it faltered when contrasting ideological differences were exposed. Finally, it returns to the general, emblematic significance of the magnet.

HARTLIB'S CIRCLE AND MAGNETIC PHILOSOPHY

From Hartlib's reaction we might assume that he was simply ignorant of books *de magnete*, and overimpressed by the work of an acquaintance. This explanation does not fit the evidence in Hartlib's papers. *Philosophia magnetica* had been a vogue science since its creation a mere thirty-five years before Gellibrand's tract by the royal physician, William Gilbert, in his *De magnete* (more properly and grandly called *A new philosophy of the magnet, magnetic bodies and of the great magnet Earth*). Its novel experiments and conclusions

---

[11] Stephen Pumfrey, '"O tempora, O magnes!" A sociological analysis of the discovery of secular variation in 1634', *British Journal for the History of Science*, 22 (1989), 181–214; Gellibrand, *Discourse*, 7.

received attention because they promised to solve both cosmological problems of celestial physics and practical, navigational problems of terrestrial magnetism. In England, the fact that it was an English author whom continentals admired as the founder of a new science conferred extra interest, and confirmed English pride in the superiority of their navigational science. As Hartlib himself noted in 1635: 'The Italians admire 3. English great wits, Gilbert, Verulam, Herbert.'[12]

Hartlib demonstrated his awareness of the major publications in magnetic philosophy and any lacunae were doubtless remedied in discussion with enthusiasts such as John Pell or Gellibrand himself. As well as Gilbert's own work, Hartlib knew of one of the earliest responses to Gilbert's publication – Guillaume de Nautonnier's *Mecometrie de l'eymant* of 1604.[13] As the title implies, this work developed a magnetic theory of position finding based on compass readings. Although it is little known today, it was promoted by the usually ultra-cautious Marin Mersenne, and vigorously refuted as a dangerous error by English practitioners. The Hartlib papers reveal that Nautonnier's son continued to hawk his father's scheme. Hartlib even knew of the very obscure English imitator of Nautonnier, Antony Linton, and, less surprisingly, of Linton and Nautonnier's illustrious opponent, Edward Wright.[14]

By 1635 the state of the art was represented by the Thomistic compendium *Philosophia magnetica* of Niccolo Cabeo, SJ, published in 1628. 'A Jesuite hase written a greate booke in fol[*io*] De Magnete,' Hartlib recorded in 1635, 'taking most out of Gilbert. Only hee hase a special thing about [*the*] hanging of the [*compass*] needle which hee [*Gellibrand*] highly approved.' After Gellibrand's death other correspondents ensured that Hartlib and his circle kept up to date with the

---

[12] Gulielmus Gilbertus [William Gilbert], *De magnete magneticisque corporibus, et de magno magnete tellure; physiologia nova* ... (London, 1600); *Ephemerides* (1635); HP 29/3/20B. Verulam is, of course, Francis Bacon, viscount of St Albans, and Herbert is the deist Lord Herbert of Cherbury.

[13] For Nautonnier, see HP 53/35/11A, in Hartlib's hand, and 71/16/6A; Nautonnier, *Mecometrie*. Mecometrie means 'longitude measuring'.

[14] 'Lintels [*sic*] Book called the Complement of Navigation his desiderata can bee the better borne withal because that his supposition upon which he builds all is false' (*Ephemerides* (1639): HP 30/4/25B). The opinion, given by Pell, was originally Wright's. See Antony Linton, *Newes of the complement of the art of navigation. And of the mighty empire of Cataia. Together with the Straits of Anian* (London, 1609). Predictably in such schemes only the 'Newes' appeared, and never the complement itself. Hartlib recorded that Wright had written the best work on navigation – *Ephemerides* (1635): HP 29/3/19A. For Mersenne's promotion of Nautonnier, see Pumfrey, '"O tempora, O magnes!"', 201–2.

(very different) compendia of Mersenne and Athanasius Kircher.[15] That Hartlib was privy to contemporary developments in English magnetic navigation is demonstrated by his familiarity with yet another infamous magnetic longitude scheme, that of Henry Bond, first announced in 1639.[16]

So Hartlib did not lack knowledge of the best books on the magnet of preceding decades when he adjudged Gellibrand's to be the best since 1435! And while we can understand that Hartlib preferred Gellibrand to Jesuits, there seems no obvious reason why he should have elevated him above William Gilbert, the founder of the discipline, in whose tradition Gellibrand respectfully and patriotically situated his own work.[17]

Yet it was Gellibrand's book that repeatedly excited Hartlib. His panegyric in the *Ephemerides* was not, so to speak, ephemeral. Enthusing in 1634 even before its publication, he urged that it 'should be immediately translated into other languages'.[18] Later in 1635 he understood that 'Sir Kelham [*sic*] Digby is gone to Paris there to print Gelebrands discourse', although he was to be disappointed.[19] And in 1639 he recorded John Pell's opinion that it was one of 'the 2 greatest magneticall experiments'.[20]

Mention of Pell shows that Hartlib's enthusiasm for Gellibrand's work was shared by his allies. Indeed the unmathematical Hartlib

---

[15] *Ephemerides* (1635): HP 29/3/29B. The reference is to N. Cabeo, *Philosophia magnetica, in qua magnetis natura penitus explicatur* ... (Cologne, 1628); Mersenne's tract is printed in Marin Mersenne, *Correspondance du P. Marin Mersenne Religieux Minime*, ed. C. de Waard, 15 vols. (Paris, 1945–83), VIII, 755–61; Athanasius Kircher's tome, of which Mersenne forewarned Hartlib, must have been his *Magnes, sive de arte magnetica* (Rome, 1641). Notice how such references show that by *magnes* Hartlib did not simply refer to magnetic needles. Gellibrand's *Discourse* might just have been the best book on that narrower subject!

[16] *Ephemerides* (1639): HP 30/4/4B. Hartlib considered that Bond 'undertakes to find out the cause of the Variation of the Magnetical needle begun to be set on foot by Gelebrand. Hee has begun to philosophat upon it but the Experiments which are made are too few'. Interestingly, given that Bond often attracted half-hearted support, Hartlib added concerning Bond's scheme: 'I suppose it necessary to speake something of it.' The papers also include an extensive extract from the appendix to Bond's *Sea-mans calendar* (London, 1639), in which Bond announced his scheme. See HP 71/16/1A.

[17] See Gellibrand, *Discourse*, 1–7. As Pell commented, Gellibrand could not both rehearse Gilbert's theory and advocate a variation of the variation. See BL Add. MS 4408, fol. 384.

[18] 'Gelebrandus edit Tr[*actatum*] de Magnete quod statim versetur in alias L[*inguas*]' *Ephemerides* (1634): HP 29/2/40B.

[19] *Ephemerides* (1635): HP 29/3/61B. Certainly no such Paris edition was published. The lack of a French translation caused problems for Mersenne when the English edition was sent to him in 1640. He was completely ignorant of its existence and had to have it translated before informing his own network (Mersenne, *Correspondance*, VIII, 690).

[20] *Ephemerides* (1639): HP 30/4/26A.

was undoubtedly led in his opinions by those to whom he entrusted the advancement of practical mathematics, which was one of his chief projects in the 1630s. At that time he mainly relied upon Pell, who in 1634 had produced for Hartlib a draft of his universal scheme, *Idea matheseos*. For a few years he also consulted Gellibrand himself.[21] Pell was immediately taken with the *Discourse*, and wrote a manuscript commentary upon it in 1635, which he was still using rather unscrupulously to further his career in the 1660s.[22] Others who shared, or formed, Hartlib's opinion included William Watts, the mathematician and divine. Watts was a friend of Gellibrand and had appended an attack on the Aristotelian curriculum of English universities to the professor's publication on longitude.[23] Samuel Ward and Theodore Haak were also competent practical mathematicians in Hartlib's circle who singled out Gellibrand's discovery.[24] Thus Hartlib and his close circle of the 1630s were united in their praise of the Gresham professor's *Discourse*, and were perfectly aware of the canon of works in magnetic philosophy against which they were measuring it.

This shows that Hartlib's opinion was not isolated, but it does not help to explain Gellibrand's reputation in Hartlib's circle. One strand of an answer must be the privileged place held by Gresham College in Hartlib's plans of the 1630s. To be precise, it was only the work of the recent mathematical professors of astronomy and geometry, Briggs, Gunter, Foster and Gellibrand that appealed to Hartlib's circle. While, as we noted above, Hartlib was especially

---

[21] For the context to, and the early 1634 text of Pell's *Idea*, see P. J. Wallis, 'An early mathematical manifesto – John Pell's "Idea of Mathematics"', *Durham Research Review*, 18 (1967), 139–48. For Gellibrand, see note 34 below.

[22] E. G. R. Taylor claimed that a copy exists in the British Library. Pell's papers are not fully catalogued, and I have found only a short exercise dated 18 July 1636 (BL Add. MS 4408, fol. 384r). Although this commences 'Out of Mr Gellibrands discourse we may gather these 3 particular experiments concerning ye Magneticall Needle', it rapidly becomes an inconclusive exercise, on its own admission, in trigonometrical geometry, exploring the possibility of shifting geographical rather than magnetic meridians.

[23] James, *Strange and dangerous voyage*. This Baconian advocacy of practical mathematics insisted that 'the careful reading of our Books of Voyages would more elucidate the History of Nature, and more conduce to the improvement of Philosophy, than any thing that hath beene lately thought upon'; (sig. s2r, quoted in Webster, 353). For Watts' first opinion that 'Gelebr[*and's*] variation of the needle [*was*] a Rare Experiment', see *Ephemerides* (1635): HP 29/3/13A. See also *Ephemerides* (1635): HP 29/3/20B.

[24] HP 34/6/9B (Samuel Ward to Hartlib, 3 December 1639): '[*Mersenne's*] Magnetical schedule hath not 2 new lines or fresh notions [not in Gilbert]* Gellibrands about the variations addes to the foregoing ... '; for Haak, see Mersenne, *Correspondance*, VIII, 685.
* later insertion.

sympathetic to practical mathematics in this period, his coterie also exhibited a longstanding distrust of the professors of the more traditional disciplines of theology, law and rhetoric. In 1649 William Petty, who was to gain the chair of music the following year, argued that of '7 lectures, There seems but 4 Usefull to this Citty viz. Those of Physick, Geometry, Astronomy, and Musick'.[25] In 1639 Sir William Boswell, the projector and patron of Pell, opined to Hartlib that the Gresham professors 'excepting few have beene very idle, [and] should bee made at least to publish all their lectures. Only Brigs Gelebrand and some other few have beene doing any thing there.'[26]

Gellibrand, then, stood out as an exponent of practical mathematics. Indeed, the mathematics professors at Gresham's in the early 1630s represented a model of achievement in the kind of learning Hartlib regarded as progressive.[27] Similar ventures with which Hartlib was associated, such as Kynaston's Academy of 1636, and his own institution in Chichester, had both failed. Pell, in particular, suffered from the Chichester failure, having been recruited by Hartlib from Trinity College, Cambridge in 1630 in order to apply his prodigious mathematical skills to 'the education of the Gentrie of this Nation, to advance Piety, Learning, Moralitie and other Exercises of Industrie'.[28] This left Gresham College as the institution most likely to spearhead Baconian reform.

As Webster noted, Hartlib's circle concentrated their endeavours in the 1630s on mechanical and mathematical sciences. This is perhaps surprising in the light of Francis Bacon's lack of interest in, and Hartlib's lack of comprehension of, mathematics. But we know that in the puritan, utopian interpretations of Bacon's books and manuscripts, practical and craft knowledges were identified as a starting point for reform, being areas where a solid base would permit advancement through 'a real and legitimate union between empiric and rational faculties'.[29] Indeed, Hartlib and John Dury were later to present Baconian proposals for education reform in which 'very little of any Science or art will remain except only the

[25] HP 71/18. The attribution to Petty is made in Webster, 548–9; see also Ward, *Professors of Gresham College*, 218.

[26] *Ephemerides* (1639): HP 30/4/29B.

[27] The period certainly represented a high-water mark. After Gellibrand's death, absenteeism, political interference and inability blighted the mathematical chairs of geometry, astronomy and music respectively. See Webster, 52.

[28] Webster, 137.   [29] Quoted in Webster, 338.

Mathematicks'. Its practical 'mechanicall' branches were 'Navigation ... Surveying ... Architecture ... Painting'.[30] Consequently, Hartlib surrounded himself with mathematical advisers such as Pell, Haak, Petty – and Gellibrand.

The Gresham tradition of work in magnetic navigation, particularly that culminating in Gellibrand's discovery, provided Hartlib with a perfect example of his 1630s model of progress. It was both learned and useful. It embodied the conjunction of the 'empiric' faculties of navigators and seamen, and the rational faculties of the university-trained professors. Its fruits were the advancement of navigation and hence the increase of the Commonwealth. Furthermore it was irreducibly collaborative. The discovery of secular variation in particular had depended on two 'Baconian' features. Firstly, as Gellibrand made clear, the measurements of variation owed much to the equipment and skills of John Marr, supplier of compasses to the navy, and of John Wells, keeper of the naval storehouses, who were treated as colleagues by the Gresham professors.[31] The professors provided calculations and the magnetic and astronomical theory. Secondly, this new truth was the result of time and of sustained collaboration. It proved vital to its credibility that everything about the crucial 1622 and 1634 measurements (the apparatus, technique, location, method and personnel) was comparable, the only difference being that Gunter had been succeeded by Gellibrand.[32]

In the 1630s, then, Gresham College was a notable foundation for Solomon's House, and Gellibrand its best servant. Certainly Hartlib had high hopes for him, which were dashed by Gellibrand's death from fever in 1636, at the age of thirty-eight. He had consulted him frequently and, doubtless recalling Pell's design for a universal mathematics library, noted that 'Gelebrand has the most of Mathematical bookes of any Man in the Kingdome and very choice.

---

[30] 'Some proposalls towards the advancement of learning', HP 47/2/1A–12B. Quotations from fols. 2A, 7B. For arguments on dating and authorship see C. Webster, *Samuel Hartlib and the advancement of learning* (Cambridge, 1970), 166.

[31] An example in the Hartlib Papers themselves is a petition conjointly submitted by Gellibrand and Wells: HP 71/12/11B.

[32] Hartlib's *Ephemerides* strengthens the hint in Gellibrand, *Discourse*, 16, that the discovery was first made by Marr and Wells, and discussed long before he later confirmed and announced it. 'Hee hase not beene an eye-witnes of those Magnet[ical] observat[ions], but hee purposes to observe hims[elf] 2. year[s] longer et then hee thought it would be a choice peece and worthy to be communicated. Gelebr[and] desid[erata] de Magnet[e]' (*Ephemerides* (1635): HP 29/3/63B).

Et so able to give us a Catal[*ogue*] of the best book's in that kind'.[33] Hartlib's *Ephemerides* also shows Gellibrand in demand for his acquaintance with logarithms, his huge collection of astronomical instruments, solutions accruing from his 'New Astronomy', numerous practical contrivances and, of course, magnetism.[34] Gellibrand's demise certainly robbed Hartlib of his leading practitioner of Baconian mechanics.

MAGNETISM AND PURITANISM I

Religious rectitude was an important factor in the judgements of Hartlib's circle of the 1630s. It certainly intruded into the assessment of Gellibrand. We know that, on occasion, Hartlib discussed theology with him – Hartlib recorded, not unsurprisingly, that Gellibrand disapproved of the 'divinity' in the *De veritate* of the deistic English 'wit', Lord Herbert of Cherbury.[35] Doctrinal connections provide the second reason for Hartlib's enthusiasm for Gellibrand and the Gresham mathematicians. While the traditionalist and 'idle' professors had no obvious puritan sympathies, the productive mathematical professors, Briggs, Gunter, Foster and Gellibrand were all known to have them in the 1620s and 1630s, when Hartlib was trying to weld those actively resisting Laud into a movement for reform. Briggs and Gunter's puritanism attracted less attention, but when tensions increased in the next decade, Gellibrand 'was brought before the High Commission, [*and*] Foster had been described as a "zealous nonconformist"'.[36] Gellibrand reputedly held conventicles at Gresham's and was prosecuted by Laud himself for encouraging the publication of an almanac in which Foxe's martyrs replaced the traditional saints. Gellibrand's case was cited against Laud at his own trial.[37]

Gellibrand was not the only puritan magnetic philosopher and mathematician in Hartlib's circle to tangle with Laud. Samuel Ward, the influential master of Sidney Sussex, Cambridge (and one of Hartlib's admirers of Gellibrand's discovery), led Cambridge resistance to Laudianism, although he remained a staunch royalist and was incarcerated by the parliamentarians. The tension of his

---

[33] *Ephemerides* (1635): HP 29/3/4A.
[34] See, for example, *Ephemerides* (1634): HP 29/2/31B, 32A; *Ephemerides* (1635): 29/3/29B.
[35] *Ephemerides* (1635): HP 29/3/48A.   [36] Webster, 152.
[37] *DNB*, 'Gellibrand'; Ward, *Professors of Gresham College*, 81–5.

position emerges in Ward's own contribution to magnetic philosophy, *The wonders of the load-stone or, the load-stone newly reduc't into a divine and morall use* of 1640, which Hartlib was, as usual, aware of well in advance. Working from the premiss that God had chosen the magnet, or loadstone, as an analogy of Himself, Ward theologized every aspect of magnetic philosophy. One deduction, from Gilbert's insistence that magnetic attraction was a non-violent 'coition', was that kings should govern 'magnetically' and not by 'slavish tyranny'. Despite this anti-Laudian advice, he dedicated the work to Charles I, adding that the magnet was 'a lively Embleme of your Most admirable Monarchicall and mild Government'.[38] Works such as these, and the militant reformism of the practical magneticians at Gresham College, remind us that, in Hartlib's world, even magnetic philosophy was conducted in contexts where it could become charged with contested religious significance. While we cannot yet conclude that the magnet was a specific symbol for Baconian millennialists, it will be the purpose of the concluding section to establish this.

Thus, in mitigation of Hartlib's judgement of Gellibrand, the professor was a friend, a colleague, an investigated puritan and an ally engaged in Baconian work in an area and institution at the heart of Hartlib's interests in the 1630s. His discovery promised to improve magnetic navigation, something which everyone, not merely pansophic millennialists, recognized as a key to peace, unification and prosperity. But 'these 2 hundred years not the like published'? Hardly. And if too heroic a picture of Gellibrand emerges from the Hartlib Papers, let us note the (unsubstantiated) conclusion of his biographer in the *Dictionary of national biography*: 'Gellibrand was a plodding industrious mathematician, without a spark of genius.'[39]

GELLIBRAND ABROAD

Confirmation that Gellibrand's work had a significance in Hartlib's world that was not recognized in other worlds is provided by the very different reception visible in the correspondence of Marin

---

[38] Hartlib reported that Ward was 'meditating upon the spiritual uses of the loadstone in Latin' (*Ephemerides* (1635), quoted in Webster, 127). *The wonders of the loadstone* (London, 1640) was a translation of his *Magnetis redactorium theologicum tropologicum* (London, 1637). For quotation, see *Wonders*, 'Dedication'.

[39] DNB, 'Gellibrand'.

Mersenne. Mersenne, the Minim friar and exponent of mechanical philosophy, co-ordinated the other great contemporary circle of savants. Hartlib had sought to establish contact with it for some time, a task he wisely left to his more physico-mathematical colleagues.[40] Thus it was magnetic philosophy, and in particular the work of Gellibrand, that provided the main vehicle for the long-overdue intersection of these philosophical networks late in 1639 and in 1640.[41]

In brief, Gellibrand's claim to have detected a secular change in magnetic variation was at first politely ignored by continental workers, then questioned, dropped and finally confirmed and accepted. I have discussed elsewhere the sociological nature of the process by which a consensus was reached.[42] Here I must focus on the broader ideological differences between the groups which may have affected their judgement of Gellibrand. It remains relevant, however, that many of the micro-sociological reasons that gave Hartlib's circle confidence in Gellibrand were necessarily lacking in Mersenne's group. In the latter he, his co-workers, and their equipment and methods were of unknown competence. Gresham professorships conferred no automatic authority, and what we now know to have been the extensive personal contacts and reputation that he enjoyed with Hartlib had little significance abroad. Nevertheless, Mersenne was also very interested in magnetic philosophy and magnetic navigation, superficially for similar reasons to Hartlib.[43]

In some ways, Mersenne and Hartlib were apparently pursuing the same ends. Both hoped, through the networks of intelligence that they sustained, to bring about the advancement of learning. They both intended to accomplish it for natural philosophy by winnowing out scholastic or other 'fantasticall and disputatious' work, and to harvest only the true and useful knowledge. Above all, they both believed that such knowledge would disclose new principles around which Europe's philosophers would unify.

But there the similarities ended. Hartlib's vision in the 1630s and 1640s was still a pansophic mixture of grand Baconian and Comenian schemes in which truth, utility and Protestant ideology were inseparable. Mersenne's was, on the surface, a more narrowly

[40] Webster, 53. [41] Mersenne, *Correspondance*, VII, VIII.
[42] See Pumfrey, "'O tempora, O magnes!'", esp. 208–13.
[43] Mersenne, *Correspondance*, IV, 102; IX, 422.

philosophical programme, where sound observations, preferably quantitative and organized into general laws, would establish a bridgehead against the twin evils of scepticism and dogmatism. These different ideologies ensured that the twelve-month correspondence beginning in November 1639 generated little common ground, even in the apparently neutral area of magnetism.

In spring 1639 Mersenne completed a little pamphlet on the new magnetic philosophy. In accordance with his anti-sceptical methodology, he had included only the phenomena he judged to be incontrovertible, and he circulated fifty copies to selected European savants. Significantly, none of them resided in the land of the philosophy's founding father. By autumn, however, a copy had reached England and Theodore Haak, who sent it round the Hartlib circle to interested parties such as John Pell and Samuel Ward.[44] Haak was now prompted to initiate a correspondence with Mersenne. He began with gifts of Pell's *Idea matheseos* and Comenius' *Conatuum Comeniorum praeludia*, works commonly deployed by Hartlib 'to stimulate interest in the pansophic system'.[45]

Mersenne was not stimulated. He criticized Pell's design for a universal mathematical library which exhibited a typically Hartlibian promiscuity. 'His plan is laudable [*Mersenne replied*]. But instead of the big collection which he proposes, it would be better to select a dozen of the best in each area.'[46] And although Haak's brief was clearly to push Comenius' ideas, Mersenne persistently refused to be drawn down this road of reform in philosophy. In turn, Haak declined to support the persecution of Robert Fludd, whom Mersenne now wished to pursue into the afterlife. For Mersenne the English mystical Paracelsian (whose books of magnetic magic he detested) exemplified the dangerous nonsense which, in his view, encouraged philosophical scepticism, and which therefore was a chief target of his very different programme of reform.[47]

Perhaps worse for Mersenne was that his own pamphlet on

---

[44] See Mersenne, *Correspondance*, VIII, 617, 754, 755–61; *Ephemerides* (1639): HP 30/4/26A; HP 34/6/9B (S. Ward to Hartlib, 3 December 1639).

[45] Webster, 54.

[46] For Pell's scheme, see Wallis, 'An early mathematical manifesto'; for Mersenne's response to 'Pelet' see Mersenne, *Correspondance*, VIII, 579–80, or HP 18/2/1A.

[47] See, for example, HP 18/2/3A–3B, 18/2/10B, 18/2/16B ('Je vous prie de me faire savoir si Fludd est mort, et quand, et quelle opinion on a chez vous de ces livres, dont le dernier imprimé à Gouda est *Physica Mosaica*'), 18/2/27A, 18/2/35B; the third book of Fludd's posthumous *Philosophia Moysaica* (Gouda, 1638) was devoted to showing that magic resulted from the properties of the 'macrocosmical loadstone'.

magnetism was badly received. Unfamiliar with Mersenne's programme of mitigated scepticism, Pell and Ward's common reaction
was that the pamphlet was derivative, dull and shockingly incomplete. In particular it omitted Gellibrand's 'marvellous' discovery of
secular variation. Hartlib noted: 'Mersennus left out the 2 greatest
magnetical experiments which Pell will suggest unto him.'[48] Pell did
so, and revealed that, in his opinion, the two greatest magnetic
experiments were those related to magnetic navigation, namely
Gilbert's correlation of magnetic dip with latitude and, of course,
Gellibrand's work on variation. Pell immediately sent Mersenne a
copy of Gellibrand's *Discourse*, together with his own commentary.[49]
When he read it, Mersenne failed to recognize something 'these 2
hundred years not the like published'. His response was merely
polite. His own tract was derivative and uncontroversial, but that
had been the point! He had left out the dip–latitude relationship
because Parisian observers could not verify it. And, reacting
guardedly to Gellibrand's 'diminution', he wondered whether it was
a real effect or an artefact of unreliable equipment, as others had
suggested.[50]

Mersenne's group successfully challenged English confidence that
the Greshamites had overlooked no hidden variables, raising objections which Gellibrand had not covered in his *Discourse*.[51] Discussion
abounded for a few months, with refutations countering confir-
mations until Descartes ruled that there was nothing further 'to say
about the declination of the needle; est questio facti'. The debate
closed, slowly, over the next few years as the facts began to build up.
It was Mersenne who persisted with the correspondence, but now
with obsessive requests to collect magnets, especially Samuel Ward's
'prodigious loadstone' for some particularly tedious experiments.

[48] For Ward, see HP 34/6/9B (S. Ward to Hartlib, 3 December 1639): for Hartlib on Pell, see
Ephemerides (1639): HP 30/4/26A.
[49] Mersenne, *Correspondance*, VIII, 617, 622.
[50] Mersenne, *Correspondance*, VIII, 636, 682; IX, 20, 134.
[51] Interestingly, Descartes wondered whether the changes had been continuous (and hence of
astronomical significance) or discrete, caused by local changes in the distribution of ferrous
materials. See Mersenne, *Correspondance*, VIII, 262, 705. Yet Hartlib recorded William Watts
wondering 'How Mountaines wil attract, or betweene 2. Mountaines one somewhat higher
than the other. The like of Earth where store of Iron-mines esp[ecially]' – *Ephemerides*
(1635): HP 29/3/20B. Together with Pell's manuscript record of a discussion with 'Mr
Gellibrand in a conference at Mayfield this Mid sommer ... [*who*] gave no reason why [*the
magnetic meridian*] should change though it can hardly stand with his discourse' (BL Add.
MS 4408, fol. 384r), these suggest a greater debate in England than I was aware of in my
first article, '"O tempora, O magnes!"'.

Haak was not alone in tiring of the requests and he brought the correspondence to a close.[52]

Thus the epistolary intersection of the two circles ended within a year. Despite their common interest in natural philosophical reform in general, and in magnetism in particular, Mersenne had been impressed neither by Hartlib's pansophism nor by the unimpeachable authority of Gresham scholarship. The Hartlibians had no fervour for refuting Fludd's Paracelsism and were repelled by Mersenne's painstakingly empiricist approach to foundational philosophy. The different continental response shows that shared audience interests in practical mathematics, magnetic philosophy, navigational science and the advancement of learning were not enough to make Gellibrand's *Discourse* the best book 'these 2 hundred years de Magnete'. Outside its Greshamite, Hartlibian, puritan context it appeared to be a vulnerable and contestable work of uncertain significance. What was for Hartlib's circle a profound advance in the science of magnetic navigation and a 'choice peece' which established the credentials of the coterie was, for Mersenne, just another contentious fact to be checked.

MAGNETISM AND PURITANISM II

We are now brought back again, in our search for an explanation of Hartlib's enthusiasm, to the special value his group placed upon the work of the puritan Gresham professors in mathematical navigation. Of course, there are many unremarkable reasons for such support. The discipline was useful, Baconian and, as we saw in the introduction, the compass was generally considered to have facilitated a new, prosperous, united world. Yet these routine reasons do not seem to me to be sufficient. In a final attempt at explanation I wish to suggest, somewhat speculatively, that the magnetic needle had an even deeper significance in Hartlib's world, as a divine token of millennialist providential history.[53]

As Hartlib and all close readers of Francis Bacon knew well, the magnetic compass was one of the three famous inventions that had become emblematic of the modern age. The fullest tribute to these so-called 'Baconian inventions' occurs in the penultimate aphorism

---

[52] Mersenne, *Correspondance*, VIII, 404; Webster, 54.
[53] The general case has been established by Webster, *passim*.

of Bacon's *Novum organum* of 1620. Although published only in Latin, the exact 'Passage Out of the L[or]d Verulem's Novum Organon translated out of Latin' is found twice among Hartlib's papers. It reads:

> It were good to take notice of the Vertue Efficacy and Consequences of Inventions, Which are scarse More Conspicuous in any then in these three, Vnknowne to the Ancients, & whose beginnings (although but of late) are obscure & without vnknowne To witt the Art of Printing, Gunpowder & the Marriners Needle, For these three haue changed the face & State of things through out the whole world ... so that no Empire, No Sect, nor no Constellation seemeth to haue had a greater Influence upon humane affaires than these Mechanicall Inventions haue had.[54]

Although the three inventions in this technological 'tryptich' of compass, gunpowder and printing have been dubbed the 'Baconian inventions', they already formed a well-worn trope by the seventeenth century, and had been pressed into a variety of ideological services. Bacon's own uses of the examples were neither usual nor straightforward. As with all rhetorical devices, to determine Bacon's meanings, and any further meanings which Hartlib's circle supplied to the trope, requires us to place it in context.

As Keller has shown, the compass figured in the first known list of post-classical inventions, compiled by the mid-fifteenth-century philologist, Niccolo Tortelli, whose purpose had been to legitimize the use of post-classical neologisms. By Erasmian humanists the same post-classical technologies were cited as proof of the vibrancy of Christian societies.[55] Bacon, however, combined two late sixteenth-century themes. Humanists such as Cardano, Bodin and Le Roy established the triptych as the three most potent proofs of progress since antiquity.[56] Bodin's eulogy to navigation, cited earlier, began: 'What, for example, is there more marvellous than the magnet? The ancients were ignorant of it ...' and concludes by 'not speaking' of artillery, nor of 'the art of printing [*which*] alone would easily be able

---

[54] Quotation from HP 63/12A–12B. See also HP 8/64/3A. For the original Latin, see Bacon, *Works*, I, 222.

[55] See Alex Keller, 'A Renaissance humanist looks at "New" inventions: the article "Horologium" in Giovanni Tortelli's De orthographia', *Technology and Culture*, 11 (1970), 345–65.

[56] For the development of what he called this 'tryptich' see Wolper, 'Rhetoric of gunpowder'. See also Alex Keller, 'Mathematical technologies and the growth of the idea of progress in the 16th century', in *Science, medicine and society in the Renaissance*, ed. Allen G. Debus, 2 vols. (New York, 1972), I, 11–27; P. Rossi, *Philosophy, technology and the arts in the early modern era*, trans. S. Attanasio (New York, 1970), chaps. 1, 2; Herbert Weisinger, 'Ideas of history during the Renaissance', *Journal of the History of Ideas*, 6 (1945), 415–35, esp. 418.

to match all the inventions of the ancients'. At the same time, as Zilsel and Rossi have shown, artisans appropriated the three inventions to demonstrate the social significance of technological skill in a culture that regarded only scholars as learned. Bacon certainly mobilized the inventions in this way too.[57]

But members of Hartlib's circle interpreted Bacon as an exponent of providential history and it is tempting, therefore, to read Bacon as having added this new dimension himself, thereby representing the magnetic compass as a gift from God with which mankind could fulfil his plan. I suspect that this is mistaken. Admittedly, Bacon interpreted the voyages of discovery as signs of the last age, as he did in *Valerius terminus*, a favourite text of 1630s puritans (and of historians of them). He invited consideration of 'the prophecy of Daniel where speaking of the latter times it is said, Many shall pass to and fro, and science shall be increased: as if the opening of the world by navigation and commerce and the further discovery of knowledge should meet in one age'.[58] However, when Bacon wrote of the technical discoveries, notably the compass, that had improved navigation and brought the prophecy to pass, he consistently stressed the accidental and inefficient nature of their invention and improvement. It was precisely the haphazard and unphilosophical practice of the arts that Bacon argued was a chief hindrance to the advancement of learning – and the need to provide philosophical order to the arts was a prime reason for Bacon's planned 'great instauration'. While man's return to an Adamic dominion over nature was, for Bacon, providentially ordained, it required hard, methodical, human work if it were to be brought to pass speedily.

Nevertheless, a conflation of a general millennialist Baconian history with Bacon's specific comments on the origin of the three inventions was an easy and obvious move for Hartlib's circle. And since they read Bacon as the 'philosophical complement' to John Foxe, they would have found the conflation already begun in his *Acts and monuments*. Foxe is the earliest author I have found who

---

[57] Edgar Zilsel, 'The genesis of the concept of scientific progress', *Journal of the History of Ideas*, 6 (1945), 325–49; Rossi, *Early Modern Era*; Bodin, 'Methodus', 227–8.

[58] Bacon *Works*, III, 221. He continues: 'However that be so ...'! He wrote very similarly in several other texts, including the *New organon*. In Aphorism 93 he read the prophecy as 'plainly hinting and suggesting that fate (which is Providence) would cause the complete circuit of the globe (now accomplished, or at least going forward by means of so many distant voyages), and the increase of learning to happen at the same epoch' (Bacon, *Works*, I, 200; IV, 92).

asserted one of the triptych to be a 'divine and miraculous invention' which, 'what man soever was the instrument, without all doubt God himself was the ordainer and disposer thereof'. The particular invention was, of course, 'the faculty of printing [*which God sent*] after the invention of guns, the space of one hundred and thirty years', in order to spread the truth cheaply and to defeat Catholicism.[59]

It seems to have been George Hakewill who extended Foxe's providentialist accounts to the magnetic needle in his *Apologie or declaration of the power and providence of God in the government of the world*, first published in 1627. John (or Jan) Johnston's *History of the constancy of nature* not surprisingly did the same in 1634. Hakewill was widely read in non-conforming circles such as Hartlib's in the 1630s and may have helped to install the magnet as an emblem of the new, more thoroughgoing Baconian millennialism.[60] The marvel of the magnetic needle had come to be regarded specifically as the gift of God, enabling the many to pass to and fro and thereby to inaugurate the last, scientific age.

Such providentialist thinking was, of course, commonly exchanged among Hartlib's correspondents. Regrettably, for the conclusion to this chapter, few of them were considerate enough to make explicit reference to the compass, and I have not found Gellibrand linking them, despite his own links with Hakewill.[61] Hartlib's papers contain three associations of the magnetic needle with an impending millennium. Hartlib himself received a letter that wrote of God's grace 'largely, fully and bountifully performed, since the Magnet of divine Love hath so covered the main Ocean and freely opened the despatches of commerce by sea and by land over the whole universe'. Another, listing signs of the approaching end, noted how 'in these last days, by means of the Magnet the entire ocean and the furthest lands have been opened up to ships ... [*Thereby*] the word of God has been spread, like lightning, through

[59] John Foxe, *The acts and monuments of John Foxe, with a life ... of George Townsend*, 3 vols. (repr. London, 1846), III, 718–22. Quotations from 719, 718, 722; for the complement see Webster, 25.

[60] Hakewill's work was first published in 1627, with a second edition in 1630. The third edition (Oxford, 1635) added a more providential dimension to his belief in the moderns' superiority. For Johnston, see John Johnston, *An history of the constancy of nature*, trans. John Rowland [?] (London, 1657). Hakewill considered Johnston's work a plagiarism. Although inspired by it, it showed 'the drift of protestant opinion ... in displaying a far greater receptivity to millenarian ideas' (Webster, 20).

[61] They both worked on bringing Henry Briggs' unpublished works to the press. See *DNB*, 'Briggs, Henry', 'Gellibrand'; Ward, *Professors of Gresham College*, 81–5.

all the corners of the Earth'.[62] Here, then, peace, unification and prosperity came through God's gift of the magnet.

Thus Hartlib's misjudgement of the significance of Gellibrand's *Discourse mathematicall* cannot be defended through the concurrence of Pell's and Watts' opinions, nor through the importance Hartlib attached to the Baconian advances made at Gresham College. The best, though admittedly circumstantial, defence for Hartlib and his circle is that they believed the magnetic needle to be a providential instrument, bestowed by God and being perfected by men such as Gellibrand, to bring about the commercial prosperity, geographical unification and religious peace that would accompany the great and final instauration.

What did Gellibrand think of providence and the magnet? He did not tell us. His *Discourse* begins: 'To write an Encomiastique of the Magnet is not my intention; the bold and confident attempts of Seamen, thorough those hidden paths of the vast Ocean, to all navigable parts of the Earth, will spare me the labour';[63] admirably Baconian, but modestly omitting any conviction that he was himself a divine instrument, let alone the recipient of a 'spark of genius', in his study of the divine instrument of the magnetic needle. And yet there can be no doubt that the uneven distribution of such contentious beliefs shaped the development of magnetic philosophy within and without the world of Samuel Hartlib. In some quarters they still do. One reads in the Book of Mormon that Nephi's father stumbled across 'a round ball of curious workmanship ... [*containing*] two spindles, and the one pointed the way whither we should go in the wilderness'. At sea, however, 'the compass, which had been prepared of the Lord, did cease to work', thereby requiring the secrets to be rediscovered in the age of Gellibrand and Hartlib.[64]

---

[62] See HP 39/12A; HP 18/24/1A. The Latin text reads: 'Hinc in postremis seculis nautis per Magnetem totus Oceanus & amplissima Terrarum spatia patuerunt: Hinc, prelo promovente Sermones Dei fulgurus instar per omnes Terrae angulos disperguntur.' Compare with Comenius to D. Sveciae, HP 7/83/1A, and the copy of the 'Sententiae Theologorum Parisiensium', HP 17/6/1A–10B, fol. 7A.

[63] Gellibrand, *Discourse*, 1.

[64] Book of Mormon, 1 Nephi 16:10; 1 Nephi 18:12. I am grateful to Alex Keller for this lead.

CHAPTER 14

Technology transfer and scientific specialization: Johann Wiesel, optician of Augsburg, and the Hartlib circle

Inge Keil

THE CAREER OF A SPECIALIST INSTRUMENT MAKER

Johann Wiesel was probably the first person in Germany to found a workshop for the manufacture of telescopes and microscopes. He was born around 1583 in the Palatinate, the region from which the ancestors of Samuel Hartlib had originated. Nothing is known of Wiesel's youth. In 1621 he married the daughter of a craftsman and citizen of Augsburg, and thereby became a citizen of the Free Imperial City of Augsburg. This enabled him to establish a workshop for producing optical instruments. Optical instrument making was a 'free art' and so he was not required to become a member of one of the craft corporations. Unlike Nuremberg or Regensburg, there was no incorporated craft of spectacle makers in Augsburg.

The first letters in which Wiesel's optical instruments are mentioned date from 1625.[1] There are references to his eyeglasses, fleaglasses (*Flohbüchslein*), burning mirrors and perspectives. He undertook contracts for several German dukes and subsequently for the German emperor Ferdinand II. He also produced instruments for King Gustavus Adolphus of Sweden following his conquest of Augsburg in 1632.[2] The period of the Thirty Years War brought devastation to much of Germany and particularly to the city of Augsburg. Besides the impact of siege and quartering of soldiers on

The assistance of Mrs Lore von Ammon, Augsburg and of Professor Silvio A. Bedini, Washington, in the preparation of this chapter is gratefully acknowledged. I also thank the members of the Hartlib Papers Project, especially Mr John Young, for their assistance during my stay in Sheffield.

[1] Copies of the correspondence between Prince August of Anhalt (Fürst August zu Anhalt) and the municipal physician of Augsburg (*Stadtarzt*), Dr Carl Widemann, are to be found in the Niedersächsische Landesbibliothek, Hanover, MS IV 341, pp. 850–64.

[2] *Der Briefwechsel zwischen Philipp Hainhofer und Herzog August dem Jüngeren von Braunschweig-Lüneburg*, ed. R. Gobiet (Munich, 1984), 554, 586–9.

the city, there were rising prices, hunger and outbreaks of plague as well as the imposition of heavy financial contributions. Moreover, the religious situation was extremely delicate. The majority of its citizens were Protestant – as was Wiesel. Yet their government was Catholic, save during the three years of the Swedish occupation. Despite all these difficulties, Johann Wiesel's workshop continued its operations. In 1638 he was assisted by Daniel Depier (De Pier), a glassworker from Danzig, who became his son-in-law two years later.

In Europe, Wiesel's products became known in particular through a book entitled *Oculus Enoch et Eliae*, written by a Capuchin monk, Father Anton Maria Schirleus de Rheita, and published in Antwerp in 1645. The author described telescope manufacture and, in a cryptogram, he mentioned a hitherto-unknown compound eyepiece for telescopes, made of three collective lenses, which would show objects upright.[3] Rheita explained that such telescopes could be obtained from Wiesel in Augsburg and from Gervasius Mattmüller (who lived in Vienna).[4] In the succeeding years Wiesel sold these terrestrial telescopes with four or more convex lenses all over Europe, as well as compound microscopes with three convex lenses. In 1650, he was probably the first optician in Europe to make use of a third lens – the field lens – in his microscopes to give a greater field of vision.[5]

By the time of his death in March 1662, Wiesel had a number of important rivals in the field of optical instrument making. Eustachio Divini had been producing telescopes and microscopes in Rome since 1646. During the 1650s, he enjoyed the reputation of being the best optician in Europe. Guiseppe Campani, who was to surpass Divini, brought his first telescopes before the public in 1662. In London, too, Richard Reeve had succeeded in grinding objective-lenses with great focal length. All these opticians had associations with the men of science of their time, those who helped to found or were active in the important scientific groups or societies of their locality. In Germany, however, interest in scientific matters waned during and after the Thirty Years War. Wiesel's successors in

---

[3] A. M. Schirleus de Rheita, *Oculus Enoch et Eliae* (Antwerp, 1645), 356.

[4] *Ibid.*, 339–40; on Rheita see Alfons Thewes, *Oculus Enoch* ... (Oldenburg, 1984); on Mattmüller see Maria Habacher, 'Mathematische Instrumentenmacher, Mechaniker, Optiker und Uhrmacher im Dienste des Kaiserhofes in Wien (1630–1750)', *Blätter für Technikgeschichte*, 22 (1960), 13–15.

[5] HP 37/144B (Wiesel to Morian, 17 February 1650).

Augsburg, Daniel Depier and later Cosmus Conrad Cuno, were both capable makers of optical instruments, but they lacked the impulse and support of scientists (especially astronomers) and no longer played a major innovative role in European science.

OPTICAL INSTRUMENT MANUFACTURE IN ENGLAND IN THE FIRST HALF OF THE SEVENTEENTH CENTURY

An interest in astronomical observation was highly developed in seventeenth-century England, and this stimulated English telescope manufacture in the years following the invention of the device in 1608. The making of a good telescope was by no means easy. It required a supply of high-quality glass, the skill to grind the lenses accurately, and finally, the ability to install them into a tube. There was, as yet, no adequate theory of optics that was usable by artisans, and so the results depended to a high degree on the skill and the experience of the 'perspective-maker', as the optician was called in the first half of the seventeenth century.

As early as the sixteenth century, ovens for glass manufacture were in operation in England, chiefly operated by Italian migrants from Murano.[6] 'Venice glass', which was more suitable to optical lenses than the common greenish or brownish glass, was thus available in England. The art of lens grinding also was known because spectacle makers had been at work in London for many years. The new optical instruments, however, required better and clearer glass, without air-bubbles and colours, while lenses had to be ground more exactly than spectacle makers were capable of achieving.

Samuel Hartlib saw in the improvement of glass manufacture and optical instrumentation the possibilities of utilitarian benefits to mankind in much the same way as he valued other scientific knowledge such as chemistry. He certainly disseminated the information he obtained from continental sources relating to telescopy and optical instrumentation to those of his circle whom he knew to be interested in such matters. These included John Pell, Benjamin Worsley, Dr Goddard, Sir Paul Neile, Christopher Merret, Christopher Wren and John Beale. As early as 1635, Hartlib was interested

---

[6] Ferrand Whaley Hudig, *Das Glas* (Vienna, 1923), 99–103.

in the optical manuscripts of Cornelius Drebbel.[7] In 1649, 'Hartlib considered the making of glass in England to be very defective'[8] and wished to have a translation made of Antonio Neri's *De arte vitraria.* Not only was the improvement of telescopes and microscopes a theme repeatedly touched on in Hartlib's correspondence for the remainder of his life, it was also an issue in the discussions and experiments of English scientists throughout the seventeenth century.

Towards the end of the 1630s, Richard Reeve, later a renowned English optician, is first mentioned in the correspondence. With the protection of Sir Charles Cavendish and under the watchful eye of John Pell, Richard Reeve attempted to grind high-quality lenses, especially hyperbolic ones.[9] At the time, Reeve was able to report no success and his disappointed patron, Cavendish, wrote: 'Mr. Reaves hath broken in his triall so much glass.'[10] These experiments were concluded when Pell left for Amsterdam in 1643. But Cavendish was also acquainted with William Gascoigne, who had already used the astronomical telescope and invented a micrometer for it.[11] Gascoigne, however, was killed at the battle of Marston Moor and shortly afterwards, a year after Pell's departure, Charles Cavendish himself left England.

WIESEL AND THE HARTLIB CIRCLE

On his arrival in continental Europe, Cavendish went first to Hamburg, his interest in optics undiminished. Almost immediately he set about gathering information on continental opticians. Rheita had stated in a letter from Cologne that he had discovered five new stars around Jupiter with his new telescope in December 1642.[12] Pell

---

[7] Stephen Clucas, 'Samuel Hartlib's *Ephemerides*, 1635–59, and the pursuit of scientific and philosophical manuscripts', *The Seventeenth Century*, 5 (1991), 38; *Ephemerides* (1635): HP 29/3/56A.

[8] G. H. Turnbull, 'Samuel Hartlib's influence on the early history of the Royal Society', *Notes & Records*, 10 (1953), 123.

[9] HP 37/47A (Morian to Hartlib, 14 November 1639); M. Feingold, 'Robert Payne of Oxford', in *The light of nature*, ed. J. D. North and J. J. Roche (Dordrecht, 1985), 265–80, esp. 272; on Reeve, see A. D. C. Simpson, 'Richard Reeve – the "English Campani" – and the origins of the London telescope-making tradition', *Vistas in Astronomy*, 28 (1985), 357–65.

[10] BL Add. MS 4278, fol. 173 (Charles Cavendish to John Pell, 5 February 1641/2) – published in *A collection of letters illustrative of the progress of science in England*, ed. J. O. Halliwell (London, 1841), 72.

[11] BL Add. MS 4278, fol. 180r (Charles Cavendish to John Pell, 16/26 August 1644).

[12] Rheita to Puteanus, 6 January 1643. This letter was published with a controversial answer by Gassendi in Paris in April 1643. A second publication accompanied by a defence of

had received a copy of this letter in 1643 from Sir William Boswell, the English representative in the Netherlands.[13] Both Cavendish and Pell strove to gain information about this discovery.[14] They heard that Rheita had left Cologne for Augsburg and Cavendish eventually received a letter from Augsburg, dated 20 November 1644, reporting that Rheita had moved on to Antwerp, but that in Augsburg there was living 'a verry excellent master in that arte, whose name is Wisell, who constantly conversed with that Capuciner'.[15] By 1648, when the Cavendish brothers were living in Paris, they had collected seven Italian perspectives from Fontana, Divini and Torricelli. Some had been brought from Italy by Sir Kenelm Digby. But there was also one from Rheita which had 'arrived in the Low countries and hath beene there tried & said to be very rare'.[16] It is not known whether this perspective was made by Wiesel or another workman or by Rheita himself. By this date, Rheita was resident in Trier as confessor to, and adviser of, the archbishop and elector of Trier.

Pell may have given important details about Wiesel's activity to Johann Morian, a friend of Hartlib and Dury. Morian, like Pell at this time, also lived in Amsterdam. Morian later became the intermediary between Wiesel and the Hartlib circle. Morian, born in Nuremberg, might well be described as an 'Optical Gentleman', the expression used by Hartlib in his *Ephemerides*. He had served from 1619 to 1627 in Cologne as a minister of the German Protestant church (Hochdeutsche Gemeinde von Köln).[17] As Protestant religious services had to be kept secret in this strictly Catholic city, Morian may have used the status of manufacturer of optical instruments as a façade.[18] Some time after he arrived in the Netherlands, he made contact with Descartes, who asked him for assistance in the

Rheita written by Caramuel Lobkowitz was published in Louvain, also in 1643; *Novem stellae circa Jovis* (Paris, 1643; Louvain, 1643).

[13] BL Add. MS 4280, fol. 107r (Pell to Cavendish, 20/30 July 1644).
[14] BL Add. MSS 4278, 4279 and 4280 (correspondence between Charles Cavendish and John Pell) – partly published in Halliwell: see note 11 above. (The numbers of the manuscript pages have since been altered.)
[15] BL Add. MS 4278, fol. 193r ('From Augsburg 1644 November 20'). I thank Dr H.-R. Bachmann, Munich, for calling this letter to my attention.
[16] BL Add. MS 4280, fol. 92r (Charles Cavendish to Pell, n.d.).
[17] *Protokolle der Hochdeutsch-Reformierten Gemeinde in Köln von 1599–1794*, 1 Teil: 1599–1630, ed. Rudolph Löhr (Cologne, 1976), 235, 334–7.
[18] Niedersächsische Landesbibliothek Hanover, MS IV 341, 861 (Prince August of Anhalt to Widemann, 3/13 December 1626: 'zue Cölln einer seii sehr perfect Inn solchen Sachen. der hab ainen gesellen Morian genandtt').

grinding of hyperbolic lenses. Morian did not follow up the request because he considered it to be impossible to grind any lenses other than spherical.[19]

In 1644, Pell told Cavendish that the reputation of an artisan in Augsburg (who can only be Wiesel) who had 'an incomparable hand for glasses' had already reached him some years earlier.[20] We may thus assume that Wiesel was known in England before 1643. He is first mentioned directly in the Hartlib Papers in October 1647 when Hartlib informed the famous astronomer in Danzig, Johann Hevelius, of the price-list of Wiesel's telescopes, a copy of which he had acquired from Hamburg in September.[21] Hartlib enclosed a copy of this price-list in German, which is now to be found among the Hevelius correspondence in the Observatory of Paris.[22] Another copy, this time in Latin, is to be found in the British Library.[23] Hartlib may well have also sent this version to Pell. This price-list is particularly significant since it is one of the earliest by a scientific instrument maker and it is now known only from these copies distributed by Hartlib.

From this list we know that Wiesel was already offering, well before the end of the Thirty Years War, all three kinds of telescopes known at that time: the Dutch or Galileian one with a convex and a concave lens, the astronomical telescope with two convex lenses, whose theoretical basis had been presented by Kepler in 1611;[24] and the newest type, the terrestrial telescope with four or more convex lenses.[25] The quoted prices were rather high.

The first Wiesel telescope found its way to England through Johann Morian in Amsterdam and the Hartlib circle. Morian corresponded with Wiesel, who used him to advertise his newly invented instruments or improvements and to circulate descriptions of them. He forwarded copies of Wiesel's letters to Hartlib and these

---

[19] HP 37/47A (Morian to Hartlib, 14 November 1639); *Observatoire de Paris, correspondance de Hevelius* (hereafter *OP Corr. Hev.*) AC 1, 2, fol. 194v (Morian to Hevelius, 9 April 1650).

[20] BL Add. MS 4280, fol. 109v (Pell to Cavendish, 2/12 October 1644).

[21] HP 7/18/1A (Hartlib to Hevelius, 28 October 1647: copy).

[22] *OP Corr. Hev.*, AC 1, 1, fol. 79.

[23] BL Sloane MS 651, fols. 173–174r. A copy is reproduced in T. H. Court and M. von Rohr, 'New knowledge of old telescopes', *Transactions of the Optical Society*, 31 (1930–1), 113–22, 117–20.

[24] Johann Kepler, *Dioptrice* (Augsburg, 1611); Albert Van Helden, 'The "Astronomical Telescope", 1611–1650', *Annali dell'Istituto e Museo di Storia della Scienza di Firenze*, 1, (1976), 13–35.

[25] A. Van Helden, 'The development of compound eyepieces', *Journal for the History of Astronomy*, 8 (1977), 26–37.

letters in Hartlib's papers are a very informative source for research
on Wiesel. Through Hartlib, Hevelius had also apparently heard
about the instruments which had been purchased by Morian, with
whom he, in turn, began a correspondence. He asked a host of
detailed, practical questions such as what shape the lenses took, how
the telescopes were assembled, and how large Jupiter would appear
in them. The Hevelius correspondence in Paris thus becomes an
important complementary source of information.[26] Two further
letters from Morian and Wiesel relating to the instruments shipped
to England have been located in Wolfenbüttel among the correspondence of Duke August the Younger of Braunschweig-Lüneburg.
H. M. Hirt, the ducal agent in Augsburg, had referred to the
shipment as a proof of the good quality of Wiesel's telescopes.[27]

It is possible that the delivery of Wiesel's instruments was delayed
by the final years of the war. In 1648, Augsburg suffered once more
from a siege, this time undertaken by Swedish and French armies.
(A report of these events can be read in a letter from Morian.) In
September 1649, however, a 'tube for night and day' with seven
glasses and eleven tubes had arrived in Amsterdam. The price was
240 guilders or 180 Reichstaler. This instrument was intended for
delivery to Benjamin Worsley.[28] Morian was greatly impressed by
the telescope and promptly ordered another, solely for use at night.
This 'astralian tube' (*astralischer tubus*) arrived in Amsterdam in
December 1649 and cost him 100 Taler. It consisted of eleven tubes
and four lenses and its outermost tube was covered with leather. It
too was sent on to England directly, probably also for Worsley.[29]

In February 1652, Morian noted that he had ordered another
telescope from Wiesel and he, as well as Pell, reported that in April
1652 they had observed the eclipse of the sun with the newly
received *tubus astralis* 'with great astonishment'. Therefore it seems
that at least a third telescope was sent by Wiesel to Amsterdam.[30]

Wiesel's correspondence also mentioned other optical instruments

[26] Copies of the correspondence are located in the Bibliothèque Nationale, MS Latin 10347.
[27] Herzog August Bibliothek Wolfenbüttel, Cod. Guelf. 98 Novi, fol. 308 (Morian to Wiesel,
    22 October 1649); *ibid.*, fols. 309r–10r (Wiesel to Duke August).
[28] *Ibid.*, fol. 308r, fol. 309r.
[29] HP 37/144A–144B (Wiesel to Morian, 17 December 1649, copy sent on by Morian to
    Hartlib, 4 March 1650). An English copy from HP 8/34A was published in Van Helden,
    'Compound eyepieces', 34–5.
[30] *OP Corr. Hev.*, AC 1, 2, fol. 304r (Morian to Hevelius, 22 February 1652); HP 8/4A (Pell to
    ?, 12 April 1652: copy); *OP Corr. Hev.*, AC 1, 2, fol. 306r (Morian to Hevelius, 28 May
    1652).

he had made, such as, for example, a small '*tubus binoculus*' or an '*opthalmoscopium*'.[31] In February 1650, Wiesel told Morian that he had made a '*microscopium*' with three lenses for the duke of Bavaria in Munich which 'makes a flea as great as a turtle'.[32] Immediately some microscopes were ordered through Morian, one of them for Robert Boyle.[33] A year later, Hartlib reported to Hevelius: 'Last week two of Wiesel's microscopes arrived by ship which we enjoyed exceedingly and which are in truth far better than all such instruments hitherto invented. One of them costs nearly 5 pound Sterling.'[34] Morian was also impressed with their performance. His judgement was of value because he had himself made compound microscopes in his earlier years, albeit ones only containing two lenses.[35]

Microscopes served many for little more than diversion and amusement. In 1648, for example, Benjamin Worsley described 'having received more pleasure and satisfaction at spare howres by looking all small and minute bodies in these glasses than almost from anything'.[36] But it also served to prove to him the immensity of God's wisdom. Nothing, it appeared, had been made by chance, and he was convinced that it would be an enormous and worthwhile task 'to discover to the world this little Atlantis or unknown part of the Creation'.[37] Robert Boyle, however, at that time in close contact with Hartlib, had already used the microscope as a scientific tool. Hartlib recorded in the *Ephemerides* of early 1651: 'He cares not for optical niceties but as they are subordinate to Natural Phil[osophy]. For by the microscopes and tubes that may bee learnt and discerned which cannot bee done neither by reason or experiments but only sense. He [*Boyle*] tried Quicksilver in very small pieces in a Microscope which presented him with a perfect Spherical figure.'[38]

It was not only to Hartlib's circle that Morian acted as distributor of Wiesel's products. Hevelius was also eager to obtain a new

---

[31] HP 37/144B (*binoculum*: Wiesel to Morian, 30 December 1649: copy); HP 37/144A (*opthalmoscopium*: Wiesel to Morian, 17 December 1649: copy).

[32] HP 37/144B (Wiesel to Morian, 17 February 1650: copy).

[33] HP 37/150A (Morian to Hartlib, 8 April 1650).

[34] 'Vergangene Woche sind 2 von seinen Microscopiis durch Schiffe geschicket alhier angelanget die uns dan uber alle maßen erfrewet v. in warheit alles was noch zuvor in diesem stück erfunden weit ubergehen. Das Stücke kostet fast 5 pfund sterl' (*OP Corr. Hev.*, AC 1, 2, fol. 215v (Hartlib to Hevelius, 20 March 1651)).

[35] *OP Corr. Hev.*, AC 1, 2, fol. 194v (Morian to Hevelius, 9 April 1650).

[36] HP 8/27/1A (Worsley to ?, Amsterdam, 22 June 1648: copy).

[37] HP 8/27/3B (Worsley to ?, 27 July 1648: copy).   [38] *Ephemerides* (1651): HP 28/2/3B.

microscope through Morian, who was able to supply one in February 1652.[39] That Morian sold Wiesel's instruments more widely is also demonstrated by a letter from Constantijn Huygens (Christiaan Huygens' father), who apparently wished to obtain another microscope from Augsburg to replace the instrument which he had lent to a friend and which had not yet been returned. By this date, 1655, Morian was living in Arnhem.[40] He was still in contact with Wiesel in 1658, planning to forward him Smethwick's *discurs de tubis* which he had received from Hartlib, and asking him for his opinion on it.[41]

Nothing more is presently known about instruments Wiesel may have sold to England during the last years of his life. That his name remained well known is demonstrated by two letters from individuals travelling through Germany. In the first, Henry Oldenburg informed Hartlib that, in the summer of 1658 'We did not neglect to see Wiselius at Augsburg, yea I bought of him a little perspective of a mans hand long, fitted for my sight, which is somewhat short, that costed a ducat. But to learne something of him, as we faine would have done', time was too short. Oldenburg in fact only spent twenty-four hours in Augsburg.[42] Three years later, and some months before Wiesel's death, Robert Southwell passed through Augsburg on his way back to England from Italy. He reported to Viviani that he had visited good old Wiesel ('quel bon veccherello') who had shown him exquisite telescopes with two, four or five glasses which had a large field of view. He saw also good microscopes and that special instrument that lets you see round a corner (a 'Polemoscopium').[43] Both correspondents later became secretaries of the Royal Society in London.

It is not known if and for how long the instruments of Wiesel were used for scientific purposes in England – those telescopes for observing the sky, and those microscopes for looking into a minute world that had never been seen before. But there is no doubt that they had been examined carefully upon arrival in England and that their design exercised an influence on local instrument manufacture.

[39] *OP Corr. Hev.*, AC 1, 2, fol. 304r (Morian to Hevelius, 22 February 1652).
[40] Constantijn Huygens, *De briefwisseling*, ed. J. A. Worp, (S'Gravenhage, 1911–16), v, 240, no. 5414 (Constantijn Huygens to Colvius, 9 June 1655).
[41] HP 56/2/1B (Morian to Hartlib, 8/18 January 1658).
[42] Oldenburg, I, 288 (Oldenburg to Hartlib, Paris, 23 June 1659).
[43] Biblioteca Nacionale Centrale Firenze, Cod. Galilaeana 254, fols. 176–177r (Southwell to Viviani, 9 October 1661). This letter was kindly drawn to my attention by Professor Van Helden.

Richard Reeve had, of course, continued trying to improve his own telescope lenses, enjoying the patronage first of Dr Jonathan Goddard and then of Sir Paul Neile.[44] In January 1651, Hartlib noted in his *Ephemerides*: 'Sir Paul Neale was mighty busy with Mr. Reeves about the Perspective-Glasses'[45] and in the following March he wrote to Hevelius: 'Our philosophers and artisans here believe that their glasses shall surpass those of Wiesel by far. But the evidence will show that best in some weeks. I myself can not yet believe that they will come with it so high and far as our excellent Augustanus.'[46] On this latter point Hartlib was eventually proved wrong. It would be some time, however, before English opticians attained their long-held reputation alongside the Italians as among the best in Europe.

The influence of Wiesel's craftsmanship and design was thus of considerable significance in England. English optical instrument makers adopted the compound eyepiece after they had observed it in Wiesel's instruments. For many years English terrestrial telescopes were constructed along the same lines as those of Wiesel: the ocular lenses were fastened in the thickest and outermost tube and the objective lens in the smallest one. In the Italian tradition, the opposite construction remained. The process of adaptation to Wiesel's designs occurred very quickly. His first microscopes arrived in England in 1651, as we have seen. In 1652 Reeve had already much improved his own microscopes along similar lines.[47] Microscopes having three lenses which Wiesel had invented were later to become known as 'English microscopes'. A good example of how thoroughly this appropriation was accepted, even in Germany, is to be found in an inventory to the Chamber of Arts of the duke of Württemberg. The collection apparently contained two compound microscopes signed J. W. A. O. (i.e. 'Johann Wiesel Augustanus Opticus'). An inspector of the chamber, to whom this inscription evidently no longer meant anything, added to the entry in the

---

[44] A. D. C. Simpson, 'Robert Hooke and practical optics', in *Robert Hooke, new studies*, ed. M. Hunter and S. Schaffer (Woodbridge, 1989), 33–61, esp. 37ff.

[45] *Ephemerides* (1651): HP 28/2/4A.

[46] 'Unsre Philosophi v. Artificis alhier thun sich sonsten einbilden, das ihre gläßer des Weisselii zu Augsburg (deren wir zwey alhier haben) weit ubertreffen sollen. Aber der augenschein wird solches innerhalb wenig wochen am besten ausweißen können. Meinestheils kan ich noch nicht glauben das sie so hoch v. weit darinnen kommen werden als unser treflicher Augustanus' (*OP Corr. Hev.*, AC 1, 2, fol. 215v (Hartlib to Hevelius, 20 March 1651)).

[47] Simpson, 'Robert Hooke', 37.

inventory: 'Engländisch'.[48] In this case-study, the influence of the Hartlib circle on the flow of technical innovation into England from continental Europe can be demonstrated to have been subtle and considerable.

[48] *Hauptstaatsarchiv Stuttgart*, Kunstkammerinventare A 20 a Büschel 23, 44. The instruments themselves are sadly no longer extant.

Improvement in Ireland

CHAPTER 15

The Hartlib circle and the cult and culture of improvement in Ireland

T. C. Barnard

From their first arrival in Ireland in the twelfth century, the English insisted that they were there to better the Irish and Ireland, and themselves only incidentally. Betterment would encompass intangible as well as tangible changes. This apologetic, hackneyed in its themes (especially its professed altruism), burgeoned after 1540 when England first sought to extend its authority and then to make the Irish conform to the changed English religion of Protestantism. These ambitions, fitfully pursued and repeatedly frustrated by Irish rebelliousness and resilience, reappeared with the conquest and settlement of Ireland after 1649. The wonderful opportunities afforded by Cromwellian Ireland to Hartlib and his friends, both for jobs and for stampeding its rulers and new or returning settlers into their programme, have been thoroughly described.[1] In revisiting this topic, I seek to add to the prehistory, context, sequels and limitations of these Irish exertions by setting them against the untidy realities of seventeenth-century Ireland.

Just as the Cromwellian land settlement, which transferred about 40 per cent of Ireland from its old Catholic to fresh Protestant owners, is best seen as a stage (important, certainly) in a process begun in the 1550s and not completed until 1703, so the Hartlibian projects which sprouted so prolifically in the freshly turned soil of the 1650s were rooted in a tradition of similar antiquity which would survive into the eighteenth century, if not beyond, thanks to the Dublin Philosophical, Royal Dublin and Physico-Historical Societies and the Royal Irish Academy, and to individual specula-

---

[1] T. C. Barnard, *Cromwellian Ireland* (Oxford, 1975), 213–48; T. C. Barnard, 'The Hartlib circle and the origins of the Dublin Philosophical Society', *Irish Historical Studies*, 19 (1974), 56–71; Webster, 57–67, 428–46.

tors, philanthropists and eccentrics.[2] Given these continuities, it may be helpful to suggest how the ingenious enterprises of the Interregnum differed from what had preceded and would follow them.

We should also ask how much the agrarian and commercial changes and the related increases in population, wealth, regional specialization, marketable and exported surpluses, fairs and markets owed either directly to the innovators or indirectly to the ideas produced by them. In this connection, the reputation of the handbook published in 1652, *Irelands naturall history*, as the first accurate and unsensational enquiry into Irish resources and potential, merits another look.

Charles Webster first postulated an origin for 'the Invisible College' among the closely knit families of Irish Protestants exiled in and around London in the mid-1640s.[3] The shock of their deracination and loss, endlessly elaborated in submissions and laments, closely matched the upheavals that had driven refugees, including Hartlib and Comenius, from the Protestant lands of central Europe into England. Throughout the 1640s, those Anglo-Irish who listened attentively to the plans of Hartlib and Dury were also actively fashioning an Irish Protestant national legend, comparable in intentions and power to Foxe's *Acts and monuments*, Crespin's *Livre des martyres* and Goulart's *Mémoires*. Concurrently, they lobbied to regain, and add to, their lost lands. From this milieu emerged what would, henceforth, be treated as the authorized history of what had lately happened in Ireland, namely Sir John Temple's *The Irish rebellion*, as well as an expedition, commanded by Lord Lisle, to recover southern Ireland.[4] From the same sources, though more circuitously, slithered *Irelands naturall history*. It was published, thanks to Hartlib, only when the island had been largely recon-

[2] Royal Irish Academy, Dublin, MS 24 E 28, 5, 7, 9, 15; H. F. Berry, *A history of the Royal Dublin Society* (London, 1915); A. de Valera, 'Antiquarianism and historical investigations in Ireland in the eighteenth century', (MA thesis, University College, Dublin, 1978), 51–93, 133–71; K. T. Hoppen, *The common scientist in the seventeenth century* (London, 1970); K. T. Hoppen, 'The papers of the Dublin Philosophical Society, 1683–1708', *Analecta Hibernica*, 30 (1982), 161–84.
[3] C. Webster, 'New light on the Invisible College', *Transactions of the Royal Historical Society*, 5th Series, 24 (1974), 19–42.
[4] T. C. Barnard, 'Crises of identity among Irish Protestants, 1641–85', *Past and Present*, 127 (1990), 49–58; T. C. Barnard, 'The Protestant interest 1641–1660', in *From independence to occupation: Ireland 1641–1660*, ed. J. Ohlmeyer (Cambridge, forthcoming); Barnard, 'The 23 October 1641 and Irish Protestant celebration', *English Historical Review*, 106 (1991), 889–920.

quered, and it was opportunistically prefaced with a dedication in which Dury groomed Ireland's new rulers as agents of its spiritual, moral and physical redemption. Often the book's value as a detailed brochure for would-be planters and investors is noticed more than its didactic purposes, akin to Temple's.[5] The account of Ireland purveyed by the Dutch brothers Boate has been reverentially praised as a major development in economic geography, which abandoned the chorographical tradition stemming from Camden. This methodical compilation, conceived within a Baconian frame, betrayed (it is suggested) the influence of recent Dutch descriptions of Brazil and of the economists Roberts and Malynes.[6] Yet the book depended dangerously on what Arnold Boate, a doctor in the state's service, remembered once he had sailed from Ireland in 1644 and on the information supplied to him and his inquisitive brother, Gerard, by the embittered Irish Protestant refugees who impatiently kicked their heels in London. Notable helpers were Sir William Parsons and his son, Richard, as well as the bishop of Dromore, Theophilus Buckworth, uprooted from his Ulster diocese, deprived of its emoluments and now moping in the fens.[7] Behind the acknowledged informants we can detect a larger network of assistants: a network that overlapped with, and may indeed have subsumed, the spectral Invisible College. Calculatedly, the Boates singled out individual settlers, such as the earl of Cork, Sir Charles Coote and Sir Henry Spottiswood, active in tapping the timber and minerals of Ireland. In this, the Boates elaborated a theme dear to the refugees: that the English were the 'introducers of all good things in Ireland' and that the native Irish, deficient alike in skill and industry, were unable to work stone or extract ores.[8] These *canards*, the stock-in-trade of baffled English encounters with Gaelic life, repeated uncritically the settlers' own estimates of what they had achieved and, by implication, of what they had lost. So the stories were published of how Lord Cork had made £100,000 from his ironworks and that Coote,

---

[5] An honourable exception is N. Canny, 'Identity formation in Ireland: the emergence of the Anglo-Irish', in *Colonial identity in the Atlantic world 1500–1800*, ed. N. P. Canny and A. Pagden (Princeton, 1987), 195.

[6] Barnard, *Cromwellian Ireland*, 234; F. V. Emery, 'Irish geography in the seventeenth century', *Irish Geography*, 3 (1958), 264–7; Webster, 428–31.

[7] PRO PROB 11/225, 36; Barnard, *Cromwellian Ireland*, 214.

[8] G. Boate, *Irelands Naturall history* (London, 1652), sig. [A7v], 59, 114, 123–4, 130, 144, 148, 159; J. Davies, *A discoverie of the true causes* (London, 1612), 168–82; J. Ware, *De Hibernia & antiquitatibus eius, disquisitiones* (London, 1654), 94–6.

employing 2,500 or 2,600 at his, enjoyed a return of 40 per cent on the (admittedly lavish) investment. Similarly, the spectacular rise in value of Coote's Mountrath lordship, through 'building, planting, hedging and the like' was reported.[9] More generally, the Boates, like Temple, depicted the rebellion as devastating a prospering Protestant settlement and attributed to 'those barbarians, the natural inhabitants of Ireland', a hatred of the English newcomers that excited actions 'quite to extinguish the memory of them, and of all the civility and good things by them introduced amongst the wild nation'.[10]

For all its grander aims of opening the cabinets of nature, *Irelands naturall history* reads, as was intended, as a manifesto for his principal patrons, the 'Old' Protestants settled in Ireland before 1641 and now, after their sufferings of the 1640s, in danger of being elbowed aside by the Cromwellian soldiers and English civilian investors. Published in the flush of triumph in 1652 and topically prefaced by Dury, the work, while giving the established their due, would also lure over more settlers. As a prospectus, however, the volume was defective and, in important details, already out of date. Thus, Boate's hubristic pride in the rarity of plague had tempted the epidemic which, after 1650, killed more than the preceding war had done, and so depopulated the country that the regenerative programmes of the Cromwellians and Hartlib group were severely impeded.[11] Some omissions are understandable since the published text was only a fragment: one of four possible books. The wish to complete it soon stimulated Hartlib to circulate a questionnaire through which the hitherto unfocused enquiries of his associates in Ireland – Child, Petty, Symner, Wood and Worsley – would be systematized.[12] This collaborative venture, so characteristic of Hartlib's dreams of collecting, collating and applying useful knowledge, began a long series, in which Molyneux in the 1680s, the Royal

[9] Boate, *Naturall history*, 97–8, 134–7; cf. Trinity College Dublin (henceforth TCD), MS 833, fol. 223.

[10] Boate, *Naturall history*, 72, 89; J. Temple, *The Irish rebellion*, 2 parts (London, 1646), I, sig. b[1], 14–16, 40–1, 83–5; II, 41.

[11] Symner's answers to Hartlib's interrogatories (HP 62/45); L. M. Cullen, 'Population trends in seventeenth-century Ireland', *Economic and Social Review*, 6 (1974–5), 149–65; *Economic writings of Sir William Petty*, ed. C. H. Hull, 2 vols. (Cambridge, 1899), II, 609; William Petty, *The political anatomy of Ireland* (London, 1691), 18–19; P. Slack, *The impact of the plague in Tudor and Stuart England* (Oxford, 1990), 66.

[12] T. C. Barnard, 'Miles Symner and the new learning in seventeenth-century Ireland', *Journal of the Royal Society of Antiquaries of Ireland*, 102 (1972), 129–42.

Dublin Society and the Physico-Historical Society in the first half of the eighteenth century, and even the Ordnance Survey in the early nineteenth, aimed to narrow the gap between Ireland's potential and actual wealth. Each ultimately ended in disappointment, although the later undertakings, rooted in a more populous and better-educated society, added more to the fertile silt first deposited in the 1650s.[13]

The *Naturall history*, owing to its silences and heavy emphases, entrenched notions that would have been better questioned. It assumed, conventionally enough, that energetic, collective enter-prises or the activity of the state could transform the material and spiritual conditions of Ireland, both through human exertions and by liberating hidden and divine forces. The Boates, beguiled by the boastful Irish Protestants, and with an eye for the dramatic and memorable, not only celebrated the achievements of the latter but lingered over the costly and unusual, such as glassworks, iron fur-naces and mines, the effects of which on the long-term development and permanent enrichment of Ireland were at best ambiguous.[14] Proudly as their begetters advertised these schemes as 'common-wealth work' – employing many hands, supplementing tenants' agricultural incomes, implanting arcane skills, inculcating a work ethic and clearing the fastnesses where the idle and rebellious Irish traditionally hid – their main allure was to turn natural assets into cash.[15]

Boate did not knowingly mislead his readers but the bald descrip-tions of the scale and profit of Coote's and Cork's ventures tempted

---

[13] J. H. Andrews, *A paper landscape: the Ordnance Survey in nineteenth-century Ireland* (Oxford, 1975); D. Dickson, 'A description of County Cork, c. 1741', *Journal, Cork Historical and Archaeological Society*, 76 (1971), 152; Hoppen, *Common scientist*, 21–2, 200–1; C. Smith, *The antient and present state of the county and city of Cork*, 2 vols. (2nd edn, Dublin, 1774), I, iii-xiii; C. Smith, *The ancient and present state of the county and city of Waterford* (Dublin, 1746), viii.

[14] S. J. Connolly, *Religion, law and power: the making of Protestant Ireland 1660–1760* (Oxford, 1992), 41–59; L. M. Cullen, *The emergence of modern Ireland* (London, 1981); L. M. Cullen, 'Incomes, social classes and economic growth in Ireland and Scotland, 1600–1900', in *Ireland and Scotland 1600–1850*, ed. T. M. Devine and D. Dickson (Edinburgh, 1983), 248–59; D. Dickson, *New foundations: Ireland 1660–1800* (Dublin, 1987), 96–127; R. G. Gillespie, *The transformation of the Irish economy 1550–1700* (Dublin, 1991).

[15] T. C. Barnard, 'An Anglo-Irish industrial enterprise: iron-making at Enniscorthy ... 1657–1692', *Proceedings, Royal Irish Academy*, 85 C, (1985), 399, n. 154; T. C. Barnard, 'Sir William Petty as Kerry ironmaster', *Proceedings, Royal Irish Academy*, 82 C, (1982), 1–32; T. C. Barnard, 'Sir William Petty, Irish landowner', in *History and imagination*, ed. H. Lloyd-Jones *et al.* (London, 1981), 201–17; T. O. Ranger, 'The career of Richard Boyle, first earl of Cork, in Ireland, 1588–1643' (D.Phil. thesis, University of Oxford, 1959), 127–71, 264–69.

others to draw unduly optimistic conclusions. Lord Cork, to be sure, made an estimated £95,000 from his ironworks between 1607 and 1643 – close to the £100,000 mentioned by Boate. His profit, however, totalled a less startling £25,000: small beer beside his annual rental of £18,000. Boate, disappointingly, said nothing of the incidental benefits which made Cork and others persevere in these troublesome ventures – the convenience of cash paid either in England or opportunely between rents on Lady Days; a supply of iron for domestic and defensive needs; the seasonal boosts to the earnings of tenants.[16] As regards the latter, Boate had waxed lyrical about the enormous colony of workers at Coote's ironworks. Since other large-scale enterprises employed no more than 400, even when ancillary helpers are counted, we may suspect Boate of repeating a traveller's (Irish Protestant) tale.[17] In the calmer years of the mid-1650s new, as well as some old, investors continued the delusive quest for hidden riches. If some reaped the less publicized benefits, their modest profits can never have approached the 40 per cent that Boate computed as Coote's return. But how much the revival of these rural industries owed to Boate's beguiling brochure and how much to the credulity and cupidity of Irish proprietors and projectors it is impossible to judge.[18]

Boate did not entirely neglect the staples for the sensations of the Irish economy, but the space accorded to the prestigious developments seriously unbalanced his account. Other omissions further reduced its utility. Boate's disdainful dismissal of the aboriginal Irish, 'in all manner of wildness' comparable with 'the most barbarous nations of the earth', uncontroversially aired the contemporary

---

[16] *The Lismore papers*, ed. A. B. Grosart, 1st series, v, (London, 1886), 205, 218–19; Ranger, 'Cork', 163–71, 386–95.

[17] Barnard, 'An Anglo-Irish industrial enterprise', 132–42 and n. 154. In 1642, the Irish Council, of which Sir William Parsons was a member, claimed that Coote had lost money on his ironworks: Historical Manuscripts Commission, Ormonde MSS, new series, II, 125. Losses reported by Coote's tenants at Mountrath after 1641 reveal industrial activity, with fustian works, iron founding and tan yards, but nothing on the scale suggested by Boate – TCD MS 815 fols 34v, 35, 38v, 39, 41, 55v, 90, 180, 240, 271.

[18] PRO of Northern Ireland (henceforth PRO NI), Belfast, D 2707/B3/2; Proposals for a joint stock company for Ireland, National Library of Ireland (henceforth NLI), MS 8646; Burlington to Capt. J. Hedges, 4 April 1691, same to Congreve, 27 June 1691, 21 July 1691, 8 October 1691, NLI, MS 13226; BL Add. MS 46962, fol. 128; articles of the society of miners of Dublin, Christ Church, Oxford, Evelyn MSS, box VIII; Charles Monck to J. Evelyn, 10 October 1694; same to same, 5 November 1694, Evelyn MSS, Evelyn period box; Barnard, 'An Anglo-Irish industrial enterprise', 132–42; Barnard, 'Petty as Kerry ironmaster', 23–31.

English opinion of Gaelic backwardness.[19] Yet in enthusing over the regimes of dunging and marling and the newcomers' skill in raising improved livestock, he accurately implied the predominance of animal husbandry in Irish agriculture. He did not, however, speculate on what these methods owed to the indigenous culture nor on how this taste for pastoralism might habituate the energetic immigrants to the endemic indolence of the Irish.[20] If Boate reflexively attributed improvements and successes to the recently arrived, he overlooked the extent to which primitive methods, although outlawed by the English state, nevertheless persisted, not so much through the obstinacy of the natives but because they suited local conditions. Any assimilation of newcomers to the customs of the country, regarded by the hostile as a prime cause of the war of the 1640s, was a theme that Boate, in common with his Protestant informants, preferred to ignore. Instead they stressed – and probably exaggerated – the diffusion by the Protestant planters of better methods.[21]

Remembering the ideological and political contexts in which he worked, it is unsurprising that Boate saw no good in the Gaelic world. More distorting was his failure to mention what successive generations of settlers from England – the Old English – had achieved between the twelfth and seventeenth centuries. The Old English, possessors still of much good land and considerable power, blocked an Irish Protestant supremacy. When the Old English hesitantly resorted to arms after 1641, they forfeited any residual credit to which their Englishness might have entitled them and joined the Gaelic Irish in the Protestants' lengthening demonolo-

[19] Boate, *Naturall history*, 7; J. O. Bartley, *Teague, Shenkin and Sawney* (Cork, 1954), 7–47; D. W. Hayton, 'From barbarian to burlesque: English images of the Irish', *Irish Economic and Social History*, 15 (1988), 5–13; A. Laurence, 'The cradle to the grave: English observations of Irish social customs in the seventeenth century', *The Seventeenth Century*, 3 (1988), 63–4; D. B. Quinn, *The Elizabethans and the Irish* (Ithaca, 1966).

[20] T. C. Barnard, 'Gardening, diet and "improvement" in later seventeenth-century Ireland', *Journal of Garden History*, 10 (1990), 71–85; Boate, *Naturall history*, 88–90, 92–3; D. Dickson, 'An economic history of the Cork region in the eighteenth century', 2 vols. (Ph.D. thesis, TCD, 1977), II, 316–418; R. G. Gillespie, 'Migration and opportunity: a comment', *Irish Economic and Social History*, 13 (1986), 90–5; V. Gookin, *The great case of transplantation in Ireland discussed* (London, 1655), 17; M. MacCarthy-Morrogh, *The Munster plantation* (Oxford, 1986), 223–43.

[21] J. Bell, 'The improvement of Irish farming techniques since 1850', in *Rural Ireland*, ed. P. O'Flanagan (Cork, 1987), 24–41; Connolly, *Religion, law and power*, 49–50; Gillespie, 'Migration and opportunity', 90–5; J. S. Kelly, 'Jonathan Swift and the Irish economy in the 1720s', *Eighteenth-century Ireland*, 6 (1991), 21–2; *The letters of Lord Chief Baron Willes to the earl of Warwick 1757–1762*, ed. J. S. Kelly (Aberystwyth, 1990), 92–3.

gy.[22] But whatever Irish Protestant publicists might now contend, the Old English, thanks to their education and estates, shared many of the assumptions and approaches of the newcomers and may well have excelled the latter as improvers. The little we know of Old English interest in agricultural and commercial innovation suggests a familiar blend of mercenary calculation, fashionable consumption and cultural hauteur towards their social and ethnic inferiors. Unwittingly the reports of Hartlib's Irish correspondents revealed what Boate had passed over: Catholic landowners as pioneers of the useful and elegant initiatives so admired by the Hartlibian virtuosi.[23] Even after 1660 when their estates rapidly contracted, those abreast of continental or English novelties still interested themselves, either as theorists or practitioners, in better husbandry and horticulture. Indeed, it was from this sophisticated and cosmopolitan world rather than from the pen of any uncouth Protestant squire that – about 1698 – emerged the first systematic treatise on how Ireland's agriculture and trade could be improved.[24]

Boate's reticence about the Old English as improvers hinted at the gestation of his tract among the impoverished and grim Irish Protestant exiles. His dependence on this group accentuated another imbalance in his work: its concentration on Leinster and Ulster. On his tours of duty, Arnold Boate had travelled chiefly in those provinces: in them also lay the estates of Parsons and Bishop Buckworth, his main sources. If, as has been argued, the stronger regional diversification of Irish agriculture occurred only late in the century (paradoxically when the country's economy was better integrated), then Boate's overwhelmingly Ulster and Leinster evidence need not have invalidated his messages.[25] But as early as the Interregnum

[22] Boate, *Naturall history*, 7–8; A. Clarke, 'Colonial identity in early seventeenth-century Ireland', in *Nationality and the pursuit of national independence: historical studies xi*, ed. T. W. Moody (Belfast, 1978), 57–71; A. Clarke, *The Old English in Ireland 1625–42* (London, 1966).

[23] Barnard, 'Gardening, diet and "improvement"', 71–4; W. J. Smyth, 'Property, patronage and population: reconstructing the human geography of mid-seventeenth-century county Tipperary', in *Tipperary: history and society*, ed. W. Nolan and T. McGrath (Dublin, 1985), 108–9, 118–21.

[24] Barnard, 'Gardening, diet and "improvement"', 81; 'The improvement of Ireland', ed. P. Kelly, *Analecta Hibernica*, 35 (1992), 47–53.

[25] Cullen, *Emergence of modern Ireland*; Dickson, *New foundations*, 96–127; R. G. Gillespie, 'Continuity and change: Ulster in the seventeenth century', in *Ulster: an illustrated history*, ed. C. Brady *et al.* (London, 1989), 104–32; R. G. Gillespie, 'Lords and commons in seventeenth-century Mayo', in *'A various country': essays in Mayo history*, ed. R. G. Gillespie and G. Moran (Westport, 1987), 44–66.

strong contrasts in ecology and climate, accentuated by varied patterns of settlement, immigration and trade, further strengthened in the early seventeenth century by the distinctive characteristics of the Munster and Ulster plantations, differentiated these provinces both from each other and from the regions less touched by fresh arrivals.[26] The *Naturall history* tells little of Munster, other than to marvel, perhaps with an unwonted note of asperity, at Lord Cork's activities.[27] It may be that Boate, in smoothing out any idea of significant local quirks, merely reflected the exiles' attachment to a loose notion of an English and Protestant Ireland rather than to specific locales. Only in the 1680s when more settlers had been longer established did they seem to identify, through their mansions, estates, kin and clients, closely with a region or county – an identification registered and perhaps hastened by the first investigations for county histories.[28] Nevertheless, it is odd that Munster featured so little in the *Naturall history* when the province was dominated by the tribe of Boyles, the very family which, among the Anglo-Irish, had most materially forwarded Hartlib's schemes.[29]

If, as is likely, the distortions in Boate's volume arose primarily because he relied on Parsons and his kind, then we can document more precisely what emphases may have been introduced. As one of Ireland's governors Parsons, a self-appointed expert on (albeit contemptuous of) the Irish and their ways, had had to quell the rising after 1641. Dissenting from the new viceroy, Ormonde, who negotiated with the insurgents, he was dismissed from the council and scuttled to England. There, in worsening penury, he took doles from Parliament, plotted revenge with other exiles and renewed his acquaintance with Boate. Parsons' attitudes, never friendly towards

26 N. Canny, 'The Irish background to Penn's experiment', in *The world of William Penn*, ed. R. S. and M. M. Dunn (Philadelphia, 1986), 139–56; W. H. Crawford, 'Landlord-tenant relations in Ulster, 1609–1820', *Irish Economic and Social History*, 2 (1975), 6–11; R. G. Gillespie, *Colonial Ulster* (Cork, 1985); R. G. Gillespie, 'The transformation of the borderlands, 1600–1700', in *The borderlands: essays in the history of the Ulster–Leinster border*, ed. R. G. Gillespie and H. O'Sullivan (Belfast, 1989), 75–92; MacCarthy-Morrogh, *Munster plantation*; P. S. Robinson, *The plantation of Ulster* (Dublin, 1984).

27 Boate, *Naturall history*, 122, 137.

28 Sir Richard Cox, 26 August 1703, NLI, MS 13247; T. C. Barnard, 'The political, material and mental culture of the Cork settlers', in *Cork: history and society*, ed. P. O'Flanagan and C. G. Buttimer (Dublin, 1993) 311–15; 'Two descriptions of County Waterford in the 1680s, ii. Sir Richard Cox's account', ed. J. Walton, *Decies*, 36 (1987), 26–31.

29 Barnard, 'The Hartlib circle', 70–1; M. Oster, 'The scholar and craftsman revisited: Robert Boyle as aristocrat and artisan', *Annals of Science*, 49 (1992), 255–76; Webster, 'New light', 19–42.

the Catholic Irish, hardened further as he raked over the wreckage of his fortune and hopes.[30] Such was the chaos in Ireland that he did not know whether a colleague in Dublin was alive or dead. (Similar uncertainty caused Boate to confess that he had not heard whether Spottiswood's 'pretty little village' on Lough Erne had survived.)[31] Settling his affairs before Ireland had been reconquered, Parsons bequeathed lands lost to the rebels in the hope that, within the next twenty-one years, 'there will be such a quietness in Ireland by the blessing of God' as would allow their peaceful occupation. He died in 1649 before he could re-enter and recreate the promised land which he had lovingly described to the Boates in London; but to the latter he had already transmitted something of his outlook and priorities.[32]

Meanwhile, a cadet of the ramifying Parsons clan had settled in the Irish midlands, where his efforts to introduce glassmaking in the 1620s were noticed approvingly by Boate. Indeed, this township of Parsonstown embodied much that the Hartlibians treasured. Protestants were attracted as tenants; the superior English modes of building, with stone chimneys, and English breeds of cattle, were introduced; industry and regular markets were sponsored; a school opened; morals were regulated.[33] Yet even before the rebellion, the idyll had been disturbed. Technical obstacles quickly closed the glass-house; Irish Catholics lived alongside the newcomers; the school was soon moved elsewhere. Later, godly discipline would be subverted by the minister.[34] After 1641, the owner of Parsonstown spent heavily, but in vain, to contain the Catholic *revanche*; but such was its force that he, like his uncle in Dublin, fled to England and there solicited Parliament for help. He, too, haunted by the memory of what had been lost, vowed to rebuild. Yet the iron had entered his soul: he forbade any of his children to marry 'with any of the Irish

---

[30] BL Egerton MS 80, fol. 20; Harleian MS 3292, fols. 26–31; Bodleian Library, Oxford (henceforth Bodl.), Rawlinson MS A. 258, fol. 37; *CSP Ireland 1647–1660*, 726, 728, 766, 767, 771, 775; Historical Manuscripts Commission, Ormonde MSS, new series, II, 272; VI, 64; H. F. Kearney, *Strafford in Ireland* (Manchester, 1959), 10, 39, 81–4, 174, 257.

[31] Boate, *Naturall history*, 73; TCD, MS 834, fols 73, 92; PRO PROB 11/215, 33; R. G. Gillespie, 'The trials of Bishop Spottiswood', *Clogher Record*, 12 (1987), 330.

[32] PRO PROB 11/215, 33.

[33] Boate, *Naturall history*, 162; T. L. Cooke, *The early history of the town of Birr, or Parsonstown* (Dublin, 1875), 35–51, 384–7.

[34] BL Add. MS 31,881, fols. 152–4; Cooke, *Birr*, 42, 47, 384.

papists' and counselled them to 'remember that horrid and bloody rebellion in Ireland'.[35]

Death cheated both Parsons from sharing in the Protestant Ireland for which each had lobbied so feverishly. Their heirs discovered that this new world, for all its similarities with pre-war Ireland, could disappoint. Sir William's eventual successor, his great-grandson, hitched himself to the Ormonde family – Parsons' old adversary – and, in 1681, was ennobled. By then, however, the inheritance was so entangled and depleted, in part through the lavish spending and loss of rents during the war, that Viscount Rosse could not live up to his new port and was reduced to borrowing from his wife and pawning his watch.[36] At Parsonstown itself after the Restoration, although the landlord procured a new market-house, the assizes, quarter–sessions and a garrison, the townspeople, 'seemingly still beggars', showed scant gratitude and once more rose against the Parsons in 1689. Moreover, for all the improvements and an increased rental, debts exiled Sir Laurence Parsons to England for most of the 1680s.[37]

Since Boate's aim was to attract, not to repel, he said little about the hazards of a landlord's life in Ireland other than to expatiate on Catholic malevolence. By demonstrating how the active, either singly or together, could amend Ireland, he not only flattered his patrons within the exiled community but repeated a popular axiom: that landlords, through their own example, prodding and spending, could animate an inert Ireland. The recent substitution of so many Protestants for the old Catholic owners further suggested the pivotal place of these newcomers in improving the island. This standard conceptual and physical framework was accepted and would be exploited by Hartlib, Boate and their disciples. In the event, only one of Hartlib's followers, Dr Robert Child, was patronized by a squire in Ireland, Colonel Arthur Hill in County Down (a connection of Sir William Parsons).[38] In time, it is true, Petty meta-

---

[35] Birr Castle, Co. Offaly, MS A/1/92; PRO PROB 11/231, 85; Bodl., Rawlinson MS A. 258, fols. 39, 44; *CSP Ireland 1647–60*, 735; Historical Manuscripts Commission, Ormonde MSS, new series, II, 289, 290.

[36] Birr Castle, MS A/1/144; Historical Manuscripts Commission, Ormonde MSS, new series, VI, 56–7, 73, 83, 86, 130–1; VII, 20.

[37] Birr Castle, MSS A/1/147–9; Cooke, *Birr*, 66–87, 391–5.

[38] Letters of Child, HP 15/5; PRO PROB 11/215, 33; W. A. Maguire, *The Downshire estates in Ireland 1801–1845* (Oxford, 1972), 2–5.

morphosed into a rich Irish landowner and would persist, quixoti-
cally, in using his remote holdings as a showcase for his smart
methods.[39] However, the other virtuosi, as public servants, looked to
their employer, the state, to promote their plans of renovation and
innovation. In the early 1650s, Child certainly testified to Colonel
Hill's dynamism as overseer and engineer of improvement in the
manner sketched by Boate. But Child also revealed how, during
Hill's frequent absences (an often inescapable aspect of landowners'
lives not discussed by Boate), the craze for building, fencing, ditch-
ing and draining bogs gripped farmers returning to, or newly
arrived in, a region already undergoing agricultural and social
change thanks to the plantation earlier in the century.[40] Indeed, an
expected function of a proprietor such as Hill, commanded in the
grants to those who undertook to settle Ulster and Munster, was to
attract tenants who would be paragons of civility, industry and
Protestantism. Boate, Child, Hartlib and Petty, in seeing the individual as the principal agent of change, subscribed to a view that
would outlast the eighteenth century. Thus, an inventive projector
of the 1720s, while conceding that the state could supply helpful
laws, trusted more to private industry, ingenious squires and prosperous farmers. Similarly, a grandee bustling around his Irish lands
in the 1730s congratulated himself: 'I inculcate the doctrine of
planting wherever I go, and I find all the tenants are coming into
it.'[41] Where Boate and other theorists failed most conspicuously was
in teaching how the whimsies of the active could be perpetuated and
diffused in a pervasive culture of improvement, for they wrote
nothing of the vital implement in improvement – the lease.

The regulation of tenurial relationships through the lease and
other legal contracts supposedly marked off the new anglicized
Ireland from the old, where economic and social relations were
organized according to military contingencies and hereditary obli-

---

[39] T. C. Barnard, 'Sir William Petty, his Irish estates and Irish population', *Irish Economic and Social History*, 6 (1979), 64–9; Barnard, 'Petty, Irish landowner', 201–17.

[40] Child to Hartlib, 13 November 1651 (HP 15/5/7–8), 26 [February] 1651/2 (HP 15/5/9), 11 March 1651/2 (HP 15/5/3–4), 23 June 1652 (HP 15/5/12–13), 8 April 1653 (HP 15/5/20–1), 7 July 1653 (HP 15/5/22–3); R. G. Gillespie, 'Landed society and the Interregnum in Ireland and Scotland', in *Economy and society in Scotland and Ireland 1500–1939*, ed. P. Roebuck and R. Mitchison (Edinburgh, 1988), 38–47; Gillespie, *Colonial Ulster*, 195–222; M. Perceval-Maxwell, *The Scottish migration to Ulster in the reign of James I* (London, 1973); Robinson, *The plantation of Ulster*, 172–94.

[41] BL Add. MS 46982, fols. 96, 98v, 99v; [F. Hutchinson], *A letter to a member of parliament, concerning the imploying and providing for the poor* (Dublin, 1723), 3.

gations.[42] Even the invitations issued by Dury to continental religious refugees (and a few magnates offered the same to desirable
immigrants in the 1660s) had to be translated into leases.[43] More
generally, leases, through their duration, rent, prohibitions and
requirements, could favour and prescribe. The prevalence of the
lease and the lessor's ability through it to command did not confer
absolute power on owners. Attractive tenants were often scarce,
especially after the wars of the 1640s and 1689–91. In times of
plenty, of course, preferential terms might be offered to solvent and
skilled Protestants. In bad times, however, arrears had to be for-
given; abatements allowed; bans, as on Catholics as tenants,
relaxed. Dues in kind, such as of butter or labour service, were
taken; and 'the custom of the country' was allowed to moderate
severity.[44] Furthermore, the owners' problems – shortage of capital
throughout much of the century, enforced or voluntary absence,
debts and other urgent financial demands – forced some to barter
away any close control over farms and tenancies by taking large cash
fines in return for granting long and secure leases.[45]

One known to the Hartlib circle who had not sacrificed personal
control was the head of the Boyle family, Lord Cork. In 1649, taking
his holdings in hand after the war, he granted leases of only one or
three years, so as to bring in a little money, to arrest any further
physical deterioration (in this spirit, his show-house in Tallow was
let to an illiterate tanner) and to keep his freedom to profit when the
situation improved.[46] By the 1660s Cork had returned to his policy

---

[42] Gillespie, *Transformation of the Irish economy*; Smyth, 'Property, patronage and population'.

[43] NLI, D. 4883; 8644/7; Nottingham University Library, Portland MSS, PW A 2324,
2326–7; Bodl., Carte MSS 36, fols. 497v–8, 521, 618; 68, fol. 617; 160, fol. 37v; *CSPIreland
1666–9*, 367; Barnard, *Cromwellian Ireland*, 57–8.

[44] Chatsworth House, Derbyshire, Lismore MSS, diary of second earl of Cork, 1 August 1666;
NLI, MSS 2322/219, 13226/1; Houghton Library, Harvard University, Orrery MSS, MS
218 22F; Bodl., Rawlinson MS A. 492, fol. 25v; Petworth House, Sussex, Orrery MSS,
general series, 29/9, letter of 26 February 1678/9; Sheffield City Library, Wentworth
Woodhouse muniments, WWM 14/17a; Dickson, 'Cork region', I, 145–92.

[45] PRO NI, D 2707/A1/1/11; W. H. Crawford, 'The significance of the landed estates in
Ulster, 1600–1820', *Irish Economic and Social History*, 17 (1990), 44–56; Crawford,
'Landlord–tenant relations', 5–21; T. P. Power, 'Land, politics and society in eighteenth-
century Tipperary', 2 vols. (Ph.D. thesis, TCD, 1987), I, 85–92; P. Roebuck, 'Landlord
indebtedness in Ulster in the seventeenth and eighteenth centuries', in *Irish population,
economy and society*, ed. J. M. Golstrom and L. A. Clarkson (Oxford, 1981), 135–54;
P. Roebuck, 'The making of an Ulster great estate: the Chichesters', *Proceedings, Royal Irish
Academy*, 79 C, (1979), 12–25; P. Roebuck, 'Rent movement, proprietorial incomes and
agricultural development, 1730–1830', in *Plantation to partition*, ed. P. Roebuck (Belfast,
1981), 82–101.

[46] NLI, MS 6143.

of granting tenancies of eighteen or twenty-one years or of three lives, stipulating detailed improvements and banning sub-letting other than to Protestants or 'British'.[47] However, except in the early 1680s when tenants vied for farms, conditions may not always have allowed Cork to insist strictly on the terms of the leases.[48] So in the pattern delineated by Boate and approved by the Hartlibians, much hinged on Cork's own performance. The second earl, like his father before him, cared for his purse and the wider Protestant interest.[49] By meticulous oversight he improved both. Rich, cosmopolitan and courtly, he introduced fashions in diet, recreation, building and consumption which gradually percolated through provincial Ireland.[50] Locally he reopened his father's ironworks while tenants in his towns developed a precarious textile industry.[51] Thanks to his wealth, his status and the deference of a powerful network of kinsmen, tenants and clients, he abetted, but did little to initiate, an improving culture. Books of husbandry and gardening were swapped and discussed; seeds, saplings, rare fruit and vegetables were exchanged; rams, stallions and bulls were lent; experiments continued into reclamation and mineral extraction; and the meritorious were subsidized and advanced. Cork's apanage, minutely overseen for much of the century, was frequently praised as the nonpareil in an English Ireland. But disregarding the problems when attention lapsed in the 1690s, even Cork, the exemplar of Protestant virtues, more often seemed a prisoner in (or passive profiteer from), rather than the architect of, a more populous, prosperous and commercialized region.[52]

It has been argued that attitudes towards land in seventeenth-

---

[47] Chatsworth, Londesborough MSS, box 1 (v), abstracts of leases; NLI, MS 6144.

[48] Farmar MSS, Dublin, letter book of William Hovell, 21 December 1683; Dickson, 'Cork region', 1, 183–7.

[49] Ranger, 'Cork', 127–71, 264–9; T. O. Ranger, 'Richard Boyle and the making of an Irish fortune, 1588–1643', *Irish Historical Studies*, 10 (1957), 257–97.

[50] Barnard, 'Cork settlers'; T. C. Barnard, 'Land and the limits of loyalty: the second earl of Cork and first earl of Burlington (1612–1698)', in *Lord Burlington: architecture, art and life*, ed. T. C. Barnard and J. Clark (London, 1994).

[51] Chatsworth, Lismore MS 28/41 and 44; Farmar MSS, Hovell letterbook, 4 January 1683/4, 24 June 1684, 8 May 1685, 9 October 1685, 27 November 1685; NLI, MS 2482, fol. 83; Dickson, 'Cork region', 11, 547–57; Walton, 'Two descriptions of County Waterford', 28.

[52] Barnard, 'Cork settlers'; Barnard, 'Gardening, diet and "improvement"'; Barnard, 'Land and the limits of loyalty'. For other direct evidence of agricultural experimentation and innovation: Chatsworth, Lismore MS 28/90; farming notebook of the Penrose-Fitzgerald estate at Corkbeg, 1652–75, Cork Archives Institute, U 257/1; BL Add. MS 46938, fol. 147.

century Ireland, different from those in England, contributed to and then in turn were further modified by the striking commercialization of agriculture.[53] A glut of cheap land throughout much of the century devalued land-owning, both in terms of its usual yield and status. Also, owners, uncertain how long they would hold estates, relentlessly realized their assets and then happily sold the land itself. Once the market for agricultural goods and pressure for tenancies grew, individual profit rather than social calculus governed economic life. Other changes, some physical, others intellectual, seemingly dissipated the benevolence of the 1650s. The state's intervention, although sought then, was condemned by the end of the century and, as Irish politics swung into a patriotic mode, English malice was contrasted with the benign potential in Irish institutions.[54] New problems engendered by rapid social and economic upheaval – of Protestant luxury and poverty – unimagined by Hartlib and Boate, called for placebos. Landlords, idealized by Boate, were later berated as vicious, self-indulgent and absent.[55] Secular and rational arguments such as those favoured by Petty when he tried to reduce all questions to 'number, weight and measure' gained ground.[56] But continuities, in problems and approach, checked these modernizing and secularizing tendencies. Accordingly, the critiques between the 1680s and 1740s routinely invoked moral as well as economic and political criteria and derived them from Scripture as much as from classical history or natural reason. Recurrent crises – Catholic warfare and vitality, famine, urban destitution and crime, shortages of skills – produced campaigns, notably in the 1690s and late 1720s, which united material and spiritual regeneration.[57]

---

[53] Gillespie, 'Landed society and the Interregnum', 43–4.
[54] J. T. Leersen, 'Anglo-Irish patriotism and its European context', *Eighteenth-century Ireland*, 3 (1988), 9–11; Kelly, 'Swift and the Irish economy', 7–36.
[55] Bowood House, Wiltshire, B/62; Petty, 'Reasons for the contempt and undervalue of Ireland'; R. Cox, 'Regnum Corcagiense: or a description of the kingdom of Cork', ed. R. Day, *Journal, Cork historical and archaeological society*, second series, 8 (1902), 70–1; R. Lawrence, *The interest of Ireland in its trade and wealth*, 2 vols. (Dublin, 1682), I, 84–9. See also A. P. W. Malcomson, 'Absenteeism in eighteenth-century Ireland', *Irish Economic and Social History*, I (1974), 15–35.
[56] Barnard, 'Petty, Irish landowner'; Barnard, 'Petty and Irish population': [R. Molesworth], *Some considerations for promoting the agriculture of Ireland* (Dublin, 1723); L. Sharp, 'Sir William Petty and some aspects of seventeenth-century natural philosophy' (D.Phil. thesis, University of Oxford, 1976).
[57] T. C. Barnard, 'Reforming Irish manners: the religious societies in Dublin during the 1690's', *Historical Journal*, 35 (1992), 805–38; Barnard, 'Irish Protestants and the Irish

Evidence of changes in ideas and structures needs then to be balanced with the weights of inertia and tradition and the pervasiveness of Christian and communal ideals. Even the poor return from lands, if it impelled some to strip and then sell them, could prompt others to diversify and experiment.[58] One activity, the reclaiming of bogs, for example, endlessly fascinated would-be improvers. Boate, as a Dutchman, revelled in describing how Irish bogs had already been drained and commended the work as conducing 'to the general good of the whole land'. Simultaneously, Child reported from Ulster the renewed zest for this task.[59] Thereafter the Protestant clergy, increasingly conspicuous as advocates and agents of material improvement, applied their funds, their talents in mathematics and 'hydrogasticks' and their quills to this subject.[60] As late as 1730, when a lay pamphleteer enthused over the recent reclamation of a bog outside Cork city, he connected its survival with its ownership until 1706 by the last Catholic grandee of the region. The bog, notorious in 1656 as a harbour for wolves and tories, was 'so drained and civilized that there is now neither shelter for one or the other'. In terms that recalled the seventeenth-century celebrants of 'commonwealth work', he concluded, 'thus, in one age, the great fastnesses of Ireland might be destroyed and even the most barbarous parts, yet not amenable to the law and civil power, rendered habitable'.[61]

Later exponents of regeneration, from the erratic moral commissar, Bulkeley, through the imperious Molesworth and practical Boyd to the public-spirited Edgeworth, clung to the hope of blending personal with communal, material with moral betterment.[62] As

---

language, 1675–1725', *Journal of Ecclesiastical History*, 44 (1993) 243–72; Kelly, 'Swift and the Irish economy'.

[58] T. C. Barnard, 'Fishing in seventeenth-century Kerry: the experience of Sir William Petty', *Journal, Kerry Archaeological Society*, 14 (1981), 14–25. Cf. J. Thirsk, *Economic policies and projects: the development of a consumer society in early modern England* (Oxford, 1978).

[59] Child to Hartlib, 23 June 1652 (HP 15/5/12–13); Boate, *Naturall history*, 114–17, 167–9.

[60] Chatsworth, Lismore MS 32/82; Berry, *History of the Royal Dublin Society*, 20; J. Browne, *The benefits which arise to a trading people from navigable rivers* (Dublin, 1729), v–vi; Hoppen, *Common scientist*, 195, 263; Kelly, 'Swift and the Irish economy', 14, 30.

[61] [G. Rye], *Considerations on agriculture* (Dublin, 1730), 74, 80–5.

[62] Barnard, 'Reforming Irish manners', 818, 833; C. Dallat, 'Ballycastle's eighteenth-century industries', *The Glynns*, 3 (1975), 7–13; T. Dunne, '"A gentleman's estate should be a moral school": Edgeworthstown in fact and fiction', in *Longford: essays in county history*, ed. R. Gillespie and G. Moran (Dublin, 1991), 95–117; Historical Manuscripts Commission, *Various collections*, VIII, 221–76.

more clergy, themselves inheritors of estates or needing to farm to live, took up the cause, they guaranteed that the utopian moderated the concrete. When, in early eighteenth-century Wicklow, a usually absent owner spectacularly converted his assets into cash, not only did he replant but he inaugurated a vigorous campaign of improvement, aptly encapsulated in his gifts of seeds and catechisms. He rejoiced to be supported by a substantial clerical tenant, 'reckoned as great an improver as any in the county'. This parson, indeed, loved his newly planted coppices as much as his Bible.[63] Such practical and philosophical enthusiasms combined in the several bishops who continued and updated the Hartlibian programme. Thus, Francis Hutchinson, bishop of Down and Connor from 1720, pleaded for a 'good' natural history of Ireland, which would collect and disseminate useful knowledge. But this, he believed, would only have its proper impact when Ireland had been converted to Protestantism. A vision of the entire community inspired him: the wilfully idle would be punished, the weak relieved, the ignorant taught, luxury and excess curbed, and work created, specifically so that the impoverished of his Ulster diocese could be stopped 'from running to America to our disgrace and loss of people'. He proclaimed how God, in creating the land and the seas, had bestowed on man 'a gift that was well worth his acceptance' and he himself set about exploiting them with gusto. Only in his designs for quickening sluggish trade did Hutchinson, also an analyst of witchcraft, move outside a scheme recognizable to the Hartlib group by deploying an irony that, alone in the circle, Petty might have relished: 'Trade is like witchcraft and works wonders; and I should be glad to see our own people a little fonder of it.'[64]

[63] Sheffield City Library, WWM 14/14; WWMA 759, 383; 764, 12–17, 23–5; 766, 7; 769, 17.
[64] PRO NI, DIO 1/22/2, 23 November 1730, 21 January 1733/4; Barnard, 'Irish Protestants and the Irish language', 260; Berry, *History of the Royal Dublin Society*, 31; Hutchinson, *Imploying and providing for the poor*, esp. 1; F. Hutchinson, *A second letter to a member of Parliament recommending the improvement of the Irish fishery* (Dublin, 1729), 3–6, 21; F. Hutchinson, *The state of the case of Loughneagh* (Dublin, 1738), 3, 5, 13–14.

CHAPTER 16

Natural history and historical nature: the project for a natural history of Ireland

Patricia Coughlan

This chapter is about the project for a natural history of Ireland which was undertaken from 1645 onwards by the associates of Hartlib who were connected with Ireland in various capacities, principally in the context of the 1640s wars, the Cromwellian military expeditions and the parliamentary and Protectorate government. Charles Webster and T. C. Barnard have already given a full account both of the scientific character of the natural history enterprise and of the mutual social relations of its participants. I am here concerned more specifically with the problem of the paradoxical relation between the ideal of the advancement of learning and the practice of English policies and actions in Ireland.[1] Broadly, the argument is as follows: the project for a natural history contained a genuine moment of enlightenment and constituted real progress in the discussion of Ireland. However, the prejudices and, to some extent, the self-interest of the group that enacted it vitiated the results. Degrees of prejudice and greed varied among the participants, as also among the body of English settlers in Ireland at large. I shall also argue that the texts the project produced were flawed in direct proportion to the level of intolerance and incomprehension of their authors. The problem thus has a broader context in the dilemma between the Baconian spirit of empirical enquiry on the one hand and the equally Baconian equation of knowledge with power on the other. Later social theorists rightly perceive the latter

---

[1] See Webster, 62–7 and 428–35; T. C. Barnard, *Cromwellian Ireland* (Oxford, 1975); T. C. Barnard, 'Miles Symner and the new learning in seventeenth-century Ireland', *Journal of the Royal Society of Antiquaries of Ireland*, 102 (1972), 129–42; and T. C. Barnard, 'Gardening, diet and "improvement" in later seventeenth-century Ireland', *Journal of Garden History*, 10 (1990), 71–85. See also his 'The political, material and mental culture of the Cork settlers, c.1650–1700', in *Cork: history and society*, ed. P. O'Flanagan (Dublin, 1993) 309–367, which affords much insight into the physical details of plantation and settlement, especially into their development in later decades.

as the domination of nature by science and technology and the suppression and repression of Otherness both within and without the self. A related paradox is the relation between two impulses which seemed to work in opposite directions: the impulse accurately to register the facts of material reality, and the utopian desire to reform the world, to change – to 'improve' – those facts into a new dispensation. This notion of a new dispensation was, of course, heavily laced in the Hartlib circle with Protestant, often even millenarian, hopes.

The natural history of Ireland enterprise was begun by two Dutch physicians, the brothers Arnold and Gerard Boate. Arnold, a Leiden-educated physician like his brother, had a long acquaintance with Ireland, having arrived there before the civil wars, in 1636. He had treated both Archbishop Ussher and Thomas Wentworth, Charles I's lord deputy, before becoming physician-general to the army in Leinster. Arnold was a prominent Hebraist and international controversialist who published several works on the question of the integrity of the text of the Bible. He was intellectually close to Ussher, who helped his medical career in Ireland, and to whom he dedicated some of his writings. Arnold, however, left Ireland in 1644 and went to live in Paris, keeping in touch with Ussher by correspondence. His younger brother Gerard's connection with the country was less extensive. Though he came to Ireland in 1649, serving as a doctor at the military hospital in Dublin before dying there in 1650, he had actually written *Irelands naturall history* in 1645 before he had any first-hand knowledge of the place. Gerard Boate and his wife, Katherine, are, however, listed among the adventurers who financed the English suppression of the 1641 rebellion, and they were granted land in County Tipperary.[2] Gerard's information about Ireland came in large part from his brother, who also, in effect, edited his text. Arnold's prefatory matter says that he communicated the material about Ireland to Gerard in the summer of 1644. They had already collaborated on an earlier project: convinced Protestant reformers in the spirit of Hartlib himself, they had in 1641 – the year of the rebellion – published in Dublin a joint

---

[2] *DNB*; and see Carl Bottigheimer, *English money and Irish land* (Oxford, 1971), 199. Gerard's descendants put down permanent roots in Ireland, playing a distinguished part in the history of Irish medicine up to the late nineteenth and twentieth centuries (personal communication by their descendant, Mr Bob Russell, who has conducted extensive genealogical research on the history of the Boates in Ireland).

work, *Philosophia naturalis reformata*, attacking the Aristotelian foundations of scholastic philosophy. When Samuel Beckett's *Whoroscope*, his early poem about Descartes, referred to 'the brothers Boot [*sic*]' who 'refuted Aristotle in Dublin', it was, albeit ironically, pointing out a moment of that demystification which is common to Cartesian rationalism and Baconian empiricism.[3]

The *Naturall history* reveals other sources besides the personal information of Arnold Boate. Gerard Boate was in close contact, while in London, with Sir William Parsons and his family from County Offaly, who had left or been driven from their large Irish estates on account of the rebellion. Parsons had been surveyor-general of Ireland since 1602 and, in 1640, he was appointed as one of the lords justices of Ireland. He was an intensely acquisitive planter who had enriched himself greatly in Irish land during most of the four decades preceding 1641.[4] Described by Hartlib as 'a very rational gentleman', he nevertheless appears as a suspicious and fanatical individual, who actively sought to provoke the two ethnically diverse Catholic factions in Ireland into merging in more and more open revolt, with the hoped-for result of having Catholic proprietors removed altogether.[5] Parsons' ambitions, and especially his extreme bitterness towards the Irish and his perception of them as uncivilized and barbarous, are conspicuously evident in Gerard Boate's text. In this it is strongly reminiscent of the bitter and anxious hostility to the Irish displayed in Spenser's *View of the present state of Ireland*, written some fifty years previously. It also, as I shall argue, raises the similar paradox, a recurrent one in Anglo-Irish history, of the poor fit between reformist, advanced Protestant thinking in the English context, and its implications on the ground in Ireland where this tended to be perverted by self-serving acquisitiveness, oppressive intolerance and revulsion at ethnic Otherness.[6]

[3] Samuel Beckett, *Poems in English* (London, 1961), 9–13.

[4] *DNB*; and see Hugh Kearney, *Strafford in Ireland* (Manchester, 1959), 174. Parsons was involved in the plantations of Ulster, Wexford, Longford, Ely O-Carroll, Leitrim and Wicklow.

[5] Hartlib's comment is in his *Ephemerides* (1648), quoted in Webster, 66, n. 113, and concerns his passing medical information to Lady Ranelagh; the paradox is emblematic. For Parsons' Irish attitudes, see *DNB*; for a blisteringly negative, contemporary Catholic view of him, see Henry Burkhead, *Cola's furie: or, Lirenda's miserie* (Kilkenny, 1645), discussed in P. Coughlan, '"Enter Revenge": Henry Burkhead and Cola's furie', *Theatre Research International*, 15 (1989), 1–14.

[6] See Ciaran Brady, 'Spenser's Irish crisis: humanism and experience in the 1590s', *Past and Present*, 111 (1986), 16–49; Patricia Coughlan, '"Some secret scourge which shall by her come unto England"', and Anne Fogarty, 'The colonization of language', in *Spenser and*

In London, the Parsons were part of the circle of Protestant Irish, many of them 1641 exiles, which revolved around the Boyles and especially Katherine, Lady Ranelagh, daughter of the earl of Cork. She was one of the leading intellectuals of the day and an active correspondent both of Milton and of Hartlib. This group was, of course, enthusiastically Protestant in religion and was simultaneously devoted to empirical scientific enquiry and experiment. The work of the great Restoration scientist, Katherine Boyle's younger brother, Robert Boyle, was nurtured in this environment.[7] In terms of Irish history and the struggles of these decades for land and power in Ireland, this group also represented a continuation of the control, cleverness and canny self-aggrandizing policies that had distinguished the career of the first earl of Cork earlier in the century.[8]

The natural history project was left incomplete by the Boates. The first part, published in 1652 by Hartlib, along with a preface by Arnold Boate, was intended to cover only the natural features of the country, together with some sections on their exploitation. The latter included such matters as ironworks, lead and silver mines, and comments on the drainage and improvements so far carried out on the land, as well as the healthfulness of the Irish climate and conditions. In the later parts it was proposed to describe Irish flora and fauna and the inhabitants, using at all times the Baconian empirical approach and the focus on economic potential which, in intention at least, sharply distinguished the work from the chorographic, anecdotal geographies that had preceded it.[9] We might put this another way by saying that the focus of the whole project was a synchronic one; it is a peculiarity of 'natural history' that, despite the implications of the term 'history', it was, of course, conceived as a text in the present tense. The interest of its compilers was usually not in how the situation came about, but in what it actually was

Ireland, ed. Patricia Coughlan (Cork, 1989), 46–74, 75–108; Patricia Coughlan, '"Cheap and Common Animals": the English anatomy of Ireland in the seventeenth century', in *Literature and the English Civil War*, ed. T. Healy and J. Sawday (Cambridge, 1990), 205–23.

[7] See Webster, 62–3, for a fuller account; J. R. Jacob, *Robert Boyle and the English revolution* (New York, 1977); and Kathleen Lynch, *Roger Boyle, first earl of Orrery* (Knoxville, 1965).

[8] See Nicholas Canny, *The upstart earl: a study of the social and mental world of Richard Boyle, first earl of Cork, 1566–1643* (Cambridge, 1982); Canny disputes what he sees as the exclusive role attributed by Barnard and Jacob to the influence of the Hartlib circle in exciting the intellectual interests and forming the scientific outlook of Robert and Katherine Boyle and other Irish Protestants in exile in the decades from 1641 to the Restoration (143–9).

[9] See Webster, 428–9.

and, in the case of these Baconians, in the ways it might be worked upon and improved, changed by will and knowledge. Bacon's ideal of the transformation by science of the material conditions of life was being applied by this group to Ireland: his vision of the 'Enlarging of the bounds of Humane Empire, to the Effecting of all Things possible' by 'the Knowledge of Causes and Secrett Motions of Things' was to be realized in the new dispensation in Ireland.[10] This programme, as Webster has amply shown, already contained within it the idea of man's dominion over nature as the desirable end and aim of his work upon the earth. Within the context of Protestant empiricism and individualism and with the resulting conviction that the advancement of learning in practice was the great task and duty of man, the scientist intellectuals of Hartlib's circle perceived Ireland as literally a God-given opportunity for scientific enquiry, experiment and the practical execution of their various schemes. They presented the horrors of the 1641 rebellion and massacres as having been sent by heaven to the Protestants as part of the divine plan, and came to understand them as a combined ordeal and signal mark of grace, a unique opportunity for radical reform. This sense of a divinely ordained moment of new opportunity is vividly expressed in the 'Epistle Dedicatorie' to Fleetwood which prefaced *Irelands naturall history*, signed by Hartlib but written by John Dury in characteristically heated millenarian language.[11]

Newness is, indeed, much stressed in their writings and those of other English arrivals in Ireland in the Cromwellian period. Images of Ireland as a clean sheet waiting to be written on, a *tabula rasa* on which could now be inscribed the lines of a reformed social order, recur in the writings of the 1650s, as T. C. Barnard has pointed out.[12] The image of English activity in Ireland as an anatomical

[10] Bacon, *Works*, III, 156; quoted in Webster, 342.
[11] The 'great and mighty Changes' in the contemporary political order are linked to the 'advancement of the ways of Learning' whereby the 'Intellectual Cabinets of Nature are opened'; the resulting gains in knowledge will in turn make possible the expansion of plantation in Ireland 'not only by the Adventurers, but happily by the calling in of exiled Bohemian and other Protestants also, and ... of some well affected out of the Low Countries'; the whole is couched in the rhetoric of imminent messianic expectation of God's breaking 'the yokes of Vanity' (*Naturall history*, sigs. A4–6).
[12] See Barnard, *Cromwellian Ireland*, 14, 268; also Coughlan, '"Cheap and Common Animals"', 214–15, for a discussion of the role of such metaphors in the development of English attitudes to and activities in Ireland, especially of Petty's Down Survey. Nicholas Canny has, however, protested at the notion that such metaphors, conveying the sense of a utopian new beginning in, as Bacon puts it, 'a pure soil', occur only in the Cromwellian or revolutionary period, citing earlier, Tudor examples; see *The upstart earl*, 145.

experiment is also evident, especially in the writings of William Petty, who had been an anatomist; one may point out, as indeed Petty himself does, that such experiments required a corpse as their material on which to work.[13] Discussing Foucault's *Birth of the clinic*, which scrutinizes some of the founding assumptions of the institutions of medicine, Jurgen Habermas has noted that 'Foucault conceives of the gaze of the anatomist, trained on the human corpse, as the concrete a priori of the sciences of man'.[14] More generally, we may perhaps understand the perspective of the *Naturall history* as what Habermas calls 'a gaze that objectifies and examines ... other subjects only accessible as the objects of nonparticipant observation'.[15] This perspective reveals a paradox at the heart of the enterprise. There *are* 'other subjects' being addressed by the Boates: there were, for example, the settlers and their prospective successors, who would, it was hoped, be enticed to Ireland by the promise of righteous economic opportunity. The Irish, however, are objectified, along with their landscape, in the polemic of their representation as savage and uncivil. Foucault's memorable assertion of an 'internal kinship between humanism and terror' and his notion of a consequently 'ambiguous liberation' in scientific knowledge seem applicable to this paradox of the scientifically progressive, ideologically questionable enterprises of these circles in relation to Ireland.[16] The idea of the anatomist's gaze as the indispensable founding moment of humanist science seems the appropriate one when the settlers' and Hartlibians' position is adopted; the sense of that gaze as objectifying and therefore destructive comes into play when one considers the matter from the point of view of the defeated Catholic proprietors of the 1640s and 1650s. T. C. Barnard puts it with a more brutal simplicity when he refers to the settlers' 'sinking deeper into the mire of self-exculpation' in which 'they fabricated myths about the aboriginals'.[17]

History, then, is the history only of evil doings; the future is conceived precisely as a break with it. Here the structure of the millenarian, utopian aspirations shows through, even perhaps to counter or distort the thorough empiricism of these investigations.

[13] See Coughlan, '"Cheap and Common Animals"', 214–15.
[14] Jurgen Habermas, *The philosophical discourse of modernity*, trans. Frederick Lawrence (Cambridge, 1990), 245.
[15] *Ibid.*   [16] Paraphrased in *Ibid.*, 246.
[17] Barnard, 'Gardening, diet and "improvement"', 72.

This raises, as I have suggested, a more general philosophical problem about Baconian thought. In the context of the application of Baconian work to Ireland, this question has two facets. The first is the possibly, though perhaps not necessarily, problematic conjunction of self-interest with intellectual enquiry. The former always possessed the potential to distort the latter, although there might be doubt as to whether a truly value-free scientific practice might be held to exist. The second facet, more evident and demonstrable, is the obliteration – physical and/or virtual and imaginative (in the form of a failure to notice them) – of existing arrangements, inhabitants, interests and a whole history embodied in actual social forms.[18] Thus, with the possible exception of Arnold Boate, the contacts of the Hartlibian investigators, arriving as most of them did either in the very late 1640s or the 1650s, during a period of war and large-scale social displacement and expropriation, were with a fairly homogeneous social group consisting entirely of the New English. These were the planters who had shown what the Irish Settlement Acts memorably called 'constant good affection' to the parliamentary and Protectorate regimes, and of other new arrivals like themselves who had functions and offices in those regimes.

What is the atmosphere of the published volume of *Irelands naturall history*? Barnard has called it 'a sober and systematically arranged account which introduced new standards of accuracy', but one may dissent from some of the terms of this praise. Systematic the book may be, but sober it is not, at least not where value-judgements about the respective merits and defects of the Irish and English are concerned.[19] Like earlier writers on Ireland for English audiences, with a view to attracting settlers, Boate does, of course, find some positive things to say. There are passages that emphasize the potential profit to be gained from the fertility and plenty of Irish land and natural resources: the many fine harbours, the 'comfort' of some towns and the existing volume of their 'trafick'. Here, the actual prosperity, certainly in the pre-war period, of areas such as wealthy Munster, shows through even in the Boates' rather sour

[18] This partly wilful, partly unconscious ignorance is especially striking in the case of the culture of the Old English, with their sophisticated European-trained Counter-Reformation clergy and their highly developed legal and political traditions. See Nicholas Canny, *The formation of the Old English elite in Ireland* (Dublin, 1974).

[19] Barnard, 'Symner', 133.

view – a prosperity and degree of infrastructural development clearly revealed in the recent research of revisionist Irish historians.[20] But the informative descriptions of physical features and material conditions are everywhere shot through with vituperative condemnations of Irish behaviour, in which the dominant themes are the rank superstition of the Irish and their lack of capacity to improve the wretched conditions of their lives. The immemorial superstitious credulity of Irish Catholics is exemplified in the devotional recourse to holy wells and to St Patrick's Purgatory. Boate scornfully dismisses the tradition of curative properties in holy wells: 'But experience doth show, that those vertues are not found in the Springs themselves, but onely in the vain imagination of the superstitious people.'[21] The text approvingly recounts the demystificatory investigation of these cults by the earl of Cork and others 'in the last years of King Iames'.[22] Altogether, the book leaves a striking impression of distaste for, and incomprehension of, the culture being described. This rhetoric of alleged uncleanness and disorder – the Protestant horror of Catholicism, the civil, urban aversion to rural, pastoral culture, the closed, clean bourgeois subject's antipathy to his shifting, unfixed, Other – is familiar from the writings of several earlier English settlers and visitors to Ireland.[23] I shall briefly cite two examples. Discussing the Irish bogs, the chapter-heading baldly says: 'Retchlessness of the Irish, cause of most of the Bogs' – that is, the bogs are there because the Irish have not drained them:

So that it may easily be comprehended, that whoso could drain the water, and for the future prevent the gathering thereof, might reduce most of the Bogs in Ireland to firm land, and preserve them in that condition. But this hath never been known to the Irish, or if it was, they never went about it, but to the contrarie let daily more & more of their good land grow boggy

[20] See especially M. McCarthy-Morrogh, 'The English presence in early seventeenth-century Munster', in *Natives and newcomers*, ed. Ciaran Brady and Raymond Gillespie (Dublin, 1986), 171–90; Liam Irwin, 'Politics, religion and economy: Cork in the seventeenth century', *Journal of the Cork Historical and Archaeological Society*, 85 (1980), 7–25; and Barnard, 'Gardening, diet and "improvement"'. See also the useful summary accounts of Irish economic geography and the material effects of the plantations in *The Irish landscape*, ed. Frank Mitchell (London, 1976), 192–203, and *The shaping of Ireland*, ed. W. Nolan (Cork, 1986), 84–103.

[21] Gerard Boate, *Irelands naturall history* (London, 1652), 72. [22] *Ibid.*, 74.

[23] See Coughlan, '"Some secret scourge"', and references therein to the large literature, now including theoretical discussions, on this topic; D. B. Quinn's *The Elizabethans and the Irish* (Ithaca, 1966) provides a very full descriptive account of the content of the usual stereotype. For a specific discussion of how the Boates reiterate these negative constructions of Irishness, see Coughlan, '"Cheap and Common Animals"', 212–13.

through their carelesness, *whereby also most of the Bogs at first were caused* *[emphasis added]*.[24]

As an empirical–scientific perspective, this seems a little unsatis-factory, not least because it is contradicted within the Boates' own text by the opinions hazarded elsewhere as to the bogs' geological and climatic origins.[25] The governing tone of the whole volume is irritation, sometimes amounting to rage, at the lack of modern skills and improving will and effort on the part of the Irish. The incom-prehension shown by the Protestant Dutch observers of a predomin-antly pastoral and recently even seasonal–nomadic culture is not, perhaps, surprising; but nowhere is this perceived Irish inertia connected to the effects of expanding plantation and imposed English settlement. It is difficult not to suspect that what Joseph Conrad, in another context, called 'material interests' did work to narrow gravely these empiricists' perspective.[26] The respective national roles are assigned: thus the section on 'Leprosie' alleges that its prevalence in Ireland was caused by the filthy Irish habit of eating salmon out of season, when they were diseased and spotty, whereas the English have now regulated this practice with laws, 'hindering those barbarians agaynst their will to feed on that poyso-nous meat'. The heralded result was that the disease had been 'almost quite abolished'.[27] The settlers' writings, of course, con-stantly approve of what we might call an 'interventionist' attitude to nature: they praise the gardens, orchards and the few planned parks and new towns of the Elizabethan–Jacobean colonization in Ireland, and nominate the native social arrangements as the anti-thesis of civility.

After the deaths of both the Boates, Gerard in 1650 and Arnold in 1653, Hartlib actively sought ways of continuing the Irish natural history enterprise. In a characteristically collective spirit, he had a set of 'Alphabetical Interrogatories' printed as an appendix to the

---

[24] Boate, *Naturall history*, 113.

[25] As, for example, later in this very passage: 'Whereunto many times also cometh the cause of the Grassi-bogs, to wit the store of Springs within the very ground; and all this in places, where or through the situation of them, and by reason of their even plainness and hollowness, or through some other impediment, the water hath no free passage away, but remaineth within them, and so by degrees turneth them into Bogs' (*ibid.*).

[26] See his novel *Nostromo*, which anatomizes the effects of the vigorously expanding, effectively colonizing capitalism of North Americans on South America in the later nineteenth century.

[27] Boate, *Naturall history*, 184.

1652 edition of his work *The legacy of husbandry* and sent them to Ireland for people to answer if they would.[28] This method of conducting the enquiry is of great interest in itself. The notion of an alphabetical arrangement of knowledge prefigures Enlightenment approaches to the assembly and classification of knowledge. Taken together with the appeal for collective participation in that ordering, also, of course, profoundly characteristic of Hartlibian practice, it manifests an ideological shift towards the notion of a shared and public universe of scientific discourse. Like other intellectual developments during the English Revolution, this might even be understood as evidence of the instatement, however short lived, of something like a proto-public sphere in Habermas' sense.[29] The idea of a tabulation of information is a further step towards executing the impulse to order the natural and social phenomena of the universe according to rational principles, to control and organize one's apprehension of, and manner of living in, the natural world. Foucault sees this as 'the nonreflexive form of knowledge proper to the Classical age', in which 'internal and external nature are classified, analyzed, and combined in the same manner – words of language in the universal grammar, wealth and needs in political economy, no differently than species of plants and animals in the Linnaean system'.[30] Foucault's aim is to point out the transparency of classical language, the assumption in such tabular, classificatory discourses that words represent things. This approach was vividly exemplified in the thought of Petty, with his project for 'a Political Arithmetick and a Geometricall Justice'.[31]

Hartlib set out to find specific successors to the Boates, successively encouraging Robert Child and Robert Wood to undertake the task. But Child's work was abortive: he found himself too limited geographically to be able to gather sufficient data, and then he too

---

[28] See Barnard, 'Symner', 134–5, and Webster, 431–3, for fuller accounts.

[29] See Thomas McCarthy, *The critical theory of Jurgen Habermas* (Cambridge, MA and London, 1978), 12, 381–2. This is suggested to me by David Norbrook's discussion of Milton's *Areopagitica* (London University conference on new historicism, July 1991); see also Francis Barker's different but illuminating application of Foucaultian perspectives to seventeenth-century discourse in *The tremulous private body: essays on subjection* (London and New York, 1984) and '"In the Wars of Truth": violence, true knowledge and power in Milton and Hobbes', in *Literature and the English Civil War*, ed. Healy and Sawday, 91–109.

[30] See Michel Foucault, *The order of things* (1970; London, 1974), chap. 5, 'Classifying', 125–65. The summary account from which I quote is in Habermas' highly critical response to Foucault's argument; Habermas wishes, *contra* Foucault, to preserve the category of a transcendental subject of history (*Modernity*, 238–65).

[31] See *Economic writings of Sir William Petty*, ed. T. H. Hull, 2 vols. (London, 1898), I, 240.

died, in 1654.[32] Petty, Benjamin Worsley and Robert Boyle were all also asked in turn to contribute observations as appropriate. But Boyle returned to England and, in 1655 and 1656, Petty and Worsley were both too engaged with the more pressing business of the Down Survey and its attendant labours to devote themselves to the project. The mathematician and decimal currency advocate, Robert Wood, who in 1656 joined Henry Cromwell's household in Ireland, proved a better prospect. He did contribute to the enterprise, sending back a sequence of replies to the Interrogatories.[33]

Wood's answers go only from 'a' to 'b', but are part of a long correspondence with Hartlib from Ireland between 1656 and 1661 which is, in itself, of considerable interest, though there is not scope to deal with it here.[34] Wood, like Symner, shows a somewhat more open mind about actual Irish conditions and characteristics than Boate. Thus he argues in August 1657 that an 'effectual course . . . to send over English Colonies' would need to be framed by 'a person that not only understands England very well, but is perfectly acquainted with the present and in some good measure with the former state of Ireland; otherwise he will be in danger to run upon many unpracticable Chimaera's'.[35] On the other hand, there is the following description of Henry Cromwell's plan, also dating from 1657, for a school in Dublin: 'in order to the propagating civilitie as well as Religion among those [*Irish*] countrymen hereafter, who tis hoped will harken to their owne country men with lesse prejudice than the English, against whom they have something of a national antipathy'.[36] Wood's air of faint surprise at the existence of this 'national antipathy' shows how partially he viewed the matter and may strike us as ironic. But he does show a serious commitment to genuinely empirical information gathering about Ireland, enthusiastically promising in May 1657 that, after accompanying Henry Cromwell on his 'Northern Progresse', he would 'be able to speake more experimentally of this land'. Wood's replies to the Interrogatories are laconic. Many of his comments are the usual account of deficiencies in Irish management of agriculture, horticulture and related matters of obvious importance to would-be settlers. Two

---

[32] See Webster, 432–3; Barnard, *Cromwellian Ireland*, 235–6.
[33] For Wood, see Barnard, *Cromwellian Ireland*, 223–4. His replies are in HP 33/1.
[34] 'Alphabetical list concerning natural history', n.d., HP 31/17/6–7. The full correspondence is in HP 33/1/1–75 and 42/1/15.
[35] HP 33/1/23B.   [36] HP 33/1/13B.

representative examples are the size of Irish barrels ('what inferiour measuers they containe') and the inevitable recalcitrance of certain classes of Irish bog: 'red bog, very unfit for drayning'.[37] With very few exceptions, however, his tone is more rueful than choleric. One example is when he notes the inferiority of Irish housing ('their scurvy fashion of houses and cottages'), a very common observation by English witnesses. Mostly he merely lists the questions that arise in relation to each topic rather than offering much in the way of answers. This produces a curious, almost parodic effect; on bloomeries, he mentions 'the fashion of them, charges of making one how many people necessary to attend them'; on beer: 'how brewed in Ireland; what severall wayes, which the best, how to make it lasting'.[38]

More important than Wood's own sketchy replies was his enlistment of Miles Symner, who did most towards the continuation of the project and whose replies, three sheets going from 'Galls' to 'Woolfe', sent to Hartlib in the summers of 1656 and 1657, are more substantial than Wood's and constitute by far the most intriguing text to come out of the whole attempt.[39] It is perhaps relevant that Symner, unlike any of the other participants, spent most or all of his life in Ireland. He was the first professor of mathematics at Trinity College, Dublin, a position which he held from 1652 to 1660 and again after the Restoration, from 1675 to 1686.[40] He had serious practical–scientific interests in many areas, including surveying, engineering and astronomy. He was a friend of Thomas Salusbury, the translator of Galileo. His projects for Irish science foreshadow those of Molyneux and the Dublin Philosophical Society in the 1680s, though it seems his work was unknown to them. He was chief engineer to the army, holding the rank of major from 1648 on, and providing expert service in the handling of fortifications during the campaigns. He participated in the Down Survey from 1656 to 1659, holding the post of commissioner for setting out the soldiers' lands alongside Petty and Vincent Gookin. Symner was well placed economically and politically as well as scientifically. He evidently did not suffer because of his prominent position in the Ireland of the war and resettlement decades although he did not make the specta-

---

[37] HP 31/17/6–7.   [38] HP 31/17/6A, 7B, 7A.
[39] HP 62/45/1A–7B. A fourth sheet existed, but has been lost.
[40] See Barnard, 'Symner'.

cular personal gains achieved by his colleague, Petty.[41] In his *History of the Down Survey*, Petty approvingly attributes to Symner a hesitant and delicate approach to his role as commissioner for distributing the army's lands: 'Major Symner, a person ever generally beloved, and especially in this very army, foreseeing the danger of incurring as much the armyes causeless hatred as he had before enjoyed their well merited good affections, could not with that pleasure attend the clamorouse part of this business, as his publicke spiritt otherwise disposed him unto.'[42]

In a 1648 letter to Sir Robert King, Symner wrote a kind of manifesto justifying his intellectual position. Thanking King for sending him a copy of Petty's *Advancement of learning* (which was dedicated to Hartlib), and expressing a renewed wish that both an 'Office of Intelligence' and the 'Colledge' – familiar from other Hartlibian writings – be set up for investigative spirits and lovers of the new thought, he remarks that his own 'scope is for reall & experimentall Learning' and states that 'I abhor all those ventosities, froth & idle speculations of the Schooles'.[43] In a manner familiar from other Baconians, he inveighs against what he sees as the intellectual emptiness and pernicious influence on the young of the training in logic and disputation which at that time still formed the major part of the university curriculum: 'for after a young Schollar hath got a little prayse for beeing able to wrangle in the Schooles about Universale a parte rei, that puff fils his sayles & makes him steere his cours to find out nothing but vanity'. He sets against this the kind of thought that could arrive at 'Axioms, usefull for further Learning, or Common life'. He modestly deprecates his own ability and instead provides, as instances of this, the attempt by the Irish architect and surveyor, Johnson, to develop a 'universal character' for printing. This had been fostered by Symner before its frustration by the rebellion. He also mentions his own invention and manufacture of 'a quadrant of 6 fot Radius' and encloses an 'Obser-

[41] Barnard notes that he had an estate at Archerstown in County Meath in 1660, and a house in Dame Street in Dublin in 1665. He was archdeacon of Clogher in 1661 and of Kildare from 1667 to 1670 ('Symner', 130–1).

[42] William Petty, *The history of the survey of Ireland, commonly called the Down Survey*, ed. T. A. Larcom (Dublin, 1851), 208. This account dates from 1659.

[43] HP 47/6/1, n.d.; the letter is dated 24 October 1648 in another copy, BL Sloane MS 427, fol. 85 (Barnard, 'Symner', n. 5). Compare the contrast Robert Wood draws between 'the learning of the Schooles' and 'this business which must be built only upon reason & experience' (HP 33/1/39A, 4 January 1658).

vation' of his own, one of several, which 'if it light on Astronomicall palates, will not be unpleasing'.[44]

The sheets of Symner's replies to the Alphabetical Interrogatories are, as I have said, rather different from the Boates' fevered distaste and fury at Irish incivility. Symner engages in no extended denunciations of the Irish as naturally savage. This may, of course, be partly because of the very constraints of the classificatory list form, but the nature of his whole approach seems to preclude totalizing generalizations. In his 1648 letter to King, he does lament the destruction by the friars at Athenry in 1641 of the precious copperplates of Johnson's experimental work. The friars, he says vividly, 'suffered the tinkers to stop kettles' with the precious plates.[45] But even this is a fairly mild and, in the circumstances, understandable reaction.

Symner's text conveys a very strong and agreeable sense of an immediate encounter with a place and a lively apprehension of its real features, positive and negative. It is neither distantly schematic, theoretical in the bad sense (like some of the more utopian schemes of Hartlibians for Ireland and elsewhere), nor riddled with prejudice (like the Boates' work). Symner, like other observers, shows a delighted astonishment at the great plenty of fish in Irish rivers and off the coast; of salmon, 'I think all the rivers of Europe yeeld not soe much as the rivers of Eirland'; of mackerel, 'I have seen great ripeling there of the water where theire scals are'; and of pilchard, 'the spies walk the hills and see where the sea is rough with them'.[46] He praises the islands, 'faire ones, with good harbours', the strawberry-trees (i.e. arbutus) at Killarney, the quality of the pearls found in freshwater crustaceans. Everywhere there is a stress on personal observation, which seems to be genuinely in the true spirit of empirical method and to fulfil a very basic Baconian prescription. In spite of our awareness of the ideologically questionable circumstances of their composition, these passages have the fresh charm of a

---

[44] Barnard details the obscure Johnson's work towards a universal character in 'Symner', 136–7; he had performed architectural work for Strafford's never-completed mansion in Kildare before the war. See also James Knowlson, *Universal language schemes in England and France, 1600–1800* (Toronto, 1975), 10. In a letter to Hartlib in March 1657, Robert Wood refers to the book of 'Mr Johnsons real Characters' (HP 42/1/15), having elsewhere expressed scepticism about the potential of the whole idea: 'I doubt the whole businesse of the Universal Character will never prove of any considerable effect' (HP 33/1B, 13 May 1656).
[45] HP 47/16/1A.   [46] HP 62/45/1A–7B.

traveller's tale: 'Our boate man hath told me ... I perswaded my servant ... coming over slew loker' (presumably Sliabh Luachra, on the Cork–Kerry border); 'I have stood on a bridge and seen him [*an osprey*] take up a pike of twenty-six inches long'; 'I have seen snow in the mountains by Dublin'; 'I have seene it [*a very large trout*] truely delineated by a painter'. His entry on hedgehogs not only refers to his having eaten them ('their flesh is very good meate roasted or baked') but also intriguingly reports how in Ireland their skins are 'only used for calues noses to keep them from [*sucking*] the Cowes'. On porpoises, he says: 'I have killed one aleven foot long' and 'my Irish boatemen did eate him like a fatt poark'.[47] Symner had travelled widely in Ireland, probably both in his war service and in the course of his work on the Down Survey. Besides places in Leinster and thus relatively close to Dublin, he mentions many others he had visited, of which the following, in counties Wexford, Kerry, Galway and Mayo, are only a selection: Duncannon, Lough Leane, Aran, Dingle Bay to Valentia, and Cleggan Bay. He was capable not just of marvelling at the potential for profitable development and civilized 'improvement' and hence in a more or less self-interested way at the achievements of the English settlers, but also of expressing wonder at the sheer strangeness of Irish natural features. For instance, he describes at unusual length the limestone pavements on the Aran islands, and in a tone of wonder:

all over the Island like the squared greate stones of some large building fallne down in as good order as a [*bricker?*] now mold a brick ... in Arann close by the coast ... there is an incredible quantitie of greate flag-stones six seauen or eight inches thick 7. 8. or 9. foot broade and som aboue 20 foot long, loose as one would iudge layd upon others, making as itt weare a pauement round about the fort.[48]

Symner, as befits his ethnic and ideological position, does, of course, show negative reactions also, especially to what he sees as the failure of the Irish to perform necessary functions in agricultural maintenance: they allegedly show a 'want of skill' to make honey; they 'cut up all young [*hop*] trees ... and neglect to plant them', showing a 'want of law and skill'; they allow jackdaws to multiply to the detriment of crops, because 'no care' is taken 'to destroy them';

[47] HP 62/45/1–7.
[48] HP 62/45/4–4A: this seems to be a description of the expanse of limestone pavement surrounding the prehistoric promontory fort of Dun Aengus on Aranmore, certainly an impressive sight.

the quality of the gunpowder is very poor because 'here is so little of the ground kept dry that wee have very little', and so forth.[49] These complaints, all to do with the Irish failure to take the land in hand and manage natural resources more actively, echo similar ones made by John Beale in his correspondence with Hartlib about fruit-growing in Ireland. Thus Beale says that the boughs of the apple-trees are allowed to grow 'soe thic, as shewd' the 'negligence, or unskillfullness' of the growers.[50]

Finally, in a characteristically down-to-earth moment, Symner registers the practical difficulties facing Irish 'improving' settlers. In the Commentary under 'gardains', the following answer appears:

I cannott commend any here very much when I thinke of the Gardains of England and other places but here are som few that endeauore to do sum small matters when the plantation is more forwards that is when Howses Barnes Stables ... trees Quicqsetts and Kitching Gardins are in som good order [*then and*] nott till then will the most desirous apply themselves to the care of procuring such delicates. The incommodity of sitting downe on waste lands when there is no wood nor artificer in many miles is nott to bee app[*rehended*] but by them that try.[51]

In 1932, T. W. Adorno delivered a lecture on 'The idea of natural history', later incorporating its main arguments into his *Negative dialectics*.[52] In it he considers 'nature' and 'history' as mutually determining concepts, each of which has a double character, both positive and negative. In the case of nature, there is a positive, materialist pole, which refers to concrete existing being, mortal and transitory, and to the material products of people's labour as well as their own corporeal bodies. The negative pole is to do with a world not yet incorporated into history, not yet penetrated by reason, and hence outside human control. Nature in this sense is what Adorno

49 An amusing shade of the Boates' type of prejudice would seem to appear in Symner's comment on how dogs 'go off' in Ireland: he says the mastiffs are 'all of English breed and they degenerate and grow into a lesser kinde here' (rather like the Norman English settlers as Spenser describes them), corrupted, presumably, by infectious Irish ways; but in some matters – climatically, for instance – Ireland seems, at least potentially, superior: 'the trees that will grow in England with difficulty I think would better grow here' (HP 62/45/1A).
50 Beale to Hartlib, n.d., HP 52/166. Beale remarks, in a spirit common to almost all these witnesses: 'I conceive the Plantation of Ireland with English, who would bee good examples to stir up a lazy people to abhor their idelenes, & to enrich themselves & yt soyle would bee of much concernement to us.'
51 HP 62/45/1A.
52 In the following passage I have drawn extensively on the discussion by Susan Buck-Morss in *The origin of negative dialectics* (Hassocks, Sussex, 1977), 52–7. See Theodor W. Adorno, *Negative dialectics*, trans. E. B. Ashton, (London, 1973) 354–8.

called the mythical, that which is eternally there as the 'fateful construction of pre-given being'. This nature, he says, is perpetuated by the unchanging rituals of the people who have submitted to its domination.

On the other hand, history too has a double signification. The positive one is 'dialectical social praxis', transmitted social behaviour, characterized by the qualitatively 'new' appearing in it. It is, as he puts it, 'a movement not running its course in pure identity' – not, one may add, eternally recurrent, but changing and changeable by collective social will. The negative pole of history is the actual history of human praxis in so far as it merely statically reproduces the conditions and relations of class (and, we may say, of various kinds of oppression) rather than establishing a qualitatively new order. A crucial point in Adorno's argument is the perception that whenever theory posited 'nature' or 'history' as an ontological first principle, this double character in these concepts was lost and, with it, the potential for what he calls 'critical negativity' – that attitude of scepticism, suspicion of transcendental positions and willingness to accommodate change which is the most salient characteristic of his truly dialectical thought. He argues that when the pole of either nature or history became singly dominant, either existing social conditions were affirmed as natural without regard for their historical becoming, or the actual historical process was affirmed as essential and, as a result, irrational material suffering was dismissed as mere contingency (as, for example, he says Hegel does) or ontologized as essential in itself (Heidegger's recourse). He argues that the result in both cases is ideological justification of the given social order. Adorno insists on what he calls the 'concrete unity' of nature and history within any analysis of reality.

While making due allowance for the fact that Adorno was working within a twentieth-century problematic, his analysis nevertheless has a clear, even a startling applicability to the Hartlibian natural history project. Without doubt, as the enthusiastic millenarian language of Arnold Boate's preface alone shows, these men were working from a sense of God's providential dispositions as the equivalent of Adorno's 'ontological first principle', and they were reading the 'irrational material suffering' of the dispossessed and unruly Irish as mere contingency, while their own trials, pains and signs of divine grace were ontologized as essential in themselves – i.e. willed by God to further the coming of His kingdom. Their Protestant sensibilities, their sense of destiny, dignified their efforts, both gains and losses. To them, especially in Boate's published text and in the writings of the most pious such as John Dury, as the passages on St Patrick's Purgatory clearly show, the lives of the ignorant, superstitious Irish were part of the people's unchanging history of submission to the domination of 'pre-given being' – for which Boate read the power of the friars in preserving the oppressive illusion of the holy places. Their own praxis, as Adorno would have called it and, by extension, the praxis of the previous generations of the righteous among the English settlers, could by contrast be understood as historical in the positive sense, characterized by the 'qualitatively new' appearing in it: this 'new' was exemplified in the improvements of the land which had been and were being carried out by these enterprising settlers: the drainage works, mining, clearing of the woods, planting of orchards and all the various experiments with new crops and strains of plant and animal which are so eagerly discussed throughout the Hartlib correspondence. The utopian character of these projections, the fervour of their insistence on making change happen in the favourable context of Cromwell's new dispensation, is the single most striking feature of these writings, even more, as I have argued, than their empiricism.

If we view these matters from the opposite position, that of the Irish and the Old English Catholics, then it seems, using Adorno's perspective, that the natural historians privileged material nature over history. They interested themselves in the natural features of the landscape, the commercial and agricultural opportunities afforded by them, the potential wealth of the country, the whole project of experiment and improvement and ultimately the establishment of its basis in accurate alphabetized description. All this took precedence over – even, we might say, obliterated – Irish history, and especially aspects such as the suppression of indigenous culture and society, the dispossession of the Catholic landowners and the depredations of the Cromwellian military reduction.

Putting it another way, and recalling the stereotyped construction of the Irish as uncivil, as 'a nation exceedingly barbarous in all the parts of their life', as the *Naturall history* puts it, we might say that these incomers, and their mentor Hartlib, who did not visit the place, assigned Ireland – social, cultural, human *tout court* – to 'nature' in the negative sense, and material Ireland to 'nature' in the

positive sense.[53] Looked at from the English and, specifically, the
Hartlibians' viewpoint, negative nature was perfectly evidenced in
the way of life of the native Irish, with their alleged barbarity
evident in so many spheres, the perceived idolatrous nature of their
religion and the extreme backwardness of their agriculture, manufacture, science and everything that could be considered progressive. This allowed the natural historians to see themselves as agents of
history in the positive sense, bringing change and a praxis of rational
action to this immemorially dark place. In so far as they acknowledged history, they dated it from 1641, endlessly recalling the
outrages of that period as a kind of negative talisman against any
doubt of the rightness of their own actions. The blessed apparent
destruction of the old order, monarchical–tyrannical as well as
Catholic, which they hoped would soon be 'breaking the yokes of
Nations' all over Europe, was to be the foundation of the new.[54] We
might recall the 'bleeding Head' in Marvell's 'Horatian Ode' which
at the foundation of the Capitol 'Did fright the Architects to run; /
And yet in that the State / Foresaw its happy Fate'.[55]

The project of discovering and describing nature, so as to achieve
control over it, is one about which, at the other end of the development of western science and technology, *we* may have reservations.
More particularly, the totalizing nature of at least some, or perhaps
most, of the Hartlibians' attitudes to Ireland – the blank space to be
filled, the duly emptied theatre now a locus for the perfect experiment, the corpse to be anatomized – must make us, at the very least,
uneasy. But there is, nevertheless, a moment in the Hartlib correspondence about Ireland that we ought also to recognize as progressive: the desire to incorporate the material world into rational human
structures, to empower people by rescuing them from what Adorno
called 'the fateful construction of pre-given being'. We do not have
to endorse the demonization of the native Irish (and of the corrupt
Old English) which flaws these writings to varying degrees, though
we must of course always keep in mind that the welcome demystify-

[53] It will be recalled that Wood worked hard during the second half of the 1650s to get
Hartlib assigned a parcel of Irish land, at Killaghteen in West Limerick (by a neat
historical irony it had once been church land and bears a saint's name: Cill Laichtin, the
church or cell of Lachtin): HP 33/1/48B, 54A. The efforts were frustrated by the Restoration.
[54] Boate, *Naturall history*, 'Epistle Dedicatory', sig. A7.
[55] *The poems and letters of Andrew Marvell*, ed. H. M. Margoliouth, revised by Pierre Legouis,
with E. E. Duncan-Jones, 2 vols. (Oxford, 1971), I, 93.

ing materialism of the natural historians is accompanied by the equally material dispossession of the Catholics (and, as modern theoreticians say, by the repression of Otherness which produces the rational bourgeois subject, the *homo clausus*, in Norbert Elias's phrase). As T. C. Barnard puts it, discussing the English planters' interest in fruit-trees, clover grass and new exotic vegetable-growing, all prime Hartlibian concerns: 'The English might garden while the Irish starved.'[56] But what William Petty ruefully calls 'the clamorouse part' of history (which, he said, Symner 'could not with ... pleasure attend [*to*]') should not be totalized, either. There must be, as Adorno also pointed out, a 'concrete unity of nature and history' within any analysis of reality. Our attitude to the Hartlibian ideals of peace, unity and prosperity should therefore include a due recognition of the genuine moment of enlightenment in the Hartlibians' thought about Ireland, together with a lively sense of historical irony. As Foucault said about humanist knowlege, it is 'an ambiguous liberation'.[57] We may justly discern, in the role of the Irish as the condemned opposite pole to the new knowledge, the trace of the oppressed Other which already reveals the incipient construction of the bourgeois subject-*ed* self; rationalism's shadow and its Other, driven forth upon the undrained bogs to assume the non-rational, wicked life of 'that wild Nation'.

[56] Barnard, 'Gardening, diet and "improvement"', 71.
[57] Foucault, *Madness and civilization*, quoted in Habermas, *Modernity*, 245.

Town and country

CHAPTER 17

Hortulan affairs

John Dixon Hunt

> Hortulan affaires doe require varietyes of novell & conceited
> amoenityes
>   The particulars of the wilde discourse, I intend to confirme
> more largely in soe many particular chapters. This I only
> shuffle together as a loose preface.[1]

My topic is hortulan affairs in the Hartlib circle and their significance for English garden history; more particularly, what role
the emphatically agricultural interests of Hartlib and his correspondents, John Beale and Cressy Dymock among others, played in
discussions of garden design. In its turn, this theme will necessitate
exploring the extent to which mid-seventeenth-century debates
about how man intervenes in the natural world through the arts of
horticulture were sustained or guided by theoretical considerations.
    At the centre of this enquiry will be a letter from John Beale,
dated 30 September 1659, probably addressed to Samuel Hartlib,
who eventually communicated it to John Evelyn, who in his turn
wrote it unchanged, though with a few crucial additions, into the
text of his opus magnum, the *Elysium Britannicum* (*see* appendix).
This material was first published by Peter Goodchild in *Garden
history*,[2] where the author presented it as an unproblematical plea for
natural gardening. This claim has more recently been supported by
Timothy Mowl, who sees Beale's ideas as picturesque landscaping
avant la lettre.[3] What is at issue in the interpretation of this most
important document is how we understand Beale's statements about
landscape and whether we can deduce from them any assumptions

---

[1] John Beale, HP 67/22/1A.
[2] Peter H. Goodchild, '"No phantasticall utopia, but a real place", John Evelyn, John Beale
and Backbury Hill, Herefordshire', *Garden History*, 19 (1991), 106–27.
[3] Timothy Mowl, 'New science, old order. The gardens of the Great Rebellion', *Journal of
Garden History*, 13 (1993), 16–35.

on which – simply because he could count on their being shared – he felt no need to elaborate. Even if we allow that the landscape Beale enthusiastically described in the late 1650s might look to us now like the sort of setting that, over a century after Beale, Uvedale Price could have endorsed, we still need to ask how each age saw these phenomena, how objects came to be endowed with assumptions and absorptions not inherent in the objects themselves, and whether similar assumptions enjoy the same genealogy at different historical moments.

Beale's letter is largely concerned with how he would landscape a site at Backbury Hill in Herefordshire. But the bottom line is clearly his commitment to what he terms 'the definition of a Garden'.[4] It was an issue of wide significance and interest. What exactly constituted the thrust of garden art? Should it evince man's control over nature; his skills or ingenuity at working with its resources; his interference in natural purposes for profit or pleasure; or his unmediated celebration of God's bounty? These were all themes in which mid-seventeenth-century England was much absorbed. Even if only a few of these ideas were actually translated into garden layouts and we were lucky enough to have adequate records of such layouts, it would still be essential to register the variety, debate, even confusion, of available theories that informed the practice.

Beale's attention to the definition of a garden emerges in his other writings: notably two proposals communicated to Hartlib for books on 'Physique' and 'Pleasure' gardens, and his 1657 publication, *Herefordshire orchards, a pattern for all England*, which had itself first taken shape as two letters to Hartlib in May 1656, prompted in their turn by the third edition of *Samuel Hartlib his legacie* (1651, 1652 and 1655).[5]

For brevity's sake (for, as Beale wrote to Hartlib, 'I must be abrupt'), four shared assumptions in these various documents will be abstracted and then glossed with some citations and commentary.[6]

Gardens were to be seen as the culmination, historically or culturally as well as topographically, of a series of human interventions in the natural world
Hartlib's *Legacie* addresses this cultural or historical development when he notes that 'Art of Gardening [*which*] is but of few years

---

[4] HP 67/22/1B. cf. the first chapter of his proposed book on the pleasure garden, which would focus on 'Howe and why a Garden': HP 26/6/3A.
[5] HP 25/6.   [6] HP 52/72B.

standing in England, and therefore not deeply rooted, nor well understood'. It was only about fifty years ago, he continues, that hortulan '*Ingenuities* first began to flourish in *England*'.[7] The recent pedigree of English gardening is a leitmotif of gardening commentary until at least the second decade of the eighteenth century, together with an equally consistent interest in how to adapt to English conditions (cultural as well as climatic) the traditions of gardening, husbandry and agriculture that can be traced back at least to ancient Greece.[8] Thus it is that modern England is claimed as the site for the recovery of antique gardening, a historical prototype that for Beale seems to meld Greek with biblical perfections.[9]

Just as gardens develop over time, deriving some of their essential forms from agricultural needs and practices, so do they in space: Hartlib's *A discoverie for division or setting out of land, as to the best form* (London, 1653) addresses this topographical scale of intervention. It is as if the view from the mansion over its gardens, orchards, pasture and tillage visually and locally recapitulated the historical sequence of a garden's evolution. In his *Discoverie*, Hartlib published a scheme submitted to him in manuscript by Cressy Dymock (*see* figs. 17.1, 17.2), austere and rigorous in its geometry, for an ideal estate.[10] 'Your house stands in the middle of all your little world ... enclosed with the gardens and orchyeards ... & all bound together as with a girdle' (this referring presumably to a circle of utilitarian buildings). Then come great quadrants of corn lands and meadows ('& all that covered againe as so (faire largeth) a cloak of meadow and tillage to which you may count the corn pasturage the cape if you please or

---

[7] *Samuel Hartlib his legacie of husbandry* (3rd edn, London, 1655), 9. But since Hartlib makes few of the distinctions between kinds of gardening that are routine nowadays, these 'ingenuities' are not *giocchi d'acqua*, terraces and so on but 'cabbages, colleflowers ... at that time great rarities' (*ibid.*).

[8] See in this respect J. Dixon Hunt, '"Gard'ning can speak proper English"', in *Culture and cultivation in early modern England: writing and the land*, ed. Michael Leslie and Timothy Raylor (Leicester, 1992).

[9] When Evelyn incorporates Beale's classical instance (HP 67/22/1A) into *Elysium Britannicum* he augments it explicitly to include biblical resonances (fol. 56).

[10] *Discoverie for division* (1653), 10. Dymock's undated letter is among the Hartlib papers – HP 62/29/1–4. It is from the latter that the references in this chapter are drawn. Mowl argues that several contemporary houses such as Snitterton, Derbyshire, seem to follow the logic of Dymock's/Hartlib's advice ('New science, old order'), though he sees such 'ruthless' geometry as part of a revolutionary radicalism rather than as, what is here presented, a mode of organizing man's relationship with the world. Doubtless it could be both at once, or rather both views of the one arrangement are possible – the question then arising as to what contemporary evidence is available for whichever point of view is thought to be expressed.

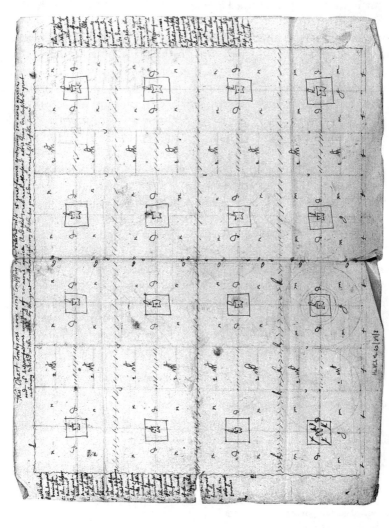

Figure 17.1 Cressy Dymock's drawing of an ideal farm or estate (HP 62/29/4A) [Sheffield University Library]

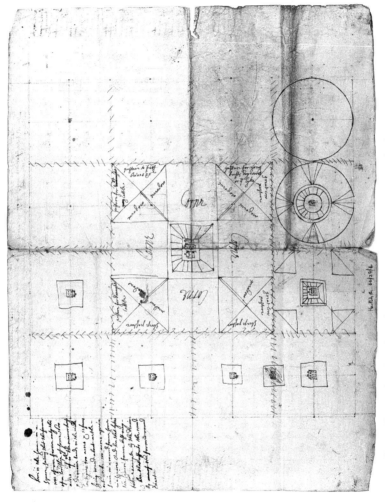

Figure 17.2 Cressy Dymock's drawing of an ideal farm or estate (HP 62/29/3A) [Sheffield University Library]

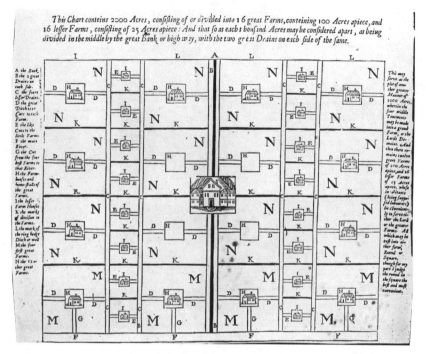

Figure 17.3 The version of fig. 17.2 published by Hartlib in *A discoverie for division*,
1653 [Sheffield University Library]

the sleeves to the coate'). Finally, beyond the furthest circle lie the
animal pastures.[11]

The 'proper domains' of each element of the estate's ensemble, as
the published plan (*see* figs. 17.3, 17.4) announces, are arranged
certainly for convenience and pragmatic purposes ('right and ample
use of every [*piece*] of ground') as well as part of a larger argument in
favour of enclosures.[12] But the layout also implicitly proposes a
hierarchy of spaces whereby nearer the mansion are those that
demonstrate greater control than those further away, more intensity
of labour and greater aesthetic delight ('refreshed with the beautye
(& Odour) of the blossomes fruit and flowers'). To this idea of scale
and relationship of parts Hartlib/Dymock gesture with such phrases
as 'and outwards to my Tillage'.[13] This anticipates the second
principle enunciated in these writings.

[11] HP 62/29/2B.   [12] *Discoverie for division*, 3.   [13] *Ibid.*, 21.

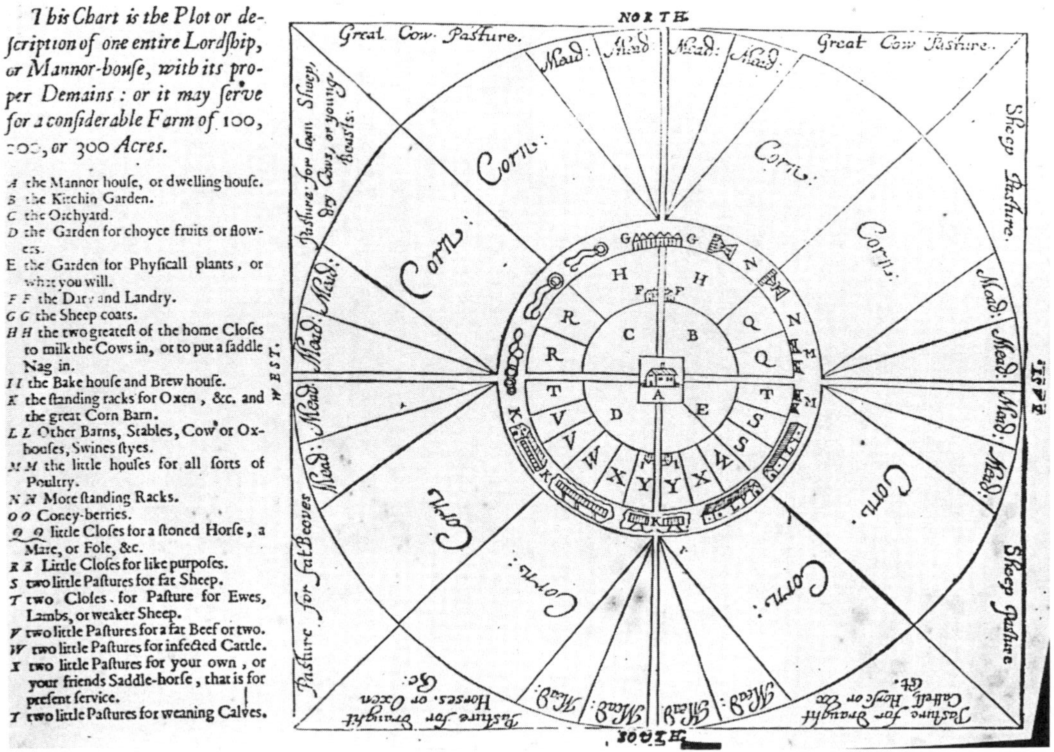

Figure 17.4 The version of fig. 17.1 published by Hartlib in *A discoverie for division*, 1653 [Sheffield University Library]

This hierarchy was physically represented on the ground in a scale of artifice
that decreased as one moved further away from the mansion

Perhaps the clearest contemporary manifestation of this palpable
representation of a hierarchy of nature was the parterre with its
topiary and embroidered beds, where the sculpture and geometry
echo the shapes and forms of both the adjacent architecture and the
interior decoration, while the green materials announce the unmediated world towards which the gardens ultimately conduct one.[14]

This gradation or scale of human intervention in the physical
world is announced particularly clearly in seventeenth-century
engravings of gardens, notably those by Kip and Knyff. But an
earlier and more interesting example that focuses in close-up on this
scale is Isaac de Caus' prospect of Wilton Gardens (*see* fig. 17.5).
Nearest the house are the intricate *broderie* patterns and the regular,
shaped shrubs. What we would expect next as the second section of
garden – the amphitheatre or 'circus', bracketed at each side by long
architectural *berceaux* – is deferred until last and placed under the
terrace walk above the grotto. In between is a wilderness, with
regularly planted trees, though crowded together to give the effect of
woodland, and this is bracketed by less architectural *berceaux* in the
form of long tunnels of greenery; furthermore, through this sector
wanders the wholly uncanalized River Nadder.

There is some dispute as to the intentions of the designer with the
River Nadder in this middle section. Strong thinks the arrangement
of the three sectors is in order to 'conceal' the river; Mowl also thinks
the river was 'conceal[ed] in a culvert instead of featuring it by a
bridge'.[15] But the central axis is indeed a bridge – and the shadows
thrown by the open balustrading show on the engraving. Furthermore, while the river is certainly brought under and so hidden by
the arbour at the right, its passage is left open and visible at the
left.[16] The idea that the river was seen as a natural feature, entirely
suitable for representation in this 'wild' segment of the gardens, is
strengthened by the engraved plate of text that draws attention to its
presence and gives its breadth as 44 feet.[17] Apart from the topo-

---

[14] Evelyn sees the flower beds as recalling both tapestry and embroidery: see *Elysium
Britannicum*, fols. 76 and 277.

[15] R. Strong, *The Renaissance garden in England* (London, 1979), 152; Mowl, 'New science, old
order', 17.

[16] In fact Strong (149) counts three rather than two bridges.

[17] Usually attributed to Isaac de Caus, *Wilton Gardens* was issued sometime in the 1640s. See
my catalogue entry 107 in the forthcoming *Oak Spring Hortus*, 2 vols.

Figure 17.5 Wilton Gardens, engraved by Isaac de Caus, 1640s [Dumbarton Oaks Garden Library]

graphical necessity of using the river at this point in the middle
sector, another reason for varying the sequence of sections might
have been to display the tripartite scale of art–nature in a more conspicuous way. Other engravings of Wilton show that beyond this
garden and its grotto-terrace was an austere, less mediated hillside
amphitheatre from which an avenue led out into the countryside
beyond.

But the princely shows of Wilton or the *Nouveau théâtre de la Grande
Bretagne* were not the only expression of this scale of mineral–vegetable or cultural–natural mediation. Beale frequently lists the consti-
tuent parts of small country estates as a sequence in which we may
intuit such gradations: 'We do commonly devise a shadowy walk
from our Gardens through our Orchards.'[18] But there is also attention to the formal means by which each zone is to be registered: his
projected treatise on 'A garden of pleasure' contains a section on
'whether the large trees of the Orchard should be admitted into the
Garden: Or the Orchard necessarily divided from ye garden',[19]
while the letter to Hartlib asks 'what sort of Trees, or what
approach of trees may be allowed for the ornament of the flowery
regions'.[20] He equally sees orchards themselves as part of a hierarchical scale of artifice – being 'the richest, sweetest, and most
embellish'd Grove'.[21]

Such assumptions were already well established in Europe by the
mid-seventeenth century, and they would also survive well into the
next century in England. When, for instance, a hundred years or so
after Beale, William Mason explained the garden's relationship to
agriculture by saying that it is 'the soil, already tam'd, [*being given*]
its finish'd grace',[22] he was still enunciating a concept of three
natures or a hierarchy of artifice, to which we have now, I think,
lost access; so it is worth sketching its salient aspects.

In the mid-sixteenth century, two Italian humanists, Jacopo Bonfadio and Bartelomeo Taegio, called the garden a third nature, a
self-conscious neologism aimed at explaining the curious conjunction in gardens of art and nature – 'nature incorporated with art',
writes Bonfadio, 'is made the creator and conatural of art, and from
both is made a third nature, which I would not know how to

[18] *Herefordshire orchards a pattern for all England*, (1657; *ed. cit.* London, 1724), 28.
[19] HP 25/6/3A (section 27).
[20] HP 67/22/1B.   [21] *Ibid.*   [22] *The garden*, Book I, line 113.

name'.[23] His coinage of '*terza natura*' must allude directly to Cicero's discussion in *De natura deorum* of what he calls a second nature, what today we might term the cultural landscape; four editions of Cicero's text were published in the years before Bonfadio and Taegio were putting their minds to garden concepts.[24] Cicero writes of sowing corn, planting trees, fertilizing soil by irrigation and managing rivers. 'In short,' he concludes, 'by means of our hands we try to create as it were a second nature within the natural world.'[25] It is language that, significantly, is readily transferable to the creation of gardens or third nature. Given the force of the Latin *alteram naturam*, Cicero clearly posits the existence of a first nature. This might be – and the ambiguity is germane to my Hartlibian preoccupations – either the gods' nature or the unmediated, uncultured landscape, what today we might term the wilderness.

Such a triad has itself three aspects – historical, topographical and evaluative. It is a historical development, in that wild terrain came to be selectively enclosed for crops, rivers would be dammed, and then gardens, drawing upon agricultural forms and technology, established. This triad of natures was also expressed topographically on the ground, as we have seen mooted in Cressy Dymock's ideal estate plan. Finally, it allows a qualitative judgement – either the sort that eventually entered English with the term 'improvement' – the more human intervention into the original first nature, whether perceived as wilderness or God's bounty, the better; or its reverse, that God's first nature is best of all.

At least until the early nineteenth century almost all serious discussion of third nature or garden design, either considered by itself or in its relationship to the other two natures, is underpinned by these concepts. As already suggested, we have lost touch with these ideas, sometimes (I believe) so obvious to their users that they received little formal exposition. It is an interesting light on the Hartlib circle, I think, that they bring such concepts so close to the surface of their discourse. One reason why they emerge as explicitly as they do in the gardening and horticultural concerns of this mid-century group of Englishmen is that the concept of a hierarchy

---

[23] This letter is reprinted in *Lettere del cinquecento* (Turin, 1967), 501; for Taegio, see his *La villa* (Milan, 1559), 155.

[24] Venice, 1508; Paris, 1511; Leipzig, 1520; and Basle, 1534. The work also existed in over a dozen manuscripts. An English translation, *Cicero's Three books touching the nature of the gods*, appeared in 1683.

[25] Cicero, *De natura deorum*, II, lx, 152–3; ed. H. Rackham (London, 1933), 268–71.

of three natures, a sequence of controls over natural resources, was a means of experiencing and understanding the natural world. Garden making, especially in an intellectual and pragmatic context of agrarian activity, was a means of understanding the physical universe and man's relationship to it. This leads to two further principles in the Hartlibian writings under discussion.

It was not always possible, owing to topographical or financial exigencies, to make this hierarchy of cultural control over territory visible on the ground. It might have to be executed approximately or piecemeal, but it was nonetheless pointed for those who grasped its underlying principle

Here we can juxtapose what we might call the drawing-board solution of Dymock that Hartlib published in his *Discoverie for division* with the empirical possibility that Beale considered for Backbury Hill in Herefordshire. Dymock proposes an ideal structure, without any local application. By contrast, Beale is constrained by topographical and financial exigencies from imposing such a thoroughgoing scheme as Dymock envisaged.

It is in the first place owing to financial considerations that Beale rules out 'Architecture', the most conspicuous ingredient of third nature, from his proposed garden rather than because he is dedicating himself to naturalistic purism as most commentators assume.[26] That this is so is clear from his statement that the garden could be created for £100 as long as that estimate can exclude ('except') both 'the charges of Architecture, conteining Walls, Statues, Summerhouses, Cesternes &c' as well as 'the charge of Plants and workmanship in setting the Plants'.[27] As it is unlikely that planting is wholly to be excluded, in even the most beneficent and fecund of sites, the reason for the exclusion of hard elements has also surely to be financial.[28] So I suggest that the proposals for regulating Backbury according to hierarchical natures differ in degree, not kind, from Dymock. But here we impinge upon the fourth and final of the principles that are at stake in these writings.

---

[26] HP 67/22/2B.   [27] *Ibid.*

[28] When Evelyn transcribed Beale's passage into his *Elysium Britannicum* he added a passage precisely on the 'addition' to Beale's landscape of various 'Artificiall decorations' (see fols. 57–8). It is a point that Beale himself seems to concede when he wrote Evelyn to say that 'you will not deeme mee so shallowe, as to dare seriously to compare our Herefordian Mountains with the Princeliee & beautifull seates which doe surround the surcharging Metropolis' – cited in M. Leslie, 'The spiritual husbandry of John Beale', in Leslie and Raylor (eds.) *Culture and cultivation*, 165.

The ultimate significance and purpose of such visible garden hierarchies of control was to educate man and woman through the contrived forms of garden art and husbandry to appreciate the ideal perfection of God's handiwork in the larger world of nature

A variant and less explicitly theological version of that perspective, as enunciated by the third earl of Shaftesbury in his unpublished *Second characters*, is that garden art represents – presents over again in its own forms – the proper character of the natural world that will be the better appreciated once a garden's version of it has been understood.

Beale touches upon this topic of representation generally and specifically. He is by no means against features such as 'mounts' or 'caves',[29] but when, as in Herefordshire, he has what Henry James might call 'the real thing' he is far less satisfied with 'poore mimical though sometimes changeable mounts and wildernesses' in modern gardens.[30] His scorn for 'our narrow, mimicall way' of garden design does not, in fact, mean the wholesale rejection of hortulan representation. If, for example, 'a gap lies in the way between our Orchard and Coppice', he suggests that 'we [*may*] fill up the vacancy with the artificial help of a Hop-yard, *where a busy Wood gives the shape of a Wood* [*emphasis added*]';[31] more explicitly he urges that 'hortulane amoenityes [*he has just instanced 'Mounts, Prospects, Precipices, & Caves'*] may sometimes bee soe representet to you'.[32]

Beale is concerned to put hortulan representation at the service of *genius loci*. One section of his proposed book on the pleasure garden was announced as 'Adviseing Not to enforce the platforme to any particular phantsy, but to apply unto it the best shape, That will agree with the nature of the place'.[33] He uses human knowledge, skill and art to bring out the potential of the landscape, perfecting its own natural resources, its special *quidditas*, just as the gardener should manipulate the micro-climates of his enclosures;[34] hence Beale's wish to improve the 'beauty and taste' of flowers, thus using cultural resources to enlarge awareness of their 'small beauty and

---

[29] HP 67/22/1B.

[30] I am referring to the witty and complex parable of art and nature in James' short story, 'The real thing', published first in 1892. Beale refers to the accidents or 'luckiness of situation' and the need to prefer a 'reall, & lofty hill' to an imitation mount (*ibid.*).

[31] *Herefordshire orchards*, 28.   [32] HP 67/22/1A.   [33] HP 25/6/3A.

[34] See HP 25/6/1A, section 16 ('To double the Sun rayes; Howe to length our Autumne, And to praeoccupate our spring').

taste'.[35] Beale's suggestion that Evelyn add a chapter on 'Entertainments' is urged because they are 'intended, as it were scenically, to shewe the riches, beauty, wonders, plenty, & delight of a Garden' – in other words they reveal its best potential.[36] Even though the Herefordshire site affords huger natural advantages to the gardener, he writes, than are available at Woodstock, Windsor and Greenwich, there is still the need to 'rectify and purify'.[37]

The Herefordshire site may, perhaps, be said to reverse the modes and directions of representation. It is a landscape that itself seems to imitate or represent gardens – a square, large green plain on the summit of one hill 'hath a perfect resemblance of an ancient flowre garden',[38] just as the system of pathways that lead to it from the house below becomes, in Beale's description, a version of garden paths and arbours, or just as Evelyn's transcription of this passage in the *Elysium Britannicum* speaks of the natural stream by the house as a 'rich and pure Fountaine'.[39] It is all what Evelyn, without ever himself having seen Backbury, calls 'a sweet and naturall Garden'; an achievement, as he finally notes, 'because Nature has already bin (as we may truly say) so Artificiall'. If we still hanker after labelling this some naturalistic or picturesque landscape vision, Evelyn's final addition to his 'source' of Spenser's 'Bower of Bliss' underlines the essential 'Idea' (his word) of hortulan arrangements that have dictated Beale's and his descriptions.

We may put this another way by saying that it is only when Beale, Hartlib and Evelyn have an idea of the garden as third nature that they can find its nascent forms in the second and first.[40] This would become, *mutatis mutandis*, the central thesis of Shaftesbury's discussion of how gardens encode and purify the characters of the natural world; thereby gardens become a school of moral vision. Hartlib and Beale, equally, saw husbandry not just as a matter of tilling and otherwise shaping the earth but as 'true and real Learning and Natural Philosophy'.

As Hartlib and his correspondents would have keenly appreciated, my commentary upon their idea of a garden – granted that it is plausible – has four further consequences for the history and historiography of English gardens.

---

[35] HP 67/22/1A.   [36] *Ibid.*   [37] *Ibid.*   [38] HP 67/22/3A.
[39] Evelyn, *Elysium Britannicum*, fol. 56.
[40] See also Wren's explanation of 'natural or geometrical Beauty' in *Parentalia* (London, 1750), 351.

The first is that English garden art had to find its own modes of procedure, suitable to climate, topography, social custom and to that whole gamut of intellectual and ideological ideas we may conveniently label 'culture'. Given the variety and flux of social and political ideas during the mid-seventeenth century, it is not surprising that different ideas of gardens, too, were canvassed;[41] if the best gardens had to show the best of England, the nation was hardly unanimous about its preferred identity. This explains, I think, the apparent diversity of hortulan ideas circulating in the Hartlib circle, ideas not always reducible to coherence by their promoters. This failure of synthesis in garden matters is most palpably available for us today in both the physical and intellectual state of John Evelyn's manuscript of the *Elysium Britannicum*, a document much interleaved, full of afterthoughts, a project never brought to conclusion despite the encouragement of many virtuosi.[42]

But a second point, concerning the Englishness of the whole enterprise, was less fraught. The Hartlib circle's focus upon husbandry meant that they inherited traditions of urging nationalist advantages in its development from the late sixteenth century, as Andrew McRae has made so clear:[43] thus we frequently encounter appeals by Dymock to the 'prosperitye ... honor and plentye of this whole nation',[44] while Anthony Lawrence, one of Beale's co-authors, explains that he writes in 'Englands true interest', for 'Hortulan Affaires are not the least of our Inland Commodities'.[45] These traditions of identifying 'country (i.e. rural) matters' with concerns of country (i.e. England) were applied in their turn to gardens, largely because the Hartlibians saw gardens or third nature as the proper refinement or extension of husbandry or second nature.[46] It is a recurring emphasis of the materials I have been

41 Mowl, 'New science, old order' sets out some of these varieties.
42 A transcription of the manuscript has now been completed by John Ingram, and the 1993 Dumbarton Oaks Colloquium on Landscape Architecture was devoted to it; a volume of the papers read on that occasion will be published.
43 A. McRae, 'Textual representations of agrarian England, 1547–1625' (Ph.D. thesis, University of Cambridge, 1992), parts of which I was able to read before its submission; see also his essay on 'Husbandry manuals and the language of agrarian improvement' in Leslie and Raylor (eds.), *Culture and cultivation*, chap. 2.
44 HP 62/29/1A: Dymock says that his thoughts on the subject of better husbandry 'I freely present to my Natyve Conntrye'.
45 Anthony Lawrence and John Beale, *Nurseries, orchards, profitable gardens, and vineyards encouraged* (London, 1677), 18 and 1 respectively.
46 Horticulture being, as the *Elysium Britannicum* put it (fol. 1), the 'noblest part of Agriculture'.

analysing that English hortulan affairs are capable of excelling all other modern and princely (i.e. continental) examples and returning England to the pure fount of antique gardening. It is, then, no accident – though, in fact, an error – that Beale's ideal garden would be established on a site so clearly marked by 'the old Britains, the silures'.[47] Henceforth, the precise adjudication of Englishness in gardens made them a battleground for national identity.

The third essential focus of the Hartlib circle follows from the first two: gardens constituted a representation of Englishness. Like other arts, garden making imitated in its own forms and modes the other natures. Gardens were, above all, ways of looking at first nature, but because husbandry and gardening were so closely identified, gardens were no less attentive to the relationship of second and third. At some stage during the early eighteenth century, the divorce of garden art from husbandry and horticulture, which threatened to taint its aesthetic ambitions, was achieved; to register this division, we have only to compare the writings reviewed here with such a basic work as Edward Lisle's *Observations in husbandry* of 1757.[48]

Now the exciting potential of seeing gardens as an art of representation was the flexibility afforded to any given garden to re-present its own locality and culture. Thus there was the opportunity to make Backbury Hill different from John Evelyn's Sayes Court in Deptford, or from the Evelyn family home at Wotton in Surrey; not only did the surrounding topography provide a different second and even first nature for the third to imitate, thus affecting and effecting a garden's design, but so too did the personal culture of each's creator, which was also an element in hortulan representation. This is clear from the elliptical reference by Beale to Méric Casaubon's *Treatise concerning enthusiasme* in its 1656 edition, which implies that those who are above worldly cares will not need formal and princely gardens (i.e. a wholly mediated nature) in which to meditate. Yet Casaubon's (and Beale's) apparent nervousness about these 'madmen' and

---

[47] HP 67/22/2A.

[48] The book is a compilation of practical hints, often culled from earlier sources, on the conduct of the kitchen garden and the 'orchard and fruit-garden'; there is no sense that the latter belong to a series of gradations in garden art, as is implied constantly by Beale, Hartlib and those writers on gardening and husbandry that I have examined in my essay in Leslie and Raylor (eds.) *Culture and cultivation.* See also the frequent conjunction of the different modes of gardening in [Pierre Le Lorrain de Vallemont], *Curiosities of nature and art in husbandry and gardening* (London, 1707), 3, 9 and 17.

their 'Ecstatie' among 'rocks and mountains, and wild prospects' surely suggests why controlled nature in gardens was the apt route or 'access to [*solid*] Truth' for the majority of humans.[49] The radical implications of the visionary's perspective were not readily assimilated by those who wished to codify, that is to say, realize and universalize, garden ideas.

This relates to the fourth point, which concerns perspective. Both Beale and Hartlib frequently imply, if they do not occasionally stress, how the gradations of intervention in the natural world are perceived in perspective: in Dymock's ideal estate we are taught to look outwards from the centre of his circle, or we learn to register Beale's orchards as the most finished or 'embellished' form of groves, or his hop-yards intervene between orchard and coppice.

It is an emphasis that became more pronounced in later writings on gardens and husbandry by people such as John Worlidge and Shaftesbury; but one of the earliest English occasions on which it was mooted was that seminal if gnomic book, Sir Henry Wotton's *The elements of architecture* (London, 1624). Wotton, whom Beale would have known at Eton and of whose friendship and patronage he makes much, made one of his precepts for architecture 'optical', which he explains thus: 'Such I meane as concerne the Properties of a well chosen Prospect: which I will call the Royaltie of Sight ... there is Lordship likewise of the Eye (as of the feet) which being a raunging and Imperrious, and (I might say) an usurping Sense; can indure no narrow circumscription; but must be fedde, both with extent and varietie.'[50] He notes that such lordship of the eye does not function with vast and indefinite views; yet a sufficient extent is necessary for us to appreciate the variety of forms.

The picturing of country estates during the seventeenth century frequently made clear what Wotton proposes and Beale utilizes in his 'definition of a Garden'. The frontispiece (*see* fig. 17.6), for instance, of Evelyn's *The French gardener* (1658), shows a couple gesturing through the built, architectural edge of a perspective that is extensive enough to take their sight across third nature (terraces,

---

[49] Beale's references to Casaubon are somewhat approximate; see, in effect, 61–2 and 68.
  That Beale was in fact both glancing at and concealing his own 'ecstacy' and prophetic dreams on Backbury Hill is clear from the letter quoted by Michael Leslie in Leslie and Raylor (eds.), *Culture and cultivation*, 165–6.
[50] See 4–5, with which also compare his later reflections on uniformity and variety in architecture, the latter being the 'great Patterne of Nature' which will yet need 'reconcilement' by the controlling hand of the former (pp. 20–1).

Figure 17.6 Frontispiece to *The French Gardener*, 1658 [Oak Spring Garden Library, Upperville, Virginia]

fountains), the interface between third and second that are regular orchards, then into agricultural land and finally into mountainous territory of first nature. We are probably most familiar with such visual representations of a hortulan scale of intervention in the natural world from the plethora of engravings of around 1700, which could be said to be the culmination of this way of looking and thinking (though, alas, we adduce these usually to exemplify not that gradation but our limited view of what is habitually called formal gardening).

It is upon the basis of such visual materials and habits as these that Shaftesbury makes his proposals for a garden art that juxtaposes along the central axis of a garden a series of less and less mediated natural forms, what he calls 'the several orders ... into which it is endeavoured to reduce the natural views'.[51] This prospect or perspective will teach the person 'who studies and breaks through the shell [*or exterior of the world*]' to 'see some way into the kernel' and appreciate the 'genuine order' of the natural world.[52] Garden perspectives, then, became for Shaftesbury a moral activity, as they initiated humans into a proper appreciation of the natural world.[53]

There were others who articulated similar views, but especially writers such as Stephen Switzer and John Worlidge who were the true heirs, I suggest, of the Hartlibian concerns I have been examining, in that they saw an intimate connection between gardening and husbandry. Thus, Worlidge's *Dictionarum rusticum, urbanicum & botanicum* (1717) noted the need for straight lines leading the eye out into 'delightful Prospect' that should not be blocked by 'tall hedges' – hence the visitor will be led 'insensibly ... into new and unexpected Varieties'.[54] Similarly Switzer argues that the countryside adjacent to a country mansion and its garden should not be blocked off with high walls or the eye forced to see 'woods misplaced' in the overall prospect or perspective.[55] Visually, we may see it eloquently set out in the anonymous frontispiece to a publication of 1707, aptly

[51] *Shaftesbury's second characters*, ed. Benjamin Rand (Cambridge, 1914), 163. For a substantial commentary on Shaftesbury's ideas as they affect garden design see David Leatherbarrow, 'Character, geometry and perspective: the third earl of Shaftesbury's principles of garden design', *Journal of Garden History*, 4 (1984), 332–58.

[52] Rand (ed.), *Second characters*, 14 and 163 respectively.   [53] *Ibid.*, 177.

[54] Second edition, 'revised, corrected and improved': under 'Garden', fols. G3r–G4r.

[55] Stephen Switzer, *Ichnographia rustica*, 3 vols. (London, 1718), I, xviii–xix. I have treated this topic of perspective and the three natures in 'John Evelyn's idea of the garden: a theory for all seasons', to be published in a forthcoming volume of the *Dumbarton Oaks Colloquia in Landscape Architecture* series (see note 42 above).

entitled *Curiosities of nature and art in husbandry and gardening* (*see* fig.
17.7). Here, as with the Evelyn frontispiece already considered, we
look out over a scale of human intervention – the third nature of
gardens (where, as Anthony Lawrence noted, 'a more curious diligence' is expended), then the second nature of agrarian territory
and finally the world of mountains and wastes; except that distant
world of first nature is inhabited by the very Muses through whose
visions we may be led to appreciate each nature only in relation to
the others. And to underline that essential dialogue – rather than the
formal battle, which is all modern commentators seem to see – the
whole scene is presented to us by the personifications of science,
knowledge or *teche* on the left and the plenitude of nature on the
right.

Now it is an important aspect of these ideas that – as in this
frontispiece and Evelyn's – we habitually look outwards from the
mansion, across the orderly parterres, beyond the garden 'wilderness', orchards, meadows and tillage to the wilder ground; such is
the privileged stance of culture or civilization. Because of that
privilege we have come, wrongly, to interpret this as some battle of
art and nature with art the clear champion. The usefulness of John
Beale's suggestions for the definition of a garden is that it enables us
to evade that narrow and fruitless opposition and to re-read the
same scene as a theatre where art and nature collaborate to bring
out the inherent characteristics of a given territory. Beale himself, in
the draft of a book on the pleasure garden, notes that one section will
address precisely 'in what points wee should disaffect the charges &
cumber of Art, when the productions of Nature wilbe more proper'.[56] For we could, in fact, reverse the perspective or 'royaltie of
sight': we could look back towards the mansion from the wild
hillside, which is in effect what Beale does at Backbury in Herefordshire; then we would value the hierarchies of intervention in the
landscape somewhat differently.[57] Put somewhat crudely ('for in
Hortulan noveltyes wee must bee phantasticall') – from the perspective of a modern and princely garden such as Vaux le Vicomte, the
Herefordshire hillside would seem somewhat disorderly, inchoate;

---

[56] HP 26/6/3A (section 6); and Beale adds that this precept is 'Confirmed by the excellent
conceipt of Sir Philip Sydney'.
[57] Visual examples of this before the mid-eighteenth century seem rare: but see Richard
Blome, *The gentleman's recreation* (London, 1686), plates facing 19 and 95.

by the A:De La Ville
now out of Print

Figure 17.7 Frontispiece to the *Curiosities of nature and art in husbandry*, 1710 (see note 48) [Oak Spring Garden Library, Upperville, Virginia]

from the different perspective of, say, the Derbyshire dales Backbury Hill becomes indeed a 'sweete and naturall Garden'.[58]

As the Hartlib circle traded ideas and perspectives, they enlarged the theoretical definition of a garden with an openness and flexibility that is, I think, unique and rare in garden theory. Of course, what garden design accomplished in practice was first a series of interventions in the natural world conceived from the house outwards, followed in the period of 'landscape gardening' by a complete reversal of the perspective, whereby the mansion was now viewed from the outside looking in, and the garden art immediately adjacent to it had little role to play in this new perspective. One of the difficulties for the Hartlibians was that it was virtually impossible to realize their ideas in practice: two mutually exclusive perspectives are only tenable simultaneously in the wide generosity of the mind's spaces – one cannot look through both ends of the telescope at once.

[58] HP 67/22/3B.

CHAPTER 18

'Another epocha'? Hartlib, John Lanyon and the improvement of London in the 1650s

Mark Jenner

In *The great instauration* Charles Webster states: 'Apart from the enterprise of the London hospitals, both local and national administrations performed traditional public health duties relating to street cleaning, sewers, and procedures to control epidemics, in much the same way as their Stuart predecessors.'[1] While this may well be true of the country at large, in the City of London this was not the case.

Since at least the late medieval period every householder dwelling within the capital was responsible for cleansing in front of her or his own property. The filth in the streets was to be swept up into heaps which would be removed by carters, generally known as rakers. They were paid from rates collected for this purpose by unpaid parish and ward officials, known as scavengers, who were also responsible for supervising the rakers' work.[2] On Christmas Day 1655, however, the mayor and aldermen made one John Lanyon surveyor-general of the City's streets, responsible for the removal of all ordure from the capital's thoroughfares.[3] With this agreement London's rulers rejected the methods by which the City had been cleansed for centuries. This chapter describes this scheme and the interest that Samuel Hartlib showed in it, and concludes with some suggestions as to why Hartlib should show such interest.

I am grateful to the archivists of Sheffield University and to the Hartlib Papers Project and the University of Lancaster for facilitating my visits to use the collection, and to the audiences in Sheffield who commented on earlier versions of this chapter. I am grateful to Steven Clucas, Roger Cooter, Mark Greengrass, Michael Leslie, Stephen Pumfrey, Nigel Smith, Frances Willmoth and especially Patricia Greene for their comments, suggestions and references.

[1] Webster, 300.

[2] For a fuller account of this, see M. S. R. Jenner, 'Early modern English conceptions of "cleanliness" and "dirt" as reflected in the environmental regulation of London c.1530– c.1700' (D.Phil. thesis, University of Oxford, 1991), esp, chaps. 2–3. I am currently revising this work for publication by Oxford University Press.

[3] Corporation of London Record Office (henceforth CLRO), Journal of the Common Council (henceforth Jnl.) 41, fols. 125–7.

In the spring of 1654, well before the founding of the college at
Durham in 1656 – a foundation which has been identified as the first
state encouragement of Hartlibian ideas[4] – the Lord Protector, who
had just issued an ordinance for the repair of highways, forwarded to
the City 'the proposicon of John Lanyon Esqr for cleansing the
streetes & Avenus within the late lynes of Comunicacon'. The
aldermen, 'conceiving itt a matter of Publique concernment as such
as if well ordered may redound to the Benefitt of the Cittie and
p[ar]ts adjacent', recommended that the mayor, recorder and others
consider the petition.[5] In November of that year it was recommended that Lanyon's proposals be taken up and the aldermen
passed the report to the Common Council for enactment.[6]

Lanyon roundly condemned both the condition of the City's
environment and the system by which it was maintained. The
streets, he wrote, 'grow daily more offensive wth dust & unwholsome
stenches in summer & in wett weather with dirt which occasions a
swarme of Coaches to the disturbance of the Citty'. This dirt was
washed into the sewers around the city and blocked them; the
Thames was thereby 'made dayly lesse Navigable'. The routes into
the City were encumbered with the carts which carried a fraction of
this dirt, and by continual spillages on the part of inexperienced
rakers. Finally, the laystalls to which this ordure was being carried
were 'soe neere the Citty' that they 'yield a great & contagious
stench offensive to Passengers but especially to the skirts of the
Towne' and any wind blew 'those noysome vapours into the Citty
itselfe somtimes to the increase if not the beginning of Infection'.[7]

Lanyon attributed this sorry state of affairs to ineffectual paving,
to workmen mixing mortar in the streets, to the lax sweeping of the
streets and to the insouciance with which rubbish was cast before the
inhabitants' doors. These offences were explicitly forbidden by City
law and, as he admitted, could be 'easily ... redressed'. However,
Lanyon argued that a lasting remedy was impossible while the old
system of street cleaning remained in force. Although there were
more than 500 scavengers and rakers labouring within the City, they
'either doe not understand or els take noe care of the worke'.

[4] Webster, esp. 519.
[5] CLRO Repertory of the Court of Aldermen (henceforth Rep.) 63, fol. 109v. The minutes of
the Council of State contain no mention of this, PRO SP 25/74, 75. For Cromwell's
ordinance see Firth & Rait, II, 861–9.
[6] Rep. 63, fols. 201v–204.   [7] CLRO Alchin Box 0/LXXVII/4: Proposals of John Lanyon.

Scavengers were 'generally tradesmen & know nothing of this Imployment'. Having made the contract with the rakers at the beginning of their term of office, they simply collected the rates in the hours that could be spared from business and reckoned themselves to have escaped lightly if they lost only five or ten pounds during their year of service. Rakers were similarly unprofessional. Their payment from rates was not sufficient and they had to 'imploy their carts otherwise'. Generally they carted building materials into the City and carried out street soil, but they would leave this behind if a more profitable load was available. What they had taken up in one precinct they often dropped in another, as 'there is not any that do superintend this worke'.

Lanyon cast himself in this supervisory role. He would 'make it his . . . sole imployment to doe this worke', taking partners to advise and assist him. He would ensure that most soil would be carried away by water rather than through the suburbs, that all laws about sweeping the streets and such like would be observed and that every day the waste would be carried away in covered carts so that 'all the annoyances & inconveniences above . . . menconed will be . . . absolutely prevented'.

In return, he desired to receive the rates at present collected by the scavengers and the fines levied upon those who failed to maintain their pavements. He asked for no money until he had performed his tasks for three months even though he 'must be constrained constantly to imploy a stock of some thousands of pounds'. As 'the charge of this worke will for many yeares farre exceed the money to bee collected or raised by the soyle', Lanyon requested that he be granted the contract for thirty-one years.[8]

The Common Council argued long and hard over these proposals. On one occasion, debate proceeded only on the casting vote of the lord mayor, Sir Christopher Pack. Finally however, in December 1654 it was agreed that Lanyon was to begin work on 25 March 1655.[9] However, Lanyon did not commence his duties as initially planned because the Corporation of the Poor intervened and delayed his undertaking. The Corporation, which was always short of money, saw a possible profit in this enterprise and offered to undertake all that Lanyon had agreed to do.

Protracted debates revealed worries that the Corporation of the

[8] *Ibid.*   [9] Jnl. 41, fols. 111, 111v–112v, 113–113v.

Poor might not be able legally to undertake such an enterprise and on 11 September 1655 the Common Council enacted that Lanyon should become surveyor-general of the streets after all, provided he pay £500 per annum to the Corporation.[10] An indenture was drawn up between him and the City and was sealed once he had found sureties for a £1,000 bond to guarantee the agreement.[11]

This sequence of events indicates that Valerie Pearl was mistaken when she described the centralization of street cleaning in 1655 as an 'attempt to run an industrial undertaking on behalf of the poor' and wrote that the plan was proposed by the Corporation of the Poor and then 'contracted out to ... John Lanyon'.[12] However, the connection she identified between members of the city government, Hartlib and social reformers associated with him, does provide a context for the enterprise.

Hartlib's commonplace book reveals not only that this scheme was being advanced several years before it left any mark in the records of the Corporation or Council of State but also that he and his circle took great interest in the undertaking. In January 1650 the puritan alderman, Thomas Andrewes, told Hartlib that 'One undertakes for the allowances that now scavengers have or far cheaper to doe whatever they had done, and moreover to keepe the whole City as cleane as never yet it hath beene. This propos[ition] was made by the new Lord Mayor Foot to the Court of Aldermen'.[13] It is probable that this projector was Lanyon, for by 1653 Hartlib was noting his scheme with keen anticipation. 'About a h[u]n[d]r[e]d y[ears] agoe', he wrote,

the streetes of London and Paris were first paved. If the cleansing of the Citty goe forward, this may be another Epocha. But then it may be not before a 100 y[ears] hence an other publick Work will be countenanced or promoted. But if this goe forward it may be that it may proove an other leading example of the present promoting of some other publick works,

[10] Jnl. 41, fols. 121v, 123–125. The Act was printed, *An Act of Common Council made the eleventh day of September ... 1655. For the better avoiding and prevention of annoyances within the city of London and the liberties of the same* (London, 1655).

[11] Jnl. 41, fols. 125–127; Rep. 63, fol. 434v; Alchin MS o/LXXVII/6. Lanyon put up £300 personally, the wealthy scrivener, Robert Yarway, £200, while William Chamberleine, Thomas White, Thomas Hampton, Edward Dodd and John Kent put up £100 apiece.

[12] V. Pearl, 'Puritans and poor relief', in *Puritans and revolutionaries*, ed. D. Pennington and K. V. Thomas (Oxford, 1978), 228.

[13] *Ephemerides* (1650): HP 28/1/64A; HP 28/1/43A–B. During 1650 the Council of State was sponsoring a bill in Parliament for repair of highways within the lines of communication and, in particular, to the east of the city: *CSPD 1650*, 5, 31, 375; *Commons Journals*, VI, 483–6, 488, 502, 529.

Magistrates and People being encouraged by the successe applause and reception of that.

Slightly later the same year Hartlib noted how it

was 30. or 40. Y[*ears*] before the Art of making of Cloth came to any progresse or perfection in Engl[*and*] it being brought hither out of Flanders ... So a hund[*red*] y[*ears*] agoe was Paris et Lond[*on*] first paved, and now Lond[*on*] is to bee cleansed by Lanio[*n*], and it's hoped the light of good Inv[*entions*] will faster advance for time to come.[14]

Why did Hartlib discuss this scheme in such enthusiastic, indeed, providential terms? Firstly, Lanyon was not simply an entrepreneur of whom Hartlib had high hopes. He was an active projector whose schemes the *Ephemerides* followed with assiduity. In 1651 he showed Hartlib's son 'a Catalogue of the Heads ... of all his Inventio[*n*]s and Exp[*e*]rim[*ents*] w[*hi*]ch amounted to 57 or 75', including 'Portable Boates and the feeding of Carps in a Cellar without any water for a whole y[*ear*]'. In this and following years, Hartlib noted more devices such as 'a great Designe to make out of English Iron and Tinn ... your Lattin-Plates in Engl[*and*]' and an improved form of awl, a prototype of which was made by the skilful London smith, Mr Owefield.[15]

Moreover, like others in Hartlib's circle of acquaintance, Lanyon acted as a conduit relaying information about technical and agricultural developments in the Low Countries in which he had travelled (and where the cities were also renowned for their cleanliness).[16] In 1651 the *Ephemerides* noted that Lanyon was 'making a Modell of the rare Water-mill at Brussels' and recorded the projector's arguments in favour of industrial espionage. 'It is as good an Invention', Lanyon apparently maintained,

to observe ... all manner of ... useful th[*ing*]s invented and practised already in other Countries as to Invent truly New ones. For the former are without any peradventure at all wheras the other are yet subject to many

---

[14] *Ephemerides* (1653): HP 28/2/50B, 52B. It is unclear where Lanyon derived this entirely erroneous chronology of London and Paris street paving, for London was paved long before the mid-sixteenth century.

[15] *Ephemerides* (1651): HP 28/2/10B; (1653): HP 28/2/56B; HP 28/2/14B–16A. See also e.g. *Ephemerides* (1653): HP 28/2/60, 69A–B. Owefield does not seem to have been in the Blacksmiths' Company, Guildhall Library (henceforth GL) MS 2884.

[16] The draft of Lanyon's contract noted that his scheme was based on 'his observacon in his Travell beyond the seas and his sole and peculiar industry here at home' (CLRO Alchin MS o/LXXVII/5). For the Dutch reputation for urban cleanliness, see S. Schama, *The embarrassment of riches* (London, 1987), 375–9.

uncertainties or seeming difficulties. Much more then are such Apodemical Observations to bee p[re]ferred before all those plausible or m[ore] rational Attempts, wh[ic]h consist only in a bare Idaea or airy notion.[17]

Hartlib concluded *The compleat husbandman* with 'Mr. Lanyon's Description of the usuall planting and transplanting (according to that of Flaunders) of those Trees called Abeales'.[18]

More generally, Hartlib's interest in urban cleanliness was not an aberration. By this I do not just mean that 'to kleanse' was one of the sixteen words whose 'Radicall Characters' he listed at the end of his 1647 text, *A common writing*.[19] In a lengthy memorandum among Hartlib's papers, the inventor William Wheeler undertook (among many other things) to drain and cleanse London's streets.[20] Hartlib also noted the undertaking of one 'Bressieux ... for cleansing Amsterdam and freeing it from all stinking waters',[21] and collected two copies of the advertisement of one Richard Wolsely of Whitefriars, who claimed to be able to cleanse privies without emptying them by turning the excrement to dust and thus avoiding any offensive smell.[22] More generally, of course, Hartlib's paeans to the benefits of manure would have encouraged Lanyon's sale of urban street sweepings.[23]

Moreover, John Dury emphasized that the governors of his 'Reformed School' had responsibility for the cleanliness of their pupils as well as their diet, exercise and sleep. Children, he wrote,

must be taught Cleanliness without Curiosity; and made in love with it, as it is usefull for Health; in which respect the Care of it must be recommended to them. 1) in their feeding, that through greediness they eat or drink nothing that is nasty. 2) in their Body, head hands feet and clothing; that they keep themselves from filthiness of sweat, from vermine, and other uncleanness. 3) in their Chamber that they defile it not with stench, or suffer it to be unswept; but that they keep it clean and sweet with refreshment of aire.[24]

---

[17] *Ephemerides* (1651): HP 28/2/14B and 15B. For the mill, see also HP 28/2/18A.
[18] S. Hartlib, *The compleat husbandman* (London, 1659), 82.
[19] S. Hartlib, *A common writing* (London, 1647), 31. [20] HP 63/2/2B–3A.
[21] *Ephemerides* (1656): HP 29/5/96A. Bressieux was an 'opticall workman' of whom Oldenburg had mixed opinions, although he also noted that he had worked for Descartes for two years: Oldenburg, I, 270, 327, 329. In 1660 Hartlib wrote enthusiastically about his optical glass: Chetham's Library, Manchester, Allen MS s373 (20 August 1660).
[22] HP 31/9/1A–B; HP 53/40A–B.
[23] Lanyon was to sell the street sweepings of London at no more than 8d a load: CLRO Jnl. 41, fol. 126.
[24] J. Dury, *The reformed school* (London, 1650), 31.

Furthermore, the imagery of cleanliness obviously carried a range of metaphorical meanings which were highly consonant with Hartlib's general philosophy. Comenius' *Patterne of universal knowledge*, for instance, expressed the hope that 'all the rivulats of thoughts and actions being reduced to their true and pure fountains ... they may acknowledge that they do agree, the ... filthinesse ... mixt therewith being now left out'.[25] The hortulan and agricultural texts associated with his circle dwelt on the sweet odours reminiscent of the Garden of Eden which improvement would produce. Similarly, improved civic hygiene was a common feature of early modern utopian writing. Streams of water ran through every street of the city in Andreae's *Christianopolis*, for instance, carrying away the 'daily accumulations' from every house.[26]

Although it is initially tempting to link this undertaking with wider concerns about the moral reformation of the capital, this plan to clean up London cannot easily be identified with any design to create a purified new Jerusalem.[27] Hartlib described Lanyon as a 'very Metallical' gentleman living with his wife and children in an Essex country house some twelve miles from the capital; he never mentioned that Lanyon had placed his metalworking skills at the disposal of Charles I.[28] At the Restoration Lanyon successfully petitioned for a royal pension, declaring that he had 'indured all the hardships incident to such as have loyally ... adhered to yor Sacred Majestie in the whole course of yor late sufferings', including sequestration.[29] He had been proposing inventions since the 1630s; in April 1633, Charles I responded to a petition in which Lanyon described inventions he had made in dyeing and in devising a substitute for lead suitable for roofing and water pipes, by granting him a licence to re-export blockwood.[30] Like other projectors and mathematical men, Lanyon became involved in gunnery[31] and

25 J. Comenius, *A patterne of universal knowledge*, trans. J. Collier (London, 1651), 6–7. See also J. Neuwirth, 'Comenius and the plague in Leszno', in *Homage to J. A. Comenius* (Prague, 1991), 105–11, esp. 109.

26 M. Eliav-Feldon, *Realistic Utopias* (Oxford, 1982), 33–41.

27 There were, however, other exactly contemporary proposals to improve London's fabric. In 1655 the Bricklayers set out a paper propounding the benefits of brick buildings: CLRO Alchin MS o/LXXVII/3.

28 *Ephemerides* (1651): HP 28/2/15A.

29 PRO SP 29/36/55, 551. Lanyon does not appear in the sequestration papers for Essex: PRO SP 28/209B.

30 PRO SP 16/236/70, SP 16/310/64. The latter is wrongly assigned to 1635 in *CSPD*.

31 A. Rupert Hall, 'Gunnery, science, and the Royal Society', in *The uses of science in the age of Newton*, ed. J. G. Burke (Berkeley, Los Angeles and London, 1983), 111–42; F. Willmoth,

although I have found no link between him and the royal ordnance factory developed at Vauxhall by the marquis of Worcester, in 1638 he was made a proof-master of arms.[32] Viscount Conway employed him to purchase books and horses for him in Flanders.[33] Lanyon served in Scotland in 1639, and in the spring of 1640 was despatched to Flanders to prove and procure arms for royal service,[34] indulging in some private enterprise on the side.[35] He brought the king a shipload of arms from London during the first siege of Hull and served as Charles I's gun-founder in Oxford.[36] Lanyon died, apparently intestate, in 1662.[37]

Further evidence about the ideological complexion of the undertaking can be gathered from the identity of the people with whom Lanyon formed a partnership to finance the enterprise. The available evidence does not indicate whether any of these people shared Lanyon's interests – whether they knew Hartlib, for instance – but it gives rare information about the people prepared to put up money in such a scheme.

The most important of the partners was a London scrivener, Robert Yarway, who would eventually take over the enterprise. Yarway was wealthy, supposedly leaving 'greate quantities of very ... rich goods Chattels plate ... and ... greate summes of ready moneyes' at the time of his death in 1665.[38] To judge by the numerous Chancery suits in which he was involved, Yarway was none too scrupulous. Bulstrode Whitelocke thought that he had been swindled by him. He dealt extensively in property, but made

'"The Genius of all Arts" and the use of instruments: Jonas Moore (1617–1679) as a mathematician, surveyor and astronomer', *Annals of Science*, 48 (1991), 355–65; S. Johnston, 'Mathematical practitioners and instruments in Elizabethan England', *Annals of Science*, 48 (1991), 319–44.

[32] Cambridge University Library MS mn-2-2, fol. 87. See also fols. 4–4v, 65–65v, 66v, 67v, 81v, 114v, 133v–134. For the Vauxhall factory, see Webster, 347–8 and 363–5. Also the marquis of Worcester, *Century of inventions* (London, 1663).

[33] *CSPD 1638–1639*, 589; PRO SP 16/415/2.

[34] *CSPD 1639*, 164–5; *CSPD 1639–1640*, 375, 416, 419, 499, 559, 605; *CSPD 1640–1641*, 118; PRO E 351/2712.

[35] *CSPD 1640*, 309, 359, 654; *CSPD 1640–1641*, 13–14, 248, and 317; *CSPD 1641–1643*, 263.

[36] PRO SP 29/36/55; C. Russell, 'The First Army plot of 1641', *Transactions of the Royal Historical Society*, 5th series, 38 (1988), 95–6; *The Royalist Ordnance Papers 1642–1646*, ed. I. Roy, *Oxfordshire Record Society*, 43 (1964) and 49 (1971–3), 28, 259, 473, 482.

[37] CLRO Mayor's Court (Equity) Bills of Complaint and Answers Box 22 (*Juxon v. Yarway*, Bill of Complaint). He had, however, regained his post of proof-master: H. C. Tomlinson, *Guns and government: the Ordnance Office under the later Stuarts* (London, 1979), 236.

[38] PRO C 7/470/18. The answers to this Bill of Complaint suggest that Yarway had few household goods and may have been in financial difficulties at the time of his death: C 7/490/26.

his fortune as a scrivener, lending out money on a large scale, on one occasion to a Wealden ironworks.[39] While Yarway was clearly well known to the rulers of Cromwellian London,[40] he may have had royalist sympathies; he was prepared to administer the affairs of sequestered Cavaliers while concealing their identity.[41]

Another of Lanyon's partners, Joseph Ash, was almost certainly royalist in sympathies. He spent the Civil War abroad, but in 1651 was examined before the Council of State for corresponding with the king and his party, and was made a baronet in 1660 for services to the royal family.[42] Lanyon's other known associates and partners are more elusive. Several were, like Ash, involved in East India trade and one was lent money by Yarway,[43] but despite a search of company, parish and testamentary records, I have been unable to discover any further information about their religious or political affiliations.

Lanyon and his associates clearly did not have an unambiguous political or religious position during the 1650s. His proposal was couched in straightforward and perhaps deliberately uncontroversial terms, stressing the benefit to public health, Thames navigation and utility with no mention of religion or morality. If anything, the partners of the undertaking seem to have been royalist in sympathy but were clearly prepared to co-operate with the established powers. Their political and religious backgrounds were comparable with other intellectuals and projectors whose careers Hartlib followed with interest during the 1640s and 1650s. Balthazar Gerbier, for instance, the education reformer, had been Charles I's art buyer in the 1630s.[44] Hartlib also commented on the technical ingenuity

---

39 PRO C 7/423/91; C 7/426/125; C 10/20/135 (this contains allegations of particularly deceitful conduct); C 10/72/170; 10/74/104; 10/487/302 (the ironworks). Bulstrode Whitelocke dealt with him and felt he was cheated: *The diary of Bulstrode Whitelocke*, ed. R. Spalding (Oxford, 1990), 468 and 620.

40 See e.g. the depositions in PRO C 24/839 Part 1 (*Yarway v. Colt*).

41 PRO C 10/74/104 and 24/890 Part 1 (*Abisse v. Yarway*). The best account of the business of the mid-seventeenth-century scrivener is T. Melton, *Sir Robert Clayton and the origins of English deposit banking, 1658–1685* (Cambridge, 1986), chaps. 2–3.

42 For a biography of Ash, see *The House of Commons 1660–90*, ed. B. D. Hemming, 3 vols. (London, 1983), I, 556–7. His brother was a Cromwellian and sat on the Committee for Compounding and appears to have served on the Committee for Trade; *Ephemerides* (1650): HP 28/1/79A.

43 *A calendar of court minutes of the East India Company 1635–59*, ed. E. B. Sainsbury and W. Foster, 5 vols. (Oxford, 1907–16), III, 254; IV, 156, 162, 223; V, 105, 113, 150, 226, 270, 346; PRO C 10/74/104. See also Jenner, 'Early modern English conceptions of "cleanliness"', 278–80.

44 For Hartlib's contacts with Gerbier, see Webster, 219–20 and HP 10/2/47A–60B. For further bibliographical information on Gerbier, see H. R. Williamson, *Four Stuart portraits*

of Sir Edward Ford, a sequestered royalist who nevertheless married a sister of John and Henry Ireton, and seems to have been pleased when the latter gained a patent from Cromwell for the construction of waterworks in Wapping and the west end of London.[45]

I would argue that Hartlib was enthusiastic about Lanyon's scheme, not because of shared religious sentiments, or for reasons of irenicism, but primarily because it might demonstrate the possibility of transforming society through technical innovations. As he wrote in 1653, 'it may proove an other leading example of the present promoting of ... publick works'.[46] Such a search for concrete examples of successful innovation reveals how insubstantial and vulnerable Hartlib's proposals could appear in mid-seventeenth-century England.

Most of the recent historiography around Hartlib has been heroic and adulatory in tone, seeing him either as an antecedent of the welfare state or fitting him into a teleology that culminates with the Royal Society and 'modern science'. To date, there have not been discussions of the relationship between his ideas and his marginal social position in the style of Stephen Pumfrey and Steven Shapin's discussions of Hooke.[47] Many scholars have shown how, in the late seventeenth century, natural philosophy and the experimental method were subjected to telling intellectual and theological critiques by Hobbes, South and others,[48] and to wounding ridicule by Swift, Shadwell and *The Transactioneer*.[49] Charles II was far from

---

(London, 1949), 26–60. In 1661 he proposed schemes to clean up London; see Jenner, 'Early modern English conceptions of "cleanliness"', 283–4.

[45] HP 26/51/1; HP 29/5/15A–B; HP 29/5/22B; HP 29/5/33A; *Ephemerides* (1656): HP 29/5/56B; (1657): HP 29/6/4B, 29/6/5B; HP 51/31A. For Ford's waterworks, see Rhys Jenkins, 'A chapter in the history of the water supply of London', *Transactions of the Newcomen Society*, 9 (1928–9), 43–51. I intend to discuss his career in greater detail in a forthcoming publication.

[46] *Ephemerides* (1653): HP 28/2/50B.

[47] S. Pumfrey, 'Ideas above his station: a social study of Hooke's curatorship of experiments', *History of Science*, 29 (1991), 1–44; S. Shapin, 'Who was Robert Hooke?', in *Robert Hooke. New studies*, ed. M. Hunter and S. Schaffer (Woodbridge, 1989), 253–83.

[48] E.g. S. Shapin and S. Schaffer, *Leviathan and the air pump* (Princeton, 1985); L. Stewart, *The rise of public science: rhetoric, technology, and natural philosophy in Newtonian Britain* (Cambridge, 1992). There are strong parallels between my arguments in the section below and those in Stewart's study, which I read only after completing this chapter.

[49] M. Nicolson and N. M. Mohler, 'Swift's "Flying Island" in the *Voyage to Laputa*', *Annals of Science*, 2 (1937), 299–334; P. Rogers, 'Gulliver and the engineers', *Modern Language Notes*, 70 (1975), 260–70; T. Shadwell, *The virtuoso*, ed. M. H. Nicolson and D. S. Rodes (London, 1966); J. M. Levine, *Dr. Woodward's shield* (Berkeley, Los Angeles and London, 1977), 85.

untypical when he laughed at the Royal Society for wasting their time on inconsequential activities such as weighing air.[50]

By contrast, modern commentators have stressed what they have claimed was the essential practicality of Hartlib and his associates, without noting that many of their proposals were potentially risible and were often in danger of collapsing under the weight of their own grandiloquent pretensions.[51] Hartlib's pamphlet, *Cornu-copia*, for instance, presents a string of fantastic invocations of fructification and profit worthy of Sir Epicure Mammon in Jonson's *Volpone*.[52] Andrew Mendelsohn has recently noted how the alchemical epilogue to *Chymical addresses* exposed Hartlib to Jonsonian satire.[53]

On occasions it is difficult to distinguish between the schemes that Hartlib followed so avidly and parodies of projection. In 1654, for instance, the *Ephemerides* noted that you could clear a room of fleas by placing a bowl of warm horse piss under your bed; Hartlib noted Lanyon's invention by which 'Ten or m[*ore*] armed men may ... go invisible into any fort or castle', his 'Invent[*ion*] of shutting of doores', and his 'boate to goe without oares with certain wheeles turned by a dog'; he passed on to Pell an account of a portable machine far smaller than any crane which could lift 120,000lb up 100 yards while also employing few men to operate it.[54]

The projectors who could feed capons on carrot scrapings, build a ship to sail against the winds,[55] construct a new theatre on barges floating on the Thames,[56] or reclaim vast acreages from the sea would not look out of place in this company.[57] Yet they are satiric portraits taken from the plays of Shirley, Brome and Jonson. Similarly, among the projects that Thomas Brugis itemized in order to ridicule in his 1641 pamphlet, *The discovery of a proiector*, was a 'new Art ... to plant great store of Fruit trees in this Kingdome, which

[50] *The diary of Samuel Pepys*, ed. R. C. Latham and W. Matthews, 11 vols. (London, 1970–83), v, 33. See also M. H. Nicolson, *Pepys' diary and the new science* (Charlottesville, 1965).

[51] E.g. Webster, 494–7, esp. 495.   [52] *Cornu-copia; a miscellanium* (London, 1652?).

[53] J. A. Mendelsohn, 'Alchemy and politics in England 1649–1665', *Past and Present*, 135 (1992), 52.

[54] *Ephemerides* (1654): HP 29/4/24A; (1651): HP 28/2/12A; (1652): HP 28/2/34A, 28/2/32A; BL Add. MS 4429, fols. 389–90.

[55] J. Shirley, *The triumph of peace* (first performed in 1634), ed. C. Leech, in *A book of masques in honour of Allardyce Nicoll* (Cambridge, 1967), 292–3.

[56] R. Brome, *The court begger*, in *The dramatic works of Richard Brome*, 3 vols. (London, 1873), I, 194.

[57] *The Devil is an ass*, in *Ben Jonson*, ed. C. H. Herford and E. and P. Simpson, 11 vols. (Oxford, 1925–52), VI, 185–9.

would arise to twelve hundred thousand pounds per annum',[58] a scheme that uncannily anticipated the horticultural and arboreal ambitions of Hartlib, Beale and Evelyn.[59] Much Hartlibian discourse was as open to parody as the pretensions of a quack's pamphlet. Moreover, as Martin Butler has emphasized, there were many attacks on projectors as monopolists in the early 1640s; invention continued to have a very mixed reputation in the Interregnum press.[60] In November 1653, for instance, *Mercurius politicus* reported that 'the wondrous ship that hath bin so long a building' was being launched in Rotterdam and listed the many wonders it supposedly could perform. In April the following year the same paper gleefully reported 'that the French Engineer who had so long filled all men with admiration and expectation' about this vessel 'is now run away, having cheated some, but deceived all'.[61]

Consequently, it seems likely that Hartlib was aware of the need to find examples with which to demonstrate the feasibility of his ambitious schemes. On at least one occasion he altered reports to make them appear more categorical than they actually were, and he often indulged in argument by association.[62] In 1650, for instance, he hailed a new fire engine shown off in London as something 'to stop the mouth of railers ag[ainst] new Inventions every body being too prone to observe their miscarriage, but very few when they ... serviceable'.[63] I would suggest that he saw in Lanyon's undertaking to cleanse London a similarly convincing example to invoke when seeking to win over sceptical patrons and investors. The political and religious complexion of inventors was less important in this context than public acclaim for their achievements. Hartlib's

---

[58] T. Brugis, *The discovery of a proiector* (London, 1641), 21. This pamphlet was recycled in dramatic form: J. Wilson, *The projectors. A comedy* (London, 1665).

[59] See e.g. *Culture and cultivation in early modern England*, ed. M. Leslie and T. Raylor (Leicester, 1992).

[60] M. Butler, *Theatre and crisis 1632–1642* (Cambridge, 1984), 212, 214, 222, 227, 229–33, 240. In addition to Brugis, note 58 above, see T. Heywood, *Machiavel. As he lately appeared to his deare sons, the moderne proiectores* (London, 1641).

[61] *Mercurius politicus*, no. 180 (17–24 November 1653) and no. 215 (20–7 July 1654). Facsimile reprint in *The English Revolution III Newsbooks 5*, 19 vols. (London, 1971–2), VIII, 98–9; IX, 254–5. Many satires of the 1630s remained current during the Civil War and Interregnum. Brome's satires of projectors, for instance, gained added currency from the publication of his collected plays in 1653, while booksellers continued to advertise Jonson's *Devil is an ass* throughout the Interregnum; Hereford and Simpson (eds.), *Ben Jonson*, VI, 148.

[62] T. Raylor, 'Samuel Hartlib and the commonwealth of bees', in Leslie and Raylor (eds.) *Culture and cultivation*, 120–1, n. 31.

[63] *Ephemerides* (1650): HP 28/1/42A.

method might be said to decontextualize the work of individuals such as Ford or Lanyon in order to reinscribe them and their work within his own millenarian and Baconian framework. His network of correspondents and his *Ephemerides* can thus be compared with many contemporary commonplace books; they were accumulations of disparate or even contradictory opinion and reports, which provided a flexible resource to be drawn on for disputation and self-presentation.[64] They might have been inconsistent, but they were also a treasure trove of projects and exempla from which arguments could be marshalled in order to convince the Council of State or the burghers of London.

Moreover, the capital was the perfect arena for such a display of practical benefit. It was from London that Hartlib gained much of his information: from the *Ephemerides* it is clear that he ransacked the commercial and artisanal culture of the capital for innovation in medicine and technology. And it was in the context of the capital that he and his circle sought to justify their innovations: Cressy Dymock supported his claims for improvements in mills by reference to the windmills on Moorfields, and Hartlib listed the Court of Aldermen and the Common Council as two of the bodies to whom inventors should give notice of their work.[65] Furthermore, the City's buildings served as a backdrop for the theatrical demonstration of new works. London Bridge, for instance, featured in the presentation of a variety of inventions in which Hartlib expressed an interest. In 1636, for instance, he noted an invention 'how both greater & smaller boates may safely . . . passe through the Arches of London bridge, whether the water be Ebbinge and flowinge', while in the early 1650s Petty took part in an experiment of 'blowing a boy or boat over London bridge'.[66] Furthermore, Lanyon's undertaking shared many characteristics with other contemporary schemes to improve and to centralize the regulation of London's life and local government, in which Hartlib was interested. These included the Corporation of the Poor, and plans to reorganize London's militia and fire-fighting capacity upon regimented and centralized lines.[67]

It is striking that Hartlib never mentioned Lanyon's enterprise

---

[64] See A. Blair, 'Humanism and the commonplace book', *Journal of the History of Ideas*, 53 (1992), 541–52.

[65] C. Dymock, *An invention of engines of motion* (London, 1651), 4–5; *Ephemerides* (1653): HP 28/2/50B–51A.

[66] BL Add. MS 4429, fol. 391v; Webster, 155.

[67] Pearl, 'Puritans and poor relief'; HP 57/4/4A; HP 31/19/1A–2B; HP 63/15/1A–2B.

after it had actually got off the drawing-board. His silence may well have been politic, for this attempt at the privatization of refuse disposal was a disaster. The scheme was bedevilled by the tensions between the undertaking and the local officials who were supposed to collect the rates. Lanyon and his partners had repeatedly to invest more money and on one occasion were obliged to relaunch the enterprise completely. Their work never came up to scratch and occasioned repeated complaints. In December 1656, for instance, the wardmote inquest of St Dunstan's in the West presented Lanyon 'for not keeping the streets cleane according to covenant'; and the inquestmen of Cornhill protested that through his negligence 'the highe streete ... and other places in the ... ward lyeth very dirtie and noysome'.[68] For their part, the partners repeatedly complained that the rates they were owed were not being collected. Shortly after the Restoration the situation came to a head and Lanyon (who had by now returned to royal service) surrendered his interest in the scheme in favour of Robert Yarway. The scrivener's confidence in his ability to run the enterprise was misplaced. By September 1661 the streets were said to be 'lyinge ... Dirty and Noysome beyond Example to the great slander and dishonour of the Government of this Citty' and Charles II had complained about them. In December 1661, the City concluded that Londoners should return to the 'old way and manner' of cleaning the streets.[69] In this case, at least, there was to be no new 'epocha'.

[68] GL MS 3018/1, fol. 139v; MS 4069/2, fol. 271.
[69] For fuller documentation of Yarway's failure, see Jenner, 'Early modern English conceptions of "cleanliness"', 236–7, 239–40, 281–2.

Appendix

COPY IN A SCRIBAL HAND OF A LETTER FROM JOHN BEALE,
PROBABLY TO JOHN EVELYN, 30 SEPTEMBER 1659
HP 67/22/1A–4B

[*67/22/1A*]

September 30.–59

Honoured Sir

Yours of September 21. I have received, & doe most cheerefully embrace this noble & friendly commerce, both for your owne Worth & as part of my manifold engagements to my dearest friend Mr. Hartlib. And now by the specimen of particulars as allso formerly by the fullnes of the Proplasma.[1] I playnely discerne, that you are plentifully provided of those Moderne Helpes of which I confest my selfe destitute. And therefore I have written to my friend (to whom my weake & imperfect delineations were in a manner preengaged) to obtaine their leave, to make this best & proper use of mine, that they may offer such hints, or advertisements, as may bee improved by your more happy compilements for the publiqve. And hence foorth I must deale with you in the manner of the old Philosophers, rather bluntly & honestly, than qvaintly & superficially: Namely, vpon this covenant, that you will resolve to receive my irregularityes with patience, & rather expect something which was not in your owne thoughts, then a servile & affected compliance, with received notions. As you give mee this freedome, so you are at Liberty to caste aside impertinencyes; And your only losse, will be the losse of time; And because that is noe small losse you may support it with this

---

[1] Beale is referring to the outline of the *Elysium Britannicum*, which Evelyn had begun circulating in the late 1650s.

357

comfort, That lesse time is lost by takeing notice of vnexpected advertisements, then by the importunity of that which is evry mans opinion, & which comes from all hande. And Hortulane affaires doe reqvire varietyes of novell & conceited amoenityes. I intend to urge you to adde 6 or 7 chapters more, than I doe yet discerne in the Proplasma. One is of Entertainements intended, as it were scenically, to shewe the riches, beauty, wonders, plenty, & delight of a Garden festivall, of which I gave a touch in my laste of very rude Latine to Mr. Hartlib. In this I shall propose Musicall instruments of a newe mode, yet resembling ancient simplicity, & exceeding all the Qvires of Italy, or Europe, either for free pleasure, or for sacred solemnity: et the charges but a triefle. Another Chapter meerely of transmutation of flowers, & improving their small beauty, & taste. Of this (if I have leave) I will give you the sure, & infallible elements & rules; & mine shall not bee hidden under the coverture of riddles, [*catchword*: vapours] [*67/22/1B*] vapours, & [*riggling?*] pretences, but reall, naturall & cleare. Another of Mounts, Prospects, Precipices, & Caves, of which, & some other matters, which will take vp full chapters. I must not now declare my meaning, till I can, (at full) shewe you what it importeth. But that you may noe longer charge mee of Modesty, I bid you expect some very strange discourses. For I shall offer you Enchanted Walkes, Pyrhian, Vaults, Legislative Mountains; The Hills of blessings, of curseings; the Muses Fountaine; but I must stop. I here put you in mind, That hortulane amoenityes may sometimes bee soe representet to you, that you dare not absolutely deny them, or blaste them; nor yet can with gravity avouch them. In these cases, you may sometimes interweave a discourse, as it were of interlocutors: not altogether scenically, or theatrically, but as you see done by that ancient & grave Romane Varro, & especially in the hortulane entertainement lately mentioned in the Latine Lettre. For I have some things to say supra fidem, yet I knowe them experimentally to be true. For such I would not prostitute my reputation, but leave evry man to judge according to his pallate, & the measure of his apprehension & capacity. Sometimes I shall offer such magnificent & yet unchergeable, yea lucrative designes, as shall rectify & purify the ogre of all the neighbouring Countrey, both for health of body & of minde; to præpare & dispose for vertue, & for sanctity; & to procure longevity. Yea to correct the Stars & to alter that which wee call the coelestiall influences. Can you hence foorth charge mee of overmuch modesty?

yet I must advance, & that you may expect Elysian raptures, This I undertake, that by reviving old Monuments I will propose: An Antique Garden, (meaning that which was anciently understood by the Words Hortus, Κηπος, όρχατος, παραδυσος, That by the luckines of situation, shall as much excell most of the rest of those moderne Gardens, which you have listed; as the Patriarches, Prophets, & true Heroes of the old World doe excell the puppet playes of our circumforaneous Agyrtæ. A good part of this Magnificence may (at small charges) bee performed at Greenewich. Most of it at Windsore: Much of it at Woodstoe; but noe where to perfection, without a reall, & lofty hill, prominent, or neighbouring over a river, & kind Vale, with parkes & lawnes, fayre boscage, or spacious [*catchword*: forrest] [67/22/2A] forrest. Thiese appendances are necessary, & cannot bee supplyed by those Vepreta, & poore mimicall though sometimes chargeable mounts & wildernesses which are enforced. If this bee not serious truth, let it nowe passe for an Antiqve enterlude. And as if it were to debate the Qvestion, & to enqvire the old sense of those words, & the definition of a Garden, & the ground of your Title, if you insiste vpon it; & as to the Enqviry, what sort of Trees, or what approach of trees may bee allowed for the Ornament of the flowry regions, & to determine, whether Viridaria, Vireta, Walkes, Mounds, groves & Prospects bee the Principall, or ought to bee soe, & the flowry area but the trimmings (as spires, pilasters, & carvd Workes in sollide Architecture); to debate whether the one, or the other bee the principall, & for such other matters conteind in most chapters of your first booke, I would take vp such a Viewe, as can bee had of Paradyse, & the most famous & most ancient Horti: In a following chapter (as if you would frame your spirit to write somewhat heartily on both sides, & leave it to the reader to please himselfe in his choice) you may recount the Moderne Gardens, to see which will bee the foyle to the other. I told you that I find my selfe fitter to doe you some service in the former chapter than in the latter. And though I am fully convinced, that God hath in later dayes very amply improvd our knoweledge, & hath given vs the Light of many very wonderfull experiments. Yet I may make bold to thinke, that Gods owne handyworke, the first Paradyse did farr exceede our Moderne Gardens: And (as if our Ancestors by Tradition continued some of the Gardens of the first Monarchy were more Magnificent, & more Heroicall; I may say, more Divine, then can bee parallelld by our narrowe, mimicall way. Having hardned you nowe to beare my immodesty, I will illustrate my Heterodoxe notions by specifying one small seate in this neighbour hood. It seemes the old Britains, the silures, or the Romanes, were very active in raysing many strong holds in this Mountanous neighbour hood of Walles; & their Princes, or chiefe commanders, were seated vpon our highest Hills. King Offa, & King Ethelbert upon Sutton hill nowe belonging to Sir H. Lingen. Another on Dinder hill, neere [*catchword*: Rother] [*67/22/2B*] Rotherwas, of Mr Bodenham: Another on Wall hill neere Ledbury. I single out the lesse famous hill called Backbury, hanging over Priours Courte, the inheritance of Mr Herbert Price his Nephewe; one Bridges nowe lives there. This commonly reputed about 100lb yearely. This is my paradoxe. If I might choose the lands that lye about it to the Valewe of 100lb yearely, adding both together (yea, I dare allmost vndertake it of this 100lb yearely alone): that (as it nowe lyes) for one hunderd pound, I would make it a fayrer Garden then many of those Princely Modern Gardens, that are in your liste. I except the charges of Architecture, conteining Walls, Statues, Summer-houses, Cesternes &c (which may bee of vaste charge) & I except the charge of Plants, & workemanship in setting the Plants; & I would take vpon mine owne charge the forming of all the bankes, walkes, sqvares, or other figures for flowres, vineyards, Myrteta, Laureta, Vepreta, Cupresseta, hedges of all sorts, for fruite, fragrancy &c. Iudge nowe howe much by the neere situation I am assisted. The Mount is of vaste height, Millions of Men & money could not easily rayse such a Mount. The ascent is nowe by severall wayes, some more obstepe, some by more gentle degrees by windings, & there are freqvent rest for our second advise, that one may alter his choice, to ascend more directly, or to take his gentle round, as hee pleaseth. One may ascend this hill by a plaine smooth passage, without bush or boscage: or, by more then semicircling trenches. Thiese trenches are perfectly dry, & of a short mossy grosse, that can not dewe the feete in any time of Winter; soe deepe, & the ends soe fenced, that I have there followed my studyes most part of the Winter dayes; shelterd from all Winds, & vnder some oakes shelterd from raine, & dropping weather: And the brims of thiese trenches are all along coverd with oakes. On the top of the hill the aire seemd allwayes gentle & pleasant, there being a very large greene plaine sqvare (called the Etans Garden) fenced every way with thickets of oakes; all the Winter long bordered, neere [*catch-*

word: vnder] [*67/22/3A*] vnder the botts of thiese oakes, with fresh primroses & some other lively plants. At a furlong distance from this Garden is a most horrid & deepe precipice called the Etans hole, over which is a prospect over a hungry vale: (called the vale of Misery, full of poore cottages), vpon many lesser hilles coverd with woods (of this I will explaine the excellency another time) or you may see a hint of it in Casaubons Enthus. Edit 2d pag.68. about the begining of 3 Ch. & pag.61. the end of 2d. Ch.[2] I pray you take notice of it for fewe doe in thiese dayes understand the Mystery. All other prospects from this Garden are most different from this, & from each other, but over severall rivers of Wye, Lug, & fromey into rich vaales, & woody hills. This sqvare is already smooth enough for a boweling greene, & hath a perfect resemblance of an ancient flowre Garden. From the West end of this high Hill you may hold (with a cleare loud voice) conference with others from the top of another hill of allmost eqvall height a deepe channell passing betweene: soe Horeb & Mount Sinai, soe Parnassus. At the foote of this Hill is the Mansion, sometimes holy ground. From the side of the hill gushes pure Water, which is conveighd through the house in a naturall streame, & then begirts the house in a moate (which I like not) & then passes to the Garden, & folds, & makes noe more stay than is reqvired. The Mansion is in the widway to a rich pasture, by a most pleasant river side. Here are the Viridaria provided. The arable, & orchards, or pasture offer the choice of our way downe to the river side, whether on a greene & vnder shade or in open ayre. In this hazle ground noe dirt is to be found in Winter, except it bee the owners neglect to conduct the springs. The Garden is vpon a rocke, yet allwayes apt to bee verdant: May bee as large, as the owner pleaseth, I designe the whole for Garden. The hill seemes to beare barberyes naturally, St Iohns Worte, Peters Worte, & other plants that shewe pregnancy. And it winds about a Vale in the middle, which promiseth a shelter for Laureta, Cupresseta & Myrteta. And the soyle of it selfe rich enough &c.

All this was to shewe, Howe little some narrowe hearted people doe [*catchword*: vnderstand] [*67/22/3B*] vnderstand their owne happines: I knowe howe much by your booke some may bee benefited, if they bee but directed to forbeare the destruction of things excellent.

---

[2] Méric Casaubon, *A treatise concerning enthusiasme, as it is an effect of nature: but is mistaken by many for either* divine inspiration, *or* diabolicall possession (2nd revised and enlarged edn, 1656).

Some would vndoe themselves to fill vp thiese precipices, & some to my knowledge have over throwne their Estates by raysing mounds, which are but as Molehills to this, which in Scriptures would bee called Gods hill, & by heathens Mons Sacer, or Mons Dei, & some vndoe themselves by enforcing a Levell, where the excellency was as hee found it not as hee made it. But where amongst us are our Laureta, Cupresseta, groves of firres, & Pines, or care of correcting the ayre? Let me dash out upon toyes. I can demonstrate, that God hath given us power to procure evning-dewes et rayne, by his blessing vpon our industry, & to alter the ayre, to death or life: Yea, our last conference with Mr Hartlib shewes, that trees doe breath, drawe & give breath, as animals doe, huge animals: They drinke vp, & diffuse the Spirite of the World, & growe to their vaste bulke of body, branch & rootes, not by devouring the earth, saith Rattray,[3] (noe more than Elephants growe by wasting the earth) but by drinking nitrous Water, or (as Dr Horne saith better): Tantus Magnes est in illa vili Arbore (vizt. Betula) ad aerem et occultum illum vitæ cibum, qvem in aere sapientes esse dicunt, attrahendum.[4] This I say, I can demonstrate, & that the breath of some plants doth cherish life in some others, & fit the place for their habitation; & doe veget diseases, & death in others, in men animals or plants. And where now is the hedge rowes of our old English friend the sweete Eglantine, or of the later lillacks? shall I adde a phantasticall toy (for in Hortulane noveltyes wee must bee phantasticall) Where is the hedge rowe of double woodbind raysd upon poles or poplars, like hops, at certaine beautifull distances, that they may perfume a whole province? From this Villa (at small charges) I would send a perfume from the hearte of this County, to all the neighbouring Countyes; & the Weatherglasse shoulde demonstrate the alteration of ayre, & experience of many ages prove the salubrity. For what historian can deny Plinyes note lib. 13. C. 1.[5] That the ayre in Cyprus by store of Cypresse trees & firres, cured the ulcers of the lungs: the ayre of Anticyra, by plenty of true hellebores, helpeth madnesse & lunacy: & the ayre of Thasus, by abundance of deadly Eughes, brought (in hot summers) epidemicall Lunacy, & the house in

---

[3] Sylvester Rattray, *Aditus novus ad occultas sympathiae et antipathiae causas inveniendas* (Glasgow, 1658).
[4] Probably quoting from an unidentified work by Joannes van Horne.
[5] Pliny the Younger, *Natural History*, book 13, chapter 1.

Spaine (mentioned by Bicsius de Aeris potestate) by beeing seated amongst elders, destroyes all the inhabitants.[6] Tis time for London to thinke of this, & to accept of a sweete & easy [*catchword*: remedy] [*67/22/4A*] remedy against the corrosive smoake of their Seawale [*miscopied* Seacoale?], that cuts off more than halfe their dayes, Sicily Sardinia, & infinite other Countreyes are fatall witnesses to this truth. I will shewe, that thiese expedients doe influence of good Angells & divine Inspirations. But our Counterfeite Enthusiasts have crakt this kind of Credite.

Sir It is now time I should answere your qvestion, but to my amazement I can not doe it. Your qvestion is, what I meane by indicative plants ch. 11. of the Garden of pleasure. I looke in my drought C. 11. & find noe mention of it, but alltogether agreeable to this the Title Directions, How to order some crosse allyes to the use of a diall yet soe as the phansy bee not too faint & to open. This all. Possibly I did correct or enlarge or alter this title in the scheme which I then sent in haste to Mr Hartlib.[7] And I well remember, that I gave notice of Indicative plants some to note the weather of the day by their morning openings (noted by Lord Bacon) to which I adde more to direct the Husbandmans harvest. Some as an Index to a diall (as suppose to a dosen of Cypresse trees, or other lesse predatory shrubs, a large lupine, or flower of the Sun, neere enough to resemble a diall) Thus I sported one summer with a Lupine which lifted all his clawes to adore the Sun; another yeare the Sun Flower (which is the largest marigold) did it. A third sort of Indicative plants are those that give sick persons the prognosticque of health & recovery, or of death, mentioned by Eusebius, Nieremb. Hist. Nat. l. 14.c.32.[8] But to this I give as little credit as is due to a Jesuite. Sit penes fidem Jesuiticam. If you would make a Chap. of wonderfull plants, Hee will give you store & style. But I can not credite him halfe way. If his nights shining tree C. 1. his gold-bearing Vines C. 2. his sad tree, C. 19. his mimicall plant, C. 20. his exhilarating tree, C. 21. The sensitive plant, C. 22. And the tree whose leaves falling on the ground, doe as soone as they touch the ground creepe about with

---

[6] No appropriate work of the title *De Aeris potestate* has been identified, though the author Beale refers to appears to be Nicholaus Biesius.

[7] See the printed texts in Appendix III, 'John Beale's draft plans for "A Physique Garden" and "A Garden of Pleasure", [1656]' in *Culture and cultivation in early modern England: writing and the land*, ed. M Leslie & T. Raylor (Leicester, 1992), 226–31.

[8] Juan Eusebio Nieremberg, *Historia naturae maxime peregrinae, libris xvi … Accedunt de miris et miraculosis naturis in Europa libri duo* (Antwerp, 1635).

an animal life. C.23. &c? But some of these are beyond my beleefe. If every lover of this Vegetative knowledge should give you two or three of his greatest wonders of infallible truth, this might prove a ravishing Chapter. Ipse symbolum conferre non dedignabor. The particulars of this wilde discourse, I intend to confirme more largely in soe many particular Chapters. This I only suffle together as a loose preface. You see the speede I have not leysure to reviewe it or to make it legible. Let mee though rudely yet to honest purpose [*catchword*: beg] [*67/22/4B*] beg your favour that when you have advertised whatever you thincke allowable in thiese papers, They may bee returned by our Common friend to your humble Servant,

IB.

Index